FAITHFUL AND FEARLESS

PRINCETON STUDIES IN AMERICAN POLITICS:
HISTORICAL, INTERNATIONAL, AND
COMPARATIVE PERSPECTIVES

SERIES EDITORS

IRA KATZNELSON, MARTIN SHEFTER, THEDA SKOCPOL

FAITHFUL AND FEARLESS

MOVING FEMINIST PROTEST INSIDE THE CHURCH AND MILITARY

MARY FAINSOD KATZENSTEIN

PRINCETON UNIVERSITY PRESS

PRINCETON, NEW JERSEY

Library of Congress Cataloging-in-Publication Data

Katzenstein, Mary Fainsod, 1945–
Faithful and Fearless : moving feminist protest inside the
church and military / Mary Fainsod Katzenstein.
p.   cm. — (Princeton studies in American politics)
Includes bibliographical references and index.
ISBN 0-691-05852-0 (alk. paper)
1. Feminism—United States. 2. Sex discrimination against
women—United States. 3. Women and the military—United States.
4. Women in the Catholic Church—United States. 5. Pressure groups—
United States. 6. Protest movements—United States. I. Title. II. Series.
HQ1421.K27 1998
305.42'0973—DC21   98-5516 CIP

For Tai and Suzanne

CONTENTS

PREFACE AND ACKNOWLEDGMENTS

THIS BOOK charts the infusion of feminist politics into American mainstream institutions. It takes as its starting point the fact that what used to be seen as outlandish has become commonplace, transforming what was once the fare of consciousness-raising sessions into the daily, routinized matter of courtroom, legislative, workplace, household, and media debates. It offers an account of how feminist activists have worked to effect change in the core institutions of American life.

The subjects of this book are neither the demonstrators of the 1960s nor the legislators of the 1990s. They are, rather, the less-in-the-public-eye feminists (mostly women) who throughout these last decades have challenged in their everyday lives the institutions where they work and live.

In this study, I take up the daily protests by feminists inside the institutions of the U.S. military and the American Catholic Church. The insistence on gender equality by feminists within these two institutions marks a new stage in the history of the women's movement. Women have long had institutions of their own: their own professions (motherhood, nursing, school teaching); their own voluntary associations (settlement houses, leagues, clubs); their own separate quarters in male institutions (convents, women's auxiliaries). Despite the women's movement's first-wave assault on exclusionary citizenship, presumptions about gender difference and the formative role such difference should play in the organization of the economy and society remained remarkably intact well into the second half of the twentieth century. It was not until the second wave of American feminism that equal opportunity in employment and university education received validation within the law, by which time women had begun to move in significant numbers into what had been firmly male-dominated domains. This conjunction of state authorization and socioeconomic change has ignited political conflict over a new range of issues in places where gender boundaries had earlier been only weakly contested. Demanding a coequal place inside *male-dominant institutions*—the legal and medical professions, higher education, publishing, film production, philharmonic orchestras, competitive sports, the armed forces, religious establishments—feminists have transported protest into mainstream institutions. In the last several decades, those who wield power in American society (mostly white, male, and heterosexual) have had to confront challenges to that power on the very terrain where they live their daily lives.

As I began my research on feminism in the U.S. military and the Catholic Church, I was struck by what different tributaries seemed to flow from a common feminist source. The very first military woman I interviewed was a navy captain working in the Pentagon. As chance had it, she had earlier been a nun.[1] Both the church, initially, and then the military represented for her an avenue toward independence and mobility. She was now a very smartly uniformed, articulate mother of several children, a woman who spoke of the problems of harassment, of the need to prove oneself at one's job, and of the career prospects women at her level faced.

The first "sister" I interviewed (a more accurate term than *nun* but one that I use interchangeably with *woman religious*)[2] was wearing jeans. She talked about Guatemala, about babies with AIDS, about the homeless, about the Vatican 24 (the sisters who were in trouble with Rome for having signed a *New York Times* ad supporting diversity of reproductive views in the church). Whereas the navy captain spoke of revamping particular policies in the military to make opportunities for women and men more equitable, the Catholic sister talked of remaking both church and society in ways that God (whose image she described as embodied in a portrait of a woman on the wall of a shelter for Latina victims of domestic violence) would deem more just. These first interviews presaged those that came later. I was soon to learn how institutional differences shaped feminist politics. By the time I commenced my research, I had begun to recognize with other feminist scholars of the 1970s and 1980s that gender was always inflected by the different life experiences of women of diverse racial and ethnic backgrounds, socioeconomic circumstances, and sexual orientations. The interviews pointed me to the power of institutions in shaping differences in contemporary feminism.

Feminist-led protest on the inside of male-governed institutions has altered the way many organizations operate. Changes in discourse, rules, policies, and institutional norms have occurred because feminist activists operating within institutional spaces have challenged many of the accepted practices of the past. Present-day "truths" have been subject to insistent contestation. Feminists and those who declare themselves opposed to that which feminism represents vehemently disagree. But the conflict over feminist ideas is often no less intense among feminists themselves. What will soon become evident in these pages is that even as most feminists are united by their opposition to gender ascription, they are separated by profoundly different versions of what feminism should be. What is at stake in this contestation is not only the viability of feminism but the vital question of why particular versions of feminism and not others come to be institutionalized within these new domains.

This book records the movement of feminist politics into the new dominion of mainstream institutions. Protest within institutions has moved center stage. Claims making by diverse groups over issues of race, ethnicity, and sexual orientation, as well as gender, have introduced into American politics a new realm of conflict and a new reality of power. It is in institutions, not merely in the electoral arena or on the streets, that the meanings of this new politics of claims making are being contested. This book reflects upon this critical juncture between feminist politics and American political history.

Some books require long, lonely hours in musty archives. The vast inventory of those to whom I owe my gratitude discloses the fact that this, happily, was not one of them. Much of the work for this book was done through interviews. I conducted about 120 interviews between 1988 and 1997, meeting or speaking with some people many times. Before I began, I had little familiarity with either the military or the Catholic Church. The women and men with whom I spoke were inestimably generous with their time even in the beginning stages of my interviewing when I needed the most basic instruction. Not one had less than brimming schedules. Invariably, I would end these conversations animated by the energy and mettle with which feminists in both the church and the military sought to challenge inequality in beliefs and practices that they often confronted on a daily basis. I list the names of all, except those wishing anonymity, at the end of this book. Perhaps this location is fitting. These individuals are what launched my interest in this book, but they are also what made it exhilarating until the end.

This project was long in germination, long enough that some of the people who were important from the start may not remember their connection to it. George Quester made it possible for me to attend a workshop on women and the military before I, at least, had an inkling that this could be an all-consuming research venture. Mary Segers patiently reviewed my first attempts to write about the church. Two then-undergraduates, Lisa Sansoucy and Amanda Sumner, wrote independent-study reports on the military and the church. Their reports were a turning point, as was Alice Amsden's advice about naming the different feminisms in the military and the church. But mostly, I could not have started on this research without the very early help of several people I regard as my first tutors in military and church matters: Carolyn Becraft, Kathy Bruyere, Pat Gormley, Rosemary Howard, Laverne Nickson, Kathy Osberger, M. C. Pruitt, Judy Vaughan, Donna Quinn, Georgia

Sadler, Margaret Traxler, Mary Daniel Turner and, somewhat later, Barbara Lee, and Lory Manning.

The exceptional competence of many students over the years made some of the most difficult parts of doing research infinitely easier. Jill Lepore scoured the early decades of the *Air Force Times.* Jean Peterson, Betsy Reed, Nadia Reynolds, Lisa Sansoucy, and James Harney were resourceful and fastidious in searching out material. Anthony Annuziato's impact is visible on every page. A now valued friend, for four years he was an unfailingly cheerful and ingenious research assistant.

Kathryn Abrams, Cynthia Enloe, Asha George, Nancy Hirschmann, Jenny Mansbridge, Sue Tarrow, Ruth Vanita, Hongying Wang, and Diane Wolf provided advice on specific questions for which I am grateful. Amrita Basu, Marie Provine, and Gilda Zwerman lavished ideas, humor, and support and were sources of strength in ways they cannot begin to appreciate. Sandy Bem read, listened, advised, walked, and played knowing exactly what was needed when. The clarity of her thinking has been a model for me for as long as I have been at Cornell. Tim Byrnes, Lizabeth Cohen, Pat Gormley, Larry Moore, Elizabeth Sanders, and Ted Lowi were wonderful readers of sections or chapters of this book. David Laitin, Steve Krasner, Eileen McDonagh, David Meyer, and Sid Tarrow, extraordinary colleagues, read every word of this manuscript, several of them more than once. They will see the results of their advice in these pages and will also recognize some of what they urged me against. Their comments were what made me revise more times than I had ever intended. I am also indebted to the painstaking and constructive comments by the anonymous readers for the press.

Sudy Shefter and Corrie Schweigler, both longtime friends, labored, cajoled, and talked me through the final editing, compiling, and arranging. I am grateful not only for their talents but also for the generosity with which they blended friendship with work and called it "fun."

Several institutions and individuals within them were important to this project. The Bunting Institute was my home for a year at the early stages of the manuscript. There, I benefited particularly from the model of scholar and administrator that Ann Bookman set. I also want to thank the Wissenschaft Kolleg in Berlin, whose support of academic spouses/ partners deserves to be widely emulated. The Peace Studies Program at Cornell provided welcome help. Sharing stories with Judith Reppy was a high point of many of these last years. I also benefited gratefully from the efficiency of Elaine Scott and Sandy Kisner. Michael Busch and the staff in the Government Department were important at every turn, not least of all for their entertaining E-mails. I am grateful for the support of the Jonathan Meigs fund, for the wonderful environment of my study in the Carl A. Kroch Library, and for the skills and exceptional courtesy of the Olin Library staff. Finally, I feel blessed by the attentive teamwork of Malcolm Litchfield and Lauren Lepow at Princeton University Press, by Malcolm's creative energy and by Lauren's calm expertise.

There are three people, Zillah Eisenstein, Uday Mehta, and Peter Katzenstein, who have been important to this book since the beginning. In its early stages, Zillah propelled me forward with a stream of inventive thoughts and an intimate sharing of life stories. Throughout, I have been sustained by the extraordinary empathy and imagination with which Uday engages people and ideas. With every conversation, he opened new doors at the same time as he left me always more surefooted.

Peter listened to, read, and lived what is in these pages. Without his encouragement and selflessness, this project and the last thirty years would have been unimaginable. Much is made of how parents do what they do in life "for their children." If Tai and Suzanne would have preferred something other than this book, they never, well, hardly ever, let on. Somehow they grew into adults with integrity and wit. This book is for them.

PART ONE

PROLOGUE

Chapter One

PROTEST MOVES INSIDE INSTITUTIONS

PROTEST in American society has moved inside institutions. In recent years, there have been only sporadic instances of marches, strikes, and demonstrations; yet the common image of protest continues to be one of placard-bearing activists whose job actions, pickets, sit-ins, and processions made lively television and news copy in decades past. What this book sets out to do is to convince those schooled to believe that protest happens only on the streets of an additional and newer institutional reality: that understanding the emergence of gender, race, and sexual politics in contemporary American society means recognizing the importance of protest inside institutions.[1] To limit the definitional purview of protest to worker strikes, race riots, civil rights demonstrations, pro-choice or antiabortion marches and gay pride parades is to be oblivious to a territory where major struggles over power, resources, and status in American society presently occur. What we have come to know as the struggle over "multiculturalism," the "culture wars," and "political correctness" stems from the spread of protest into mainstream institutional spaces of both the state and civil society.

We forget, I think, just how new the insistent ethnic, race, and gender claims making is within the dominant institutions that govern American society and the economy. This assertion of group interests has, of course, long existed within the domain of electoral politics. But powerful economic and societal institutions have been relatively exempt from the contestation over status and resources. Not only in the nineteenth but for much of the twentieth century, the preeminent Protestant, white, and male-dominated private and state-run universities, most prominent medical, law, or business practices, the fraternal orders, and the establishment press were not institutions within which women, the Irish, Italians, Jews, or African Americans, *as groups*, demanded a share of decision-making power. Individuals from each of these groups gained entry and sometimes success and recognition in these elite domains. But, for the most part, women, newly immigrant, and nonwhite groups sought to advance within American society from the confines of separate institutions—women's associations, parochial schools, Black colleges, Polish and Irish parishes, Jewish law firms and business houses, the urban Irish-dominated police forces. Throughout the nineteenth and during the first half of the twentieth century, power struggles in institutional spaces, based on ethnic, racial, or gender identities, occurred inside these separate institutions rather than in the elite institutions of American society.[2] The control of Protestant-white-male-dominated institutions was one-sided with elites declaiming the reasons for continued policies of exclusion and nonelites gaining access to institutional arenas only on the condition of quiet acquiescence.

Political parties and unions were, by contrast, important exceptions to this rule. In party and union politics, it was a two-way proposition: the upwardly aspiring strata of society were courted, and the newly enfranchised and even the not-yet-enfranchised sought political favors.

But what occurred in parties and unions makes all the more vivid what was absent in the elite institutions of American society where ethnic, race, and gender claims were largely out-of-bounds. In higher education, class-based claims by farmers had made democratizing inroads into universities.[3] Well into the twentieth century, however, either individuals from other nonclass unrepresented strata were admitted as clients into the dominant institutions of American society or (and sometimes "and") they launched critiques of exclusionary practices from separate institutions (church organizations, colleges, and occupational niches) located outside the white, Protestant-dominated mainstream of American society.[4] W.E.B. Du Bois, a member of the Harvard class of 1890, was one of six commencement orators. Many decades later, he might well have played a more adversarial role from within the university community. A brilliant historian, he functioned largely from outside the formal academy: Peter Novick writes about Du Bois's later career, ". . . with the exception of an article by W. E. B. Du Bois in the *American Historical Review* in 1910, almost all of the work of Black professional historians including Du Bois himself . . . appeared in the *Journal of Negro History* or in privately printed monographs and was generally disregarded [by historians]." By the late 1960s, African-American historians held positions inside the academy and were engaging in vehement critiques of the Eurocentric biases of the professional canon.[5]

It is interesting to think, also, about the absence of Jewish identity politics or political protest inside the institutions of higher education in the early decades of this century. Jews were a "problem" in higher education—mostly because their growing numbers were seen as threatening the institutional identities of prestigious universities.[6] But Jewish students made few political demands on the universities in which they were enrolled. To be sure, Jewish students in the 1920s and 1930s stood outside university buildings passing out leaflets or giving speeches. But these appeals decried as foolhardy a particular governmental action or extolled the merits of a political party that pledged needed reform. In the 1920s when Jewish students entered higher education in America in significant numbers, issues of *institutional* change—the diversification of the curriculum, the extension of special facilities, broader faculty representation, or the redirecting of university investments—were not matters about which students thought to protest.[7] This was partly because, as the late political theorist Judith N. Shklar writes about Harvard in the 1950s, there was strong pressure to conform to a more Anglo-Saxon ideal:

> The real ideal of many teachers at Harvard in the '50s was the gentleman C-er. He would, we were told, govern us and feed us, and we ought to cherish him, rather than the studious youth who would never amount to anything socially significant. There was, of course, a great deal of self-hatred in all this, which I was far too immature to understand at the time. For these demands for overt conformity were quite repressive. Harvard in the '50s was full of people who were ashamed of their parents' social standing, as well as of their own condition. The place had too many closet Jews and closet gays and provincials who were obsessed with their inferiority to the "real thing," which was some mythical Harvard aristocracy, invented to no good purpose whatever.[8]

The present-day calls for a multicultural curriculum, a more diverse student body and faculty, Latino/a, African-American, Native American, or gay/lesbian residential units have few counterparts in earlier times.

There are at least two explanations for the recent decades' growth of protest within institutions: The first is the growing representation of diverse groups in middle-class institutions no longer segregated by race, ethnicity, or gender. Second, the "rights revolution" in the courts and legislature has given new legal recognition to claims based on race, gender, and other nonclass identities.

Gradually over the last half-century, some significant portions of the ethnic groups of different immigrant generations, African Americans, and women have made their way into the middle class and into institutions that were previously the preserve of a far more homogeneous elite. The entry into mainstream societal and economic institutions began for some groups well before the postwar civil rights resurgence. The economic dislocations of the 1930s caused Catholic communities, Lizabeth Cohen writes about Chicago, to look outward in the face of the failures of their own separate institutional structures to provide needed relief in times of hardship.[9] By the 1950s, many second- and third-generation Catholics had moved into the mainstream of American socioeconomic life.[10] For other groups, the entry into formerly white, male, and Protestant-dominated elite institutions is of more recent vintage. In the twenty-year span between the mid-1970s and the mid-1990s, the numbers of Asian, Black, and Hispanic students in public and private four-year colleges rose rapidly, more so than comparable figures for white students.[11] In the thirty-year period between 1960 and 1990, the Black representation within a number of middle-class occupations has more than doubled.[12] The numbers of women lawyers and physicians by 1990 had reached over 20 percent of the professions, and the numbers of computer systems programmers and analysts close to 30 percent.[13] In the last several decades, socioeconomic mobility, affirmative action, less overt discrimination, and changing aspirations have all contributed to the increasing presence of diverse groups in today's mainstream institutions.

This does not make the institutions (unions, parties) to which the weaker sections of society have turned in the past immaterial, but it does mean that these groups now possess the wherewithal (education, resources) to do battle on their own behalf in the many institutional arenas where their issues emerge. The decline in Democratic Party strength and union muscle, in fact, may both reflect and reinforce what might be thought of as a strategy of diversification of political resources by middle-class groups as they hedge against adversity by investing their political claims making in an ever broader range of institutional possibilities.[14]

But presence is not voice. The ascendance of "identity" politics and the political coming-to-life of a vast array of "status" (as opposed to "class") groups in the population—the handicapped, women, African Americans, senior citizens, Latinos/as, gays/lesbians, among others—is associated with the rise in demand making throughout American societal institutions.[15] Identity politics is not new in America: Catholic, Polish, Irish, Jewish, African-American "identities" have had a long history in this country, as has gender-identity as a basis for political claims making. But the last decades' shift from "presence" to "voice" registers a much newer judicial and legislative certification that the claims a group makes have some validity in law. The momentous 1954 repudiation of the "separate but equal" doctrine in *Brown v. Board of Education* marked an ideological turn in the discourse of state authority that was broader than race. Over the next several decades, the language of civil rights and equal opportunity was repeatedly deployed in Congress and in the courts to authorize the claims to equality by an array of different groups. The 1963 Equal Pay Act affirming women's right to equal pay for equal work and Title VII of the 1964 Civil Rights Act, which barred discrimination in employment on the basis of sex, and which preceded the emergence of the women's movement by several years, recognized legally for the first time women's right to make claims in the workplace. These complex socioeconomic and political changes led to an increasing incidence of institutional protest by a growing array of groups inside America's mainstream institutions and to an enlargement in what Charles Tilly has referred to as the available repertoires of collective action.[16]

THE MEANING OF PROTEST

This book is about contemporary feminist protest located inside the core institutions of both state and society. Since the 1970s, feminists have voiced demands for equal roles within the U.S. armed forces, within the institutional spaces of most religious denominations, within prison management, the health sector, universities, police forces, the professions, unions. Indeed, no major institution has been untouched. Feminist groups inside these institutions have pressed for equity in pay, hiring, and promotion, for the end to harassment and sexual abuse, for greater attention to everyday needs as defined by the realities of women's lives (day care, flexible work times, a more nurturant work environment).

In calling this demand making the politics of protest, I wish to highlight the way in which its purpose is often disruptive. Feminist organizing in institutional contexts may not press for the instant cessation of daily business sought by the earlier sit-ins or the demonstrations that led to the destruction of property or clashes with police. But feminist organizing (in its most adversarial and even sometimes in its more accommodative forms) does seek to transform the world. *Even* some of the most narrow versions of feminist politics that decline to embrace antiracist, antiheterosexist, and antipoverty agendas intend through their focus on equal jobs, promotions, harassment, rape, and other forms of sexual violence to fundamentally change the way American institutions function. In the 1990s, protest pursued in the byways of institutional life can be as disturbance-making as that orchestrated on the public staging grounds of earlier social movements.

I use the term *protest* despite the fact that the women whose activism I describe are far from lawless, rarely use civil disobedience, and never resort to violence. Less lawbreaking than norm-breaking, these feminists have challenged, discomfited, and provoked, unleashing a wholesale disturbance of long-settled assumptions, rules, and practices. Mostly this is intentional or at least, as many advocates of equality would say, inevitable. Sometimes by their mere presence, but more often by claiming specific rights, and by demanding in certain facets the transformation of the institutions of which they are a part, feminists have reinvented the protests of the 1960s inside the institutional mainstream of the 1990s.

Frances Fox Piven and Richard A. Cloward are right to focus on disruption as the defining feature of protest actions. Disruption, they argue, occurs when people "cease to conform to accustomed institutional roles, withhold their accustomed cooperation, and by doing so, cause institutional disruptions."[17] For some of the working and nonworking poor, as they maintain, demonstrations, strikes, and even riots are the most forceful expression and maybe even the only available means of withholding cooperation. But for other groups, I will argue, there may be a wider pool of actions and words that convey exactly this refusal to "conform to accustomed institutional roles." When advocates of gender equality in the military proclaim that gender alone should not bar women from flying bomber missions, when feminists in the Catholic Church write that the words of the gospel provide for a church that would include women in all its ministries, they are violating firmly established institutional norms and participating in role-shattering behavior. This too is protest. This is not mere "resistance" to the power of dominant elites; it is proactive, assertive, demand-making political activism. If groups inside institutions were not in organized ways making these kinds of demands, if these forms of institutional activism were not deeply unsettling, the fear-laden conservative backlash of the last twenty years might well have been, one can only speculate, less virulent.

It is limiting, I think, to define protest in terms of any preestablished, particular set of political tactics or events.[18] What constitutes nonnormative behavior, disrupts existing understandings, and challenges established roles is context-specific. To fail to see disruption as situation-specific can be to misrepresent the course of social movements themselves. Marking the beginning or ending of social movements by the rise and decline of media-covered protest "events" or by the requisite use of particular demonstrative actions (sit-ins, demonstrations, marches) may leave much convention-breaking speech and action unremarked.[19] To recognize protest requires knowing as much about the "who, when, what, and where" as it does about the "how."

Feminist activists, I argue in this book, have confronted through a variety of political strategies those who seek to preserve traditional gender roles in institutional contexts. Contesting inequality in the institutional locales where they work, play, love, or worship (in places of employment, in athletics, in the family, in the pews), feminist protesters have brought their own form of disruptive politics into the mainstream institutions of American society and of the state.

UNOBTRUSIVE MOBILIZATION AND CIVIC ASSOCIATIONALISM

What I have called protest inside institutions is only part of the repertoire of American feminism. Institutional protest exists alongside and

would not exist without the rich associational activity that has constituted feminist activism in the 1980s and 1990s. This associationalism
has outlived the marches, the litigation, the cascade of legislative activity
that marked the first decades of the contemporary women's movement
and won much media attention. Even as these dramatic days of demonstrations, court cases, and legislative battles have mostly faded, there
continue to be vast numbers of organizations operating in the inter-
stices of society, doing the important work of what I call unobtrusive
mobilization.[20]

Protest inside institutions is different from unobtrusive mobilization.
When activism inside institutions turns into protest, it is almost never, in
the sense of escaping public notice, unobtrusive. When institutional
routines are disrupted and the norms of an organization contested, it is
almost always because the public gaze has been focused on these institutions and institutional elites feel exposed.

What I am calling unobtrusive mobilization occurs both inside institutions and in the space outside institutions, in what Susan Hartmann
has elsewhere designated as the work of autonomous feminism.[21] What
is specific to *institutional* mobilization is its connection to a parent organization. Formed or re-formed with the intention of holding a parent-
institution accountable to feminist concerns, activism inside institutions
ranges across different sectors of the workforce from women's studies
programs in universities to women's groups located in the larger professional associations of lawyers, engineers, doctors, and scientists, to the
Congressional Caucus for Women's Issues of the U.S. Congress, to the
Coalition of Labor Union Women in the union movement.

These institution-based organizations are different from more autonomous women's organizations. Autonomous organizations (although
they may receive governmental or foundation funding) think of themselves as more free-floating, situated outside government and less directly beholden to institutional supervision. Institution-based organizations are more connected administratively or financially to the political
institutions they intend to influence. They may receive funds, may have
overlapping memberships or meeting spaces, and may share a common
normative or ideological purpose with the larger, male-dominated institutional body of which they are a part. They must also on a more daily
basis than autonomous feminist groups negotiate the often hazardous
terrain where influence and access are traded against independence and
critical distance.

It is the case, of course, that much organizing inside institutions es-
capes public notice. Feminist politics in institutional locales is often not
designed around publicity-arousing strategies. But activism in institutions turns disruptive often just when advocates of equality start seeking

publicity, contacting the press and conducting actions intended to draw media attention.

Institutional activism is not what comes to mind in any usual description of the feminist movement. The women's *movement* more likely evokes images of autonomous feminism. Independent of party politics or institutional affiliation, autonomous groups such as the Redstockings or the Feminists of the 1970s or the National Abortion Rights Action League, the Black Women's Health Project, Business and Professional Women, or the National Women's Political Caucus are conventionally thought to be at the heart of feminist activism. Unobtrusive mobilization is, however, a vital form of women's associationalism that courses through the bloodstream of American civic life.

Much of unobtrusive mobilization mirrors the long-standing voluntarism of American political life remarked upon in the early nineteenth century by Alexis de Toqueville.[22] Voluntary associations were the primary vehicle by which women exercised influence in the public arena throughout the nineteenth and into the twentieth century. With time, women's voluntary associations began to be understood in more differentiated terms as philanthropic, charitable, or social reform organizations, as nonprofit and nongovernmental organizations in the terminology of more recent times, as well as in specifically political terms as interest-group and movement organizations—with the lines inevitably blurring among categories.

Exemplary of erstwhile unobtrusive but now quite visible autonomous organizing in recent times is the work of local and grassroots rape crisis organizations and battered women's shelters. But many more organizations, much less in the glare of media lights, operate to keep the projects of feminist activism alive. There may be no way to quantify this decentralized, dispersed form of organizing. Nor can we know if these less visible organizations have burgeoned or leveled off. We do know, however, simply by the range, specificity, and diversity of the groups of women they represent that they are prolific.[23] As I tell colleagues about my interest in women's organizations, both inside and outside institutions, I am consistently directed to look at this caucus or that organization. What about the Chicago Women in Trades who are pipe fitters, electricians, laborers, and elevator repair–workers?[24] What about the Women in Scholarly Publishing (WISP) whose two-pronged goal (consciousness-raising and self-help) is advanced through newsletters about career opportunities, a task force on gender-biased language, and a range of other activities, or the Women in Film, an organization of two thousand women in the entertainment industry?[25] What about the Women's Caucus for Art, or Cassandra, a group of mostly lesbian/bisexual nurses who describe themselves as radical feminists committed to ending oppression of women in nursing and health care? What about Sisters in Crime, started when a woman mystery writer drew attention to the fact that Mystery Writers of America had failed to award a woman the prize for best novel any time in the previous fifteen years? Had I known of Guerilla Girls (women who dress in gorilla costumes to make early morning assaults on New York's metropolitan museum and post the walls of Soho to protest the exclusion of women artists in important exhibitions)? What about the Coal Employment Project, whose Coal Mining Women's Support Team in Tennessee sends mimeographed newsletters in pastel pinks, greens, and blues alternating news of women who have fought discrimination and harassment in the mines with birthday wishes to one subscriber and condolences on a family illness to another?[26]

Had I seen the *Wall Street Journal* article on the first International Women's Brass Conference (IWBC), where the conference agenda covered issues not likely to be taken up at the conventions sponsored by the Tubists Universal Brotherhood Association, including a workshop titled "Pregnancy and Playing a Brass Instrument"? (Mahler's Third Symphony and the Berlioz Requiem, the workshop discussions note, are particularly risk-prone.)[27] What about the Women's Law Enforcement Association, which has encouraged women police officers to sue the New York Port Authority on grounds that women cops are discriminated against in hiring, promotion, and pregnancy-leave policy,[28] or the Special Agent Women Interested in Fair Treatment (SWIFT) at the FBI,[29] or the National Lesbian and Gay Journalists Association?[30] Did I know of the recently recognized clerical union at Harvard, the Women's Bar Association (WBA) organized at the state and national levels,[31] the Women's Rights Committee of the American Federation of Teachers (AFL-CIO), the Women's Caucus of the American Public Health Association,[32] the American Jewish Congress' Commission for Women's Equality that has printed battered women's hotline stickers to be affixed inside synagogue bathroom stalls where women can copy phone numbers of support services in private?

Some of these organizations are clearly inside institutions, others outside; for still others, differentiating between inside and outside requires far more knowledge than their names, alone, provide. Any proper classification requires more specific knowlege of how directly organizational activists see themselves as accountable to institutional authority.

Associational activism in American politics organized with the purpose of reshaping some facet of gender relations is nothing new. It is unclear, given the widely dispersed and often inconspicuous character of much of women's organizing, whether the degree of associational activism that has accompanied second-wave feminism is much the same as in earlier times, greater than before, or whether (as seems unlikely) it has declined over time as Robert Putnam claims is the case with civic associationalism in the United States more generally.[33] What I call unobtrusive mobilization by women has always existed in profusion in American society. What is clearly new is its development inside male-dominant organizational environments—the media, law enforcement, the churches, universities, business, prisons, unions, and engineering, to name just a few of these institutional locales. In these new environments, feminists have spurred debates over hiring and promotion, rape and harassment, child care, and workplace benefits (including coverage for lesbian and gay partners); they have sometimes enagaged in intense contestation over how the quality of work and the fairness and worth of what men and women do should be assessed. If the profusion of unobtrusive feminist networks, caucuses, associations, coffeehouses, bookstores, Internet lists, informal and formal organizations, both inside and outside institutions, is any indication, civic associationalism not only is present but can provide a breeding ground for a form of protest politics that operates within both arterial and capillary corridors of society and of the state.

FEMINIST PROTEST IN THE U.S. MILITARY AND THE CATHOLIC CHURCH

This has been a long prologue, in the course of which I have scarcely mentioned the two institutions that are the subject of this study. Why the U.S. military and the Catholic Church? What makes these institutions important to an analysis of protest inside institutions? It would be disingenuous if I claimed to have initially chosen to focus on the military and the church because of any prior thought I might have given to case selection and hypothesis testing. My choice of these two institutions in the beginning was due simply to their centrality to the American state and to American society. If I were to convince a readership of the vitality of current-day feminism, I had persuaded myself, it would be best to do so through a description of institutions that could not be dismissed as operating on the fringes of mainstream America.

But as I delved more deeply into the research, I became engrossed by two puzzles, one about the similarities, the other about the differences characterizing feminist protest in these two institutions. As I spoke with activists in both the military and the church, I was persistently puzzled by their readiness to speak out in the face of what seemed to be often overwhelming institutional pressures to keep silent. Sex discrimination in many other sectors of society is as much de facto as de jure, and the practices against which women must rail are sometimes subtle and indirect, often part of institutional cultures rather than matters of rules or law. In the case of the U.S. military and the Catholic Church, by contrast, discrimination is not subtle. Much prejudice takes the form, to mistranslate the Latin expression *prima facie*, of "in your face" discrimination. Because you are a woman and cannot be ordained, you are barred from the deaconate, priesthood, and all higher offices of the Catholic Church. Similarly, in the military, even with the policy changes of the early 1990s that permitted women to fly combat missions and serve on surface warfare ships, there are still combat roles from which women are explicitly barred. For lesbians, of course, there is legalized exclusion from the armed services in its entirety. But provocation is one thing and activism is another. What needed making sense of was why feminists, women and men, did speak out when to do so could invite the negative sanctions of institutions whose capacity for repression is greater than that of many others in contemporary times. As I detail in later chapters, in the church, the powers of excommunication can and have been used against those who espouse feminists ideas, specifically support for women's reproductive choice. For other expressions of dissent from institutional teachings, feminists have been fired from their jobs in church institutions or officially silenced; scheduled speeches have been canceled, and pressures have been put on religious communities to rein in aberrant members. In the military, the risk to promotion and job security is no less real. The military lawyer who refuses to prosecute a suspected gay or lesbian servicemember risks possible court-martial for disobeying an order, or the necessity of resigning his or her commission; the whistle-blower or complainant who reports illegal harassment risks retaliation in the form of a blocked promotion or unwelcome job assignment. Distinct to the military, specifically, is the widespread experience of feminists and women in general who face daily harassment from male peers in the form of comments, jeers, gossip, rumor—all amounting to accusations about their sexuality or their alleged incompetence at their job.[34] The puzzle is, in the face of the pressures and institutional penalties that exist in *both* the military and the church, why speak out as a feminist?

A second puzzle preoccupied me even more intensively: Despite the strong similarities between the military and the church—the deeply gendered assumptions embodied within institutional doctrine, the hierarchical structures, and the coercive measures that can be deployed against internal criticism—feminists in the two institutions pursue very different political objectives and use different political strategies. For most feminists in the military a gender-equal society is one in which qualified women have the same opportunities as qualified men. What this reformist vision requires, many military women would say, are better laws, policies, and education. For many activists in the Catholic Church, by contrast, feminism is inseparable from the all-encompassing goal of antimilitarism, class equality, race and gender equity, a homophobia-free society, and social justice on a comprehensive scale. This is a radical vision that demands, many Catholic feminists believe, nothing less than a reconstructed world achieved through an entire restructuring of societal institutions. No doubt both institutions have been unsettled by feminists in their midst. And yet feminists in each of these institutions might be just as unsettled by the version espoused by their counterparts in the other of what it means to undertake activism on behalf of gender equality.

Indeed, in much of Europe, American Catholic feminists are viewed as among the most outspoken exponents of feminism with their language of radical equality that combines a sharply etched critical analysis of institutional hierarchy and clericalism with a critique of societal inequalities, racism, patriarchy, imperialism, and militarism. Given what is widely acknowledged as the historical frailty of radicalism in the United States more generally, this American "exceptionalism" inside the church adds grist to this second puzzle.

It might be easy, too easy I will argue in later chapters, to cite the different institutional traditions in the military and the church as explanations of the different political visions to which feminists have turned, although the church in America does have a history of radical politics— the Catholic Worker's Party—and models of prophetic thinking are legion in the church. It might also be plausible to attribute the difference in institutional feminisms to individual self-selection. Are more conservative women drawn to the military and more radically inclined women toward the church? If this is the case, I was not able to discern it. The navy captain, former nun, whom I interviewed at the outset of my research was the first of a stream of Catholic women whom I met in my interviews with women officers in the military.[35] It is possible, of course, that had I had refined measurements of attitudes and personality characteristics, I would have discovered differences that led to a self-selection among women entering and exiting these two institutions. But numerous interviews suggested otherwise. Many of those I spoke with emphasized that their political ideas were not at all fully formed at the time they became nuns or joined the military, or that their politics had little to do with why they chose to become what they became. One air force colonel had been a Sister of Christian Charity. She joined her order at a very early age and left (or, as she explained, was asked to leave) when she was twenty-one. ("I talked out then, and I still do. What I couldn't take was the hypocrisy, the belief in love, as disciples of Jesus and yet the view that we were apart, somehow better, or that friendships were unacceptable.") When I asked her whether she had joined the order because of some early commitment to fighting poverty or injustice, she said, "What do you know when you are young? . . . You are just what your parents have brought you up to be. I wasn't my own person until later. I was very religious, very idealistic, I thought I had a vocation." Why did she join the military? Because a friend's friend was going to school, paid for by the military, and that possibility, given her desire to earn a master's degree, was decisive.[36] If the Catholic women who joined the military (the navy in particular, it seemed) came from one socioeconomic sector or geographical region, and those who joined religious orders from another, I did not detect it.

As I proceeded with my research, I became increasingly convinced, although I could not claim the observation to be more than impressionistic, that some of the differences in political outlook of Catholic women in the military and Catholic women in the church were a function as much of the institutions they inhabited as of the individuals they had been before they joined (usually by age eighteen in the case of the church or age twenty one in the case of the military). If, among my interviewees, the military women who had previously been nuns had stayed in their religious communities, would they too, I began to wonder, have become like many of their religious contemporaries—advocates of sanctuary for Central American refugees, activists against racist and homophobic practices? As my research progressed, I began to think the answer was yes.

What convinces me that we must look beyond the "different institutional traditions" or the "self-selection" explanations of feminism's differing manifestations in the military and the church is the fact that women's attitudes have not always *been* as different in the two institutions as they are now. Until the mid-1970s, what was striking about the attitudes and practices of military and church women was their similarity, *not* their differences. In the first half of the twentieth century, the organizational affinity of the two institutions seemed to correspond to a similarity in women's understandings of their roles within the two institutions. In neither the military nor the church did women expect to exercise an equal voice in governance, and in neither institution did women expect to be considered equal partners with men in daily affairs. Rather, women in both the military and the church saw themselves in relation to men as fulfilling a different but complementary role. Why is it that in the last two and a half decades when women in the military and in the church turned to feminism, they did so in very different ways—to an interest-group (influence-seeking) liberal feminism in one case and to a radical, discursive politics in the other?

How is it, then, that feminist protest has managed to disrupt—and it plainly has—two institutions with the force and authority of the military and the Catholic Church? And why is it that when women in these quite similarly structured institutions turned to feminism, they were propelled toward very different conceptions of feminist politics?

INSTITUTIONAL PROTEST IN ITS DIFFERENT FORMS: INTEREST-GROUP AND DISCURSIVE POLITICS

It is important to understand the differences between feminism in the military and in the church as part of a larger universe of protest that exists inside institutions. What bears emphasizing is that protest inside institutions is not monolithic. The objectives and forms may vary hugely. Some protest internal to institutions aims at moderate change, some at the radical restructuring of the institution. Some protest emphasizes influence seeking in order to shape policy; other instances emphasize the crafting of language and the formulation of meanings in print and speech. I have called feminist protest inside the military "moderate, interest-group, influence-seeking" politics and that within the church "discursive radicalism." But these do not exhaust the possibilities of institutional protest. The accompanying diagram suggests at least four kinds of protest where objectives and form are differently combined. The four quadrants represent different examples of protest inside institutions. Influence seeking may be the tool of radical change, as was the intent of German radicals who sought to "march through the institutions." Discursive politics may be the instrument of moderate-minded activists, as is the case with activists who mobilize around the issue of date rape in universities, hoping to create new understandings but not necessarily to remake the institution. The other two quadrants represent the feminist protest described in this book.

It is not difficult to envision what feminists do when they engage in *interest-group* politics. We can readily visualize feminist lobbyists walking the corridors on the Hill. We can fill in the words by rote: Feminist organizations, often Washington-based, endeavor to influence political elites to support or oppose particular legislation, regulations, or policy decisions. In the United States, interest-group activism is the way many feminists do politics. Not that this form of feminist politics necessarily elicits public acclaim. The selection of Geraldine Ferraro as a Democratic vice presidential candidate provoked accusations that feminists had acted as an interest group, "biasing" the selection of Walter Mondale's running mate. Some feminists, too, are disquieted, albeit differently. When feminists do interest-group politics, some suspect, they

Four Types of Institutional Protest

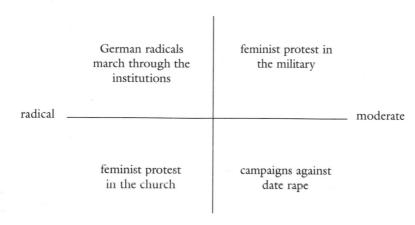

influence-seeking

German radicals
march through the
institutions

feminist protest in
the military

radical ———————————————————————— moderate

feminist protest
in the church

campaigns against
date rape

discursive

have bought into a world of political compromise. But on the whole, interest-group politics is seen as politics-as-usual.

Discursive politics requires greater elucidation. Most succinctly, it is the politics of meaning making.[37] By discursive, I mean the effort to re-interpret, reformulate, rethink, and rewrite the norms and practices of society and the state. Discursive politics relies heavily but not exclusively on language. It is about cognition. Its premise is that conceptual changes directly bear on material ones. Its vehicle is both speech and print—conversations, debate, conferences, essays, stories, newsletters, books.

These two kinds of politics are ideal types. In real political life, organizations combine something of both. Feminist interest groups are often very word-conscious, usually out of calculated instrumentality as to what phraseologies will "work." Feminist interest groups are also well aware of the need to change *understandings* of gender stereotyping. For feminist interest-group activists, questions about gender identity—who women and men are, what they want—are real but not at the forefront of their immediate concerns. For feminist interest-group activism, the balance is struck in favor of instrumental change. In discursive politics, the careful thought given to word choices and language is sometimes instrumental but more often expressive. Its intent is to articulate clearly the differences in perspective, the revisioning of a feminist worldview.

Less attention is paid to measuring the progress or acceptance of these newly voiced perspectives. Preeminent emphasis is on expressing with clarity and integrity a true vision of societal change.

I have considered terms other than *discursive politics: cultural politics, the politics of ideology, transformative politics, identity politics. Cultural politics* has too much the connotation of operating on the plain of music, art, and literature; and it evokes the glacial process of changing deeply embedded norms. Discursive politics is also intended to challenge deeply held beliefs. But it directly interrogates the way people write and talk about these beliefs. That process is more immediate, more malleable. *The politics of ideology* is simply too weighted by pejorative luggage. *Transformative politics* presumes an answer to the question that needs to be posed: what, if anything, does discursive politics transform?

Discursive politics is very much of a piece with identity politics. Part of what feminists do when they think and write is to ask, Who am I? Who are we as women? In what ways are women different from men, from each other? In what ways do gendered identities and experiences shape political understandings and authorize different groups to speak? These identity questions are connected to a larger discursive undertaking that requires a reexamination of the norms and rules by which society operates. I prefer the term *discursive politics* over *identity politics* because its emphasis is outside the person, focusing less on the individual (detractors would say, the navel) but stressing, instead, the terms of debate in which the project of political analysis is to be conducted.

I do not mean to draw too neat a line between interest-group and discursive politics. All political activism does interpretive work using language and symbols, so in this sense all politics is discursive. Similarly, all political activism is, in some ways, about advancing the interests of some sectors of society over others. I am suggesting, however, that political activism is at any point in time (whether by choice or by default) more fully absorbed by one kind of political project than by the other—by the intention to influence policy and shape immediate outcomes or by the effort to deploy language and symbols to convince others of new possibilities.

Feminism in the military engages in an influence-seeking *interest-group* form of politics. It is grounded in norms of equal opportunity and a belief in social change through adherence to institutional rules. It is common to hear women activists in the military speak of the need to be mission-oriented, team players, to work for change from within, to follow the chain of command (phrases distinctly absent from the vocabulary of women in the church). Military activists often welcome the attention of the press and have on occasion looked the other way when information was leaked to the news media, but going public with a *New York Times* advertisement, or undertaking the kind of public protest that armband-bearing sisters presented during the pope's visit, would be unthinkable for women who intend to pursue a military career. I use the term *interest-group* to describe what women advocates in the military do to emphasize their interest in influencing decisions and policy. Women activists in the military pay attention to who wields influence in the military hierarchy and in positions of political importance outside the military, and they endeavor to build connections to those who can make change happen. At the same time, what they aim to do is to play by the rules and change the gendered assumptions embedded in the norms of the institution.

Feminism in the Catholic Church relies heavily on a discursive politics that self-consciously invokes the language of "radical equality."[38] I emphasize the discursive aspects of radical politics in the church to call attention to the energy that feminists in the church devote to language and interpretation—to seeing the meaning of God, of church, of ritual, of justice through a feminist, antiracist, globalist, nonelitist, and non-heterosexist politics. Most feminists in the church (both sisters and lay activists) work for a living in paid jobs not unlike those of women generally. They spend significant amounts of time, however, and most would spend far more if they could, reading, writing, attending (and planning) conferences, engaged in creating a new vision of church and society in prose.

In both the U.S. military and the American Catholic Church over the last twenty years women activists have worked to create a consciousness that challenges discriminatory institutional practices. In both institutions, feminists have created organizational habitats (formal groups and informal networks) within which feminists (mostly women) share stories, develop strategies, and find mutual support. In both institutions, numerous initial-and acronym-denoted organizations carry the burden of keeping gender equality on the institutional agenda. In the military these include groups like the Defense Advisory Committee on Women in the Services (DACOWITS), composed of civilian appointees and military advisers, whose "mission is to assist and advise the Secretary of Defense on matters and policies related to women in the Armed Services";[39] the Women's Officers Professional Association (WOPA) of women military officers in the sea services; and Women Military Aviators (WMA), an organization of pilots and other aviators attracting officers, primarily from the navy, air force, and army. In the church, these organizations include the Women's Ordination Conference (WOC), the Leadership Conference of Women Religious (LCWR), the National Assembly of Religious Women (now defunct), the (ecumenical) Grail, Las

Hermanas (a Catholic Hispanic women's group), the National Coalition of American Nuns (NCAN), Call to Action, and numerous others.

Despite this common project of institutional change, and despite the existence in both institutions of woman-made organizational spaces within which those at odds with institutional practices gather energy and devise plans of action, there are profound differences in their agendas.

In describing interest-group feminism in the military and feminist discursive radicalism in the church, I wish to defend the usage of two words. The first is military *feminism*. Only about half of those I interviewed described themselves as feminists. Those who did often laced their self-description with humor, irony, or a touch of bravado—used as they are to the sense of embattlement such terms provoke:

> I remember thinking [when I was a cadet at the academy] how incongruous we were. The situation was like, "We exist, therefore we're feminists!" Am I a feminist? I dance around it. I don't deny it, but hey, "them's fighting words." (Air force officer)[40]

> If you're thinking I sound like a feminist, it's because I am. I believe in organized activities to advance opportunities for women and, yes, you can quote me on that. (Air force officer)[41]

> Was I always a feminist?! Ooh Yaa [laughter]. As I got more senior and would go around giving talks, I'd begin by saying, "I'm a radical feminist." All the women would smile. The men would grimace. (Navy officer)[42]

Others eschewed the feminist label, occasionally expressing impatience with my question. One former high-level civilian official in the Pentagon, who played an active role in recruiting other women for posts in the Carter administration's Defense Department, and who forcefully opposed efforts to bar women from securing abortions in military hospitals, retorted when asked whether she or others identified themselves as feminists:

> Why would we have done that? It would have been death, do you hear me, death?! What you may not realize is that we were dealing with people who thought that feminism had totally destroyed our society. To have seen things in those categories would have been to shortchange everyone.[43]

Many military activists are what I would term "feminists by any other name." Feminism-by-any-other-name describes the civilian Barbara Spyridon Pope, a former Goldwater staff member, a Reagan-Bush appointee, and the first woman assistant secretary of the navy. Throughout the Tailhook investigation, following the 1991 navy sexual scandal at the Tailhook Association convention, Pope adamantly opposed procedures that she saw as veering in the direction of a whitewash. Rumors of her shouting match in a Pentagon corridor with the commander of the Naval Investigative Service (who had been quoted as likening women aviators to go-go dancers) made the rounds of Washington with lightning speed. Accurately or not, Pope was described by a *Wall Street Journal* editorial as having said that an important task ahead was "weeding out the white male as norm."[44] And yet when described as a liberal feminist, Pope is quick to reply, "The people that know me know that is far from the truth."[45] I would argue that feminism-by-any-other-name encompasses a Lieutenant Paula Coughlin, the lead plaintiff in Tailhook, who has not generally described herself as a feminist, but who insists that it is important for ". . . everyone to understand that what happened at Tailhook happened to a woman who could be your daughter, your sister, or your wife, and you'd better sit up and pay attention because it happens to zillions of women out there and you're looking at one of them."[46] Although I use the term "advocates of gender equality" when I am aware that the people I speak of prefer that nomenclature, I nevertheless talk generically of feminists in the military because of the work all activists do in challenging at least *some aspect* of a system of institutional inequality based on gender.[47]

Second, I believe it is no less important to explain the term "radical" as I use it to describe feminism in the church. By the term, I mean that feminist activists in the church seek an understanding of the *structural* or *systemic* bases of inequality in the church and in society. When the planners of the November 1995 Women's Ordination Conference wrote that the meetings were premised on a mutual dedication to the goals of radical equality, what they meant was that the "women, too" view of equality was not enough. It was not enough merely to ordain women; a true "radical" equality demands a reenvisioning of church hierarchy itself, including ritual and prayer and all elitist structures of church and society. When feminists in the church describe their dedication to radical equality, they do not mean the kind of commitment to the poor evinced by a Mother Teresa with her ministries to the sick and dying. What feminists mean is the identifying and rooting out of the very *systems* that cause the poor to be poor, the homeless to be homeless, and that cause people to die of poverty or oppression.[48]

Inevitably, using terms like *radical equality* or, as I do, *discursive radicalism* is problematic in certain respects: The terms *radicalism* and *extremism* are labels that can always be used to tarnish the credibility of what is being said. Indeed, sections of the church hierarchy have in the last ten years invoked such terms to denounce feminism in the church.[49] Ironically, describing feminism in the church as radical is likely to be viewed as problematic by those who believe that most feminist activists do not really live by radical principles, are too weakly committed to eradicating class or race inequalities, or are insufficiently engaged in battling heterosexism in the church—that to be a true radical means being on the front lines of organizing among the poor *or* declaring loudly one's alliance with gay and lesbian activists in the church *or* refusing (as a male) to be ordained until women too can be admitted to the priesthood *or* taking a pro-choice stand *or* . . . There is no radical activism in history that is not subject to such kinds of litmus-test critiques.

The advent of feminist protest inside institutions is part of a larger story about the last half-century in American society. Prior to the 1950s, the political rights (the vote, specifically) granted to Blacks, to immigrants, and to women were unaccompanied by privileges of citizenship in the reigning social institutions of the time. Or to put this claim differently, either social citizenship was granted on the condition that it was exercised in separate institutions (Black colleges, women's colleges, Black athletic leagues, parochial schools, Jewish resorts), or admission into prestigious institutions was extended provided individuals did not make group claims on the institution. By midcentury, sections of each of these groups had become middle-class, had gained in some cases a foothold, in some cases substantial representation in the educational, occupational, and cultural institutions of mainstream society. At the same time, beginning in the 1950s, laws and court decisions recognizing this right of entry provided these diverse groups with authoritative language through which to make claims within their institutions. The conjunction of these patterns of mobility with the legislative and judicial affirmation of equal rights has given rise to the proliferation of claims making within institutions. Feminist protest inside the U.S. military and the Catholic Church is party to this history. This book takes up the question of how protest fares inside institutions—what supports it, what contains it, and what shapes its different expressions.

I begin this discussion by describing in chapter 2 the institutionalization of feminist protest over time, asking whether the boundary making that typically demarcates protest inside and outside institutions needs to be rethought. In the next four chapters, I turn to the cases of the military and the church. Chapters 3 and 4 present, respectively, a description of feminist activism in the military and an account of why it takes the form it does. Chapters 5 and 6 repeat the same sequence of a descriptive chapter followed by an analytical one, first tracing feminist activism in the Catholic Church and then exploring the opportunities and norms, both intra- and extrainstitutional, that gave rise to discursive radicalism in the church. The final chapter returns to the significance both for feminism and for American politics of protest inside institutions.

Chapter Two

LEGALIZING PROTEST

NOT UNTIL the 1970s did feminists inside the male-dominant institutions of mainstream society have the "right" to act on their long-held sense of injustice and to protest discrimination on their own behalf. When women gained the franchise in 1920, they triumphed in battle but not in war. Women won equality of opportunity in the realm of voting rights but little else. As the 1920s was to demonstrate, women lacked the right to be treated the same as men beyond that of their newly secured "political citizenship." By the 1970s, the law extended the right of equal opportunity to women seeking equality in jobs and education by embedding equal opportunity provisions in statutes that barred discrimination in pay, employment, university and college admissions, school and college athletics, credit, insurance, disability provisions, and many other specific institutional arenas. Whatever else these rights may or may not have meant, one clear result has been to "legalize" claims making inside mainstream male-dominant institutions of American life.

This process of legalization is nothing less than the institutionalization of feminist protest. To institutionalize, the sociologist Philip Selznick said, is to "infuse with value beyond the technical requirements of the task at hand."[1] Institutionalizing protest means ascribing legitimacy to the place of protest within an organizational environment. By this I mean establishmenting habitats, or protected spaces,[2] for feminists within institutions.

In most ways this story resembles that told by scholars of social movements who analyze how structures of opportunity (legal provisions, in this case) give rise to political mobilization. The opportunity to gain access to the courts and to legislative redress, I argue, has made possible the eruption of feminist protest inside institutions in the last several decades. But the language of "opportunities" does not entirely describe the process by which feminists come to challenge inequality inside institutions. By categorizing, ranking, and validating, the law also shapes how those vying for power think about themselves and others, and how they define the meaning of the world around them. This multilevel significance of the law for women who sought equality within institutions is the focus of the first half of the chapter. In the chapter's second part,

I turn to a discussion of what it means to be protesting from "inside" institutions as a caution against the view that inside activism signals the end of the challenges that movement politics initiates.

THE 1920S: LIMITING FEMINIST CLAIMS

Unless social movements take hold in some way inside institutions, the challenges they pose in the drama of the mobilizational moment collapse. It is interesting from the perspective of the twentieth century's end, with the theater of feminism's second wave largely over, to look back at the period following suffrage. There are similarities, but there are also differences.

In both periods, organized feminist activism (associations, caucuses, and autonomous women's groups) continued well after the marches and demonstrations of the initial mobilization ended. In both periods, moreover, women activists looked to the electoral arena in their attempt to assert their social and economic agendas. In the two periods, the age-old question of women's sameness with and difference from men continued to be intensely debated by feminist activists as well as by power-holders responding to feminist claims. But two developments are original to the last several decades: the legislative and judicial legitimation of gender sameness and the changing educational and employment patterns of large numbers of women. The consequence of the shifting law and shifting numbers has been the emergence of feminist protest inside *male-dominant* institutions.

Political activism among women did not collapse with suffrage. Like the late 1970s and 1980s, the 1920s was a period in which new groups emerged taking activism into new arenas. Countering the long-prevailing view of the 1920s as a period of political quiescence for women following enfranchisement, Nancy Cott describes the twenties as rife with organizational activity. Although the number of women in the National American Women Suffrage Association (NAWSA) was never matched by any other single organization, the League of Women Voters together with new partisan organizations drew thousands of women, and ". . . where one large or vital pre-1920 women's organization declined or ended, more than one other arose to take its space, if not its exact task."[3]

Women's activism operated effectively in several domains. Robyn Muncy describes the reformist impulse that played "a particularly prominent part in bridging America's two periods of reform, the Progressive era and the decade of the New Deal."[4] The reformist activism that Muncy calls a "female dominion in the mostly male empire of policy-making" consisted of a network of governmental agencies (the Children's Bureau, the Women's Bureau, the Women's Joint Congressional Committee) and a host of women's organizations and feeder institutions in educational establishments. Kristi Anderson describes women's activism in party and electoral politics in the 1920s, which she argues had far-reaching consequences for the conduct of politics more generally, not because women were assimilated in large numbers into party or policy-making positions, but because women's difference reshaped the boundaries of policy definition and political exchange.[5] Many of the women—Susan Ware counts twenty-eight—who became officeholders in the New Deal, had learned their activist skills in the suffrage campaigns or the reformist movements of the Progressive period and the 1920s.[6] Another domain in which women played a leadership role was, of course, the movement to secure protective legislation for wage-earning women. Supported by the National Women's Trade Union League, the National Consumers' League, and several other groups, protective legislation that limited the hours women could work, and stipulated wage, labor, and working conditions lasted into the 1960s.

Two features are striking about these domains of women's organizing: The first is the evidence they provide of the intense level of organizing by women in the decade following suffrage. The twenties was by no means a period of quiescence, as might be mistakenly inferred from the low levels of voting participation by women after suffrage. The second is the continued premise of gender difference that seems braided through the kinds of activism these groups undertook. Many women continued to organize in women-segregated spaces, voluntary associations, clubs, leagues, outside of male institutions, and they continued to organize around traditionally feminine concerns—children and family issues, the health and well-being of workers, and other issues of social reform. Even where women were incorporated into male arenas of party politics and policy making as they gradually began to be, they dedicated themselves to issues related to the concerns of mothers, children, the poor, and societal well-being, issues that had occupied the women reformers of earlier eras. The endurance of women's activism premised on gender difference is a striking feature of the 1920s.

But claims based on assumptions of a gender-differentiated world met with a mixed record of policy success. The child labor amendment suffered defeat in the course of the decade. The Sheppard-Towner Maternity and Infancy Protection Act was passed over the opposition of the American Medical Association in the early years of the twenties, but by the end of the decade the renewal of the act failed to win the support of Congress.[7] The Cable Act, which did allow a woman to base her claim to citizenship on her own national status rather than that of her husband, became law in 1922 but with provisions that still treated women differently from their spouses.[8]

These groups and their issues had more success than was true for activists within the equal rights domain of women's organizing. Reformers espousing equal rights for women on the basis of sameness, not difference, and outside the political realm (of the voting booth, office holding, or naturalization) met much stronger opposition. The National Woman's Party's Equal Rights Amendment, which was intended to strike down the profusion of laws specifying different treatment of men and women, was fiercely debated but went nowhere as a national legislative proposal.[9]

Even within the male-dominated professions, arguments over the meaning of equality—its basis in sameness or difference—continued. Most women's organizations in male-dominated professions supported the equal rights approach, opposing protective labor laws that they saw as compromising women's job opportunities. The Women's Press Club, various women's medical associations, the Women's Lawyers' Association, the Women's Real Estate Association, the Federation of Women Dentists, and businesswomen's associations joined with the equal rights organizations in New York and in other states to oppose protective legislation.[10]

But the position taken by particular groups of professional women depended in part on the norms of each individual profession. The example of women in medicine is an interesting case in point. Women in medicine were advocates of both difference and sameness positions. More readily than in some other professions, women in medicine could carve out for themselves professional roles that were consonant with the traditional images of women as nurturant caretakers. Their support for the Sheppard-Towner Act, which the National Woman's Party equal rights feminists saw as reinforcing the view that all women were mothers (and which their parent institution, the AMA, opposed), was consonant with the obligation many women doctors felt they had to the welfare of women and children.[11] Patricia M. Hummer writes that women doctors were particularly engaged in preventive medicine and humanitarian causes. They founded the American Women's Hospitals, seventy-two in number, throughout France, Serbia, Turkey, Russia, Armenia, and Japan, whose work was largely ignored by the male medical journals but was covered in the *Medical Woman's Journal.*[12]

Women in medicine also pursued an equal rights approach attempting to make claims on their own behalf. The Medical Women's National Association, for example, recommended that coeducational institutions put women representatives on their admissions committees, denouncing, as Hummer remarks, "the trend developing in many schools at the end of the decade [of the twenties] of intimidating female students by admitting only one per class."[13] The MWNA endeavored to collect data on discriminatory practices in medical training and service in order to challenge the bias in acceptances to internships and residency programs and lobbied for changes in policies that barred women doctors from the military and the upper ranks of government medical service. Historical analyses of the 1920s describe women's groups in male professions as working to gather data, discuss issues of common concern, pass resolutions, guide women in career choices. The MWNA is described as an effective lobbying group,[14] and women lawyers and business and professional women as working in some states to block protective legislation.

But not surprisingly, these organizations of women in medicine, in law, in universities, or in business did not deploy the strategies that became the trademark of feminist groups inside male institutions fifty years later—undertaking litigation, initiating media exposés, or in other vociferous, demonstrative ways protesting the denial of opportunities that women in male-dominated institutions faced. The reasons gender politics inside institutions was more contained in the 1920s are not hard to discern. Women's numbers were small. Women in certified law schools and women in medical schools hovered in the range of 5 percent of all graduates, and only one-third of those in medicine at its peak joined the MWNA.[15] More important, there was no reason to expect that a court of law would look favorably on any assertion that women were being denied equality of opportunities on the basis of their sex. The Supreme Court held fairly closely to the view that the differentiation made in the law between women and men did not contravene any constitutional guarantee. The famous 1873 *Bradwell* decision—in which a concurring judge went well beyond legal justifications to invoke not only the civil law but "nature herself" in affirming a lower court decision upholding an Illinois statute excluding women from admission to the bar—was still "good law" in the 1920s.[16] In *Muller v. Oregon* (1908), the court cited "women's physical structure" and the "burdens of motherhood" in upholding an Oregon law that prohibited women from working more than a ten-hour day.[17] When the court finally (and only temporarily) struck down a (minimum wage) law that differentiated between women and men, in *Adkins v. Children's Hospital* (1923), the upshot of its decision was to "allow" women workers to negotiate a minimum wage on the same basis as men—hardly an opportunity in and of itself to enjoy equality in the world of work.[18] In fact, a cartoon of the period pictured the *Adkins* justice transmitting his decision to an emaciated "woman wage earner" and saying, "This decision, Madam, represents your constitutional right to starve."[19]

It is not necessary to look far in order to explain why in the decade of the 1920s, feminist claims based on assumptions of gender sameness did not make much headway in male-dominated institutions outside the realm of electoral politics, where women's rights had, as a result of years of campaigning and constitutional amendment, finally been acknowledged. In 1920, after a government report revealed that women were barred from taking 60 percent of all civil service tests, the Civil Service Commission ruled that all exams were to be open to both men and women, but allowed department chiefs to continue to specify preference as to the gender of the prospective appointee. No further congressional provision was made to ensure equality of opportunity in employment or education during the decade. But the difficulty was not only one of access or opportunity; it was also one of norms. This inactivity in the legislature and the continued affirmation in the courts of gender difference (with the brief exception of *Adkins*) could only have dampened the aspirations women had of acting on their own behalf, wishing professional success for themselves, believing themselves entitled to demand economic rights for women on a par with those of men.

Equal rights feminism failed to be institutionalized within male-dominant arenas of the economy and of society in the 1920s. The idea of gender difference and the need for protective legislation continued to be espoused by those who sought to speak on behalf of wage-earning women. Equal rights feminism had its strong adherents among professional women inside male-dominated institutions, but given their scanty numbers and without the law on their side, the politics they pursued within their institutional environments remained subdued.

THE 1970S AND BEYOND: UNLEASHING FEMINIST CLAIMS

The turn toward equal rights in the second half of the twentieth century ignited feminist politics within institutions. This might not have occurred, however, were it not the case that the structure of women's lives was changing. With declining birth- and rising divorce rates, and with the decline in male employment and wages in the manufacturing sector, more women of all social backgrounds sought paid work (half of all women with preschool children in 1985 were in the labor force),[20] including higher paying jobs in previously male-domains of work.

The shift of women into male-dominant spheres of work has been dramatic. As Johanna Brenner reports, in the late 1960s, women had become 18 percent of orchestra members, rising to 28 percent in 1985 (and 47 percent in metropolitan orchestras). By the mid-1980s women were 39 percent of all employed economists, 34 percent of computer systems analysts, and 25 percent of all associates in law firms (although only 6 percent of partners). By the mid-1980s, women were 23 percent of all graduating dentists, 31 percent of medical school graduates and MBAs, and close to 40 percent of law school graduates.[21] By the mid-1990s, women had become 17 percent of all circuit court judges, 14 percent of all District Court judges, and 20 percent of all full-time U.S. magistrates. Women's numbers in the military rose from 3.8 percent of all officers in 1972 to 13 percent in the mid-1990s, and from 1.6 percent of all enlisted personnel in 1972 to 11.8 percent in the mid-1990s.[22] By the mid-1990s, women were counted as 12 percent of all electrical and electronic equipment repairers, 36 percent of all machine operators, assemblers, and inspectors, and 15 percent of all police and detectives.[23] As Victor R. Fuchs writes, "In 1960 the higher-level professional and managerial occupations were almost exclusively male preserves. Only 6 percent of the *new* lawyers, physicians, and doctoral degree recipients were women, whereas 94 percent were men—a ratio of 16 to 1. By 1985, more than one-third of the new entrants to those high level jobs were women—the ratio was less than 2 to 1."[24]

The proliferation of equal rights legislation and court rulings in the 1970s and the shifting educational and occupational trends among women led for the first time to vocal claims making within male-dominated societal and state institutions. The 1980s Reagan and Bush administrations ushered in an intently conservative period. But the language of rights that had developed in the 1960s and 1970s within Congress and the courts gave feminist activists inside institutional spaces the capacity to continue some of the contentious and disruptive politics that the second wave of feminist activism had initiated.

In the decade and a half leading up to the 1960s, in what Verta Taylor and Leila Rupp have aptly dubbed "surviving the 'doldrums,'" feminism existed largely in elite provinces of political life. The National Woman's Party, the core of the feminist efforts of the period, continued to push for the Equal Rights Amendment, but the fifteen-year period between the Second World War and the early 1960s saw little happen in the legislative or judicial arenas.[25]

Beginning in 1963 with the Equal Pay Act, however—followed closely by the passage of Title VII of the Civil Rights Act of 1964 barring discrimination in employment based on race, color, religion, national origin, and sex; Executive Orders 11246 and 11375 in 1965 and 1968, which required firms contracting with the government to undertake affirmative action programs in an effort to meet equal opportunity goals; and Title IX of the Educational Amendments of 1972, which barred discrimination in all federally financed educational programs—the language of equal opportunity was broadly diffused.

It is easy to forget that the constitutional guarantees of equal rights have been available to women only within the most recent past. Astonishingly, it was not until 1971 in *Reed v. Reed*[26] that the equal protection clause of the Fourteenth Amendment was used to strike down a law considered to be discriminatory on the basis of sex (discounting *Adkins*, where any antidiscrimination outcome was likely to be dubious at best).[27] From the 1970s onward, the courts have been flooded with equal protection (Fourteenth Amendment) and Title VII hiring, promotion, and harassment cases, Title IX cases challenging discrimination in education and sports, challenges to unfair credit and insurance practices, and discrimination claims in all conceivable institutional arenas. The courts together with the legislature have enunciated reams of decisions and policies that provide as well as bar opportunities for claims making on the basis of sex, and which, in so doing, authorize certain conceptions of gender equality, discouraging others.

For much of the 1970s and 1980s (a process that continues through the present), feminists have pushed the legislature and the courts to expand and strengthen the reach of equal rights legislation and the Fourteenth Amendment's guarantee of equal protection. Over the decades the courts have been faced with seemingly limitless questions: Could an employer prefer one sex over another by stipulating that a job involved a bona fide occupational qualification? Was work that was comparable in value, rather than identical in job description, covered under equal rights provisions? Was sexual harassment a form of sex discrimination that could be litigated under Title VII? Was trafficking in pornography an act of sex discrimination? Should discrimination based on sex be dealt with under the same strict standards as discrimination based on race? Were single-sex educational institutions necessarily discriminatory? Were laws or policies distinguishing between men and women on the basis of conditions (such as pregnancy) that are distinctive to female biology a denial of equal protection? Any standard undergraduate text reviewing the case law on gender and equal rights as it has developed since *Reed v. Reed* (1971) covers between fifty and seventy-five significant cases.[28]

Without doubt this torrent of cases registered the increasing power of feminist claims making. But the shift from assumptions of difference in the early part of the century to the equal treatment approaches of the contemporary legal system is not, from a variety of feminist perspectives, unproblematic. The intense debates within feminism about the adequacy of equal treatment as a remedy for gender inequality have generated at least three important critiques: The first is the problem of false gender neutrality. Sandra Bem refers to this as seeing the world through the lens of androcentrism, whereby the apparently objective standard being utilized is based on experiences born of male biology and male biography.[29] When, as was true in the much cited case of *G.E. v. Gilbert* (1976), for instance, the company's insurance policy excluded pregnancy, the court ruled that such a policy was not discriminatory since it differentiated between "pregnant women and nonpregnant persons" and did not protect male employees from any risk from which women were not protected and vice versa.[30] According to this critique, difference is discouraged and inequalities are addressed through pressure on those who are different to accommodate themselves within a single, male-centered standard of conduct.

A second critique focuses on the problem of the preexisting construction of difference, which an equal treatment approach ignores. In *EEOC v. Sears, Roebuck & Co.* (1988), for instance, the company claimed that the absence of women in their high-paying sales jobs was not discriminatory but simply reflected the long-standing disinterest of women in applying for this kind of nontraditional "big-ticket" work (selling large appliances).[31] Under equal rights law, there is no presumption that preexisting inequalities will be rectified by equal treatment under the law.

A third critique is an umbrella category for a range of different criticisms that might be thought of as the problem of "classification" in general. Through the stipulation that some category of people should not be denied equality of treatment given to another category of people, certain "differences" are privileged and others rendered invisible. Kimberlé Crenshaw writes about the importance of rights law for those denied power in American history, describing at the same time, however, the failure of equal protection to take into account the experiences of those who are at the intersection of recognized categories. Thus African-American women who charged General Motors with discrimination could demonstrate neither that they were victims of race discrimination (since there was a representative number of Black men on the assembly line) nor that they were victims of sex discrimination (since there was a sufficient representation of white women in the secretarial group from which they had been excluded).[32] The difficulty of demonstrating discrimination on the basis of sex where sex is constructed as sexual orientation and the near-impossibility of seeking judicial remedies for discrimination based on class[33] raise the specter in equal protection law that some categories will be reified while other very real inequalities will be obscured. Under the rights revolution, this critique suggests, the category "women" comes to assume (much as with the androcentric

standard in the case of men) the experience and bodies of white, heterosexual, and middle-class women. This critique points to the ways that
equal rights both provides and denies opportunities for claims making at
the same time as rights law fashions the norms by which groups come to
see themselves and relate to one another.[34]

Exactly how the institutionalization of equal rights has shaped the
politics of feminism inside male-dominant institutional spaces and
whether these critiques are empirically borne out as problems that severely undercut the promises of equal treatment are the questions this
book addresses in the analysis of feminism in the military and the
church. For the purposes of this chapter's discussion, however, it is
enough to note that in contrast to the decades following the first wave
of the women's movement when feminism lacked state "authorization,"
the "legal" promulgation of equality of opportunity in the second wave
was principally responsible for exciting feminist activism within institutional spaces.

LAW AS OPPORTUNITY, LAW AS NORMS: THE STUDY OF INSTITUTIONS

The opportunity the law furnishes and its effect in generating political
activism are true to the account offered by the "political opportunity"
school of social movement scholars. Sidney Tarrow, writing on the role
of political opportunity structures, identifies four kinds of openings: access to the political system, instability of political alignments, the possibility of elite alliances, and cleavages among elites.[35] The legislative and
judicial turn to equal opportunity in the last decades fits this description
of the importance of political access. Rights law created an opportunity
for claims making inside male-dominant institutions, just as it is also the
case that political activism inside institutions, reciprocally, led to a profusion of rights activity in the legislatures and courts, creating new opportunities for political agitation.[36]

But the way opportunities affect political activism can only be fully
understood in dynamic relationship to the normative environment in
which activists operate. What the analysis of political opportunities, by
itself, cannot explain is why openings for activism are not necessarily recognized as such, or why some opportunities are simply not seized
whereas others are.[37] Emphasizing the interactive relationship of opportunities and norms, Lee Ann Banaszak makes a compelling argument for
discerning how opportunity structures shape beliefs, preferences, and
values. Observing that feminist politics in America was molded by its
marginalization within the Republican Party (where women activists

had in earlier days found a receptive home) and by its alliance with the Democrats, Banaszak argues, "Thus, by constraining certain networks and expanding others, the political opportunity structure may alter the values, beliefs, and tactics of a social movement and its activists."[38]

Following Banaszak and others,[39] I argue here that the law does provide an opportunity for activism; but it does so in part by shaping the values, beliefs, and preferences that activists hold. When the American women's movement mobilized around the Equal Rights Amendment, which defined equality in terms of what men had that women were denied, it would have been a mistake to presume that women had less need for social provisions better subsumed under a "difference" than under an equal rights framework—such as child care, Medicaid-funded abortions, or family leave. The movement's focus of greater attention on equal rights than on "difference" issues, Anne Costain argues, was a result in part of the ways the legislature and governmental agencies (and the courts, it could be added) reacted more responsively to equal rights claims, influencing in turn the values and priorities of the women's movement in the 1970s and 1980s.[40] This is about the opening of opportunities to influence policy, but it is also about how legal institutions shape the perceptions and behavior of the actors involved.

Aligning opportunities with the social environment is the concern of those who study institutions. Institutions are what an organization or set of organizations comes to "represent" in the minds of some relevant group of people. Institutions, like organizations, have structures, functions, and rules. Unlike organizations, however, institutions are denoted by a set of norms and beliefs shared among a given population.[41] As organizations, Harvard, Yale, and Princeton, for instance, function to instruct students and conduct research, for which they must recruit and support teachers and research scholars. As institutions, Ivy League universities are believed to stand for certain norms—educational excellence, the anointing of elites, the primacy of academics over football and "frat" life, among other shared values. When I refer to institutions in this book—to the Catholic Church, the armed forces, and the law as institutions—I am specifically intending to convey that these institutions do more than structure people's daily routines; they also assign value to what people do, and they shape the very self-definitions people come to hold.

The "new institutionalism," the study of institutions in political science, is a capacious term that covers a wide swathe of analytical approaches. Walter Powell and Paul DiMaggio are right when they say that it is easiest to describe the new institutionalism in terms of what it is not.[42] What it is not is a rationalist view of politics that starts with the individual and takes interests and identities as exogenously given, external to institutions, and unnecessary to an analysis of individual actions or choices.[43] Institutionalism, by contrast, sees the norms, rules, structures, and routines of institutions as formative. For the rationalist, research begins with questions about what individuals want and how they conceive of their interests. For the institutionalist, research begins with context; institutionalist approaches ask how the acts of an individual or collectivity can be understood in the context of how institutions promote particular opportunities, ideologies, interests, and identities.[44]

The study of institutions in comparative politics and international relations has generated an important concept described as "nesting" that refers to the interconnecting locations of different institutional contexts.[45] If we think of institutions as nested, Russian doll–like, one within another, it is certainly the case, as David Meyer argues, that there are different amounts of space for movement within what he calls "wiggle room" or political "slack."[46] The force of a given institution's norms, rules, or structures in exacting conformity from those within it may be related to the proximity of that institution to a broader institutional environment exerting similar kinds of pressure. Take the example of the association of women's historians, known as the "Berks." The "Berks" was begun by a group of women historians who felt on the margins of the history profession. For many years, they met as a small group in the Berkshire Hills during an annual weekend when they discussed issues of common interest. Initially, what drew them together was their shared identity as historians. They were not students of women's history, and they did not come together around any identity as feminists. In the 1970s, interest and pressure from younger, feminist historians led to the establishment of a bigger Berkshire conference—what has now become a major women's studies event, resisted by some of the original women founders.[47] This expansion (a better word than "takeover") might not have been possible had the original "little" Berks been closely nested within the larger institution of American historians, and had it been able to invoke the authority of the larger organization. But since the original Berks was, itself, an insurgent organization, uneasily "nested" within the broader institution of historians, its members had little reason to exert authority to resist the change coming partly from within (and partly from outside) its own borders.

Although the literature on institutions provides useful insight into institutional nesting, it has remarkably little to say about the situating of marginalized groups located within institutional locales. Studies coming out of the organizational behavior tradition are inclined to ask questions about efficiency and productivity, about why organizations that might be expected to diverge in character resemble each other, and about organizational conformity, rather than asking how contending groups vie for institutional power.[48] For the most part (the newer analyses of gender and organization excepted)[49] institutional studies do not ask who benefits and who loses as a result of particular institutional arrangements, how power is allocated, or what might cause different groups to gain or relinquish institutional control. And yet, by highlighting both opportunities and normative environments within which activism operates, the focus on institutions provides useful tools for the analysis of power relations in environments where activists endeavor to challenge existing inequalities.[50]

It is a mistake to view the norms of an institution as either shared by all or frozen in time. The now-vast literature on gender describes the biological and sexual, materialist, psychological, cultural, and discursive systems that construct difference.[51] Indeed the very project of feminism has been about understanding the way identities are differentiated in gendered terms through systems of male dominance. In the light of the discussion of gender, race, and other differences, it is useful to consider institutions as defined not only by shared values but also by disagreements. What David Laitin argues about culture is also true about institutions: that part of what describes collectivities (whether institutions or culture) is agreement on what requires debate.[52] To observe that in recent decades feminist protest has been institutionalized is to recognize that feminist issues now compel discussion. From a feminist point of view, this can be read as progress, but it is not inconsistent with what commentators such as Susan Jeffords and Susan Faludi describe as the resurgence of cultural conservatism.[53] Without the institutionalization of feminist protest, there would have been no need for the assault on feminism that both Jeffords and Faludi describe.

For protest to occur inside institutions, there must be protected spaces or habitats where activists can meet, share experiences, receive affirmation, and strategize for change.[54] These may be physical spaces—a regular table in a lunchroom, a locker room, an office, a newsletter—or they may be shared cognitive habitats. Lesbians in the military, for example, have a wealth of signs and behavioral codes (as well as sports teams and social meeting places) that provide for mutual recognition and validation, even as overt lesbian organization inside today's military is out of the question.

By focusing on institutions and the spaces for activism within them, this book endeavors to identify the ways that activists are influenced by the norms of their localized environment and make choices about goals and strategies in reaction to existing institutional opportunities. Over the last decades the incorporation of rights language within the law and the broader institutional diffusion of equality of opportunity norms have led to the "legalization" of protest inside institutions. What this legalization means in terms of both norms and opportunities is a central question of this study.

INSTITUTIONS: INSIDE AND OUTSIDE

The idea of protest existing inside institutions clashes with the usual understandings about the location of political activism. Conventional wisdom assigns the role of disruption exclusively to social movements, to extrainstitutional organizing. Institutional actors (lawyers, judges, politicians, employers, and journalists) are definitionally precluded from being social movement activists—except after hours. Those who wield influence inside institutions are denoted as "third parties" called upon as professional allies of, rather than as actual parties to, a movement's effort to effect change.[55] Movements are assisted by institutional actors but institutions are not, in this view, actual sites of mobilizational politics.

The presumed inconsistency between movement politics and institutional politics is based on a frequently drawn linkage of location, form, and content. When social movement actors doing street politics (location) opt for or ally themselves with those who utilize conventional modes (form) of political activism such as lobbying or voting, a social movement is generally deemed to have crossed the threshold separating protest politics from institutional politics, and the result is presumed to be deradicalizing (content).*

There are three hazards one would do well to avoid in specifying the relationship between movements and institutions. The first is the tendency to presume a dichotomous, rather than more continuous, distinction between outsiders and insiders. One need not go the full distance of Michel Foucault's minimization of state power or of broad, systemic (racial, patriarchal, capitalist) discourses in order to recognize (with Foucault) that the dispersed disciplinary power of organizations creates a world where sharp demarcations between those who are part of "the" establishment and those who are outside it are inadequate.

The second hazard is the tendency to elision, blurring political space, political method, and political claims. Their linkage needs to be demonstrated, not implied, and the conditionalities that shape their connections should be specified.

Third is the presumption that what holds for one social movement applies equally well to others. Whatever definitional distinction is made

---

* It is ironic that we tend to believe that when our *opponents* move into power-wielding educational, cultural, or political institutions, they are gaining real power—whether it is establishing a foothold or a stranglehold on the instruments of power. Conservatives believe this about liberals and the liberals are similarly convinced about the power conservatives exercise within institutions. But when each sees its own gaining access to institutions, there is fear that political commitments will be diluted, and compromise and cooptation will ensue.

between movement and institution is likely to elucidate the political iterations of some social movements better than others. Freedom fighters in nationalist movements staged violent protests or civil disobedience and then joined legislatures. If this trajectory also captures important aspects of civil rights history in the United States, it does a less successful job of describing the women's movement. Constrained by traditional gender role stereotypes and by political choice, feminist activists' arsenal of political strategies has drawn only fleetingly on demonstrative protest activities and even more rarely on violent activism. This raises the question of whether the very definitional distinction of conventional and unconventional political forms is situated in the experience of freedom movements and, most particularly, in the era of the 1960s male-dominated New Left and civil rights movements.

It is only through the attempt to circumvent these three conceptual traps that it is possible to account for this book's twin claims: That, on the one hand, disruption-provoking feminist activism has burgeoned even within such restrictive institutional environments as the military and the church, and that, on the other hand, despite the strikingly similar hierarchical and command-based structures of the military and the church, feminist protest therein developed along dramatically different lines.

INSIDE-OUTSIDE: A THREE-DIMENSIONAL CONTINUUM[56]

It is possible to explain how protest can survive on the inside of institutions—including such "total" or "greedy" institutions as the military and the church—only if we abandon the binary notion of inside and outside.[57] Even with institutions that are voraciously demanding of their members' time and loyalty, those on the inside are often not fully sequestered. Those on the outside, moreover, often are not as autonomous as might be presumed because of ties to institutional funding, links to institutional networks, or shared ideological positions. A distinction between inside and outside needs to be made, but these locations are at two ends of a continuum, and there is much shared space in between.

To define activists as outsiders or insiders based on the degree to which they are critics of a given institution is problematic even as it is usual in common parlance. It obscures the very question that should be examined: *What* about location shapes the form and content of a group's politics? In a useful definitional discussion of social movements, Paul Burstein, Rachel L. Einwohner, and Jocelyn A. Hollander address the question of what outsider status means. One set of approaches they consider and find wanting defines social movements as engaged in giving voice to outsiders who lack representation in established institutions or who are politically unmobilized.[58] They observe, I believe correctly, that these approaches definitionally preclude the possibility of meaningful movement activity once insider status or representation has been gained. They argue, joining Doug McAdam, for limiting the definition of outsider status to groups that use noninstitutionalized and disruptive movement *tactics*: "Noninstitutionalized tactics," they write, "customarily have two defining characteristics: They involve activities that (1) are not part of the formal political process and (2) are intended to be disruptive (whether they are legal or illegal). Sit-ins, mass marches, and boycotts are examples. Not included are legally regulated components of the political process such as voting and lobbying; unregulated but non-disruptive tactics such as letter-writing campaigns; and sometimes disruptive but institutionalized forms of participation such as continuous court challenges to proposed regulations (a tactic often employed by environmentalists, for example)."[59] Because the intention of this book is to elucidate what effect location has on choice of strategies and on outcome, however, it would be problematic to define insider or outsider location in terms of tactics and disruptive intent or outcome. One cannot define location in terms of the very same concepts whose causal relationship one is trying to assess.

One approach to avoid any presuppositions about the tactics or disruptive intent of outsiders or insiders is to focus, instead, on the lines of accountability that bind people to institutions.[60] Insider or outsider location, then, is discernible by the degree to which activists believe themselves to be accountable to the institution of which they are a part. It is crucial to recognize, here, that accountability is multidimensional. Accountability is *financial* (who funds whom, who scrutinizes whose budget), *organizational* (who reports to whom) and, in Jane Mansbridge's useful words, *discursive* (whom activists identify with).[61] Activists may be organizationally accountable to their own institution, for instance, but discursively accountable to groups or a set of ideas that originate outside. Discursive accountability, Mansbridge suggests, is evident in the questions activists ask themselves or are asked by others, such as, "Is this a feminist way to think/to act?" Inside or outside location, then, can be seen in terms of a three-dimensional scale of accountability.

Acknowledging such multidimensionality, we can recognize most feminist activists as neither wholly insiders nor outsiders. Hester Eisenstein writes that "femocrats," a term coined in Australia to describe feminist bureaucrats, are often seen by feminist movement leaders as unresponsive bureaucratic loyalists, but by government colleagues as feminist fanatics.[62] Patricia Hill Collins writes about African-American women as "outsiders within" to describe the simultaneity of experiencing a situation through the knowledge gained of having multiple accountabilities.[63]

Just as feminists inside institutions are rarely entirely insiders, activists working in autonomous lobbying groups are often tied to institutional authority. Claire Reinelt describes the dynamics that ensue from the now common funding assistance given to battered women's movement organizations by the state—the concern, too, of Sandra Morgen's work on the women's health movement.[64] The result has been, Reinelt states, "The blurring of boundaries, between who is and is not a movement activist, between hierarchical and collective processes, and between movement and mainstream institutions. . . ."[65]

AVOIDING THE CONFLATION OF LOCATION, FORM, AND CONTENT

Rather than assuming (or defining) activism inside institutions as involving certain kinds of political strategies and outcomes, one must rise to the challenge of specifying the conditions under which activism assumes particular forms and leads to particular results. It is plausible to hypothesize, for instance, that the more connected or accountable institutional activists feel themselves to be to those on the outside, the more likely they may be to take risks and protest institutional practices. The accountability to the outside may take organizational, financial, or discursive form. An example of this organizational accountability to the outside is suggested in an interesting essay by Cheryl Gilkes. Gilkes describes Black women heads of social service agencies who sought to transform the rules in their institutional environments. By serving on each other's organizational boards and thereby creating dual organizational accountability for themselves, they sought to advance this transformational project.[66] A counterexample may be suggested by what some feminists see as the growing depoliticization of feminism inside academia. Feminist scholars have become increasingly accountable, the charge reads, either to their specific disciplines or to new interdisciplinary but still professionalized standards of scholarship that may work at cross-purposes with sustaining connections to feminist projects outside the confines of academia.

The conditions for sustaining activism on the inside may also vary with the degree to which activists see themselves as accountable to their institution. The closer to the institution the activists are on all three dimensions (financial, organizational, and discursive), the more necessary it may be for extrainstitutional organizations to make contact and maintain pressure. To use a stark example, prison activists can simply not organize effectively in the absence of alliances with external groups.

Juanita Diaz-Cotto describes the efforts of Latina prisoners to get access to decent medical care and improved prison conditions. Without litigation by third parties and persistent monitoring and communication by outside groups, it is hard to see how groups on the inside might have sustained their organizational efforts.[67] If, as I suggest earlier in the chapter, the "legalization" of equal rights has been important in galvanizing protest inside institutions, it follows as likely that the greater the proximity inside activists have to legal authority, the more likely that protest can be sustained.

The multidimensional character of accountability and the linkages among those who are differently placed along an inside-outside continuum help to account for the fact that activists often do not assimilate fully into the norms of an institution. A simple inside-outside binary may obscure the reasons for the present reality and the future possibility of protest inside institutions.

MOVEMENT TRAJECTORIES

There are multiple accounts of the sequences by which political activism moves from movement to institution and vice versa. One prototype, deriving more from common wisdom than from social science literature, sees institutions as the retirement home of movement leaders who abandon the drama and sometimes violence of street politics for the routines of mainstream occupations. That is how, for instance, the examples of Bernadine Dohrn and Tom Hayden are sometimes interpreted.[68] A second portrayal, suggested by Sidney Tarrow's study of Italy, notes the incubating or protective function of institutions that are the home to protesters whose activism may later help to spark a broader societywide wave of mobilization.[69] A similar view, suggested by Aldon Morris, describes institutions as the soil where seeds of movement consciousness are cultivated. "Throughout time," Morris writes, "for significant numbers of oppressed people, the groundwork for social protest has been laid by the insurgent ideas rooted within their churches, labor unions, voluntary associations, music, informal conversation, humor, and collective memories of those elders who participated in earlier struggles." Institutions are where "oppositional consciousness matures and becomes combat-ready."[70] A third depiction, drawn by Verta Taylor, speaks of institutions as "abeyance structures" harboring activists until the next movement cycle gathers speed.[71]

The Tarrow, Morris, and Taylor accounts provide useful correctives to the version of the 1960s events that portrayed protesters as materializing spontaneously on the streets "outside the system" and expiring once "inside the establishment." For the protester of today, it is as if the handbook of Chairman Mao has been supplanted by the essential writings of Michel Foucault. Most feminists of the second wave live their lives inside institutions—inside universities, churches, professions, unions, hospitals, social service agencies, schools, police forces, military corps, athletic teams. They have learned that the linkages connecting those on the inside to those on the outside are multilayered: language, money, and organizational networks work in complex fashion to link the inside and outside. The question for today's activists is what sets of these complicated conditionalities make protest possible.

CONCLUSION

The institutionalization of protest in the United States is both old and new. It is old in the sense that the drama of social movement politics on the streets has always had an institutional antecedent and an institutional echo. It is new in the sense that the incorporation of the language of rights within the documents of congressional legislation and judicial decision making has provoked unprecedented levels of claims making inside institutions.

What is also new is the presence of increasing numbers of women inside once male-dominated institutions. This new demography and the new democracy of rights have galvanized the outbreak of feminist protest in the core male-dominated institutions of the American state and of American society. Changes in U.S. law have established opportunities for feminist claims making within institutions. In their normative dimension, laws have also shaped feminist values and self-definitions.

Located in differently nested institutional habitats, feminist activism is often both inside and outside of established centers of power. Discursive, financial, and organizational linkages often bridge feminist movement and institutional authority. "Power and authority," as Biddy Martin has eloquently written, "are no longer vested in a central point, not in Foucault's analysis or in the actual workings of power in our world. Nor does resistance arise from a single point. For that reason, a very different form of political organization and struggle suggests itself, an alternative to the frontal attack on the state led by the One revolutionary subject. . . ."[72] But how these multiple institutional locations, together with the concurrent turn to the courts in the pursuit of equal rights, blunt or sharpen the critical voice of feminism inside institutions is the question to which this book turns in the next four chapters. The military and the church are particularly important institutions for this study because of their very different relationships to the institution of the law. Activists in the military enjoy greater proximity to the legislature and courts than do their feminist counterparts in the church; this distinction allows us to ask how the language of rights has been utilized, by whom, on whose behalf, with what effect, in the face of which alternatives?

PART TWO

THE MILITARY

Chapter Three

INTEREST-GROUP ACTIVISM

"HERE TODAY in the East Room of the White House," President Lyndon Johnson declared in 1967, "we will end the last vestige of discrimination—I hope—in our Armed Forces."[1] The bill he signed, PL 90-130, lifted the ceiling on promotions for military women officers and the restriction on the recruitment of women that had been set by law at 2 percent of the forces. Nineteen sixty-seven was, however, less the end of sex discrimination than it was the beginning of feminist political protest within the military environment. The new language of rights that the law unleashed and a shift in the demographics of the armed forces implanted feminist protest within the U.S. military. In 1973 the draft was replaced by the All-Volunteer Force (AVF), causing the military to turn to women recruits in the face of a dearth of qualified men. The invocation of equal rights together with the entry of rising numbers of women set the stage for the ascendance of feminist institutional activism.

A long walk down the narrow Pentagon corridors leads to a small suite of offices of the Defense Advisory Committee on Women in the Services (DACOWITS), which monitors women's issues throughout the military. Less than a mile from the Pentagon, in the Navy Annex, another three-person office houses a navy captain and her assistants, who are the designated clearinghouse for women's policy issues in the navy. Across the Potomac, in the District of Columbia, are an array of lobbying, research, and policy organizations: The Women and Military Project of the Women's Research and Educational Institute monitors the progress of military women and runs workshops that address current issues of concern; the Servicemembers Legal Defense Network tracks policy and provides support for uniformed gays and lesbians; and the National Women's Law Center drafts legal analyses of military policy as it affects women—to name merely a few of the relevant organizations. Back on the Beltway, toward Maryland, is the home and office of the editor of *Minerva*, a journal that specializes in reporting on women's activities within the military. Clear across the country, in the environs of the Air Force Academy, a legal rights organization called WANDAS files suits on behalf of uniformed women who are charging the military with discrimination. Women from each of these organizations all know each other. They are also the information sources for a network of journalists and academics who write about military and gender issues, and who stay in contact by fax, email, and phone.[2]

This network is part of a longer list of feminist groups that constitute the institutionalization of feminist protest in the military. For two decades, advocates of gender equality inside the military, supported by civilian feminist activists, have been pressuring political and military leaders to make equality of opportunity into operative policy. From their habitats located within the Department of Defense or in the environment of the military, activists pressure policy-makers to take gender equality seriously. The institutionalization of feminist politics does not yet mean that equal opportunity norms prevail within the institution; what it means is that a feminist organizational presence within the armed forces is there for the duration.

My purpose in this chapter is primarily to describe the appearance (remarkable, given its unlikely institutional setting) of feminist interest-group activism in the military. I defer until the following chapter an analysis of how the law sustains military feminism in its particular influence-seeking, interest-group form and how the law simultaneously restricts feminism's reach. In this chapter, I begin by recounting the 1991 efforts of women aviators and their civilian supporters to pressure Congress to amend the combat exclusion, an example of the influence-seeking, pragmatic politics of military feminism. I then turn back in time in order to describe how military women once accepted the logic of gender difference, abandoning it in the 1970s for equal opportunity norms. In the next section, I discuss how the pursuit of equal opportunity has been dependent on the collaboration of military insiders and civilians who are in varying degrees insiders and outsiders. The chapter concludes with a discussion of the inadequacy of terms like *co-optation* or *de-politicization* in describing feminist protest within the armed forces. The story this chapter tells is about how equal opportunity feminism came to life within the institution of the military.

INTEREST-GROUP ACTIVISM AT WORK IN THE HALLS OF CONGRESS

In the military, feminist protest takes the form of interest-group politics. The objective of military women's activism is to influence policies set by Congress, formulated in the courts, or promulgated within the military itself. Military feminists demand the right to job assignments based on competence, not gender, the right to work in an environment in which sexual harassment against military women is not business as usual, and the right to be treated with the same respect as the men next to whom they work. In the setting of the military, these are radical goals. In the context of feminism more generally, what military women seek is more liberal or conservative than radical. But given the deeply masculinist character of the military, the sexual caste system that is only now just beginning to change, the punitive capacities of an institution that has little tolerance for dissent, and the resolution it takes to be a feminist in uniform, labels like "liberal" or "conservative" for military women activists are inadequate descriptions.

I employ the term "interest-group feminism" in preference to the range of alternative terminology in order to emphasize two aspects of military feminism. The first is uniformed feminism's focus on concrete "interests"—jobs and careers. Military women are concerned above all with securing women's rights to do whatever work women can prove themselves capable of doing. Because this also means demanding a change in the system and culture of discrimination in the services, women advocates also address themselves to questions about the character of the academies, harassment, rape, day care and family support services, body weight standards, and a range of other issues. Women activists always frame their claims in terms of enhancing military preparedness. A fighting force that is fit and prepared, they argue, cannot be one in which those best suited for the job are denied training and advancement based on gender alone.

My second reason for describing women's activism in "interest-group" terms is to emphasize the way these concrete demands entail the kinds of compromises and bargaining that are a defining part of what interest-group politics means more generally. But to say that women activists are prepared to compromise is not to say that over the years institutionalization has been synonymous with de-radicalization or co-optation. Over the years, the norms of what is acceptable have changed. In ever evolving ways, feminists have tested those boundaries, seeking at the same time to maintain the credibility that comes with being, at heart, institutional loyalists.

Lobbying to Change the Combat Exclusion Laws

"I've been here two years," a legislative aide to Senator William Roth (R-Delaware) commented, "[and] I can tell you that this was a model of interest-group politics all the way around."[3] Those working the issue, the aide went on to explain, were organized, they presented themselves well, they tracked the votes carefully, they were strategic, and they were ready to make critical compromises to ensure a successful legislative outcome.

The "model of interest-group politics" that Roth's aide, Mark Forman, was referring to was the tightly organized lobbying effort by women's groups to secure support on the Hill for the 1991 legislation that amended the combat exclusion of women. Women activists, both civilian and military, had organized an intense lobbying effort to repeal the law that had kept women aviators from flying combat aircraft.[4] This historic end to the legislative ban on women fliers' serving in combat was passed by both houses in summer 1991 as a provision of the Defense Authorization Act and signed into law by President Bush in December. The events of summer 1991 illustrate why military women activists believe it is worth speaking up in the language of equal opportunity.

On the heels of the Gulf War, women who had been energetically promoting gender equality within the military recognized that the moment was propitious to mount an effort (once again) to challenge the combat exclusion rules.[5] Despite their declared intent to protect women from risk of combat or enemy assault, the exclusion rules had failed to keep women from being targets of enemy fire. The deaths of both male and female soldiers in the army barracks of the Gulf had been a recent reminder of that truth. Combat restrictions did, however, obstruct women from holding the high-level jobs in the services in which experience in combat related specialties has always been close to a requisite for promotion to the higher ranks.

The Gulf War made clear that this issue of equality was not a routine matter of everyday discrimination on the job. It was now evident that women were risking, indeed sacrificing, their lives in combat situations, while their "right" to serve in combat and to be recognized for their military accomplishments was being officially denied.

About thirty-five to forty thousand military women were deployed in Operation Desert Storm.[6] Six women were killed in action, and three were taken prisoner by Iraqi forces.[7] Although women were a significant part of wartime military operations, the images presented by the media conveyed that reality only in part. As had been the case in Panama, restrictions on the news media's access to the site of combat operations meant that reporters sought out human interest stories, devoting considerable space to women's military presence. So stories of military women were not scarce. The problem was, however, that repeated stories and photographs of military mothers departing for the Gulf, leaving behind small children, reinforced stereotyped gendered images of women, suggesting that women were merely dressing up in men's clothes and playing at war. These portrayals, as Cynthia Enloe put it, of "Womenandchildren" were the dominant images relayed to the public of women's presence in the Gulf. But other interviews with uniformed women conducted from the barracks and work sites did convey the striking messages of women who knew they were facing dangers, who were struggling to overcome both boredom and fear. However mixed the message, television transmitted images of uniformed women to the American public in ways that left little doubt as to women's presence as part of an American fighting force.[8]

According to Major General Jeanne Holm (USAF—ret.), army women of the 101st Airborne Division Screaming Eagles were flying Black Hawk and Chinook helicopters transporting troops and supplies fifty miles into Iraq.[9] Women marines helped establish forward positions in the desert (driving trucks, setting up communications, digging bunkers), miles ahead of the "frontline" infantry. Women flew jet tankers refueling bombers and fighters in midair, bringing women pilots hundreds of miles across and into Iraqi territory. Women were loading and fusing five-hundred pound bombs on B-52s, launching Patriot missiles, driving and repairing trucks and heavy equipment, and refueling tanks.[10]

It was the very real threat, indeed, the reality of death that proved catalytic. The often grim news of military women's risking their lives was met with a renewed determination by activist women to end the hypocrisy of the combat exclusion.[11] When the first report came over the airwaves of a woman missing in action, one woman activist queried rhetorically, "Can you see her father in a committee hearing listening to some senator say that his daughter did not fight or die for her country?"[12]

In April 1991, the Defense Advisory Committee on Women in the Services (DACOWITS) passed a resolution at their spring meeting urging the secretary of defense to support repeal of the 1948 combat exclusion statutes, a vote that, as Jeanne Holm recounts, met with a standing ovation from the military women present at the meeting. In the course of the spring, even a small number of civilian and military leaders alluded to the anachronism of existing combat exclusion restrictions.[13]

Congresswoman Patricia Schroeder (D-Colorado), long a member of the House Armed Services Committee, submitted an amendment to the defense authorization bill that sought to dismantle the ban on women's flying fighter planes in the air force.[14] Her fellow Democrat, Congresswoman Beverly Byron (Maryland), chair of the House Military Personnel and Compensation Committee, moved to place her own imprint on any successful legislation, proposing that women pilots in the navy similarly be permitted to fly combat missions. The bill was passed in the House by voice vote with little opposition.

The amendment, however, met severe opposition in the Senate. Senate hearings in June had given critics time to mount a campaign against repeal. All four service chiefs openly opposed a change in the exclusion rules. If women aviators had wondered how their service commanders viewed them, the congressional hearings made it perfectly clear. A remarkable exchange between Senator William Cohen (Maine) and air force general Merrill McPeak registered how fundamental the belief has been in women as second-class members of the military.

> *Senator Cohen*: Suppose you had a woman pilot, she is an instructor pilot of superior intelligence, great physical conditioning, in every way she was superior to a male counterpart vying for a combat position. Would your personal judgment be because you would not want to see the risk to her life increased by putting her in a combat role that you would pick the male over the female under those circumstances?
>
> *General McPeak*: That is correct.
>
> *Senator Cohen*: So in other words you would have a militarily less effective situation because of a personal view.
>
> *General McPeak*: Well, I admit it doesn't make much sense, but that's the way I feel about it.[15]

McPeak's words were well received by women lobbyists such as Phyllis Schlafly and Elaine Donnelly from the Center for Military Readiness, long and reliable opponents of women in combat. Indeed, these opponents were in a position to promote a lobbying campaign of their own.[16] As Schlafly commented at a Heritage Foundation event, "The oft-stated goal of the radical feminists is a totally gender-neutral society, and the military is the cutting edge of this fantasy."[17]

It was at this point that pro-repeal women activists mobilized. The key pro-repeal players were two groups: the increasingly active organization of Women Military Aviators[18] and the hand-selected circle of women put together by Carolyn Becraft, then the foremost civilian policy strategist for women's military concerns. A "command and control" center was set up in Senator Roth's office under Becraft's stewardship. Becraft had directed the Women and Military Project of the defunct Women's Equity Action League and had since brought the project to the Women's Research and Education Institute (WREI). Understanding the unique opportunity before the Congress, she organized a lobbying effort of such efficiency that it hardly seemed handicapped by the group's scarce funds and limited organizational resources.

Becraft drew together a small but diverse coalition of women. It included a lobbyist (and former army nurse) from the American Nurses Association, a woman activist from a liberal women's law group, a conservative Bush appointee to the National Security Council who had served on the Defense Advisory Committee on Women in the Services (DACOWITS) and whose early resignation from the NSC allowed her to participate in discussions on the Hill,[19] and a National Organization of Women lobbyist who had come to NOW as their lesbian rights advocate. Briefing packages were prepared and distributed to senatorial offices.[20] The former NSC member was dispatched to meet with key conservatives, the NOW member with Hill liberals, Becraft and the others with the remaining key senate figures.

Women pilots, primarily from the navy, flew into Washington.[21] Although precluded from outright lobbying, they accompanied individuals from the coalition on their visits to congressional offices, providing information and briefings as permitted by their military status. Well aware of the visual effect that their uniformed presence created, activists sought to arrange for a triservice representation of women to accompany each of the visits that women lobbyists made to Hill offices. When congressional members wanted to know whether women could "pull nine g's" (endure the gravitational force of extreme acceleration), whether women were ready to fly bombing missions, to be captured or killed, these highly accomplished and articulate uniformed women were present to give first-person accounts.[22]

The aviators who arrived on the Hill were an extraordinarily well-spoken and self-possessed group of women, no surprise to anyone familiar with the highly selective military recruitment and promotion process through which they were chosen. To many, if not all, of these women, the very idea of needing congressional assessment of their capacity to pilot combat aircraft seemed almost offensive. Some of the women were highly experienced and had, indeed, been training male pilots for decades. Then-commander Rosemary Mariner had flown for twenty years. The first woman to fly a tactical jet and a frontline attack plane, and the first woman to command a navy aviation squadron, Mariner commented wryly that she hardly needed Congress or some national commission to tell her whether she could fly a plane.[23] Senator Roth's aide was right to have remarked on the textbooklike elements of interest-group politics manifested in this mobilization. All the features were there: the organized pursuit of group claims, compromise, bargaining, logrolling. The women's coalition lobbied for their particular claims in the name of broader national objectives: enhanced national security, military preparedness, military professionalism, equality. The participants put differences aside in order to present a unified front. The NOW lobbyist who had carried a card specifying her involvement in lesbian rights issues was advised to utilize other identification. The contacts she would establish on the Hill, she was told, would prove of benefit later to her antidiscrimination work on lesbian and gay matters; but this lobbying effort demanded a separation of issues.

Ultimately the legislation that passed was itself a compromise. Congress was well aware that military policy-makers were anything but enthusiastic about opening up fighter pilot positions to women. Defense secretary Richard Cheney had first appeared willing to support the repeal of combat exclusion for women pilots, at least according to his press secretary Pete Williams.[24] In fact Senator Roth's office had drafted his legislation not only with an eye to keeping faith with the House bill but also with the intent of conforming to Secretary Cheney's expressed view that the services should not be required to utilize women on combat aircraft, but neither should legislation prevent them from doing so. When the bill was on the Senate floor, Cheney's office repudiated Pete Williams's earlier assertion that the secretary supported repeal.

With Senate support for the legislation anything but assured, two things became critical: the contacts between DACOWITS members and conservative senators, and the willingness of the Kennedy-Roth team to compromise by agreeing to the appointment of a presidential commission to study a range of questions about women and the military as a quid pro quo for support of the legislation. Many military women who had served in women's organizations were appalled at the suggestion of yet one more study; women's military performances had been assessed from every possible angle in scores of studies since the All-Volunteer Force (AVF) was first established in 1973. But the lobby team realized that Kennedy-Roth would need to make this concession as a condition of passage. By accepting the commission proposal, an idea most legislative proponents saw as without merit and sure to be slanted by conservative appointees, the team removed a major obstacle to the passage of the legislation.

The compromises to ensure passage were thus struck: The legislation permitted but did not require the combat utilization of women pilots, and the presidential study commission that would delay any Pentagon enforcement of the repeal was accepted.[25] When time came for the Senate vote, a number of military women watched the proceedings from the Senate gallery. Describing what transpired in ways that were reminiscent of the 1920 suffrage vote, one officer said, "I stood and threw my arms up in the air; this is what I was hoping for all my career—to see this law repealed. I went right away to phone Jeanne Holm [a retired air force general who was for many uniformed women the military's foremost advocate of women's equality] and Becky Constantino [DACOWITS chair]. Then they talked to each other and they were in tears."[26]

Organizing the presence of military women was no small feat. Owing in part to an admonition delivered by one senator to the navy congressional liaison, the navy was largely supportive of its pilots who chose to participate in the discussions on the Hill. The air force generally sought to discourage the participation of its women aviators.[27] In conversations between General Merrill McPeak, chief of staff, and other Defense Department personnel, the leadership entertained a variety of positions, from seeking to prohibit women from appearing on the Hill at all, to considering barring them from appearing in uniform, to finally acknowledging their democratic right as citizens to be present during the legislative process—as individuals on their own time. A number of women were explicitly told that if they wished to spend time on the Hill while the legislation was under consideration, they were to do so only on the condition that they took it as vacation time, a stipulation of considerable irony given the fact that no such requirement was imposed on many of the aviators who attended Tailhook—which the navy later insisted was not an officially sponsored event.

One high-ranking woman said she took meticulous care to protect herself from criticism that she was using her position to attempt to influence the political process. She contacted people on her own time, went out and bought her own fax machine, and made calls at her own expense. Another woman approached her commanding officer asking for permission to spend time on the Hill and was rebuffed with a comment that the issue being discussed in Congress was unrelated to her job. Fearing the consequences if she disregarded these instructions (the ever-present tool for exacting compliance is a negative remark on a performance report), she stayed at work and watched videotapes of the congressional hearings and debates at night.

This cameo of interest-group politics on the Hill portrays all the key features of military women's activism. First, it is a statement about both the political conservatism and the political radicalism of military feminism, registering as it did women's rights to be full-fledged combat-ready participants in America's military mission; second, it revealed how critical the support of the law is to military feminist goals. At least some of the service chiefs would have endeavored to block this reform effort on their own. No less in this case than throughout its history, feminism in the military has depended on the support of either Congress or the courts.[28] Third, the process revealed how lobbying and interest-group politics require compromise. The absence of space for doctrinally pure politics was, here, clearly revealed by the necessary concession made concerning the presidential commission whose prospect feminists loathed.[29] Fourth, the organizing on the Hill recorded the inevitable risk taking that feminist politics among uniformed women involves. Knowing that the chiefs of their services and many of their own colleagues regarded the legislation with deep aversion, it is far less surprising that some women stayed away than it is that other military women (one congressional aide estimated the number at thirty or forty) made their way to the Hill. Fifth, this episode of women's activism revealed the way feminist issues have been largely segmented from other issues to which they are logically connected. Combat exclusion of women was in many ways both similar to and interconnected with the ban on gays and lesbians. But most military feminists were convinced that to have coupled the two would have secured victory for neither.

FROM DIFFERENCE TO EQUAL OPPORTUNITY, 1940s–1970s

Any description of how women activists have endeavored to influence the policies of the contemporary military should begin with an earlier history. There have always been women leaders in the military who looked out for the interests of other women who served. But the definition of what has constituted women's interests has changed. Well into the 1970s, as long as the separate women's line components (the WACs, WAVES, Air-WACS, and WASPS)[30] endured, most of those who looked after women's interests operated from a premise that women's and men's "natural" differences should be the basis of military assignments. With the All-Volunteer Force (AVF) and with the influence of second-wave feminism, women activists sought to influence military policy to reflect their belief that merit and competence, rather than untested assumptions of difference, should govern the assignment of personnel to military jobs.

In this early phase, prior to the 1973 establishment of the AVF, the directors and staff of the WAC, WAVES, and other line components dedicated their leadership to maintaining the highest standards within the women's components. They sought to improve the training, the living conditions, and the morale of the women under their command. They did not endeavor to claim that women deserved the same or equal opportunities as male servicemen. From the 1940s until well into the 1960s, the military felt little need to confront issues of gender equality. As Colonel Bettie Morden's account of the Women's Army Corps begins: "Women in the Army? Never."[31] It was only with World War II and the war-induced manpower crises that the military saw a need for an organizational place for women. Established in World War II and eliminated finally by the second half of the 1970s, the women's services (or line components) were structurally adjunct to the male military.[32]

During World War II, the navy, coast guard, and marines brought women into separate components of the reserves. The army created a women's corps, initially refusing its members military status. But soon women were assigned to a wide range of positions. In the army, Morden writes, women were "mechanics, weather observers, radio operators, intelligence analysts, photographers, carpenters, parachute riggers, postal workers and heavy equipment operators."[33] After the war, in recognition of their wartime service, women were incorporated into the military on a regularized basis through the Women's Armed Services Integration Act of 1948. The act limited women enlistees to a maximum of 2 percent of service strength. No officer except the line component director could hold a rank higher than lieutenant colonel or navy commander. As Morden notes, "The idea was not to provide equal opportunity for women or to set a precedent for society; it was to relieve as many men as possible from administrative jobs so that they would be available for combat."[34]

At the end of World War II, the idea of distinct gender identities persisted. The women directors were no less ready than the male leadership to see women dispatched from their wartime positions; they urged women to return directly to civilian life.[35] The directors of the women's line components shunned efforts to upgrade their positions to star or flag rank. According to Holm's account, the line directors strictly opposed such efforts in the late forties because they were apprehensive that if legislation designating them as eligible for higher promotions had been pursued, the 1948 integration act would have been jeopardized. Somewhat later, the women directors again objected to legislative efforts that would have opened up promotion to star or flag rank on the grounds that women would be seen as too "grasping" and ambitious.[36]

By the late 1960s, military women had fewer options than those who had served in the 1940s and 1950s. Women had ceased doing the broad range of tasks that had been open to them in World War II and Korea. Jeanne Holm writes, "Unlike their predecessors . . . American women were no longer to be found driving trucks, taxiing aircraft, teaching aerial gunnery, running motor pools, staffing post offices, repairing engines, manning airborne radios, or aiming aerial cameras." By Pentagon policy, women were not to be employed in jobs that were "not in conformance with the present cultural pattern of utilizing women's services in the country."[37]

There was little questioning of the separate and distinct identities of the women's components. The women directors did not assert women's rights to equality but worked instead to see that women were well-trained and well-treated: They fought for decent housing, better uniforms, high standards for recruitment. They spoke out against the image, incessantly propagated, that women who signed up for military service were loose, fair game, or consorts to serve the sexual needs of the male military.[38] Ironically, despite the repudiation of, as Morden observed, "changes that appeared to make women more like men," at least one of the directors of the women's components opposed any waiving of rules that might allow pregnant women or women who sought an abortion to remain in uniform.[39]

The emergence of the women's movement in the mid-1960s posed the issue of gender equality in new terms, and the women's rights movement raised a host of new issues: Should women be registered or drafted? Should enlistment qualifications (which were and still are higher for women) be equalized? Should women serve in combat? Should pregnant women, married women, or women with children under their guardianship be barred from military service? Should women be admitted into the reserve officer training corps and into the academies? Should the separate women's organizations within the military be eliminated?[40] These questions posed a new vision of gender equality in which women were to be recruited, educated, trained, assigned, and promoted in ways that were similar to rather than different from those experienced by their male counterparts.

These issues divided women in the line services. Morden's chronicle of army history suggests that on the whole the younger members of the WAC supported change, including the dissolution of the corps itself: "Although no poll was taken," Morden writes, "probably 50 percent of the WAC favored dissolution of the Corps and the office of the director. They believed this would free them from an inferior status and increase their value as career soldiers."[41]

The "difference" perspective was not shared by all the line component directors. When the integration of the military academies was proposed, air force colonel Jeanne Holm saw it as a move forward for women. Captain Robin L. Quigley, the director of the WAVES, opposed integration. To the WAVES director, the idea that women might be sent to sea, or might seek to fly navy planes, promoted a vision of equality that sharply departed from previous assumptions.[42]

The belief in difference for some was based on the conviction that a separate women's military structure empowered uniformed women. "For the WAC the chain of command had special significance because it was composed of females. Fort McClellan was a post composed entirely of females. The structure had a unique power, that of a chain of women, protecting, encouraging, and looking out for other women in a world of men. . . . With the WAC attending to its own promotions list, deserving women were unlikely to be passed over, and of course they could never be passed over in favor of men."[43]

But as Brigadier General Evelyn P. Foote commented about the corps, this powerful sense of distinctiveness was counterbalanced by the fact that a segregated structure placed women in a subordinate status:

> In the corps you knew everyone and we basked in a special esprit. But as long as you had a special corps, you had two different kinds of soldiers, two different training. Actually women in the corps were never referred to as sol-

diers. . . . They were never trained to defend themselves or to defend their units. They were trained for administrative, personnel, medical, public relations work. They were not permanently detailed to the army: They were detailed only temporarily. But there were fantastically gifted women, highly educated. Many had graduate degrees. There was a tremendous sense of who we were.[44]

The predominant perspective before the disestablishment of the women's services, then, emphasized quality over equality and self-esteem over self-advancement. But some of the women prominent in the women's components such as Major General Jeanne Holm (USAF—ret.) and Brigadier General Evelyn P. Foote (USA—ret.) bridged the two eras and became powerful exponents of equality and mentors to military women in the integrated forces. On the whole, however, the actions and speeches of the line directors can be seen as protofeminist in the *pragmatic* rather than *strategic* sense. Maxine Molyneux writes that strategic interests are derived "deductively . . . from the analysis of women's subordination and from the formulation of an alternative, more satisfactory set of arrangements to those which exist." Practical interests, like those that arose in the early era of the women's separate line components, were determined "inductively [arising] from the concrete conditions of women's positioning within the gender division of labor. In contrast to strategic gender interests, these are formulated by women who are themselves within these positions rather than through external interventions."[45] Until the late 1960s, those who spoke on behalf of military women were largely military women themselves. Their concerns were not to challenge the gendered assignment of military roles but to cultivate the image and improve the reality of military women's lives within the existing definition of gender difference.

With the societywide dissemination of equal opportunity norms in the 1970s, military women began to insist on women's similarities to men. The emergence of the feminist movement in the mid-1960s, trumpeting ideas about equal opportunity, and internal developments in the military itself converged to bring issues about equality to the forefront. By the mid-1960s, morale among women officers was suffering. In 1949, Jeanne Holm notes, there were 108 women majors and merely 2 lieutenant colonels in the WAC. By the mid 1960s, there were 237 majors and 77 lieutenant colonels, of whom half were in the promotion zone for colonel. But because they were women, under the 1948 integration act still in force, they could not be considered for promotion.[46]

DACOWITS, which was charged with helping the Defense Department recruit women, began to address itself to inequities that women in the military faced. The emergence of DACOWITS as one of the most important organizations protesting inequality within the services is remarkable given the function for which it was initially devised. DACOWITS was established in 1951 during the Korean War to assist the Department of Defense in its effort to recruit women. It was hoped that the appointment of bluestocking, well-bred women to such a committee would upgrade the image of the military in the minds of parents who might have thought the military an unbecoming place of employment for their daughters.[47] At the inaugural dinner, Anna Rosenberg, then assistant secretary of defense for manpower, addressed the committee of women attired in glittering dresses and fur stoles: "We expect counsel from this group to help us evolve policies that will make military service an attractive duty and that will assure parents that we are genuinely interested in the welfare of their young women in the services."[48]

For the first two decades of its existence, DACOWITS mostly served as a public relations arm of the Defense Department. In 1967, however, the committee assumed a public role going to bat to galvanize Congress to lift the ceiling on women officers and to lift the quota on women's enlistee numbers. Nevertheless, for much of the early 1970s, DACOWITS was regarded as a committee that exercised little clout. In 1972, it was described in the *Army Times* as "a nice little group that doesn't do very much."[49] The reporter noted that there was poor turnout for the biannual meeting (only thirty-one of the fifty-member committee attended the fall 1970 meetings); that the DACOWITS office made little attempt to track committee members' activities (lobbying or recruitment visits) and thus had little way of evaluating committee effectiveness; and that a committee composed of women who were part-timers serving on DACOWITS as a philanthropic undertaking could not be very effective.

But signs of change were visible. In 1973, the Center for Women Policy Studies sued to force DACOWITS to open its meetings to the public.[50] In 1974, the committee placed itself squarely in support of the integration of the military academies (although three of the four former directors of the women's components opposed it).[51] This boldness won DACOWITS attention in the press, which noted that the committee was "becoming more militant."[52] Again, in the mid-1970s, there were signs of a slough. The support staff of DACOWITS was severely reduced, and for a period in 1977 its administrative functions became the collateral duty of a male army officer in charge of overseas schools. Understaffed and lacking its own office space, DACOWITS momentarily seemed to be on the brink of folding.

But the committee was revived over the course of the Carter administration. The staff and office space were restored. The reconstituted group was made up of about thirty civilians, nominated by the secretary of defense and appointed by the president, and military women were deputed to be advisers to the committee. The Carter administration eschewed the politics of patronage that had operated in earlier years, giving careful consideration instead to the potential political efficacy, knowledge, and experience of its appointees on DACOWITS.[53] As Carter Defense Department appointee Kathleen Carpenter commented, nevertheless, it was not so much that the DACOWITS women became more committed as that the Defense Department "stopped giving them the tea-party treatment."[54] In the four years of the Carter administration, the committee pursued a vigorous agenda.[55]

The language of equality and discrimination had started to appear repeatedly in the committee's proceedings. "Equality" as a word entered into committee discussions over the treatment of married women in the military (1969); relating to "inequities" in severance pay (1969); "inequities" in housing (1970); "equality" in entitlement to dependency allowances (1973); and support for the Equal Rights Amendment (1973). By 1980, the committee was even to take the services to task for the "male oriented approach" in its recruiting material, emphasizing instead the "importance of depicting men and women as *equal* partners in a variety of traditional and non-traditional occupations. . . ."[56]

The mobilization to establish equal opportunity within the military took off in the late 1970s under the Carter administration. With rising numbers of women recruited into the all-volunteer military, the time was ripe for the new cadre of Carter appointees, both women and men, to make an issue of equal opportunity concerns. The Carter years brought an unprecedented number of women into prominent positions within the defense establishment. Brian Mitchell, whose book *Weak Link* is an attack on gender equality in the military, enumerates these appointments, which he describes as the "infiltration of feminists."[57]

> Those near the top in the Pentagon included: Kathleen Carpenter as Deputy Assistant Secretary of Defense for Equal Opportunity; Deanne Siemer as Defense Department General Counsel; Antonia Handler Chayes as Undersecretary of the Air Force for Manpower, Reserve Affairs, and Installations; Jill Wine Volner and Sara Elisabeth Lister as General Counsel of the Army; Mitzi M. Wertheim as Deputy Undersecretary of the Navy; Patricia A. Szervo as Deputy General Counsel of the Navy and Mary M. Snavely-Dixon as Deputy Assistant Secretary of the Navy for Manpower.

Mitchell's roster could have been even longer. It should also have included Ginger Green, deputy assistant secretary in the air force later succeeded by Gail Berry. Several of these appointees helped to recruit other women. Wertheim brought in Chayes, who later recruited Carpenter. They constituted an informal network and, as one woman put it, provided each other "camaraderie." "Occasionally we'd get together," one woman recalled, "and in the navy tradition, have a glass of port."[58]

Individually, many of the Carter appointees were strong proponents of equality. Carpenter, especially, was an outspoken advocate of *both* gender and racial justice. Flamboyant and articulate, and unafraid of ruffling feathers, she was once referred to as the disco-dancing deputy, a reference to her efforts to follow up on reports that German clubs discriminated against Black soldiers.[59] Chayes was an outright feminist who paid explicit attention to a battery of women's issues. She directed the service to double the air force accessions of women; she worked on developing a policy about pregnancy at the academies; and she testified forcefully on dismantling the combat exclusion policies. Without question, gender equality had new legitimacy within the Harold Brown Defense Department.

Although they recognized themselves as women pioneers, not all women in this network entered the Pentagon as self-identified feminists. Many viewed themselves simply as staunch professionals. Some who vigorously supported appointments for women in the department eschewed any explicit identification with feminism.

But these Carter appointees often used the term "we" to refer to what they recognized themselves to be—a group of trailblazing women. Repeatedly, they noted the importance of women's pitching in to help each other in an environment that had been largely male-dominated. "I'd come in, in the morning," a Carter appointee noted," and there would be a copy of traffic [exchange of memos] that a secretary would have left anonymously in an unmarked envelope. Other women saw to it that I knew what was being said about me, what to expect."[60] Large numbers were lawyers, some with impressive administrative credentials. These were women who in their individual positions supported antidiscrimination policies. Some spoke the language of feminism. Many did not. Hardly an organized group, let alone the "cabal" implied by Mitchell's vocabulary of "infiltration," these new appointees recognized their novelty as women in a male-commanded Defense Department environment. They were aware that some people would see women as a collectivity whether they were or not. As one Carter appointee joked, "They saw us as one brain in multiple bodies."[61]

By 1980, however, Carter was out and the Reagan administration was in. The courts, which had endorsed equal opportunity claims related to sex discrimination consistently through the 1970s, reversed course. In 1980, President Carter had requested congressional authority for permission to register women for the draft. Congress rejected the request, and in 1981 the Supreme Court, in *Rostker v. Goldberg*, refused to hold male-only draft registration discriminatory, making clear the limits to which it was willing to go to support an equal opportunity military. The military leadership could scarcely wait for the Reagan administration to take office. They knew to expect a freer hand in setting their own personnel policies, and within months the military got down to the business of slowing the process of gender integration. By spring of 1980, the army declared a "pause" in women's accessions. The air force, less conspicuously but no less determinedly, lowered its targets for women's recruitment as well.[62] In 1982, the navy did not lower its targets[63] but did initiate investigations on several ships into the conduct of a number of women suspected of being lesbians.[64]

Throughout the decade, the military conducted an elaborate dance whose footwork was continuously rechoreographed. Women were excluded here, included there, reexcluded, and reintegrated. The rules governing the access of women to particular military occupational specialties came and went under the then-operative regulations: the army's Direct Combat Probability Coding (DCPC), the navy's Defense Officer Personnel Management Act (DOPMA), the air force's "high probability" of combat or exposure to hostile fire policies, and the cross-service 1988 risk rule (abandoned in 1994). Odd practices resulted: Women could launch Titans but not Minutemen. They could serve on civilian Military Sealift Command ships but not their military counterpart, the Mobile Logistics Support Force (MLSF) vessels, which were not considered combat ships until, with a flourish of a pen, they were redesignated as Combat Support Force;[65] and women were even shipped in and out of combat zones as the military decided, backtracked, and then determined again that women could actually do certain kinds of jobs. As one retired air force officer noted with a wry laugh, when the subject came up of whether women had been sent as part of the Grenada deployment: "How do I know? The army [police] women went in, then out, then in again [of Grenada]. Our planes were ferrying them back and forth across the damn Atlantic."[66] Study group after study group, survey after survey, task force after task force produced mounds of reports—the gist of which was a double-edged message that on the whole women could do a lot of tasks in the military that the military was in no rush to see them do.

Paradoxically, despite the conservative tide, women's numbers in the military continued to grow throughout the 1980s, and an increasing number of occupational specialties were slowly opened to women as well. What this reflected, at least in part, was the burgeoning activism of organized feminism within the military environment. In the 1980s, feminism became institutionalized within the military. Women's groups both inside the Pentagon and in the Washington area worked assiduously to pressure anyone with influence. Women activists approached military leaders whom they believed might listen; they contacted the service secretaries and their Defense Department civilian counterparts; they sought out sympathetic members of Congress; and, as a last resort, they brought cases to the civil courts and to the media, inviting public scrutiny when their grievances were otherwise ignored.

Throughout the 1980s, activists defended women's barely established gains, put out brushfires, and anticipated problems that might arise in the future. The issues were myriad: combating the army's policy recruitment reversals incorporated in the army's "womanpause";[67] getting women into the Minuteman launching silos; ensuring that navy women whose on-sea duty was limited by exclusion from combat vessels could still be assured reasonable career paths; fighting the exclusion of women from the navy's Mobile Logistics Support Forces (MLSF) and the Marine Embassy Guard Duty; pressuring the air force to cease penalizing male officers whose wives worked off-base; and, over and over, calling attention to the existence of sexual harassment that was an inveterate problem within the military.

In the course of the 1980s, a broad range of groups and individuals (largely women but also men, uniformed and civilian) constituted formally organized as well as informally networked collectivities that set about "working" both the state and the institution. They collected and shared information about the status of women at all levels of military employment. They conducted surveys about harassment, participated in working groups to study inequality, ran training programs, wrote memos and letters, submitted reports, and sought meetings with military and civilian policy-makers. They submitted and pursued cases through the military's judicial process. Informally, they shared knowledge about episodes in which women were the targets of job discrimination and sexual violence. They talked about job assignments and compared notes about individuals who could be either helpful or obstructive. They challenged job definitions that designated certain assignments as combat-related, thereby excluding women from entry. The 1980s saw a constant hum of institutional activism. The pressure that women's groups created, and the controversy that attended the issues they raised, make it no surprise that Lawrence Korb, secretary of defense for manpower affairs under President Reagan, would later say, "No issue has taken more of my time than women in the military."[68]

THE INTERDEPENDENCE OF FEMINIST ACTIVISM INSIDE AND OUTSIDE

By the end of the 1970s, the separate women's components had been dissolved. Their impending dissolution created a temporary vacuum, raising the question of who would speak for military women. But this space was not vacant for long. The vacuum left by the end of the line components was quickly filled by networks of uniformed servicewomen working out of various offices throughout the Defense Department and the individual services. In addition, an array of lobbying and rights organizations engaged questions of gender equality within the military environment. One of the important lessons the feminist politics of the last decades conveys is about the mutual dependence of activists located along an insider-outsider continuum. Uniformed activists depend on feminists outside the military to say in bold language what they must sometimes express in more guarded tones. Activists in lobbying networks are better able to release information to the media that cannot be attributed to military sources. Feminists on the outside are also critical in their role as organized pressure groups, since uniformed activists are proscribed officially from lobbying Congress—as illustrated, for instance, by the lobbying efforts to modify the combat exclusion in 1991 described earlier in the chapter. Feminists on the outside are also able to request information from the military itself that might be awkward for an insider to secure. Feminists on the outside, reciprocally, rely on uniformed activists for vital information and reality checks about what problems exist, and about how to frame an issue in language that will prove persuasive to military insiders.

It bears reiterating that insider and outsider designations are relative terms indicating location along a scale rather than binary categories. As I narrated stories of the military to colleagues, it was revealing that the very labeling of groups as insiders and outsiders proved to be difficult. Was DACOWITS (with offices in the Pentagon, with uniformed military advisers and staff, reporting to the secretary of defense (but with a civilian membership) more inside or outside the military? Were civilians teaching at the Naval Academy on Department of Defense paychecks (several of whom had called the media's attention to discriminatory practices) more outsiders than insiders? The different dimensions of financial, organizational, and discursive accountability make the insider-or-outsider classification an oversimplification. Although the labels rarely capture the full complexity of the situation, what can be emphasized is the vital interdependence of groups located along different points of a continuum, proximate to or distant from the institution. Schematically, there have been four sorts of habitats that house advocates of gender equality both inside the Pentagon and in the feminist-activist world more broadly.

Military Offices and Organizations

Within the services, particular offices have been designated formally or informally as the place to which issues about women are directed. The navy, alone among the services, specifically assigned women's issues to an office within manpower, personnel, and training that was given responsibility for tracking issues relevant to women's progress in the service. In the other services, sometimes more informally, particular individuals within the offices of personnel management or the judge advocate general's offices, individuals within the orbit of sympathetic secretary-level appointees, as well as people in particular equal opportunity offices and on the faculty of the different service academies, were either designated or became known in their environment as the people to whom problems relating to discrimination or gender issues should be taken.[69] Within the Department of Defense, the Defense Advisory Committee on Women in the Services (DACOWITS), in existence since the early 1950s, grew to be, in the course of the 1980s, the most visible, armed forces–wide habitat where issues of concern to uniformed women could be addressed. In the 1980s, women officers formed associations as well. The Women Officers Professional Association (WOPA) for women in the navy and marine corps began as an informal network in 1978, formally incorporating in 1984. WOPA was the most active of the associations throughout the 1980s.[70] By the end of the decade, Women Military Aviators (WMA) was incorporated, offering a forum and important meeting space for women pilots, navigators, and those involved in the aviation community.[71]

Lobbying and Nonprofit Organizations

In Washington, several women's movement organizations became directly engaged in the 1980s in tracking and lobbying around issues of gender equity in the military. The most active organization was the Women's Equity Action League (WEAL) Women and Military Project begun in the early 1980s. The project later moved to the Women's Research Education Institute (WREI). Periodically, groups like the Women's Policy Institute and the National Organization for Women (NOW) involved themselves as well. But the feminist pro-peace and antimilitarist position of much of the movement's membership kept gender and military issues off the agenda of many movement organizations. By the late 1980s, the issue of the homosexual exclusion was taken up by a number of the gay/lesbian Washington-based organizations. But for most of the decade, WEAL was the major movement organization in town working on military issues, and it focused almost exclusively on gender discrimination.[72]

Legal Rights Organizations

The Women's Rights Project of the ACLU, and the legal offices of several women's movement organizations, provided legal counsel in lawsuits brought by military women throughout the 1970s. When the issue of sex discrimination and draft registration worked its way through the courts, in the early 1980s, women's groups generated reams of material in the form of legal briefs and memoranda. In recent years, the National Women's Law Center has done public policy and advocacy work on military issues. Throughout the 1980s and into the 1990s, the ACLU project on gay and lesbian rights, Lamda (an organization supporting the legal rights of lesbians and gays), and more recently the Servicemembers Legal Defense Network (SLDN) have all assisted uniformed gays and lesbians (or those so charged) who have fought their involuntary discharge from the military.

Media

The media was an integral part of the institutionalization of military feminism in the 1980s. Editors and journalists attentive to gender equity played a crucial role in pressuring the military to confront inequality and discrimination in the services. Beginning even before the 1980s, the service newspapers that are officially independent of the military (such as the *Navy Times* and the *Air Force Times*) began to pay increasingly close attention to gender issues. The service papers that into the 1970s continued to carry pinup photos began to run copy on issues about military wives' wanting careers of their own, rape on military bases, and the numerous controversies revolving around policies that women's groups were labeling as discriminatory.[73] By the 1980s, mainstream papers such as the *Washington Post* and *New York Times* had regular correspondents informed about and eager to cover issues about gender inequality in the military.[74] In 1983, the journal *Minerva: A Quarterly Report on Women and the Military* was established, undertaking to provide contemporary updates as well as more historical and scholarly analyses of gender and military issues.[75]

The importance of civilian-uniformed interdependence is evident in the risk taking that military feminists engage in when they organize on their own. Concerned that the services discouraged uniformed women's associations, DACOWITS in 1984 asked each of the services to comment on whether they provided support for women's organizations. The navy expressed the belief that such associations provided useful professional benefits to its women officers, remarking that the chief of naval personnel, Vice Admiral William Lawrence, had been the first speaker at the newly incorporated WOPA luncheon.[76] The marine corps in distinctly less enthusiastic language noted that the service "does not object" to the participation of its members. The air force said that "concerted efforts" had been made to "maintain formal and informal lines of communications among personnel," observing further that service authorities "have no control over informal communications among personnel," but that "formal communications addressing personnel policies, such as housing, uniform needs, medical information etc. are distributed to keep Air Force Members aware of current policies and developments."[77] The comment skirted recognition of any need to discuss harassment or job discrimination either for "all personnel," for uniformed personnel, or for women-in-uniform specifically. The air force communication did go on to acknowledge that all women working for the government were entitled to join Federally Employed Women, a national organization of largely civilian women with numerous chapters including some located at air force bases. The army, in a refreshingly frank statement, "voiced some reservations about efforts on behalf of women only."[78]

The services' wariness stemmed from a recognition, no doubt, that all-women's military venues can be politicizing. In January 1982, two years into the Reagan administration for instance, navy and marine corps officers in WOPA invited navy secretary John Lehman to address their association. In front of a gathering of about 250 members and guests, Lehman was asked what the implications would be of recently enacted changes that would group navy women and men together for the purposes of promotion board assessment. His response that these changes were a "non-issue" and his apparent casualness toward what many of those present perceived as the most vexing career concerns of navy women officers sparked sharp criticism. "I wasn't actually there," one navy officer commented, "but as I heard it, Lehman was just unprepared for the question. He responded vaguely, indicating that he hardly took the issue seriously at all. Some of the women were livid. They said what they thought. And the press was there."[79] The navy quickly attempted to smooth the troubled waters by sending Lawrence Korb, assistant secretary of defense (manpower, reserve affairs and logistics) to "clarify" the navy's position at a WOPA session soon thereafter.

The important role that nonuniformed activists can serve in bringing pressure to bear on an institution by making inside issues visible to the outside was well illustrated by the USS *Safeguard* incident: In 1987 the executive committee of DACOWITS went on what was known as the WESTPAC trip to inspect navy and marine installations in the Pacific. If a tour was ever designed to confirm the skepticism of feminists about the possibility of a committee like DACOWITS's reshaping the system from within, this was it. The inspection sites were chosen by the services, which were intent, presumably, on showing off their best. Indeed, one of the ships on the tour, the USS *Safeguard*, was considered to be a model ship under the command of a lieutenant commander who had been heralded for his excellent service record. Members of the committee, moreover, included not merely Republican women but at least one member with close ties to Phyllis Schlafly's Eagle Forum, who, prior to the trip, had been vocally dismissive of such issues as sexual harassment, terming it a problem that women invited on themselves. In talking with women crew members aboard the *Safeguard*, DACOWITS members were joined by local military personnel. In the course of the discussion, information emerged that the ship's commander had sponsored onshore parties involving public sexual displays with crew members present; over the ship's radio he had, reportedly, "jokingly" offered to "sell" female sailors to Korean "clients." The women sailors had apparently felt there was nowhere to turn. Instilled with the military creed that problems should be taken to the chain of command, here they faced a chain of command that was, indeed, the problem. Several of the DACOWITS members and military women officers were scandalized not merely by the reported events but also by the fact that navy authority had been unaware that the command of this presumably model ship seriously flaunted professional rules of conduct. So serious was this, in the eyes of a number of women who were informed of these events, that they made sure the facts of this DACOWITS tour were available to the national press. Rather than dismiss these incidents as errant deportment, the chairwoman of DACOWITS, Jacquelyn Davis, wrote to the Pentagon that such "encouragement of a 'macho' male image contributes to behavior that is at best inappropriate and at worst morally repugnant. . . . Such behavior," she wrote, "should not be considered surprising given *the Service's support* [emphasis mine] for such on-base activities as 'peso-parties'. . . [at] enlisted, NCO, and Officer's Clubs, noon-time burlesque shows and 'dining-ins' that emphasize sexually-oriented entertainment." In wording reminiscent of Susan Brownmiller's phraseology in her feminist account of rape,[80] Davis wrote, "The issue of moral acceptability aside, on-base activities such as these contribute to creating an environment in which all females are regarded with little or no respect and abusive behavior toward all women is not only passively accepted and condoned but encouraged."[81] Davis's report was submitted as testimony in a congressional hearing and was distributed to the media by the Women and Military Project of the Women's Equity Action League.[82] This anticipated public airing was followed by an intensive self-study by the navy and another by the Department of Defense.[83]

Civilians also depend on uniformed insiders for information and language. At one of the twice-yearly meetings of DACOWITS in the early 1980s, a high-ranking air force spokesman was asked to address the committee on the issue of placing women in the Minuteman silos. Titan crews had finally been opened to women in the late 1970s, but the air force balked at integrating the Minuteman crews, arguing that many air force wives were opposed to having their husbands stationed for long

periods of time in close and isolated quarters with military women. Going into the DACOWITS meeting, the military women had briefed the
civilian committee members not merely with questions to be posed to
the air force leadership but with appropriate follow-ups to the anticipated answers. "We knew he'd explain why women couldn't be there in
the silos one-on-one with a man. They'd say, 'Well, we talked to the
wives and they were not happy.' So we prompted the committee members with the follow-up: 'Sir, can you tell me the last instance when air
force policy was made by military members' wives?' "[84]

Organizations on the outside have been important coordination
points for strategizing among activists who are both inside and outside.
Under Becraft's six-year direction, WEAL's Women and Military Project built a powerful organizational network.[85] It was an official and un-
official clearinghouse of information in which fact sheets about military
women were produced and made available to the media and to the public, and in which informal information about discriminatory treatment
could be shared that was difficult to disseminate across military circuits
alone. As one air force officer commented, "We'd hear of something
that just happened. Someone would get a new piece of information and
you'd say, 'Get that over to Becraft.' "[86] Reporters covering gender and
military issues, staff from congressional offices, DACOWITS committee
members, military women, other women's organizations—all were in
touch with Becraft's office.

Activists who are not in uniform are better positioned to speak vociferously and publically than are feminists in the military, as attempts to
alter the culture of the military academies suggest. A few years ago an air
force officer, a faculty member at the Colorado Springs Academy, urged
the school to consider replacing the inscription etched in stone above
the ramp that is the portal for new male and female cadets as they enter
the academy each year. It reads, "Bring Me Men." Even the contro-
versy-ridden all-male Virginia Military Institute (VMI) boasts a less gendered welcome ("You may be whatever you resolve to be") above its
once all-male barracks. An exchange of memos occurred. There was debate within the academy but no outside media was involved; the debate
soon subsided, and the exclusive words still welcome cadets to the academy. Remarking on the strength of character required even to broach
this kind of challenge to accepted norms, a colleague of the faculty
member observed, "My sense is that as a woman, if you stick your neck
out of the trenches, you get shot at."[87] At the Naval Academy, where
civilians are a larger percentage of the faculty, nonuniformed instructors
have sought to invite debate about the culture of the academy by seeking a more public forum for their concerns. Carol Burke, a folklorist and
former faculty member at the academy, released to the mainstream press
some of the older marching chants and ditties still sung that midship-

men had brought her in the period when she was at the academy. Members of the Male Glee Club, she reported in a *New Republic* article, would sing on their bus rides home from trips away a scurrilous variation of the song "The Candy Man" (entitled "The S & M Man"):[88]

> Who can take a chain saw
> Cut the bitch in two,
> Fuck the bottom half
> and give the upper half to you. . . .

> The S & M Man, the S & M Man
> the S & M Man, cause he mixes it with love
> and makes the hurt feel good!

> Who can take an ice pick
> Ram it through her ear
> Ride her like a Harley
> As you fuck her from the rear. . . .[89]

In 1997, a civilian faculty member of the academy whose twenty-six-year career in the marines has given him credibility normally denied to civilians precipitated a debate about academy culture by directly targeting the arguments against women's presence in the academy that one of the academy's icons, former secretary of the navy James Webb, has endeavored to keep alive. In extraordinarily candid prose, Professor Paul Roush took his critique of Webb's argument against women in combat, and by implication against women at the academies, to the pages of the naval journal *Proceedings*. Scrutinizing point by point the logic of Webb's position, Roush dissected Webb's contention that hyperstress and abuse are what make warriors in the academy, and that women's presence undermines this goal. In one characteristic passage, Roush wrote:

> Consider the implications of this particular theme: If the presence of women in the college experience prevents the brutality that is necessary to the inculcation of warrior-hood, the Marine Corps is in deep trouble. After all, Naval Academy graduates are a minority within the Marine Corps officer cadre; most of that cadre went to college with women and missed out on being physically abused by upperclassmen. Does that mean that the majority of the officers in the Marine Corps are incompetent warriors?[90]

These wars of words at the academies are interesting in several respects: They demonstrate the importance of discursive politics as an albeit secondary strategy where influence-seeking pressure politics aimed at changing policy is the primary mode of operation for feminist activists. They are also evidence of the crucial part played by activists who operate at different points along the spectrum of inside-outside politics.

INSTITUTIONALIZATION AS DE-RADICALIZATION?

It is often presumed that the institutionalization of activism is synonymous with the de-radicalizing of a group's claims. Those who once voiced challenges on the outside, it is sometimes supposed, are induced by their dependency on institutional status and income to assume the norms of the organizational environment. In the effort to engage the institution, as Margaret Levi and Meredith Edwards have stated it, there is an "exchange of ideological commitment for institutional power."[91] Two points can be made about this claim. The first is that feminist activism in the military is not co-optation in the classical sense that outsiders have been brought into an institution with the result that their more radical objectives have been diluted: Activists in the military came to their feminism from within the institution and were not co-opted from the outside. Second, although it is the case, clearly, that activists are deeply influenced by the norms of the institution—and although in the effort to be strategic and thereby influential, they often avoid the most controversial issues or temper their presentation—there seems to me little evidence to suggest that these practices have led to a de-radicalization over time.

Most activists in the military environment developed their views of gender issues in the institution itself. Although she had no "movement" experience in a formal sense, one of the foremost advocates of gender equality, Carolyn Becraft, was hired in 1982 by the Women's Equity Action League to run their Ford Foundation–supported Women and Military Project. Herself a former army officer, the daughter of an army colonel, and an army officer's spouse, Becraft came to her new job well informed and well connected. Becraft had been through an experiential feminist "boot camp." Trained as a nutritionist, an army captain appointed to be chief of the Food Service Division in a five-hundred-bed hospital, she had a promising career ahead of her. After marriage, although she outranked her military husband, her change in marital status meant a cut in her housing allowance and assignment based on her husband's position. When she became pregnant, she left the military since women could not then be in the service and have a family.[92] With her husband stationed in Germany, Becraft began work for an M.A. in education and elected to write her thesis in 1977–78 on the influence of the women's movement on the wives of military officers.[93] In Germany, Becraft was asked to make presentations to wives' clubs and federal women's programs on her thesis topic. After the presentations, she would be swamped by women coming up and saying, "I thought I was crazy; I know what you mean; thank God you're saying this."[94] Back in the United States in 1980, Becraft became a group facilitator at an Army Wives Club symposium and then chair of the After Action Committee that made recommendations to the army chief of staff on family policy. By the time she reached WEAL, Becraft had accumulated direct knowledge of equity issues in the armed services. A number of activists have held memberships in women's organizations. Captain Patricia Gormley, trained as a lawyer and working actively on behalf of gender equality in the Judge Advocates General (JAG) office of the navy, had been involved early on in her career in a local NOW chapter in Newport, Rhode Island. A number of others joined women's organizations in mid-or late career—several recruited by the Women and Military Project of WEAL. Captain Kathleen Bruyere, a plaintiff in the *Owens v. Brown* suit in the late 1970s, whose work to advance women's opportunities in the navy spanned the 1980s, was also unusual in her organizational links to the women's movement. Her résumé, distributed by her office, described her as an "outspoken advocate for women's rights in and out of the service," a member of NOW, the National Women's Political Caucus, and WEAL.

The uniformed women who worked on behalf of gender equality, were, by and large, self-educated feminists. Captain Georgia C. Sadler (USN—ret.), recently head of the Women and Military Project at WREI, observed, "Most military women are drawn from pretty conservative backgrounds. If they became feminists, they mostly did so after being on the job."[95] Sadler describes herself as having become "at least a moderate feminist" after having been assigned to direct the women's program section of the navy in the early 1980s.

> I had done a lot of staff work in Washington where you see a problem, you identify a process, you outline a solution, you proceed towards a resolution. In women's issues, you'd see something that makes sense, but you'd get a very emotional response. In those days, we were addressing the pregnancy separation issue. It was easy to hit sensitive buttons. For instance, the P-3 aircraft: Men in that community were a bit on the margins. Putting women in the squadron underlined the fact that these men were not in combat positions. There were extremely strong feelings.[96]

What is clear is that feminist networking in the military—to the extent that it emerged out of the women's movement at all—arose as a response primarily to the general diffusion of egalitarian ideas in society rather than to any outright organizational seeding in the military. In the 1980s, military women activists were not, by any means, steeped in feminist literature; but most were familiar with Betty Friedan and Gloria Steinem and made use of the the vocabulary generated by the movement. "Equal pay for equal work" (which many military activists say is one reason why they stay in the military), "sexual harassment," "male chauvinism," "sex discrimination," "hostile environment" were phrases that women activists in the military learned to deploy in the 1980s. Military activists recognized this discursive link to the movement. At one point, planning to meet some friends at a talk Betty Friedan was delivering in Washington, a navy captain joked, "We decided it had been too long since we'd gotten our last feminist fix."[97]

Activists in the military are the first to admit that to be successful they must choose their goals strategically and choose when to risk speaking out and when to hold back. The frustrations of this exigency are patent. As one retired navy captain who had served as an articulate and effective director of DACOWITS (half-)joked: "You have a choice. You can speak out and leave. Or you can be quiet."[98]

Even activists who were not on military payrolls but who hoped to influence military policy had to be strategic. At WEAL, Carolyn Becraft chose her priorities self-consciously.[99] Job discrimination (including sexual harassment) and family issues were central to her agenda. Abortion and sexual preference questions were not. Under Becraft, WEAL did not shy from controversial issues. The project lobbied against the appointment of secretary of the navy James Webb.[100] It provided legal assistance to women who brought discrimination suits against the military, helping civilian submarine technician Pamela Doviak Celli, for instance, in her case before the Equal Employment Opportunity Commission. And the project responded to requests for support and advice, as in the case of the wives of two Griffiss Air Force Base officers who were being pressured by their husbands' commander to leave their off-base jobs in order to conform to expectations about the on-base social obligations of officers' wives.[101]

Becraft also framed issues in bold language. Speaking in ways that would make people sit up and listen was her trademark. Talking about the military's presence overseas and the issue of prostitution on the perimeter of military bases:

> "It's a contradiction. You can't do the humanitarian stuff by day, feed the kids, and then rape the women after dark."

To those who would question "why Paula Coughlin or other women at Tailhook would have gone to the third floor, anyway":

> "Nobody in their right mind would say, 'Gee, I haven't been sexually assaulted today. I think I'll go up on the third floor.' If you want to blame military women, you're blaming the victim."[102]

But for Becraft, being political and pushing the limits in ways that were sure to invoke institutional enmity nevertheless required careful decisions about which battles could be fought. In Becraft's judgment, to challenge the ban on homosexuals was asking for more trouble than even she could handle. Becraft describes her choice of issues as having been based on the calculation that the project must begin by addressing controversies in which it had a fair chance of prevailing. "I decided early on," she comments, "that I wasn't going to touch the issue of homosexuality. I just wouldn't get anywhere with it. When you start out, you have to *win* some issues. In the beginning I was going to go with the issues I could win."[103] By the time Becraft left the project, there was a perception at WEAL that the project was now firmly established and could afford, indeed, *must* begin to take on new if riskier issues.

Becraft's successor, Vicki Almquist, who took over in 1988, chose to define her agenda more radically. With the endorsement of the WEAL staff, Almquist tracked a number of the military proceedings against women charged as lesbians and helped to form a network of organizations ready to act together to address the issues that such proceedings raised. Almquist, together with lesbian activists, brought the issue of the Parris Island "witch-hunts" before one of the 1989 DACOWITS meetings by utilizing the time slot reserved in DACOWITS meetings for public presentations. Several women accused of being lesbian testified before DACOWITS to bring to the committee's attention the way procedural due process was being violated in the investigation of suspected homosexuals. The issue was framed as a problem of sexual harassment since, as Almquist argued, the homophobia of military culture meant that all women were potential subjects of harassment and lesbian baiting. The committee was divided about how the issue should be handled and whether DACOWITS should respond at all. But the committee ended up drafting a resolution, forged as a compromise by one of the military members. The resolution did not take issue with the military's ban on homosexuality but, rather, questioned the procedures by which investigations may be conducted against innocent parties and used as a method to discredit all women. Before it became apparent whether WEAL could have pushed the gay/lesbian exclusion issue any further, the organization (in the late 1980s) shut its doors.

Many activists in the military maintain that political protest has not followed a linear course, becoming more radical *or* less radical with time. Rather, how much activists push depends, some maintain, on an equilibration between what is necessary and what is possible at any given time.[104] But this does not mean that activism lapses during a conservative presidential administration. The Reagan period tested this proposition. As soon as the three-year term of the remaining Carter appointees lapsed, DACOWITS committee slots were filled by new, conservative, Reagan nominees. These were well-heeled and well-connected

Republican women. They included the past president of the National Federal Republican Women; the president of American Agri-Women, who is the wife of chicken magnate Frank Purdue; the assistant secretary of state from Florida; the general director of personnel with General Motors; the University of Oklahoma provost; the chairman of a New York public relations firm; and others drawn from the professional and corporate world.[105] Referred to, at least on one occasion, by skeptical military personnel as a "gaggle of women" whose visits to foreign installations are punctuated by interludes of shopping, DACOWITS women had a frivolous image to combat. But in the case of some DACOWITS members, being strong Reagan supporters was not synonymous with a conservative perspective on gender discrimination.[106] The appointment of Jacquelyn Davis as chair in 1986 was a case in point. Dr. Davis, a foreign policy analyst,[107] was an imposing director of the committee, in part because she was extremely well-informed herself and was undaunted by technical talk and military jargon. Although Davis disavows the feminist label, she acknowledges with some bemusement that she was probably selected as a woman known to be a forceful conservative on foreign policy issues on the assumption that she was no less conservative on issues of women's equality. But if that was the presumption, it was clearly mistaken. Renewed twice in her role as chair for an unprecedented three-year term, Davis used the continuity of her position to build a powerful agenda. According to one of the DACOWITS attendees, the committee under Dr. Davis began to make full use of its "subpoena" powers. As before, the committee continued to ask for briefings from a particular service on a given issue.[108] But increasingly, it was the highly ranked flag officer or department secretary, rather than a lower ranked designee, who appeared before the committee to do the presentation.

As chair, Davis took resolute charge of the committee. She orchestrated meetings in a way that left little to chance. Strong pressure was put on subcommittee members to give their full energies to committee work.[109] Meetings were tightly run. Problems were aired before the meeting and a consensus reached prior to formal deliberations. Committee members came to the meetings well prepared, ready with pre-planned questions and follow-up queries. On her return from the infamous WESTPAC trip, in her official report, Davis minced few words: "With respect to both Services, but especially the Navy, there is a widespread perception among female officers and enlisted personnel that the institutional hierarchy and Command Structure of each of the Services are biased against women."[110] Davis's strong leadership predictably earned her detractors, particularly within the marine leadership with whom she had gone toe-to-toe. As one member of the military familiar with DACOWITS work commented, "If you do a karate chop to the throat, which is the way it felt to them, you can make them dislike you pretty bad."[111]

Although it would be wrong to characterize feminist protest within the military as becoming de-radicalized over time, it is the case that activists have been slow to take on issues of racism and for the most part continuously reluctant to address questions about homosexuality. Since over 30 percent of uniformed women are African-American and 14 percent of women officers are identified as "minorities," the inattention to race-specific issues is striking.[112] Throughout the last few decades of DACOWITS's deliberations, the issues that might particularly concern women of color—whether, for instance, attrition or promotion rates were similar or different for Hispanic, African-American, and other women of color; whether women of color in the military perceived issues of discrimination and sexual violence as white women did, or differently; whether facilities for single mothers were adequate; and how officers and enlistees fared with respect to health and pregnancy, including abortion, needs—have not been central to the committee's agenda.[113] This is presumably because DACOWITS personnel have perceived race issues as the charge not of the committee but of the equal opportunity offices. Yet, until recently, it seemed of little worry to the committee that such a division of labor existed and that the concerns of Black uniformed women or other women of color might fall through the cracks.[114] Even the language of committee recommendations or summaries showed little of the political consciousness of diversity that has now become canonical in many feminist circles.[115] In 1993, at the fall conference, several of the minority women on the committee approached the chair of DACOWITS and expressed "their concern that their voices had not been fully heard."[116] Perhaps because the committee's push to address the combat exclusion issue was now behind them, committee members were more prepared to turn to other issues. After the fall meetings, the DACOWITS subcommittees were restructured and a committee called "Equality Management" (a term drawn from the corporate world that semantically seems to highlight the need for administrative order rather than political voice) was instituted. This committee subsequently turned its attention to issues of equal opportunity training and education and has begun to review data about perceptions of military life among diverse groups of women and men in the military. Important as these changes are, in the eyes of some members of DACOWITS the committee could still be a lot more emphatic in its resolutions about the need for service attention to diversity and about "getting the word out" that this is now one of the committee's priorities. It is, nevertheless, a sign of the changing perspectives of the committee that the women pictured on the cover of the DACOWITS briefing books regularly now include women of color.[117]

If the race issue was slow to be put on the agenda because it was "unseen," the issue of homophobia has been perceived as politically treacherous and mostly avoided. In 1990–91, as the issue of the combat exclusion began to heat up, the homosexual exclusion was becoming simultaneously politicized. With the exception of the NOW representative, those lobbying for the overturn of the combat exclusion wished to avoid merging the issues.[118]

With the legislation now passed, for DACOWITS's civilian personnel to face the issue of the homosexual ban head-on is possibly unstrategic, but it is not unimaginable. When DACOWITS committee members are called to testify before Congress, it is perfectly conceivable that they could make the kind of comment offered by former NOW president Molly Yard when she testified that the department's own analysis (in this case, the Defense Personnel Security Research and Education Center) called into question the validity of some of the claims made in support of continuing the military's proscription.[119] Certainly this would be easier for DACOWITS than for uniformed personnel (lesbian uniformed personnel, most particularly), who jeopardize their careers in raising the issue of the ban or in providing any indication of their own sexual identity.[120]

The avoidance of the homosexual exclusion issue by DACOWITS, by WREI, in the early days of WEAL, and by other feminist groups has left organizing around the questions of witch-hunts and expulsions entirely to gay and lesbian rights groups.[121] The Servicemembers Legal Defense Network (SLDN) along with Lamda and the ACLU gay and lesbian rights project are three of quite a number of gay/lesbian groups that have organized against the ban. The SLDN is the primary group doing direct legal counseling of gay and lesbian servicemembers. SLDN not only pursues legal routes but also, according to Michelle Benecke, one of its cofounders, attempts to "work on the cultural level as well." Across the country, about three hundred cooperating (mostly volunteer) attorneys have contacted local field commanders or higher level military personnel, informing them of ongoing situations under their command that may transgress the law. In the wake of Tailhook ". . . people are scared of being accused of having someone in their unit being seen as perpetrating harassment," so there is some self-education taking place. Although women's organizations have not explicitly intended their actions to address the gay issue, it is clear that the consciousness-raising around sexual harassment has been useful for gay/lesbian organizers.[122] Several years past the combat exclusion victory, even those women who see no point in the homosexual ban have been silent on the issue. And no more than a very few military women (active or retired) or civilian women in the military environment have worked in alliance with organizations addressing gay/lesbian issues.[123]

Most activists who work within institutions believe that they must negotiate a fine line between their desire to goad the institution toward change and their understanding that to command support for the work they do, they must prove themselves to be institutional loyalists. Such balancing means that activists are likely to withhold or blunt some critiques of the institution that, were they on the outside looking in, they might be inclined to make forthrightly. But at the same time, the deradicalization thesis imprecisely describes military feminism. Military activists were not *de*-radicalized; they did not move from an earlier, more radical feminism to a more conservative position. Military feminists were not radical to begin with, but they have not become *less* radical over time. They may indeed have been pressured to avoid issues to which they might otherwise have been more openly sympathetic — lesbian/gay rights, in particular. But this suggests that the more appropriate model to describe military feminism would be a counterfactual one about the averting of radicalization rather than one that describes the history of feminism inside the institution as a de-politicizing move away from a more radical agenda.

CONCLUSION

Up until the dismantling of the separate line components, most women leaders defended women's interests largely on the basis of the view that they were different from men. The leadership of the line components had worked hard over the previous decades to look after women's concerns, to ensure proper training and good housing, and to win women respect and status in the services. The model was of a military where women were to be differently trained and assigned to support jobs, thus freeing men to fight. By the 1970s, however, military women such as Major General Jeanne Holm (USAF) and Brigadier General Evelyn P. Foote (USA), began to lead the military in another direction.

From the late 1970s on, women activists attacked policies and practices that barred women from being treated as equals alongside men. Women activists with the Women and Military Project that was first at WEAL and then at WREI, the navy/marine women of WOPA, the civilian and military women at DACOWITS, the aviators of WMA, and individual women throughout the Pentagon and in the military environment consulted, researched, parleyed, plotted, and lobbied tenaciously. Throughout the 1980s, military feminists challenged policies that maintained male-only occupational preserves, calling into question long-standing practices, such as sexual harassment, that had maintained the line between the "real" military and the women who were also in uniform. Feminism in the 1980s had found protected, institutionalized spaces from which these challenges could be mounted.

At the end of the 1980s, Phyllis Schlafly termed DACOWITS the "feminist thought-control brigade"[124] of the U.S. military, improving on the coloratura of *Navy Times* reporter Brian Mitchell, who described DACOWITS in his book *Weak Link* as a group of feminists inside the federal government "who oversee the progress of the march" toward "full sexual equality" by summoning high-ranking military officers before their committee only to assault them with their feminist questions like "pop-up targets."[125] Much as military feminism *is* challenging the institution, it is only slowly, in the 1990s, beginning to engage a feminist vision that focuses on race and sexual identity, and that includes attention to gender equality beyond the confines of American women's experiences.

This chapter leaves unanswered *why* feminism was able to locate itself within institutional habitats in the 1980s, in the decade in which conservative political winds began to sweep through national politics. Why was the claims making by feminists not more successfully arrested as the campaign to end the ban on homosexuals was? Was feminism allowed to survive as long as certain boundaries were not crossed? To address these questions requires that we turn to the complicated and contradictory role of the law.

Chapter Four

LIVING BY THE LAW

NOW in her forties and recently a mother, in 1990 Rosemary Mariner became the navy's first female jet squadron commander. She spent the initial twenty years of her career "operational"—not behind a desk but behind the controls of anything she was allowed to fly—from helicopters to high-performance jets, racking up over 3,500 flight hours. Flying was a childhood dream for Mariner, a dream she announced early on to the principal of her Catholic girls school. Along with becoming a proficient pilot, testing planes and training male aviators for combat missions that she was not by law permitted to perform herself, Mariner became an activist promoting gender equality in navy aviation. She had not always been outspoken. In the mid-1970s, Mariner was asked to join in the *Owens v. Brown* class action suit in which women were suing the service to open up navy ships to uniformed women. At the time, Mariner was establishing herself as an up-and-coming young aviator in a fighter community. Going it on her own seemed smarter than calling attention to herself as part of a cadre of discontented women. ". . . I basically wimped out. Because I had it good, I didn't want to get in trouble with the Navy. And I consider that moral cowardice on my part."[1]

By the late 1980s, however, Mariner had become an unrelenting advocate of women's career advancement. "I definitely call myself a feminist—though I don't agree with everything feminists do," Mariner told the *Los Angeles Times*. "It's very important for professional women to acknowledge that a lot of things would not have changed if not for bra-burners."[2] As squadron command leader, Mariner worked self-consciously to support women who were seeking training and promotion. In the late 1980s, Mariner became the head of Women Military Aviators, a six-hundred-person organization that networked in support of equal opportunity. As with most women activists in the military, this was not a feminism Mariner brought with her into the armed forces. It was a commitment to gender equality that Mariner discovered and made her own *in* the military itself. A southern Californian product of parochial schools and Orange County Republicanism, Mariner had become an outspoken advocate for women's equality while losing none of her dyed-in-the-wool patriotic love of country. Mariner's story, writ large, frames the question this chapter addresses. When the pressures are monumental to conform and keep silent, why do some women and men put themselves out front? How has feminist activism managed to emerge within the military when the open advocacy of gender equality so often invites opprobrium?

Neither the experience of gender discrimination nor military women's career calculations adequately explain the emergence of feminist activism. Real as the experience of discrimination is for many military women, those who confront gender biases still must choose, in Albert O. Hirschman's phrase, "exit, voice, [or] loyalty."[3] In the face of discrimination or bigotry, some leave the military determined to live their lives in more open environments; some are silenced but remain in uniform; only some choose voice inside the institution. Career concerns, too, are only part of the motivation for activism. Although overturning the ban on women in combat aviation, for instance, was crucial to the careers of women aviators, career mobility cannot explain the presence in 1991 of individual military women on the Hill. For the senior-most aviators who visited legislative offices in anticipation of the debate on combat exclusion, the rewards of any legislative change were likely to be too late; for the younger cohort of activists, it was hard to know whether they would benefit from the changes themselves or, on the contrary, face retribution for publicly advocating a change in policy that their prospective colleagues and superiors in the warfare community of aviators clearly decried. Because the costs of activism are frequently high, it is often far more rational to leave political work to others. Why be outfront, when it is possible, as Mancur Olson has observed, to free ride on the activism of others?[4]

In an institution, I argue in this chapter, where masculine attributes have for centuries defined prevailing standards of conduct, the emergence of organized feminist activism would not have been possible without the law's legitimation of equal opportunity. In the language of social movement theory, the law's very recent affirmation of equal rights has provided the political opportunity for the emergence of feminist protest. The courts and congressional endorsement of antidiscrimination norms gave advocates of equality a voice that otherwise might well have been overpowered within the institution. But the law's role has been more far-reaching than what is conveyed by verbal imagery about the opening or closing of opportunities for activism. The law has also steered the kind of activism military advocates of gender equality have been prepared to undertake. The law's relationship to gender claims within the military, I will argue, has discouraged the creation of alliances across lines of race and sexuality, and has curtailed women's full integration into the military, by extending women's right to compete for jobs and promotions without fully confronting the question of whether the maintenance of an efficient fighting force requires adherence to traditional masculinist models of military prowess. The law, thus, not only frames opportunities; it also defines the normative boundaries that distinguish "legitimate" claims from those believed to be "beyond the pale."

THE PRESSURES TO CONFORM

When I asked military women activists what they hoped to see in the pages of this book, they would repeatedly respond with some version of the request: "Tell them about the daily indignities, hurdles, affronts . . . about how hard it is to be a woman in this kind of male environment." Every single military woman with whom I spoke (those who called themselves feminists and those who did not; those who had obviously established themselves as successful and those who were facing uncertain career futures) had a story to tell. If the stories spoke to a single theme, it was to their struggles as women to be taken seriously. No less important, the stories also revealed the continuous pressure on women to find individual rather than collective solutions to problems and to do so without making waves.

It is not my purpose, here, to describe in detail the lives of military women. There are numerous excellent autobiographies as well as reports that give military women a chance to speak in their own voice.[5] I am explicitly not describing here how peer culture and institutional policy make life difficult, sometimes miserable, for military women. The stories of routine harassment and (unreported) rape, of the perpetual putdowns, the taunting, and even slander, would be another topic entirely.[6] What I present, here, is rather a schematic view of the "gatekeeping" that activist women and men encounter. Women who speak out confront at least three modes of rebuff:

(a) *The first is, simply, the refusal on the part of peers and superiors to acknowledge inequality as an institutional problem.* The way this repudiation is expressed runs the gamut, from outright opposition to women's presence and more particularly the failure of institutional leadership to curb this hostility, to comments that some event, occurrence, or scandal is just an unfortunate anomaly that is not representative of what goes on in the military as a whole. As Dr. Edwin Dorn, then a senior staff member at the Brookings Institution and a specialist in military and personnel issues, has suggested, comparisons between the different ways in which senior military leadership sometimes react to racial hostility and to gender hostility can be revealing. Testifying before Congress after Tailhook, Dorn observed:

> It is worth contrasting the situations of blacks with those of women, and General Holm just did when she talked about the incidents in Las Vegas. I, like her, was struck less by the "wilding" that occurred on the third floor than I was by the complete failure of senior officers to assert leadership during an earlier seminar, when a young woman asked a serious question about her career opportunities as a Navy flyer and was greeted with derision. An officer who responded so dismissively to a question about opportunities for blacks would have been disciplined rather severely.[7]

When military leaders do take an active role in trying to reshape the hostile climate for women by making accountability a priority for those at the highest ranks of military leadership, accusations of "political correctness" are likely to swiftly follow, along with charges that the military is being used as an institution for social experimentation. Former secretary James Webb has made this argument in several *New York Times* op-ed pieces, and such charges repeatedly surface in publications aimed at a military readership.[8]

In the academies, opposition to the services' alleged "political correctness" is evident in the derisory comments to which women students are repeatedly subjected. The proportion of women who hear fellow students commenting that standards have been lowered in the academy, one recent study indicated, was 64 percent at West Point, 33 percent at the Naval Academy, and 38 percent at the Air Force Academy. The proportion of women hearing fellow students say that women do not belong at the academies was 45 percent at West Point, 19 percent at the Naval Academy, and 22 percent at the Air Force Academy.[9] These figures may underestimate the actual opposition to military women's presence in the academies since, according to one Naval Academy study from 1990, 45 percent of entering midshipmen believe that women do not belong in the academy, and one-third of graduating male midshipmen share that view.[10]

Women in the academies, whether or not they are feminists, are often "accused" of being women's libbers if something they say can be construed as defending women's interests. This "monitoring" is often directed at women and men, whether in the academies or elsewhere, who assume institutional roles as advocates of gender equality. Without exception, all the servicemembers I interviewed who were conspicuous proponents of gender equality had anecdotes to tell about having been offered (often unsolicited) advice cautioning them against the risk of being outspoken on gender issues. Whether the advice came from a spouse, a friend, a parent, or a commander, whether it was delivered in an avuncular fashion, as a joke, or in a manner meant to chastise, the messages were intended to warn activists against stepping across some boundary onto the terrain of unacceptability:

> My [surrogate] Dad didn't want me to be tainted. I talked with [him], he was trying to persuade me out of this, and I said, and it was really hard, "Look, you've got this great idea about what you think I should be doing next, but no one really cares what *I* want to do." (An air force officer who was working to challenge the combat exclusion provisions)

> I was told to be more careful about what I was saying, that these kinds of comments wouldn't be good for my career.(A young officer at an academic workshop who had referred to academy studies reporting that male students were less, rather than more, tolerant of gender difference after several years in one of the service academies)[11]

Sometimes, admonitions are offered in the form of "good-natured" put-downs:

> "So, you took bitch law, fag law, and law-law." (Comment made in a locker room to an air force major [a male] who took several courses on discrimination and constitutional law at an East Coast law school where he was on an air force fellowship)[12]

More often, gatekeeping rebukes take the form of rejoinders that acknowledge some event but deny its representativeness or connection to the larger picture. These kinds of remarks can best be termed "isolated incident" rebuttals. Some examples:

> From a ROTC commander who had attended a workshop in which a film on "hazing rituals" had been shown and a paper presented that recounted some of the academy rites (lewd marching chants, references to navy women as WUBAs, and WUBA jokes). The commander's reaction to this account was, "The academy is not the navy; operational environments are very different."[13]

> Although Rear Admiral Virgil L. Hill, Jr., then superintendent of the Naval Academy, took the unusual action of sending personal letters of reprimand to the midshipmen who chained classmate Gwen Dreyer to a urinal, he commented to the press after the incident that the Dreyer affair represented "a very, very isolated incident."[14]

The "isolated incident" response is often accurate in a strict, literal sense. Many of the fraternity-like rituals that exist at the academies do not exist in training environments elsewhere, and chaining women to urinals is not routine at the academy. But what the "isolated incident" response ignores is the continuities that exist between these kinds of incidents and others like them that can be found more broadly in the academy or in other locations within the military. The chaining of a woman to a urinal could be seen as connected, for instance, to the still ongoing practice at the academy of the "paddling" that is given to the midshipman who is "punished" for having had (at a social event) the "ugliest" date. The academy hazing and lewd marching chants could be seen as connected, by the same token, to what Eric Schmitt of the *New York Times* reported from Fort Bragg: "For Specialist Trenee Maddox, it was sexist innuendo from leering sergeants about her appearance. For Capt. Priscilla Mondt, it was sexually suggestive lyrics in soldiers' marching cadences. For Former Specialist Pamela Metras, it meant an assault in her barracks. At Fort Bragg, one of the Army's largest bases, women encounter the same kinds of sexual harassment that many women have complained is common in the Navy."[15]

(b) *A second mode of social control exists in the form of discouraging women from finding common cause with each other.* As Carol Barkalow comments in her account of West Point,

> . . . despite all the flap that goes on in the military about how desperately men need to bond with one another, male soldiers seem categorically unable to perceive or to forgive a similar need in women. In fact they often appear to possess an irrational fear of women's groups believing that, in their midst, men will be plotted against or, perhaps worst of all rendered somehow unnecessary.[16]

Women spending time together draw attention. Women who might socialize together as a group, arrange to meet together, or sometimes even just stop to talk to each other in a public place are the subject of jokes or inquiries: "Female conspiracy?" "A cabal?" "Hen party?"[17] In Barkalow's words, "fitting in meant not making too much of women's 'solidarity.'"[18] In the words of another cadet from the first integrated class at West Point, "fitting in" meant "putting up with treatment that might be unfair, never turning the corps against you, never getting to be known as a crybaby, staying exactly on line, never sliding one bit, never letting down your guard or goofing off, being in sum 'ultra-professional.'"[19] Fitting in means above all handling things on your own.

These comments are no less relevant to today's military: A 1994 General Accounting Office study of sexual harassment at the academies found that over 80 percent of the women believed that a "victim" reporting harassment would be seen as a crybaby; 60 percent felt that she would be shunned by her classmates; and close to 35 percent felt that she would actually receive lower military grades.[20]

There are few environments in the academies where it is easy for women to socialize together, although the sports teams and locker rooms may provide the one relatively safe space for sharing experiences (aside from the dormitory room). But even the "teams" are not risk free. As one former army captain commented (not about the academy but about her experience on a base), "As an officer, I worried about joining the women's softball team. Would it draw attention, inviting inquiries about whether or not I was a lesbian?"[21]

The charge of lesbianism is one of the most punitive means of gate-keeping used against women. Women who report violations have suffered retaliation in the form of investigations into their alleged lesbianism. One incident involving a young enlistee who reported that she had been assaulted by male fellow soldiers was recently reported by the Servicemembers Legal Defense Network (SLDN):

> In South Korea, a young Private First Class reported that male soldiers assaulted and threatened to rape her. The soldiers then spread false rumors that she was a lesbian. Rather than investigate the men who attacked her, the command in South Korea investigated her. The command tried to force her to confess to being gay. She refused. The command threatened her with prison if she did not identify suspected lesbians in her unit. She refused. The command started discharge proceedings against her based on the same trumped up allegations. She still refused to buckle. In July 1995, after ten months of intense efforts by her family, Servicemembers Legal Defense Network and its cooperating private attorney, the Army finally dropped all charges and retaliatory actions against her. Her new command is excellent but she and her family should never have had to go through what they did. What happened to her is common. Straight or gay, the "Don't Ask, Don't Tell, Don't Pursue" policy has been used to retaliate against hundreds of servicemembers.[22]

SLDN reports that the numbers of discharges have actually increased under the supposedly ameliorative policies of "Don't Ask, Don't Tell," which indicates that this kind of gatekeeping (investigating as lesbians women who speak out) has become increasingly repressive.[23] The lengths to which air force investigations have gone are particularly alarming. In keeping with an official 1994 air force memo from the service's top uniformed lawyer at the time, air force investigators are instructed to question parents about the sexual orientation of their children as well as to interrogate close civilian friends, high school guidance counselors, and other mentors. Doctors, psychologists, and other health care professionals are also instructed to turn in servicemembers who reveal their homosexual orientation.[24]

  (c) *A third source of women's silencing is the chain-of-command-system that structures military accountability.* The expectation that complaints will be first channeled through the "chain of command" may both counter and heighten the difficulty of speaking out.[25] The responsible commander can use the power of a commander's position to ensure compliance with military regulations. But an irresponsible commander or fearful NCOs and junior officers may exacerbate existing problems. As has been documented repeatedly in harassment and race discrimination cases, the chain of command may itself be the problem.[26] But even where commanders are not themselves the miscreants, they can be subject to cross-pressures about reporting or acting on problems within their units. In acting on a problem of harassment (or alcohol, or other unlawful behavior), commanders may feel apprehensive about drawing attention to their unit and worried that any problem that makes their command appear troubled will be held against them in their career promotion.[27]

FEMINISM BY ANY OTHER NAME

Given the gatekeeping that deters uniformed servicemembers from speaking out, it is understandable why most women (and men) would be reluctant to identify as feminists. In an excellent analysis of gender roles among air force officers, Karen O. Dunivin discusses women's understanding of their marginalized status in a "male- and masculine-dominant military."[28] Dunivin entitles her report "There's Men, There's Women, and There's Me." Drawing on Betty Friedan's three-sex theory, Dunivin observes that women may accept that they are not men at the same time as they see themselves as different from most women. "Instead, they saw themselves as the classic exception. . . . They distanced themselves from other women, internalizing an individualistic identity. They even shared sexist attitudes with men, describing other women (including fellow Air Force female officers) as 'airheads,' 'bubbleheads,' and 'wimps.'"[29] One message Dunivin's data convey (although these are not Dunivin's own words) is that there is little reason to be a feminist when it is bad enough in many military environments to be a woman.

Dorothy and Carl J. Schneider's 1984–85 interviews with over three hundred women from all ranks in all the military services revealed a clear reluctance to identify with feminism.[30] Many servicewomen equate the women's movement with a dangerous liberalism or radicalism; with a brand of pacifism that condemns the military; with lesbianism; with telling other women what to do; with forcing other women into jobs they do not want; with denying other women freedom of choice—particularly the freedom to join the military; and with focusing on trivia instead of real issues.[31] Karen Dunivin notes that in her sample of air force officers, 86 percent "emphatically said they were not feminists."[32] The reasons given ranged from distress with feminism's radicalness, the supposed abrasiveness of feminists, the fear of being tarred with the lesbian brush, to the desire to situate oneself as a traditionalist.

Dunivin's report, however, indicates less of a condemnation of feminism among military women than the negative comments would intimate. The air force officers she interviewed, in fact, convey mixed messages. "Kim," one of Dunivin's respondents who was most antipathetic toward feminism ("I don't like the feminists. They are too radical. . . . for me. They make speeches and are abrasive . . .") goes on to say, "the feminist movement has been good for America and the military. It's opened people's eyes about the competence of women when given a chance."[33] In fact, 89 percent of Dunivin's respondents "acknowledged the positive influence of the feminist movement, generally, for society."[34] Disassociating themselves from feminism may be less a rejection of feminism than it is a strategy used by some military women to divert attention from and perhaps deny even for themselves the clearly feminist actions in which many engage. Many military women, I would argue, are feminists by any other name.

Given the pressures preventing women from naming themselves as feminist, how is it that there are enough uniformed women choosing advocacy over quiescence to enable the survival of feminist habitats within the institution? Their experience of the abuse of discrimination may be part of the answer. But the ordeal of discrimination is itself not sufficient to account for women's speaking out as feminists. If it were, there would be far greater numbers of feminists in the U.S. military.

POLITICAL OPPORTUNITY AND THE LAW: THE 1970S

The key to the viability of women's advocacy in the military has been the courts—more specifically the validation the courts provided women's claims against the military in the 1970s. Throughout the 1970s, coinciding with the early days of the all-volunteer force, the courts sided with women who sued the military for sex discrimination. This judicial sponsorship—despite its reversal in the 1980s—was essential in motivating uniformed women together with their supporters in nonprofit and lobbying organizations to wage an overt, active struggle for equal opportunity. Facing hostility from within, women activists had reason by the end of the 1970s to believe they could go outside the institution and receive legal affirmation. Although the courts pulled back from equality of opportunity norms in the 1980s, by that time military women and their lobbyist allies were already invested in the promises of equal opportunity.

The 1970s tells a remarkable tale. It would have been less remarkable if the courts had been generally disposed to support those who sought redress for perceived harms experienced within the military setting. But this was not the case. In the face of most kinds of litigation, the courts rarely restricted the military from setting its own standards of conduct. In stark contrast with their usual practice, however, throughout the decade of the 1970s, the courts refused to allow the services the autonomy to practice sex discrimination. During this decade the court was prepared to instruct the military, time and again, to redress problems of sex discrimination that the courts found to be constitutionally unacceptable.

In what Stephanie A. Levin calls the *Stanley* line of cases, the Supreme Court articulated a highly deferential standard of judicial review.[35] In *United States v. Stanley* (1987),[36] an albeit slim majority of the court refused to uphold a suit brought against the army by a sergeant who had been given LSD without his knowledge in an experimental program designed to test protective clothing and equipment.[37] In the *Stanley* set of cases, Levin suggests, the court majority repeatedly asserted that "military life calls for a different standard of constitutional review than civilian life."[38] Under this higher standard, the court failed to protect First Amendment rights not only in situations where combat engagement and military mobilization were immediately at issue but even in situations where combat readiness or military discipline was a much more distant concern. In 1974, in *Parker v. Levy*,[39] it is not surprising that the court declined to overturn the conviction of an army captain and chief of dermatology who refused to train Special Forces aides for service in Vietnam, and who claimed that his conviction was a violation of First Amendment rights. With the Vietnam conflict ongoing and in light of Levy's explicit opposition to the war and his declared support for those who might refuse orders to deploy, the court's deference to the military is hardly startling.[40] But two subsequent 1980 cases continued the separate standards perspective even in a situation that was neither wartime nor fully pertinent to combat readiness.[41] In 1986, the court went on to rule that an Orthodox Jewish air force captain had no First Amendment right to wear a yarmulke while in uniform.[42] Both under constitutional standards and also under tort law, generally claimants have had little success in suing the military.[43]

In light of this history of judicial deference toward the military, it is striking that in numerous instances the courts in the 1970s required the military to dismantle sexually discriminatory policies.[44] Rather than exempting the military from equal protection claims as might be expected given the courts' record of holding the military immune to First Amendment claims in the *Stanley* line of cases, the courts repeatedly throughout the 1970s upheld claims of sex discrimination against the armed services.

This readiness to support equal protection claims was evident in the 1970s decisions of both the Supreme Court and the lower courts. In 1973, the Supreme Court ruled that policies requiring military women but not men to prove spousal dependency in order to qualify for family allowances was unconstitutional.[45] In 1975, the court denied an equal protection case brought by a male navy officer but, rather than holding that the military was immune to equal opportunity challenges, found that the navy's promotion system, which treated men and women differently (allowing women extra time in rank), was justified by the different situations of male and female service personnel in the navy.[46]

The willingness to impose equal protection standards on the military was evident in lower court cases as well. In 1974, the D.C. circuit court overturned a lower court ruling that had upheld the prohibition against women's admission to the military academies.[47] In 1976, following an abundance of cases challenging military policies that required pregnant women to be discharged, the second circuit court ruled that the automatic separation from the military of pregnant servicewomen was a violation of equal protection and due process guarantees.[48] In 1978, the D.C. district court held that an absolute bar on the assignment of navy women to sea duty was a denial of equal protection.[49] Citing *Frontiero*, Judge Sirica noted that the court ". . . shows not the slightest hesitancy about reaching the merits even though military affairs were involved."[50] In both *Frontiero* and *Schlesinger*, the court reached its decision by considering the relevant equal protection standards that were developing at this time in nonmilitary cases. In the disagreements between the court's majority and dissenting opinions, the chief issue preoccupying the bench was not whether the military was due special deference but which equal protection standards should be applied. Should a rational basis test or strict scrutiny be applied? Should women's and men's positions be viewed similarly or differently? Such questions are the stuff of equal protection debates, not military concerns. In 1978, Judge Sirica concluded his decision in the *Owens* case with the comment: "In sum, then, neither deference for the decisions of the political branches of government in the area of military affairs, nor concern about undue judicial intervention, nor the likelihood of influencing legislative efforts to revise section 6015 affords a principled basis for avoiding a decision on the precise [equal protection] claims raised by plaintiffs in this case."[51]

In the case of women's claim to a right to serve on navy vessels, it would have been easy for the courts to invoke military exigency, deferring to military or congressional judgment about the requirements of national security. Judge Sirica chose otherwise.

The courts' insistence on equality of opportunity was for the most part unwelcome, if not unexpected, among the military leadership. The different services had constituted committees to anticipate what the passage of the Equal Right Amendment (ERA) and the courts' interpretation of equal rights were likely to mean. In 1972, expecting the ERA's passage, the army appointed a committee to assess its likely effects and to make recommendations about prospective army policy. As Bettie J. Morden recounts: "The committee believed the courts would take a balanced approach involving the military services and national defense and would uphold differences in housing policy to preserve privacy between the sexes; involuntary discharge on pregnancy to preserve mobility; and exclusion of women from combat to preserve tradition. The committee actually recommended opening up West Point to women (irrespective of the ERA's passage and the courts' likely reaction). But this recommendation carried little weight when, several years later, the Army Secretary who was a West Point graduate, vigorously opposed integration, a sentiment shared by the USMA Superintendent who temporarily considered resigning when Congress mandated the admission of women to the academies."[52] In the early part of the decade, the military vehemently opposed the integration of the military academies. Although the air force had begun to plan for integration, the three service chiefs issued statements directly opposing the admission of women to the academies and ultimately opened the academy doors only in response to pending litigation and legislative directive.[53]

The armed forces watched legislative and judicial developments, carefully assessing the likelihood that they would be called upon to comply with injunctions not of their own making. For the most part, particularly in the first half of the 1970s, the military simply resisted change, making gestures in the direction of equal opportunity only when instructed to by Congress and the courts. The military was reluctant to alter its policy requiring pregnant women to leave, preferring to grant individual waivers rather than undertake any wholesale policy change. As Judith Stiehm details, three cases in the early 1970s found the military taking orders from the courts rather than setting its own agenda for change: In one, the judge advocates general of the air force believed that they were unlikely to win the case that Susan Struck, a pregnant air force nurse, had appealed, so they recommended that Struck be given a waiver that would allow her to remain in the service. The air force granted two other waivers—to Lieutenant Mary S. Gutierrez and to Airman Gloria D. Robinson—whose cases were also both in the district courts in the early 1970s.[54]

By the mid-1970s, the services were beginning to inch forward as they saw the writing on the wall. Although for twenty years since a 1951 executive order, the military had required women with minor children to leave the service, the WAF director had by the early 1970s extracted from the legal office of the air force the admission that such a policy was likely to fail in the light of equal opportunity legislation.[55] By 1974, the Department of Defense considered initiating action for repeal of the discharge policy that pregnancy and parenthood triggered. But by the 1976 *Cushman* decision, the department's rules still stood. Similarly, the navy began to examine their women-at-sea policies, which in the mid-1970s still barred women from serving on all seagoing vessels. Anticipating the need for change, the navy went to Congress with a proposal to allow women on noncombat ships. But before legislative debate was concluded, Judge Sirica handed down his ruling in *Owens*.[56]

As always, it should be noted, the military did not speak in a single voice. Individuals such as Admiral Elmo Zumwalt were active proponents of egalitarian reforms. Well before *Owens*, for instance, Zumwalt directed the navy to integrate one ship on an experimental basis, urging as an ultimate goal the assignment of women to ships at sea.[57] Besides Zumwalt, there were other military leaders who encouraged women's careers and, as in the case of one of the *Owens* plaintiffs, even endorsed the actions of women who were challenging discriminatory practices in the military.[58] But the men and the women who were overt, outspoken advocates of gender equality were the exception, rather than the rule. Without the law on their side, they would not have survived within the institution.

Women's movement organizations—the Women's Equity Action League (WEAL), NOW, the women's rights project of the ACLU, and others—played a crucial part in supporting military women's claims in court. These organizations brought with them a range of different agendas. Some, such as NOW, were pulled between antimilitarist views held by some of their membership, on the one hand, and a liberal belief in a woman's right to exercise choice, including the choice to fight in wars.[59] In their legal briefs and statements before congressional committees, NOW and the ACLU tended to stress the denial of equality to women in terms quite different from those of WEAL, Business and Professional Women, or the American Association of University Women. NOW's 1981 *Rostker* brief read: "The requirement to register and be classified for eligibility for induction into the armed forces is a responsibility which NOW believes, *if imposed at all* [emphasis mine] must be imposed equitably on all members of society."[60] The brief goes on to cite extensively not only relevant case law but also feminist texts connecting an all-male military to images of women as weak and unfit, linking this, in turn, to the "staggering incidence of rape and domestic violence."[61] The *amicus* brief submitted by WEAL jointly with a number of other women's organizations also emphasizes the impact of an all-male draft in reinforcing sexual stereotypes and in denying equal rights and responsibilities. Their brief, however, displays no ambivalence about the draft itself and is presented in a conventional style of legal argument. The different mode of argumentation aside, these women's movement and legal rights organizations played a central role in seeing that gender inequality issues in the military became part of the state's legal agenda.

In sum: By the end of the 1970s, military women had reason to believe that if they took measures to challenge discriminatory practices within the military, they would get a hearing outside the institution. Feminist activists in movement organizations had assisted military women in bringing their cases to court. And the courts had made it clear that their doors were open.

The Backlash

In the 1980s, the doors to the courtroom swung shut, and there was little legislative activity directed at expanding opportunities to military women.[62] But there was no turning back. By 1980, women's groups had situated themselves within the institution and were working relentlessly (as the previous chapter detailed) to keep gender equality issues on the agenda.

The backlash set in immediately with the 1980 election of Ronald Reagan. Anticipating Reagan's election, the army instituted a "pause" in the accession of women soldiers, and the other services considered slowing their integration of women. Whether because of the conservative tide or because the court possibly viewed itself as being asked to face an issue that more fundamentally tested the question of whether women belonged in the "real" military (that is, in combat), the luster of the 1970s' equal opportunity days appeared to dim. In *Rostker v. Goldberg* (1981),[63] that decade's spate of equal opportunity decisions on military and gender issues came to an end. Asked to treat men and women the same with respect to draft registration, the court, as William Brundage observed, seemed to approach "the defining nucleus" of the military mission.[64] Writing for a six-judge majority, Justice Rehnquist claimed that draft registration directly related to conscription and thereby to combat. The dissenting judges claimed that women could be registered or drafted without their necessarily being implicated in combat duties. In language that was significantly absent in the 1970s sex discrimination cases brought against the military, Justice Rehnquist affirmed the importance of a "healthy deference to legislative and executive judgments in the area of military affairs."[65] Moving from dependency allowances, to the pregnancy issue, to the matter of women's service on ships, the court began to approach what many saw as the core definition of a masculinist military, the composition of a fighting force.

Plaintiffs protesting discrimination, whether on gender, racial, or sexual orientation grounds, had reason to find the 1980s a discouraging decade. Two civilian employment discrimination cases that plaintiffs might well have won in the 1970s met only partial success in the courts. Pamela Doviak Celli, an engineer technician working at Portsmouth, New Hampshire, was denied the right to participate in submarine sea trials and sued the secretary of the navy. The Equal Employment Opportunity Commission ruled in her favor, but the navy procrastinated, moving slowly in its compliance. Eventually, Celli won back pay and attorney fees from the military, and, in 1987, the navy changed its policy to permit women technicians on submarines for testing purposes. But when Celli, represented by Isabelle Katz Pinzler of the Women's Rights Project of the American Civil Liberties Union, took her case to court, the Federal District Court of Maine refused to accept the claim that Title VII covers personnel decisions in the military. A similar case, however, brought by Glenda Bledsoe, a civilian electronics technician at Miramar Naval Air Station in San Diego who was denied embarkation on an aircraft carrier, won a favorable ruling in the ninth circuit court of appeals.[66]

In the 1980s, if Blacks in the services felt that they might look to the courts, they were disappointed. Black enlisted men who sued their commanding officer for damages in a discrimination suit, claiming a violation of their constitutional rights, were rebuffed in 1983 by a Supreme Court that reiterated the often cited position that the military and civilian systems of justice were separate entities.[67] In the same year, another group of Black servicemen sought unsuccessfully to establish cause of action for alleged discrimination by their commanding officers. A unanimous Supreme Court ruled against the servicemen.[68] This repudiation was all the more troubling given the harsh treatment in military courts of many Black servicemembers. One notorious case was that of Corporal Lindsey Scott, convicted in 1983 for raping the wife of a white marine and sentenced to thirty years although he did not match the initial description given by the victim and was reported to have been seen at a shopping center by a security guard at the time of the crime.[69] A similarly disturbing episode involved the USS *Norton Sound*, in which twenty-four sailors were placed under investigation for being lesbian; the case ended in the conviction of two Black women, one of whom denied throughout the trial that she was a lesbian.[70]

With the 1980s, the courts were once again relying on the language of "deference." In a 1989 case involving the discharge of a military officer identified as a lesbian, the seventh circuit court returned to the earlier stance: "[I]t is difficult to conceive of an area of governmental activity in which the courts have less competence. The complex, subtle, and professional decisions as to the composition, training, equipping, and control of a military force are essentially professional military judgments, (albeit—ed.) subject *always* to civilian control. . . ."[71]

For the ten years following *Rostker*, the legal chill probably kept women from challenging the constitutionality of the 1948 bar on women in combat, but the challenge remained imminent. In 1989, in fact, DACOWITS did finally pass a resolution calling for the end of the combat exclusion, and women aviators would likely have taken the issue to court soon thereafter had the Gulf War not propelled the issue to prominence. Nor have lesbian or gay activists been fully deterred by the legislative rebuff of the Clinton directive that upheld the proscription on gays and lesbians but instructed the military to cease "pursuit" of uniformed homosexuals.

Paradoxically, it is less the legislative or judicial proscriptions than it is the establishment of equal rights itself that has kept feminist activism from developing in more radical directions. Because the law has legitimated the claims making of feminist activists, there has been little reason for them to pursue a more mobilizational strategy. Rather than seeking out alliances with critics of race discrimination or the exclusion of gays and lesbians, many feminist activists in the military have believed that they are best served by limiting their claims to issues of gender alone.

This is repeatedly explained in strategic terms. DACOWITS members, for instance, have believed at least until recently that they would not be well advised even to make race issues a priority despite the military's own explicit affirmation of antidiscrimination policies on race. Early on, as one navy captain explained it, "We needed to keep focused. We didn't take up race issues, but we didn't take up family issues either or many other issues. It took years, for instance, before they [DACOWITS] could [even] turn to reserve or guard issues."[72] DACOWITS, many of its members believed, was specifically charged to deal with women in the services, whereas race issues were the priority of the equal opportunity offices, a division of functions that inevitably has slowed identification of the concerns that women of color might raise.[73]

Feminist activists are even more reluctant to address themselves to questions of discrimination against lesbians and gays in the military for fear of discrediting their own claims by allowing them to get entangled in a set of issues that have even less legitimacy than challenges to gender inequality. As one activist explained in recounting why WOPA had declined in the mid-1980s to arrange a proposed session about the homosexual exclusion, "[S]ome said, 'Well, they're fearful enough of us [feminists] already as it is. . . . it was one of those, you know, 'better not to scare the horses.' "[74]

This reluctance to seek alliances among the different groups challenging discrimination is partly a function of the law itself. The denial of equal opportunity can be challenged only on the basis of segmented identities—race *or* gender *or*, prospectively, sexual orientation. It is not surprising that until recently the institution has replicated this functional specialization (gender issues in DACOWITS, race issues primarily in the offices of equal opportunity), and that many activists' reluctance to make the links between inequality in its different expressions reproduces that of institutional leaders who fail to see in military culture the convergence, as law professor Kathryn Abrams argues, of an inseparable complex of androcentric assumptions.[75] These categories also make it very difficult for those who stand at the intersection of legal categories (women of color, for instance) to make claims on their own behalf.

To recapitulate: In the 1970s, the law encouraged feminist activism by responding favorably to women's claims against the military. Although the courts went on in the 1980s to play a more restrictive role, their reversion was in some sense too late. By 1980, the courts had transmitted to women the message that in certain basic respects, under the Constitution, they were entitled to equal treatment. This was vital in lending legitimacy to women's advocacy groups. The response women received outside the institution, in courts of law and in what through the 1980s was a Democrat-controlled Congress,[76] validated the institutional standing of offices within the military in which women worked on behalf of gender equality. The opportunity the law created for activism produced ongoing protest within the institution. But it is also the case, ironically, that this "opportunity" encouraged feminists to train their sights narrowly on gender-specific concerns. Since feminists generally believed that they did not need the support of other groups challenging discrimination and in fact, in the case of gays and lesbians, saw any possible alliance as potentially counterproductive, the law's responsiveness and the categorizations that the law itself encourages had the paradoxical effect of limiting feminism's agenda.

BEYOND OPPORTUNITY: THE LAW AND INSTITUTIONAL NORMS

It is important to recognize that the law does more than widen or limit opportunities for activism. By signaling the acceptability of some claims (and denying the validity of others), the legislature and the courts shape the normative environment within which activists define themselves, their concerns, and their priorities. The law is more than *dictum*, rules that allow or disallow. Through its influence on institutional norms, the law also affects the language, customs, and rituals through which activists come to form their sense of self and their relationship to others. The law does not, for example, simply provide opportunities for feminists to make gender-based claims and deny similar opportunities to those who wish to challenge discrimination based on sexual orientation. By upholding the homosexual exclusion, the law also fosters an institutional discourse (climate or culture) in which homophobic jokes are acceptable, gay- and lesbian-baiting is encouraged, and males are pressured to prove their masculinity and females their femininity whatever the requirements of the job or social situation. The law thus shapes institutional norms that bear on how the meanings of feminism itself are likely to be constructed.

The law's multiple functions bear comparison with the three dimensions of power described by Steven Lukes and John Gaventa. They contend that power is not merely the capacity to shape decisions or to influence political agendas. It is also the ability, they argue, to influence how at a most basic level people come to imagine what they want for themselves and for others.[77] When the law frames equality as "equal opportunity," feminists whose work lives are shaped by legal norms are likely to think of equality within the framework the law itself sets. When the law focuses on equal protection, for instance, it is easy to think about equal opportunities to compete for jobs. The right to serve on ships fits within this framework. The practice of frequenting prostitutes when "on liberty" does not.

That is perhaps why Tailhook came as such a shock. Rape, prostitution, and sexual assault along the lines of the Tailhook incidents are hardly new to military life. When the Tailhook Association met in the Las Vegas Hilton in 1991 and staged its infamous third-floor gauntlet, the convention was the group's thirty-fifth. The Defense Department investigative report records: "It is important to understand that the events at Tailhook 91 did not occur in a historical vacuum. Similar behavior had occurred at previous conventions. The emerging pattern of some of the activities, such as the gauntlet, began to assume the aura of 'tradition.'" What is remarkable is how few people over the years seem to have considered this form of behavior inappropriate, unprofessional, demeaning of women, or hostile to the standards of gender equality, let alone in certain respects (the gauntlet assaults) criminal. The Tailhook convention—what is described in the investigative report of the Defense Department as "the professional aspects of Tailhook 91"—was attended by flag officers; the squadron suites that planned the "social entertainment" (drinking, strippers) were organized by junior officers. Military women clearly participated in some of the raucous partying. This was "equal opportunity night life" with the entertainment defined in a tradition that was as masculinist as it comes: Even after Tailhook '91, in which according to the Defense Department report eighty-three women and seven men had been assaulted,[78] the president of the association, Captain Frederic G. Ludwig, Jr., wrote: "Without a doubt, it was the biggest and most successful Tailhook we have ever had. We said it would be the 'Mother of all Hooks,' and it was."[79] Although the comparison to a frat party or spring break behavior is often used by those who would wish to downplay the seriousness of Tailhook, the analogy is not entirely accurate. Unlike a frat party where the university administration may, in albeit troubling ways, turn a blind eye, in the case of Tailhook the counterpart of the dean and provost actually attended the events year after year. Journalist Gregory L. Vistica writes that when the invitation to Tailhook arrived on the desk of the administrative assistant, Marybel Batjer, to navy secretary H. Lawrence Garrett, III, she scribbled on the invitation: "Yuk, yuk, no, no. You can't go to Tailhook." But as Vistica writes, since Tailhook '91 was to be a "celebration of the swift and stunning American victory in the Gulf War and one of the biggest and most important conventions in the association's history," Garrett could not decline.[80]

If the third-floor gauntlet constituted assaultive behavior, as Paula Coughlin (whose complaint launched the exposé) claimed both to the media and in court, and if the sexualized-male-predator-as-soldier was to be repudiated as normative behavior, neither the civilian nor the military courts provided clear messages to that effect. When Tailhook first broke in the media, the navy clearly recognized the damage that the wildfire publicity might inflict on the institution, and initial indications seemed to suggest that the navy would act speedily and punitively. But the eventual results of the Tailhook prosecutions proved otherwise. Initially, Pentagon officials intimated that of the 140 navy and marine corps officers under investigation and being considered for discipline, more than a dozen officers might be court-martialed, and that up to twelve admirals could be forced to retire or could expect to be reprimanded.[81] Not a single officer, however, was court-martialed.[82] Navy secretary Lawrence Garrett resigned almost immediately; later, chief naval officer Frank Kelso was pressured to take a two-month early retirement. Kelso was, however, promoted just prior to his retirement,[83] although the confirmation of his four-star rank was opposed by six of the seven women senators in Congress at the time;[84] Vice Admiral Dunleavy retired at a two- rather than three-star rank.

In the civilian courts, some of the women plaintiffs reached monetary settlements with the Tailhook Association and have been successful in their suits against the Hilton; but the courts—in keeping with the pattern of deference resumed in the 1980s—imposed no sanctions on the military.[85] In 1994, a federal judge dismissed most of the claims against the navy brought by five women who claimed to have been sexually molested in the third-floor gauntlet.[86] The difficulty of prosecution was immense given the determination of the brotherhood of aviators to protect each other and to remain silent about what they knew.[87]

This judicial paralysis seemed to have been too much even for Senators Strom Thurmond and Sam Nunn of the Armed Services Committee, who took the unusual step of requiring that the navy notify the committee when one of the officers being selected for promotion was on the list of the 140 potentially culpable aviators. Later, in a letter to navy secretary John Dalton, Nunn and Thurmond said that they would not have confirmed the promotion of Commander Robert Stumpf (a highly decorated pilot who once commanded the Blue Angels aviation demonstration team) had they known the charges against him, sending Stumpf's case back to the navy for reconsideration. (Stumpf was said to have flown to the convention in navy aircraft and to have been present at a frocking party his squadron held in one suite during Tailhook, where a prostitute stripped and performed a sexual act on a junior officer, although Stumpf reputedly left before the party finale.)[88]

The absence of any court convictions could only have instructed military women in the perils of coming forward and could only have validated the image of a sailor-on-liberty as beyond reach of the law.[89] In Congresswoman Patricia Schroeder's words, the idea that justice was done in the aftermath of Tailhook "doesn't pass the giggle test."[90] Others, such as former navy secretary James Webb, maintained that Tailhook was a lesson in political correctness run rampant, leading to witch-hunts, scapegoating, and the persecution of valued military leadership.[91]

The public response of military women activists was to invoke equal opportunity language. As long as women were unwelcome in combat aviation, they claimed, women were likely to be seen as second-class citizens, perhaps as sexual prey, but not as peers or professionals. Activists eschewed taking any public position in support of the Tailhook plaintiffs, nor did they express a position on the inquiry, the judicial processes, or the appropriateness of the penalties imposed.[92] Whether the actual presence of more women in combat aviation will ultimately change the character of this military subculture (acknowledged widely as more "macho" in character than the still all-male submarine or now-integrated surface warfare subcultures) remains to be seen. But the fact that Tailhook could transpire despite two decades of equal opportunity law suggests some of the law's limitations. As a normative framework, equal opportunity law has successfully provided grounds for protest against the form of discrimination that exists when women are denied that which men have access to. Equal opportunity is then necessarily limiting as a normative framework if sexual predation is to be challenged.

The limitations of equal opportunity law were also visible in the litigation against the single-sex Virginia Military Institute (VMI) and the Citadel. Although these were not military-run institutions, military officers were deputed to them as part of the ROTC arrangement on the campuses, and the two institutions received public funds. The outcome of the VMI and Citadel cases was bound to have at the least symbolic importance for those who have long opposed the presence of women at the navy, army, and air force academies, as well as for those who have claimed that their integration was right both for the military and from the viewpoint of legal justice.

Although the case against VMI was ultimately upheld in the Supreme Court, the limitation of the court decision raised some of the same difficult issues as those evoked by Tailhook. The Supreme Court ruled 7–1 against VMI, requiring that the institution open its doors to women. Writing for the court, Justice Ruth Bader Ginsburg quoted from VMI literature, noting that "Entering students are incessantly exposed to the rat line, 'an extreme form of the adversative model' comparable in intensity to Marine Corps boot camp. Tormenting and punishing, the rat line bonds new cadets to their fellow sufferers and, when they have completed the 7-month experience, to their former tormentors." The adversative model, she also notes, is built on a hierarchical "class system" of privileges and responsibilities as well as "*a dyke system*" (emphasis mine) for assigning a senior class mentor to each entering class "rat."[93]

The majority decision did not question the validity of the "adversative" system for educating "citizen-soldiers." What Justice Ginsburg emphasizes, rather, is the unacceptability of excluding qualified individuals who happen to be female from such a system based on generalizations about women as a class.[94] By ruling that all-female institutions do not provide equivalent military education, the court debunked the lower court ruling affirming the VMI position that women need "nurturance not competition."[95]

But without being able in the context of the specific issues raised in the VMI case to either scrutinize or regulate the form of education offered within the to-be-integrated VMI and Citadel, the court potentially reinscribes the idea of military education as the cloning of Rambos-in-uniform.[96] There was little the court seemed willing or perhaps able to do to alter the way the military had in the past fused hypermasculinity and aggression with the idea of what it means to educate a class of military leaders.[97]

The ruling "against" VMI and the Citadel ensured that women should have the opportunity to compete in a male environment. But no question was raised about whether that environment was the optimal one for producing a modern-day soldier.[98] To require the admission of women to the last two publicly supported all-male military institutions is to open doors. But given the kind of institutions whose doors are being opened, this is a weak victory for military feminism. Perhaps a more fundamental challenge might be to ask whether the sorts of programs in military leadership offered at VMI's and the Citadel's sister institutions—where students are "generally supported rather than harassed"[99]—might in some ways offer better preparation for the next generation of military leaders. But this was not a question that could be asked within the framework of the equal opportunity issues that the court had before it.[100]

It goes without saying that equal opportunity norms provide no possibility for feminists who might wish to challenge the war-making functions of the military as masculinist. In two Gulf War cases, a woman army reserve physician was jailed for eight months in a military prison for refusing duty in the Gulf. Declaring the war "immoral, inhumane and unconstitutional," Captain Yolanda Huet-Vaughn appeared at antiwar rallies, stressing the "disastrous environmental and political consequences" of war. Captain Huet-Vaughn was convicted at court-martial in August 1991.[101] Chaplain Garland Robertson was discharged from the air force for writing a letter to the Abilene, Texas, newspaper questioning the use of force against Iraq two weeks before the Gulf War—this despite the fact that Robertson had served in the air force for twenty years and had been decorated for his service as a pilot in Vietnam. Prior to his discharge, he was ordered to undergo three psychological examinations to determine whether he had a personality disorder.[102] Neither

Huet-Vaughn nor Robertson claimed to be challenging the military on grounds that had anything to do with gender equality. But the harsh punishment meted out indicates that any radical antimilitarist definition of feminism would have little chance of survival within the military itself. Equal opportunity norms have encouraged feminism, but its possible meanings are limited by the norms of the institution.

CONCLUSION

A decade after Rosemary Mariner declined in the mid-1970s to join the *Owens* suit, feminism had been institutionalized within the military. Throughout the 1980s, military women and their civilian supporters worked actively through DACOWITS, WOPA, WEAL, *Minerva*, and the various offices within the services that were assigned the task of monitoring gender equality. By the late 1980s, Mariner herself had been installed as head of an organization of women aviators eager to open up combat aviation to women. The previous chapter described the establishment of organizational habitats from which advocates of gender equality within the military were able to generate challenges to the status quo. The present chapter has advanced an explanation of how this process of institutionalization was set in motion—the validating role, that is, played by the the courts and the legislature in the 1970s.

In the face of the hostile attitudes and routine derogatory commentary to which many military women have been subjected, the risks of being seen as a "women's libber" are all too apparent. Without the affirmation of the law and the consequent establishment of spaces within the institution for those who sought to work on behalf of equal opportunity for women, feminism within the military could not have survived. With the law on their side consistently throughout the 1970s, women activists were not "troublemakers" pure and simple; they were now entitled by law to be troublemakers.

When the courts and Congress stipulated that the most prestigious of the military academies must open their doors to women, that pregnancy and motherhood must not bar women from military duty, that dependents of military women should be treated similarly to dependents of military men, that women should not be blocked from serving on ships, and most recently that women aviators should be brought into combat aviation positions, such legal nods of encouragement from outside the institution motivated women to be active within.

In certain respects, women's activism pushed both the law and the institution much farther than those who originally framed the terms of equal opportunity laws and policies intended to go. Neither Congress, the courts, nor the military leadership in the 1970s or 1980s expected or desired to see women flying combat planes or serving on combat vessels. Nor was it clear in the early stages that women's claims to equality would mean not only that they would demand entry into the academies and formerly all-male job environments (significant in itself) but also that the perquisites of a masculine military (where male power could command female sexual compliance) were now assailable. Required by law to shift institutional rules and policies, the military has adjusted incrementally to a range of new realities. Each of these challenges has caused agitation, and yet many of the changes, extended over several decades, have come to be assumed as "natural." As Colonel M. C. Pruitt, a former executive director of DACOWITS, remarked, "If you asked them whether such and such a policy was desirable, they'd have objected. But once it was in place, they accepted it." "With each change," she noted with amusement, "they'd say, 'Well, things are about right now, just the way they are.'"[103]

But the very responsiveness of the law has also narrowed the agenda of women activists. The success of women's groups in realizing many of their claims has meant that they have little reason to look for alliances with other groups that have also sought to change military practices. The law has effected this agenda narrowing, partly by outright proscription. The continued legal ban on homosexuality in the military and the punitive treatment of uniformed conscientious objectors make any alliance between military feminists and gay/lesbian or pacifist/antimilitarist groups likely to be at best discrediting, and at worst ruinous.

The law's influence, however, is not exerted merely through legal rules specifying what is allowed and disallowed. The law also acts discursively[104] as a lens through which those who seek change come to define the kind of change they want and think is possible. Equal rights law instills institutional norms that encourage women to be given the same opportunities as men. As a normative framework this enables feminists to develop challenges to exclusionary practices on the job. But these same norms do not effectively equip feminists with a ready critique of sexual predation or machismo-embued definitions of a model soldier.

The story of feminist protest inside the U.S. military can be read as an account of the perseverance and fortitude it takes as a feminist in a male-dominant environment to be out front leading a cause whose legitimacy is constantly under attack. The story of military activists can also be read as a lesson in how the state constructs a politics of gender equality whose reach the state, through the courts and the military, is able to control. What braids these two seemingly opposing interpretations into a single narrative is the way in which, as this chapter argues, women's activism is both the producer and the product of its institutional environment. In the case of the military, the law's regulation of the institution has been both catalytic and controlling. In the case of the church, as we shall see, the law is absent. From the point of view of women's activism, this absence is decisive.

PART THREE

THE CHURCH

Chapter 5

DISCURSIVE ACTIVISM

I N THE American Catholic Church, unobtrusive mobilization by women has taken the form, largely, of discursive politics. By discursive politics, I mean the politics of reflection and reformulation. Much of this politics involves words and images. Practitioners of discursive politics speak, write and publish, talk, hold workshops, compose and record songs, draw, make cards, print T-shirts, direct plays, and produce newsletters; they write memoranda, letters, pamphlets, news releases, and books. The feminist women and men who do this intensely political work are engaged in the construction of a knowledge community whose view of the institutional church and of society is self-consciously at odds with the present-day Catholic hierarchy.

In its vision and in much of its lived reality, this is an explicitly radical politics. Feminist activists in the U.S. Catholic Church call for nothing less than a restructuring of both church and society. Some espouse a renewed priestly ministry in which women will be ordained into a democratized church. Some reject ordination, and the hierarchy it implies, altogether. Most seek a society where dominance by the few is replaced by a sharing of power among people of all races, genders, and sexual orientations, and where the chasm dividing rich and poor is erased. Many of those who endeavor to live this vision have committed themselves to working with the homeless, prisoners, people with AIDS, Central American refugees. The positions they take, often publicly, on church organization, homosexuality, abortion, and a range of social justice concerns mark them as outliers either in the institutional church or in society, or both. I confront the puzzle of why feminism in the church takes this direction—both discursive and radical—by first simply describing in this chapter the route pursued by activists in the church. In the chapter that follows, I turn to a more explanatory account of why feminism in the church and in the military diverged so dramatically.

AN EXAMPLE OF DISCURSIVE FEMINISM:
"A DISCIPLESHIP OF EQUALS"

Gathering in Crystal City, Virginia, in 1995, the Women's Ordination Conference (WOC) identified the "discipleship of equals" as their watchword for the conference.[1] This phraseology, drawing on Elisabeth Schüssler Fiorenza's writings, signaled WOC's attempt to engage a "new paradigm."[2] The WOC conference program introduced this rethinking with the statement "Through the plenary rituals and panels, and through the smaller focus groups, WOC will demonstrate that the ordination of women does not resolve the problem, and that nothing short of a major deconstruction of clericalism, patriarchy, and hierarchy . . . will do."[3]

Coming from WOC, this repudiation of reformism was particularly noteworthy. As one of many feminist organizations within the church, WOC had consistently made its distinctive focus the ordination of women. What WOC members had always sought was ordination within a "renewed" church, but it was ordination nonetheless. In 1995, the WOC conference planners set about opening up for discussion the very idea of ordination as fundamentally flawed. Insisting that "ordination" means "subordination," Harvard Divinity School theologian Schüssler Fiorenza criticized the "elite, male dominated, sacred, pyramidal order of domination" in the institutional church. As Peter Steinfels's report in the *New York Times* noted, the conference's espousal of a "discipleship of equals" suggested the pursuit of a "church without hierarchy and without priests ordained for life and bestowed with special power to administer sacraments . . . a model of the church [that] is associated more with New Testament ties, with the radical wing of the Protestant Reformation and with movements like the Quakers rather than with Catholicism."[4]

This invitation to debate was taken up many times over by conference participants. Criticizing the possibility of abandoning the goal of ordination, Sister Maureen Fiedler, herself a member of the WOC board and a well-known activist, exclaimed at one of the open mike sessions, "If I were a bishop and I heard that this group no longer wanted the ordination of women, I would say, 'Thank God, they are off our backs.' Every institution in this country is patriarchal. . . . Am I going to tell women not to run for Congress, not to take tenured positions in universities? No, I am going to tell them to take that chisel and chisel from inside . . . even as we need people outside the walls blowing the trumpet."[5]

Throughout the debate over ordination, speakers warned against dualist thinking, a theme repeatedly sounded by women activists. Endeavoring to insist that the conference agenda was not rejecting ordination, Georgetown theologian Diana Hayes commented:

> What we are trying to explain with the "discipleship of equals" is a wholistic vision . . . not either/or. We're saying both/and. We need to have women ordained as priests but we also need to be about changing the structure of the

church . . . the challenge is, how do we do that? How can we be thorns, embedded so deeply that nothing can pluck us out?

Elisabeth Schüssler Fiorenza added her voice:

> I'm very happy because what we are experiencing here is *ecclesia* [a "real" church—involving democratic debate]. I fully agree with what Diana has said . . . it is both/and, not either/or. We have said yes and that is why we are here. We have said yes; the question is to what will we say no?

But the debate never turned, at least in the setting of the conference ballroom, to strategy.[6] Did it make sense to seek ordination to the deaconate as a way station? Should there be an attempt at mobilizing women on a mass scale—to withhold parish contributions, to pressure sympathetic clerics against ordaining men into the priesthood until women could be similarly ordained, to engage in symbolic protest acts such as the time women performed foot washing outside the Bishop's Congress or something far more directly challenging of the "sacred," such as women's going onto the altar? What about organizing around extrainstitutional issues (welfare, military spending, violence against women, reproductive choice—one of the hardest issues for feminist activists in the church). Perhaps these questions had been on the agenda for so long and with such little effect that conference planners preferred to turn their attentions elsewhere? Perhaps it was assumed that the appropriate forum for strategy questions was the smaller workshops, not the larger plenaries?

Rather than focusing on concrete next-steps, the discussion in the conference ballroom revolved around visions of a restructured church. Participants wanted to debate the place of ordination, to articulate their understanding of an inclusive spirituality, and to summon in words the meaning of faith. In the discussion facilitated by open mikes, a number of conference participants expressed their distress at the near-invisibility of Christ within the themes of the conference. Commenting from the audience, Sister Joan Sobala from Rochester (the originator and erstwhile editor of WOC's newsletter) said, "A Unitarian friend could accept the draft [of the conference "Declaration of Radical Equality"] the way it is. I would like to preface it with 'Members of WOC acknowledge with gratitude and joy that we are disciples of Jesus Christ, our brother and our savior. . . .'"[7] As Pamela Schaeffer recounted in her conference write-up for the *National Catholic Reporter*, "Explicit mention of Jesus or of Christ was rare in [the conference] liturgies, although Schüssler Fiorenza, in her keynote talk, referred often to Jesus and the gospels."[8] As one audience member commented, "The role of Christ here is entirely ambivalent. He is my god. He is the person I wish to be ordained to serve. Who are we, then, disciples of? My feeling is that the god has become equality itself."[9]

The conference debates and discussion seemed almost secondary to the rituals—liturgies, song, dance—that were woven throughout the program. Speakers were introduced with an audience-sung refrain used in other liturgical settings that feminists in the church had developed to offer a collective blessing, for and with the speaker—

> Bless Sophia
> Dream the vision
> Share the wisdom
> Buried deep within—[10]

or with the sung lines,

> Give me a woman who can ride the tallest mountain, give me a woman who can inspire me. . . .

This was sometimes followed by the gaily offered exhortation, "Who do you need to say no to . . . do it while you dance":

> So I say . . . No, no, just open up your ears and say it, no, no, no . . . Just as a woman so you say . . . but within me rages passions strong, and I have lots to say, I say no, no, no, a thousand times no, it's so clear, just open up your ears. . . .

Sometimes the follow-up was the more somber song (dedicated to Ivone Gebara, a Brazilian nun silenced by the Vatican):

> We will not be silenced
> We will not be silenced
> We will not be silenced
> We will gather, we will gather
> In her name.[11]

The singing continued through the three days, often repeated, with words set to simple, memorable tunes:

> Say it . . . Say it . . . Sister . . . Don't Hold Nothing Back.

And this song's Spanish refrain:

> Rompe, Rompe, Hermana el Silencio Ya
> Rompe, el Silencio y greta la Verdad![12]

Or still another reminiscent of the rousing militancy of the 1960s with a feminist difference:

> I'm crossing the lines for justice

Crossing the lines for liberation
Crossing the lines for you.[13]

Each session was peppered with singing, between speakers as well as at the beginning of each plenary session, often in both Spanish and English. Some of the Spanish songs were written and sung with stirring emotion by Rosa Marta Zarate, a sister originally from Mexico who came to work in the Los Angeles diocese and, after being fired from its employ, sued the church:

Por Nada Me Devuelvo (For Nothing Will I Go Back).

By Sunday, the words, tunes, and rhythms of many of the songs already felt familiar. The booths selling discs and tapes did a brisk business.

The songs were only a part of the carefully thought-out conference dramaturgy. There was no conference "podium" but a slightly raised stage in the middle of the ballroom, with the audience on all sides. Speakers turned around talking equally to people on all sides of the stage. The evening dinner was preceded by a long set of rituals of lighting candles, breaking bread, sipping wine.

The conference itself brought together the most illustrious representatives of feminist activism in the church—but, perhaps out of an attempt to avoid the re-creating of hierarchy, seemed to feature as many of the well-known activists as could be brought to Virginia. Hence the program offered an entire galaxy of the "who's who" of feminist activism in the church. The book, tape, and craft booths lining the hallways to the ballroom were taking orders in quantity. The books written by speakers at the conference were featured among the densely packed displays of what is now a thriving industry of books on religion and gender, sexuality, poverty, liturgies, spirituality, and racism, in the United States and globally.

As with other feminist workshops and conferences, the planning committee made a concerted effort to see that the program included people and issues responsive to a diverse agenda. Silvia Cancio, the Hispanic president of the WOC board, spoke. Two African-American women, Diane Hayes and Dot Jackson, were part of the plenary program. A session devoted to "struggles and visions around the globe" featured a woman from Ecuador, a woman from Kenya, a Native-American woman, and a Chinese American. Jeanine Gramick, co-founder of New Ways Ministry, which addresses itself specifically to the lesbian and gay Catholic community, was also a speaker. All plenaries were accompanied by someone who signed for the hearing-impaired.

In comparison with the speakers' rosters of many conferences or workshops in academia, the WOC conference speakers and workshop presenters manifested an impressive diversity. There was not much talk of lesbian/gay identity issues, although it was unstated whether, as seems likely, this was because most activists already share the view that homophobia has no role in a renewed church, or because there was still awkwardness among the group about lesbian and gay issues.

The speakers represented a more diverse group of women than did the participants, among whom were few women of color. As one Hispanic woman from Texas commented about the attempts at inclusivity: "To ask for scholarships [to come to the workshop] is difficult. We need to not do this in hotels. We need to go out into the community. They need to come into my barrios. I need to go into African-American communities. We're used to this. I'm sorry. But this is very white. They try. But. . . ."

This was not the only criticism of the conference. For some, the ritual seemed to be too theatrical. In the midst of the lengthy liturgy that began when participants sat down to dinner but before food was served, one conference-goer was overheard by a *National Catholic Reporter* journalist to remark, "I'm from the McDonald's generation; Bring on the food."[14] For others, WOC seemed to have "lost its focus," perhaps moving into a "post-Christian model of Woman-Church."[15] But for many the conference seemed to serve as a chance to gather strength. As various participants commented,

> I miss ritual. I don't go to church on Sunday. When we come to a gathering like this, it sort of touches something in me that I no longer have. (Nun, recently resigned from her community)

> Every community has ritual that helps to define community. We tried very hard [here] to fit the old model of liturgy and ritual into something that has no history so I wasn't really comfortable with all that new stuff, but the best part about it is that it is new . . . not connected to a male expression of ritual. (Laywoman)

> It's a way of breathing deeply what I believe. (Bilingual teacher, active member of a self-constituted community of believers)

> I'm pretty isolated . . . there are very few places where I feel completely safe. A place like this can make me say, all right, the world isn't safe. But I'm going to keep going anyway. When I think of what Dana was saying about sacramental moments, a special meeting with God. Here we are meeting God in one another, telling stories; those are sacramental moments for me. It is about bringing justice. (Lesbian pastoral counselor)

> I am fairly isolated where I am. I don't have family; my community is scattered. This is where I come to get my sustenance. It is where I come to catch

my breath. I come to see acquaintances. We go a long way back [points to a Sister sitting next to her]. (Nun from Los Angeles)

The everyday lives of many people at the conference is very hard. They work with AIDS patients, people in prisons, people who have a tough time in life. Part of what they may look for at a conference like this is a chance for some relief. The singing, the dancing is healing. (Nun from Washington, D.C.)

The workshops touched on each of the critical themes of discursive politics in the church: finding a place that is neither fully inside nor wholly outside, challenging the norms of hierarchy and dualism, searching for an inclusive community, endeavoring to discover a faith that is built on "radical equality"—a phrase invoked repeatedly throughout the weekend.[16] The final Sunday morning session included a specially commissioned musical suite ("Call to Action"), a closing liturgy, a blessing by the assembled gathering of those who felt called to a variety of different ministries. Many embraced each other, musicians and singers moved to the stage to play and sing, and people moved slowly from the ballroom. Nearly everyone, it seemed, went home with suitcases brimming with paper, books, tapes, pamphlets. As they left, conference participants dropped the conference evaluation forms, a fixture of every church-related feminist gathering, in the waiting containers.

FEMINISM AND CONFESSIONAL CONFERENCING

The contemporary history of feminism in the American Catholic Church can, in fact, be sketched as an account of conferences, writings, and speeches. In the 1970s the combined force of Vatican II and the dawn of feminism's second wave galvanized women (both lay and religious) to reexamine their lives and the world around them as women. Particularly at the beginning, much of this process seemed to pose questions about identity: In what ways can we believe in women's equality and be Catholic or Christian? In what ways is this patriarchal church our church? To what spiritual and secular ends should we dedicate our lives? As women asked themselves these questions, however, the answers they formulated required a reanalysis of both church and society.

In the 1970s, groups of sisters and laywomen began to meet together in conferences and associations, initially to discuss the issue of women's ordination. But as feminist groups proliferated, their concerns and agendas soon multiplied. In November 1975, the first Women's Ordination Conference was held in Detroit. It was called "Women in Future Priesthood Now: A Call to Action." Attendance exceeded twelve hundred, and another five hundred people were turned away. The mood was one of excitement and promise as participants joined in liturgies and listened to talks on such topics as "Moral Imperatives for the Ordination of Women" and "Models for Future Priesthood." The willingness of the bishops and church authority to engage in dialogue on ordination was questioned in bold, frank terms, but on the whole the speeches reflected hopefulness that the church would prove open to women's ministry. In a talk that anticipated the more radical themes of the 1980s, Rosemary Radford Ruether wondered about the wisdom of seeking ordination without "questioning fundamentally this concept of clericalism."[17] But there was no disputing the sense of empowerment that came from women's gathering together around a single issue—and the issue in 1975 was the priesthood.

In 1978, the second Women's Ordination Conference, this time in Baltimore, took on a more feminist and polemical tone. Shortly after the Detroit meeting, the National Conference of Catholic Bishops had affirmed the proscription against women's ordination issued by the Vatican in October 1976. It was thus abundantly clear to the Baltimore participants that church authority was uncompromisingly opposed to the claim around which the conference had gathered. Some participants continued to focus on the issue of ordination and change within the institutional church, but a substantial group sought to connect the issue of ordination to a much broader call for systemic change. Sister Elizabeth Carroll, vice president of the Religious Sisters of Mercy, Pittsburgh, told the conference, "Unless the women who are to be ordained are deeply conscious of the oppressions of the poor and racially different, unless they are deeply converted to the necessity of uprooting the mindset of dominance and dependence on which these oppressions rest, they will all too easily fall into the institutional framework of clericalism which now hampers the church."[18] The discussion had clearly moved beyond ordination.

In 1979 John Paul II made his first papal visit to the United States. On 7 October, when the pope was to visit Washington, Sister Theresa Kane was asked to offer a short welcome.[19] As head of the Sisters of Mercy and then-president of the Leadership Conference of Women Religious (LCWR), Kane was no radical. But with television cameras recording her words and with fifty-three women religious wearing blue armbands to protest the pope's opposition to women's ordination, Kane made church history. As she thought over her remarks in advance, she called several sisters she had worked with in LCWR:

> I also called one of the sisters who had been the president of LCWR, an older woman who I had great admiration for. She said, "This pope has really worked hard to have people aware of the poor of the world. I think it would

be important for you to say, 'We acknowledge your priority, and we're in solidarity with you on the poor.'" So I had my (four) points there.[20]

As so often with feminists in the church, antipoverty and other issues of oppression and discrimination are braided into the consciousness-raising about gender. Dressed in a gray suit rather than a traditional habit, she addressed the pope in words that were to reverberate well beyond the walls of the church. She urged him on behalf of women both lay and religious to open up all ministries of the church to women and to be "mindful of the intense suffering and pain of many women in these United States . . . who are desirous of serving in and through the Church as fully participating members."[21] With women no nearer ordination than before, Sister Theresa was later to address a convocation of women activists in 1987, observing, "The core of courage is rage. For each of us I pray for a passionate holy rage; a just anger in the face of injustice not to be confused with hatred or hostility."[22]

By the early 1980s momentum had gathered for national conferences that would be framed around a set of issues broader than ordination. The Women's Ordination Conference had postponed the meeting scheduled for 1981 in favor of continued local conferences, thus creating space for a rethinking of the direction a new national conference effort might take.

The numbers of meetings proliferated. In the course of the 1980s, the gatherings broadened beyond specific concerns about reforms within the institutional church. Increasingly, they addressed themselves both to broad social justice concerns and to the discovery of how a life of faith could be lived within a reimagined church. The 1983 conference, held in Chicago, marked a departure from the Women's Ordination Conferences of the previous decade. Called "From Generation to Generation: Women Church Speaks," it marked the formalization of the movement that created what came to be called "Women-Church." Many of the sessions were presented in a bilingual format in English and Spanish; Hispanic women made up 10 percent of those attending and included migrant workers from Florida and women from the low-income neighborhoods of New York. The emphasis was no longer on ordination or on desired changes in the institutional church that church authorities were sure to repudiate. Instead conferees began to reflect on ways of creating a spirituality and a praxis for themselves. Rosemary Radford Ruether spoke of women's being "Women-Church not in exile but in exodus." Mary Hunt, also a theologian and the co-organizer of a recently formed feminist ethics group, spoke of women's claiming "a new baptism—a baptism into a Church which acknowledges that it is guilty of sexism, heterosexism, racism and classism."[23]

The next years were filled with meetings:[24] The National Assembly of Religious Women (NARW) held their annual meetings. WOC scheduled a smaller gathering in St. Louis in 1985, and many local meetings were held. Immediately after the Chicago conference, the Women of the Church Coalition broadened to become Women-Church Convergence, a coalition of some thirty groups whose names indicated the growing geographic and social dispersion of women's activism. In 1987 the latter group sponsored a second Women-Church conference held in Cincinnati, which drew on increasingly broadened constituencies. As before, it was organized to include Spanish-language sessions. The conference attracted increasing numbers of lay participants. Along with feminist theologians and well-known activists in the church, the conference was addressed by leaders of the secular women's movement (Gloria Steinem, Eleanor Smeal, Charlotte Bunch). Only a small number of sessions concerned the institutional church; most covered a broad social agenda: the sanctuary movement, racism, abortion, sexual assault, lesbians keeping faith, community organizing South Bronx–style, women and AIDS, economic literacy. On the Saturday evening of the conference, what was billed as a feminist Eucharist celebration ("Women-Church shares in the breaking of many breads and drinking from many cups") was scheduled for a ballroom-sized crowd. Attended by three thousand participants, this second Women-Church conference was named, significantly, "Claiming Our Power."

In 1993, when the Women-Church Convergence held their third meeting ("Mujer-Iglesia: Tejedoras de Cambio; Women-Church, Weavers of Change") in Albuquerque, New Mexico, the planning discussions and postconference analysis focused on the issue of diversity.[25] As the theologian Mary Hunt inveighed, "Our concerns are how to be inclusive, not in a liberal or token way." It soon became clear that the issue of ethnic and race inclusiveness raised another issue of diversity— whether the strictly Catholic focus of the gathering should be broadened. To represent true ethnic diversity meant, some believed, a willingness to open the meeting to a greater "spiritual diversity."[26] Plans were made to include rituals led by Buddhists, Native Americans, Quakers, Jews, and Rose Vernell, the woman priest ordained by George Stallings of the breakaway Imani Temple, as well as by Catholic nuns. Was Women-Church, the headline of the *National Catholic Reporter* queried, "Adrift from Catholicism?" Some Catholic feminist activists worried aloud about the direction the conference was likely to take and about the future identity of Catholic feminism. Jeannine Gramick, the well-known leader of lesbian and gay ministries in the church, observed, "From the publicity for the Convergence and from planning committee reports, this [Women-Church gathering] does not appear to be a Catholic conference. The conference brochure does not use the word Catholic. The word *liturgy* was changed to *sacred events* because the former word is too much associated with Catholic ritual."[27] At the conference conclusion, some activists extolled the success of the efforts to broaden the conference program. Humility of Mary Sister Madonna Kolbenschlag exclaimed, "This event is an incredible sign that women are able to do what the institutional church is called to but which it has failed to accomplish: Create ways for people of diverse customs, beliefs and cultures to become a people—ecclesia."[28] Others were more critical: In a *Commonweal* editorial, Catherine Walsh contended that the weaving of a communal basket that conference attendees were invited to help create was a metaphor for the conference more generally. Although the basket was intended to represent the weaving of diverse dreams and hopes of the women present, Walsh said, "To weave something that endures—like a Navajo rug—requires faithfulness to a tradition even while expanding it. Women-Church hasn't defined yet what it really believes and thus its long-term impact is still a matter of conjecture."[29]

THE INSTITUTIONALIZATION OF FEMINISM

The abundance of conferences and workshops reflected the existence, by the 1980s, of institutionalized feminist spaces within the church. Feminism in the church operated from five kinds of feminist habitats. Religious congregations themselves constituted one such habitat. From the late 1960s and to this day, many religious orders held discussions in their regular assembly meetings about gender and race issues. These discussions were general self-explorations as well as specific debates about matters of particular relevance to individual religious orders. Should the congregation support the ERA? What does racism mean in the everyday lives of sisters? How to think about the meaning of inclusive liturgy? Should a particular resolution on sanctuaries be adopted? In the case of particular orders (say, the Sisters of Mercy) there might be discussions, for instance, over the responsibilities of Sisters of Mercy–run hospitals for women's gynecological and reproductive health care. Smaller networks were also formed within a congregation. When particular subgroups within an order wished to address themselves to an issue not necessarily involving the whole congregation, measures were taken to constitute community-connected associations. Loretto Women's Network, formed by a group within the Loretto Sisters, and the network's newspaper, *couRAGE*, represent one example.[30]

Church renewal and social justice organizations provided a second habitat for the development of a feminist voice within the church.

Renewal organizations surfaced with the momentum driven by Vatican II and the women's movement.[31] Women religious were the founders and core activists of many of these groups. One of the first organizations to be established was the National Assembly of Women Religious (NAWR), later to change its name to the National Assembly of Religious Women (NARW) to reflect the participation of laywomen. Founded in 1968, NARW endeavored to give voice to a more grassroots expression of views by women religious than was at that time possible in the Leadership Conference of Women Religious, and remained until its demise in 1995 one of the groups most actively involved in tackling class and race issues within the movement of Catholic feminism.[32] The National Coalition of American Nuns (NCAN) was formed in 1969 with the intent of speaking out on a range of social justice and human rights issues.[33] In 1971, the Conference of Major Superiors of Women changed its name to the Leadership Conference of Women Religious (LCWR), clearly signifying an effort to reconceptualize their view of authority within the church. Approval for the change in name was withheld by the Vatican for three years.[34] In 1971 as well, Las Hermanas, an organization of Hispanic sisters and laywomen engaged in the struggle against poverty and discrimination, was also founded. The Women's Ordination Conference (WOC) was founded in 1974, the same year that Chicago Catholic Women (CCW) was established. In 1974, Catholics for a Free Choice (CFFC), directed by Frances Kissling, was founded to support the right to legal reproductive health care, including family planning and abortion; it was later declared by the Vatican not to be an official voice of the Catholic Church. Other multiple-issue groups also date from this period (the Quixote Center, the Eighth Day Center for Justice, Call to Action), all of which worked toward the advancement of gender equality as part of their broad agendas.[35] In 1977, Sister Jeannine Gramick and Father Robert Nugent founded the New Ways ministry to work toward reconciliation of church teachings and gay/lesbian issues. In 1982, Mary Hunt and Diann Neu founded the Women's Alliance for Theology, Ethics, and Religion, which organizes workshops and resources for an ecumenical constituency. In 1987, Mary's Pence was established to raise and distribute money for women's causes. (Peter's Pence collections raise money for the papacy.) The feast of Teresa of Avila, 15 October, has been selected as Mary's Pence Day, but because many of the fund's donors are not churchgoers, much of the fundraising occurs through other avenues. In 1995, the fund distributed sixty thousand dollars—a surprisingly high sum given that Mary's Pence has not been approved for entry in the *Kennedy Book*, which lists sanctioned Catholic charities.[36]

These organizations gained a visibility that was striking in light of their tiny staffs and limited budgets. Skilled in the arts of communications and media, all the renewal organizations, no matter how small, produced quantities of literature—newsletters,[37] resources for workshops, liturgies, and press releases. The spokeswomen/men for the organizations were also spending large amounts of time on the road, interacting with others in projects, conferences, and educational endeavors. From this brief inventory, two facts stand out: that the 1970s and 1980s propelled feminist thought into the contemporary affairs of the American Catholic Church, and that women religious were absolutely at the core of this development.

A third habitat for feminism within the church has been academic institutions housing feminist scholars. By the 1980s, feminist theologians, historians, and sociologists had secured, in fairly significant numbers, tenured places in American universities.[38] These positions have provided not-always-safe spaces from which feminist scholars have been able to produce hundreds of volumes about church teachings and church history. Feminist theologians have developed an array of new ideas about what church, spirituality, and ritual might look like in the context of a Catholic faith dedicated to equality and justice within its own institutional practices. This was not a smooth road. The obstacles were evident from the beginning, with the tenure battle over Mary Daly's promotion at Boston College, a Jesuit institution, and with the controversy over the promotion of Charles Curran at Catholic University in the late 1960s.[39] By the 1980s, feminist theologians were being appointed in significant numbers to posts that were, unsurprisingly, as much in non-Catholic institutions as in Catholic colleges and universities,[40] but it is not unexpected that some of the most vociferous and critical voices in feminist theology from the 1970s and 1980s came out of institutions where Rome's approval was not required.

It was of no small importance to feminism's institutionalization that feminist theological writings found outlets in prominent commercial presses (Harper and Row, Simon & Schuster, Beacon) in addition to the presses that produce largely religious publications.[41] It is also telling that by the late 1980s, women were one-quarter of all students enrolled in American Roman Catholic theological schools.[42]

A fourth habitat where feminist voices have found an albeit limited protected space within the church has been in the parishes themselves. The women who have become pastors in so-called priestless parishes bring feminist perspectives to much of their work almost by virtue, alone, of being on the frontier.[43] Ruth Wallace estimates that there were about three hundred priestless parishes in the early 1990s (2 percent of all Catholic parishes in the United States),[44] approximately three-quarters of which are "pastored" by women.[45] The number of women who have assumed lay ministry positions (as pastoral associates, liturgists, in positions responsible for the elderly or the sick, among other roles) has certainly also increased. I know of no study that systematically explores the dissemination of feminism among lay ministers. But it seems to be the case that in numerous parishes male priests are under pressure from at least some parishioners to use more inclusive language, to allow female altar servers, to utilize women in liturgical ministries (as lectors, choir directors).[46]

A fifth habitat that feminism came to occupy in the 1970s and 1980s was the liturgy groups and base communities that sprang up in numerous locations. Those who have become frustrated with the institutional church, with the Mass, or with a particular priest or parish have often gravitated to such communities. Groups meet in community centers, in parish basements, or in someone's living room. Many are feminist although most liturgy groups identify themselves in broad terms as endeavoring to constitute themselves as egalitarian communities. One member of a group that calls itself St. Harold ("because we meet in the Harold Washington apartments . . . we canonized Harold Washington") is constituted by members of a Chicago parish that began to meet separately after experiencing frustration with the constraints a newly assigned priest had begun to impose. The group includes a sympathetic priest but, as one member of the community explained, "We basically got to the point in our liturgies where we all preside together." One night at a party, this member explained, the priest turned to her and said, " 'Lee Ann [not her real name], do you have mass tomorrow or do I?' I thought I was on another planet."[47]

Discursive Acts

To say that contemporary Catholic feminism can be described through a narrative of conferences and workshops, an account of *ideas* rather than *policies*, is not to say that women (both lay and religious) in the church do not "act" in the "real world" to effect social change. Many nuns as well as many committed Catholic laywomen are engaged in direct social justice activism (in prisons, shelters, hospices, and sanctuaries), working to redress problems of poverty and racism as they affect both women and men. Others have sought positions in the church (as educators, pastoral assistants, chaplains, and in a range of different ministries) from which they hope to work toward a more just as well as faith-driven society. But much of the work women activists do when they come together is discursive: rewriting through texts and symbolic acts their own understanding of themselves in relationship to both church and society.

It may be helpful in specifying the character of feminist discursive politics if I say a little more about what it is not: For the most part feminist groups in the church do not lobby either the state or the church. Network, a sister-run organization with offices in Washington, is an exception. It explicitly monitors legislation on a range of social justice and peace issues, conducts letter-writing campaigns, and undertakes the requisite visits to congressional offices.[48] Within the context of church politics, for a brief period in the 1980s, women's groups strategized in "interest-group" fashion, discussing who the sympathetic bishops might be, and how it might be best to frame an issue so as to be "heard" by the clerical hierarchy, but few feminist activists devote much time now to this form of strategizing.[49] The LCWR probably does somewhat more of this kind of strategic thinking than other organizations. Because the LCWR sees itself as representing religious communities to Rome[50] and thus makes an attempt if not to "lobby" at least not to alienate the papacy, they too spend time discussing acceptable approaches to voicing concerns with the Vatican. But in their efforts to engage with elite decision makers in the government or in the church, both Network and the LCWR are more the exception than the rule among feminist activists.

What is more noticeable is how infrequent "protest acts" are used among the repertoire of feminist challenges to the church. Nuns have readily participated in civil disobedience (to protest nuclear missiles) or demonstrations to bring attention to the needs of migrant farmers or the poor, but comparable actions are rarely directed against the church. There have been some dramatic 1960s-style moments: The spontaneous action of women at Marjorie Tuite's funeral in 1986 was one such instance.[51] As Ruth McDonough Fitzpatrick recounted it, the priest reminded those in the church that only Catholics were to come forward for Communion.

> At the consecration, the priest on the altar was surrounded with women. He was trying to elbow them back to give him his sacred space. But all of us extended our hands and said the words of consecration so loudly that you could hear it in this huge New York church. Now we've said consecration at many of our liturgies, in living rooms and smaller places. That's the first time in my life I've ever heard a consecration said from a parish church. Finally, we could really hear it. Before communion, Maureen Fiedler got out of the pew and went up and down the first seven rows saying, "Everybody, please come to communion; everybody is very welcome."[52]

There have been other dramatic occasions as well: Drawing for inspiration on the blue-armbanded nuns who stood in protest during the pope's 1979 visit to the National Shrine of the Immaculate Conception in Washington, D.C., some Chicago nun-activists decided to take their protests inside the church. For a period in 1980–81, Chicago women chose to disrupt ordinations—"Franciscans, Benedictines, Jesuits,

Dominicans and parlor-variety diocesan priests."[53] Barbara Ferraro describes the occasions:

> The taking of Holy Orders is a sacrament in the Catholic Church. The ceremony itself is inserted into the ritual of the Mass. The men waiting to be ordained lie facedown on the floor before the altar rail, and the bishop comes down from the altar and calls them forward.
>
> "Joseph McGhee, come forth, you are called to be ordained," says the bishop. And the ordinate rises and replies, "I am ready and willing."
>
> The first time we had tried our new protest, no one suspected anything. I guess they thought we had settled for symbols when they saw our arm bands. So they were surprised when, after the last man was called to be ordained, we began popping up, one after the other, all over the church, and calling out, "I am ready and willing."[54]

Women have also engaged in foot washing on Holy Thursday; in Ash Wednesday protests outside the church—in one case with ashes from a burned copy of the Vatican statement banning ordination; in the regular Chicago Mother's Day demonstrations outside the Holy Name Cathedral ("for a Eucharistic Celebration") protesting the ban on ordination.[55] Recently, too, a small group of nuns, organized by NCAN, carried banners (one reading "They are meeting about us—without us") across the piazza outside St. Peter's during the Synod on the Consecrated Life in October 1994. The reporter for the *International Herald Tribune* commented that "the police who patrol St. Peter's Square could scarcely believe their eyes . . . [as] American nuns marched into the cavernous piazza. . . ."[56] But on the whole, feminists in the church have mostly eschewed the kind of demonstrative "disobedience" engaged in by ACT UP on several occasions in the early 1990s both inside and on the steps of St. Patrick's Cathedral in New York City.

At the same time, few activists explicitly engage in parish politics. Of the many activist nuns and laywomen with whom I met, only a small handful regularly attend Sunday Mass. It is not unusual to hear activists speak of church services as "abusive" or "assaulting." As one sister asked me, rhetorically, "Why should I go to Sunday service every week and then have to spend all the time in between recovering from abuse?" The vehemence with which she appeared to feel punished by what she saw as the misogyny of regular church services was more typical than atypical of those with whom I talked.[57] Recognizing that an activist can engage in parish politics only as a committed parish member, most activist sisters consider the route of direct parish mobilization to be foreclosed. Indeed, few groups aim at directly mobilizing women in the "pews." Parish politics, rather, is left to those feminists who are willing to take on ministry within the church (on necessarily conditional terms) and to those who seek change by engaging in liturgical rethinking and in the production of church language that is inclusive rather than male-centered. As Elizabeth Johnson, SSJ, explained, in discussing her motivation for writing her recent book, *She Who Is* (insisting that God is both male and female), "Language doesn't just reflect what we think, it shapes what we think and defines our world."[58]

Sharing Johnson's premise, activists have spent much of their time in reflection and deliberation, fashioning new words and meanings to describe their changing understanding of women in society and church. But it would be a mistake to see these words as "simply" the literary or scholarly exercises of armchair radicals. Judging by the attempts of the church hierarchy to silence those who speak out (as described at length in the next chapter), words are believed by both feminists and the church clerical leadership to have very real consequences.

Women-Church

One of the most dramatic expressions of feminist discursive politics is the linguistic construction "Women-Church." The concept grew out of the need shared by many feminists in the church to find a home and identity within Catholicism. Unwilling to leave the church, yet to varying degrees alienated from its institutional practices, many women found connection and validation in the knowledge community that the phrase Women-Church evokes.

The term itself was adopted from the Second Vatican Council's affirmation of the laity's role, expressed in the phrase "We are the Church." In the 1980s, women who saw themselves as deeply spiritual with life roots in Catholicism, and yet felt themselves to be a subordinated class within the institutional church, adopted the Vatican II language, declaring, "We are the Church and it is Women-Church."

Women-Church is less an organization than an idea. Organizationally, there *is* a coalition of the groups that came together under the auspices of the Women of the Church Coalition in 1983 and Women-Church Convergence in 1987. But there are other women, not active members of the twenty-five to thirty-five groups formally associated with the umbrella organization, who also find spiritual identity in Women-Church. Many women who are part of local liturgical communities reconceptualize their connections to the church in terms of Women-Church. Two women writing for the newsletter of the National Assembly of Religious Women explain:

> The ever present reality of patriarchy and clericalism forces us to consciously and deliberately marginalize ourselves from much that is "Church." Still we choose to remain, in identity and practice, Roman Catholic. . . . Functioning as a "base community" or "house church," our WomenChurch group gathers

regularly for inclusive liturgy, story sharing, and potluck meals. The leadership is "roundtable"; we take turns planning, hosting and presiding at liturgy. Our affiliation with WomenChurch energizes and empowers us. It gives us the hope we need to continue as women in the church.[59]

The creative reconceptualization of women's identity within the church in terms of a critical rethinking of women's relationships to the power of the institutional church is captured so precisely by Rosemary Radford Ruether that I quote her at length:

> Women-Church means neither leaving the church as a sectarian group nor continuing to fit into it on its terms. It means establishing bases for a feminist critical culture and celebrational community that have some autonomy from the established institutions. It also means sharing this critical culture and sense of community with many women who are working within existing churches but who gather, on an occasional or regular basis, to experience the feminist vision that is ever being dimmed and limited by the parameters of the male-dominated institution. . . .
>
> One must refuse the institutionally defined options either of continuing on its terms or of cutting off all connections with it and becoming sectarian and hostile to those who are working within established institutions.[60]

In her book on the theology and practice of Women-Church, Ruether offers alternative liturgies for the use of Women-Church celebrants. Included are rites of healing from incest, wife battering, and rape, and a coming-out rite for lesbians. Passages instruct women on the remembrance of foremothers, on the exorcism of patriarchal texts, on the blessing of symbolic foods (bread, wine, milk, honey, the apple). The text, Ruether emphasizes, is not a prayer book "with words and forms to be repeated." Rather it "assumes that the creation of liturgy is properly a function of local communities who are engaged in a collective project woven from the fabric of many concrete stories that make up the lives of each member of that body."[61] The discursive politics of remaking the rituals, customs, visions, and norms of feminist worship as a collective endeavor is thus central to Ruether's project.

LCWR: REVISIONING WOMEN

Not all women engaged in equality issues in the church identify with Women-Church. Nevertheless, even those who may not utilize the vocabulary of Women-Church have been deeply engaged in discursive politics. The Leadership Conference of Women Religious (LCWR), the official umbrella organization representing 90 percent of women religious in the United States, is generally on the more cautious, moderate side of feminist encounters with Vatican authority. It has nonetheless struggled over the last decades to foster deliberations, pass resolutions, and engage in discussions that subject issues about religion and society to major reexamination.

Constituted under Vatican direction in the 1950s, the LCWR has provided a forum in which the changing mission of American sisters has been debated and the delicate relationship between religious orders and the Vatican has been negotiated. Its early founding and official position give it a different cast from the politics of more recent (and in different ways more radical) groups such as Catholics for a Free Choice, the National Coalition of American Nuns, or the National Assembly of Religious Women. There is no question, however, that all these groups have been seen by the present-day Vatican as troublesome sources of feminist politics.

Lora Ann Quiñonez and Mary Daniel Turner's exceptionally vivid history of the LCWR tells an important story of discursive politics:[62] For the first decade of its existence, the organization looked inward, focusing on the religious life of the membership. With the Vatican II call for renewal and the societal changes in the 1960s that swept many American sisters into the civil rights movement, the women's movement, and third-world political issues, the LCWR began its own self-examination. The 1971 bylaws redefined its mission as the "development of creative and responsive leadership" by conference members "within their communities but in the church and, through the church, in the world."[63] The changes precipitated opposition both inside and outside the LCWR. Inside, some sisters worried that the spiritual essence of the body's mission was being diluted. In Rome, when the new bylaws were submitted to the Vatican's Congregation for Religious, discussions led to the reinstitution of language acknowledging a "due regard for the authority of the Holy See and of the bishops."[64] Even the new name, particularly the use of the word *leadership*, met with objections from the Vatican. In one meeting both the conference president and the Vatican ambassador sat with dictionaries looking up the words *leader* and *leadership*. According to a former LCWR president, church authorities could not tolerate the association of women with leadership.[65]

Over the years numerous disputes arose between Vatican officials and the LCWR, as well as within the LCWR. The sources of disagreement ranged widely: What should be the nature of religious life? What was the relationship between the sacred and the secular? In what way, if at all, did religious authority demand attention to experience, history, culture? In what way should religious life be seen as an unchanging essence? These questions translated into specific, often intense, disputes about sisters' apparel, about the rewriting of the constitutions of religious orders, about deference to Vatican authority, about the disciplining of sisters who were seen as disobedient. Debates grew intense over particular resolutions: supporting theologian Charles Curran, developing a deeper understanding of the right-to-life issue, bolstering the legitimacy of conference alliance with communities in conflict with church officials.[66]

Throughout, the LCWR reflected on epistemological issues, particularly the place of experience in shaping how sisters should be guided in their lives. The LCWR, like other organization in the church, came to insist on the authenticity of experience as a source of moral decision making. The surveys and research into the views of individual sisters in member congregations were themselves an indication of the early attention that the conference felt should be paid to women's experience. The "Sister Survey" gave legitimacy to women's own experiential understandings and became an instrument of politicization.[67] In national assemblies, LCWR women were encouraged to tell their stories. It became understood that members would be seated in circles of eight to ten persons, and that in place of speeches, there would be questions posed to generate discussion: "Would you tell about a time when you felt powerless?" "What are the themes you want to include in a statement about the Vatican's censure of Charles Curran?"[68]

The LCWR leadership was very self-conscious about the role of language. As Quiñonez and Turner state, "Names signify. . . . The power to name a group can be the power to position it socially and politically. . . . To study the progress of American sisters in the past thirty years is to become aware of the exquisite attention lavished upon naming, more particularly renaming."[69] At times the attention to language is instrumental. Quiñonez and Turner recount the huddles in the dimly lit basement down the street from St. Peter's Square where LCWR officers would rehearse for their meetings with Vatican officals: "They played roles, trying out language. They tagged words that under no circumstances should cross their lips because they evoked such hostility ('team,' 'empowerment,' 'dialogue'); others (like 'ministry') they would decide to risk . . . because they thought meanings need to be expanded."[70] But more often the attention to language was expressive rather than instrumental. A word was tried and chosen not with regard to how far an idea could be pushed, not in the context of calculation of its reception, but because the word expressed an idea that required articulation. As Quiñonez and Turner remark, the discussions at national conferences were considered indispensable for moral growth. But as ideas were explored, "to secure official approval of their views was not their primary object. Comprehending their own diverse views was."[71]

Other groups have taken their discursive politics more purposefully into the public arena. The signatories to the 7 October 1984 *New York*

Times advertisement supporting a diversity in views about abortion were clearly targeting public opinion. So also was Catholics Speak Out when it commissioned a Gallup Poll in spring 1992, the results of which were strategically released the day the U.S. Catholic bishops met to discuss the third draft of the pastoral on women. But for the most part, feminist organizations in the church—in conferences, discussions, workshops, newsletters—have aimed primarily at self-reflection.

ANTIRACISM

Given the continuous reflection directed at imagining a more egalitarian world, how has feminist activism in the church endeavored to incorporate antiracism into its politics? For many activist women of color, "feminism" is about what white women want in a reenvisioned church. *Mujerista* or womanist theology is the term by which a number of Hispanic and African-American activists prefer to designate the faith by which they feel guided. *Mujerista* theology, as Ada María Isasi-Díaz discusses it, endeavors to speak from the experiences of Hispanic women but attempts to avoid speaking in a single voice.[72] Recognizing that women from various parts of the Spanish-speaking and Catholic world have experienced church in relation to gender in a multiplicity of ways, Isasi-Díaz emphasizes the importance of the term's remaining "open, in flux, alive."[73] At the same time, Isasi-Díaz undertakes to specify a methodology by which this diversity of understanding can be arrived at. She emphasizes the importance of creating a *Mujerista* theology from lived experience, recognizing the need for interpretations existing in dialogue with those experiences—by researchers, analysts, speakers. But these interpretations must be based, she argues, on close listening to how it is that Hispanic women live their faith:

> For example, some Hispanic theologians give great importance to scripture. Their goal is to present Jesus in such a way that the common folk can relate to him. . . . *Mujerista* theology, on the other hand, using the lived-experience of Hispanic women as its main source, pushes out the old parameters and insists on new questions. In the case of Jesus, for example, we ask why it is that the majority of Hispanic women do not relate to Jesus. What does this mean about their understanding of the divine and the presence of the divine in their lives?

The roots of *Mujerista* theology grew in part from the discrimination that many Hispanic sisters experienced within their own religious congregations. In 1971, Las Hermanas was founded, bringing together sisters with Mexican-American roots who challenged discrimination within the church (including their own religious communities), and who wished to focus their work with farm workers and Mexican Americans in order to strengthen Hispanic ministry.

The importance of defining faith through experience, an experience which is often very different from that of white women, is echoed again and again by women of color. Reporting on the comments of Joan Martin, an African-American campus minister at Temple University at a Women-Church conference, Gretchen E. Ziegenhals wrote, "[Martin] defined herself as a sister of women in women-church, but not as a part of the movement. Name yourselves as women-church she urged, but don't name me. Although for white women women-church may now be a necessity, Martin made it clear that women-church is still a luxury that womanist or black women can't afford. Womanism is about race as well as gender. The black church is the only institution that blacks own."[74] Not all women of color would disassociate themselves from women-church. But common to the diversity of voices among women-of-color theologians and activists is the exhortation that white feminists in the church not "speak for" but "listen to."[75]

Just as it is important to avoid homogenizing the experiences and theological positions of women of color, it is important to specify some of the distinguishing charcateristics in the politics of various white-dominated feminist organizations within the church. Some organizations such as NARW whose principal staff was for many years primarily White made antiracist work one of its foremost goals. NARW's newletter, *Probe*, devoted the bulk of its contents to articles, stories, poems, and narratives by women of color in the United States and abroad: accounts by migrant workers in the United States, poems written by homeless women, first-person accounts by women who were tortured or whose families disappeared in Central America. NARW was also one of the earliest organizations to make a wholehearted effort to go beyond tokenism in drawing women of color into all aspects of national board involvement and conference planning.[76]

In some ways NARW was exceptional among feminist organizations in the church. But in comparison to feminism in other institutional settings (the military, business, medicine), not just NARW but also other feminist organizations in the church have been relatively attuned to issues of diversity. Most renewal organizations and many religious congregations by the 1990s have made some significant efforts to reflect on their own history of racism, to print narratives by women of color in their organizational literature, to achieve diverse representation when speakers are chosen, to introduce Spanish-language materials. Because many sisters and laywomen are involved in settings that are multiracial (prisons, farm worker organizing, shelters, hospitals, Central and South American missions) and because of the diffusion of the spirit of liberation theology, feminism in the church is less insular than American feminism in a number of other organizational contexts.[77] At the same time, white feminists in the church are continually made aware by women of color with whom they interact that the eradication of racism in their midst is far from realized, and that the job of "listening" is far more difficult than might at first appear.

The 1993 Women-Church Convergence Conference was emblematic both of the miles traveled and the distance still to be traversed. This dual message was evident right from the beginning. Conference planners decided to focus the meetings on the issue of diversity itself. Among the first letters that the planners sent out was one that listed thirty-five organizations, including Las Hermanas, Conference for Catholic Lesbians, New Ways Ministry, Dignity/USA (the latter three focusing on gay/lesbian church issues), and that read: "Women-Church Convergence (W-CC) invites you to join in the preparations for a Women-Church Conference to be held in 1993, *Specifically we are asking you to gather a small group as diverse as possible in race, ethnicity, sexual orientation, education, age, class, etc. etc.; to review the enclosed materials; and to send us your feedback.* We believe that human survival—locally, nationally, globally—depends on our learning to live with each other, dealing with our differences not as threats that divide but as opportunities to enrich each other."[78]

In the course of the conference planning, however, members of NARW indicated that they were "deeply disturbed by the lack of diverse women participating in the convergence," stipulating that ethnic/income diversity should be a highest priority at the Convergence table and in the member organizations. This precipitated an exchange of memoranda during January–February of 1992 about the goal of diversity. The representative of one of the Convergence organizations reacted to the NARW challenge by suggesting that the goal of diversity was not the core mission of all Convergence groups (as it was with NARW) and that, in effect, diversity should be one among a number of values pursued by activists in the church but need not be the foremost priority of all.

The conference itself, held in New Mexico and attracting twenty-five hundred participants, featured Hispanic, Filipina, Muslim, Native-American and African-American keynote speakers. One newspaper account described the multiculturalism as including "welcomes in Spanish and English, Native American drum and pipe ceremonies, an Isleta Pueblo Indian buffalo dance and prayers invoking Our Lady of Guadalupe as well as various gods and goddesses."[79] But in the evaluation session, a number of women of color at the conference spoke about "spiritual hucksterism" (the mass marketing of ethnic traditions), about their voices' being unheard, and about the small numbers of women of color who were there as participants in the conference. Several women spoke critically about the ways that the dominant Euramerican culture was appropriating in an exploitive sense the rituals of other cultural groups. This frustration came to a head during the final speak-out of the conference, when an American-Indian woman present asked conference women who were not of Indian heritage to forgo using Indian drums.[80] Diversity within feminist discursive politics in the church is very explicitly honored as an idea and not yet fully embraced in its daily reality.

But in the end, the meaning of a commitment to radicalism is best set in context. A short anecdote recounted to me toward the end of my interviewing situates the phrase "discursive radicalism" as I think it best describes American feminists in the present-day Catholic Church. A few years back, a group of sisters who were about to make their perpetual vows were studying and living together in Rome. The novices were an international group, including sisters from Poland, the Philippines, Korea, India, Ireland, Germany, and the United States. According to one member of the group,

> When we said, "God, He . . . ," the American sisters wanted to say, "God, He/She" to use inclusive language. The Polish sisters were saying, "What's going on? We are saying 'He' without being exclusive." Then the American sisters wanted to have an Indian Eucharist, to have us all eat rice. But the traditional host is not rice. When we took our final vows, they wanted the person who presides to be a woman. We had a Jesuit priest, but they invited a sister from the United States. They wanted to have a liturgy in which one of us was to preside. The majority resisted saying, "Oh, no, you're going too far." We finally compromised on a para-liturgy. I'll tell you, the Polish sisters went to "real Mass" the same day.[81]

CONCLUSION

It is telling that the recent vituperative book-length attack on feminism in the church, Donna Steichen's *Ungodly Rage: The Hidden Face of Catholic Feminism*, devotes nearly its entire four hundred pages to what feminist activists say and write.[82] Indeed, Steichen is right to focus her attentions there. Speaking and writing is a lot of what feminists in the American Catholic Church do. It is not surprising that Steichen finds feminism threatening. What feminists propose and the directness with which they propose it from their now institutionalized habitats within the church are of little comfort to those who, like Steichen, would defend both the societal and the ecclesial status quo.

To summarize in a paragraph or two what is laid out in the numerous texts, speeches, conferences, workshops, memos, letters, news releases, newsletters, and books that feminists produce is at once both preposterous and possible. On the one hand, it represents anything but a homogeneous set of beliefs: Feminism within some quarters adheres closely to a Christ-centered faith, in other quarters to a goddess-based neopagan religious practice. For some, reproductive rights is a just cause; for others, it offends fundamental church doctrine. For some, ordination of women is central to religious reform; for others, it risks reimbedding feminism within the conventions of inequality and hierarchy. To do justice to the varied sorts of priorities and claims among Catholic feminists would require a much elaborated discussion. On the other hand, there *are* certain common precepts. Feminist activists in the church share a belief in the distinction between the "institutional" church and the "true" postconciliar (Vatican II) church of the people; in a church that represents a broad diversity of beliefs and of peoples, both in the pews and in the sanctuary; in a church that demands the same kinds of equality and justice of itself as it does of society at large.

Feminists in the church are deeply reflective and troubled by a myriad of questions about how to live their belief in "radical equality." Is the work feminists do—in prisons, with the homeless—merely ameliorative or is it revolutionary? How much of the creation of new liturgies, the singing of songs, the speechifying, and the writing of texts is opting out of politics, and how much of it is doing politics? How much can one be outside the institutional church and still of the church? How much, as Mary Jo Weaver asks, can one celebrate diversity and "the dream of pluralism" and not be "confronted with the nightmare of total relativism . . ."?[83] But how it is that women religious and laywomen even arrived at these kinds of questions after decades in which, as John M. Huels, OSM, notes, "women's role, in relation to clergy and other men, was to be passive, subservient, and docile—to 'pray, pay, and obey'"—is the question the next chapter can now address.[84]

Chapter Six

IN THE LAW'S ABSENCE

WHEN Pope John Paul II once again in 1994 affirmed the church's ban on women's ordination, declaring that "this judgment is to be definitively held by all the church's faithful,"[1] American women religious responded quickly and publicly:

The pope has apologized for the way Galileo was treated. I believe that someone, in the future, will apologize for the way he is handling the issue of women in the church. (Sister of Mercy Teresa Kane)

[The pope's statement] continues the macho practice that has provoked serious problems here in Peru and in other parts of Latin America. The pope's ban on women priests indicates to many men their superiority and their capacity, therefore, to dominate women. (Sister of Mercy Elizabeth Carroll)

Until the official church is willing to face the implications of acknowledging the full personhood of women and their inclusion as equal members of the church, this issue will continue. The idea that you can cut off dialogue by fiat is simply a delusion. We will never get a different statement on women's ordination until the church admits to its character as patriarchal and clerical and begins to address that issue. (Dominican Sister Nadine Foley)

[This is] [t]he second incident of the week that is aimed at the control and elimination of women.[2] . . . After 2,000 years of teaching errors on matters as global and major as official anti-Semitism, usury, the Inquisition, slavery, the nature of the universe, and meat on Fridays, it is hard to believe that concern for the recognition of the fullness of grace in all creatures can be considered a distortion of the faith. I'll take my chances. (Benedictine Sister Joan Chittister)[3]

These are not voices from unknown women religious. Each one of these sisters is a visible, highly esteemed member of a well-known religious order. Each of the four is, in fact, a former head either of her own religious community or of the umbrella organization of orders, the Leadership Conference on Women Religious.

If there is a Vatican file marked "feminism," it is likely that references to American Catholic sisters constitute the bulk of its contents. I would conjecture that, in the eighties and nineties, the Vatican has been more familiar with and apprehensive about the writings and the activities of American sisters and laywomen than about women religious or laywomen elsewhere around the globe. This is not to suggest that Catholic women and feminists are inactive elsewhere. To name only a few examples—numbers of Latin-American women religious have long been deeply engaged practitioners of liberation theology and members of base communities and, together with lay activists, have spoken out about church teachings;[4] feminist theology in Holland has established an institutional base;[5] recently, laywomen in Germany and Austria have become very vocal; and individual outspoken women religious in various corners of the world have attracted the attention of the Vatican—as evidenced, for instance, by the 1995 silencing of Brazilian Sister Ivone Gebara.[6] But there are reasons that American feminists may be particularly worrisome to the Vatican: their open and direct critique of the institutional church; the media attention they receive; their prolific written and published and readily reproducible work, which, in English, is disseminated across international networks; and the willingness of at least some Catholic feminists, lay and religious, to address issues of reproductive choice. Only someone within the Vatican could estimate the quantities of ink that have been spilled informing Rome of the statements or activities of American women religious or advising American bishops and the directors of religious communities about the need to require obedience from outspoken nuns. But we need no insider information to recognize the high state of Vatican alert evident in the immediacy with which Rome counters the expression of feminist views in the American church, and the energy devoted to sending delegations directly from the Vatican itself to manage and make an example of American sisters who are deemed to have "caused scandal."[7]

Indeed, the insistence among American Catholic feminists on a discursive radicalism—what feminists name "radical equality"[8]—is striking. It is especially so in light of the acknowledged frailty of left-wing radicalism in the United States more generally. Whether in the arena of worker struggles, academic scholarship, anti-imperialist or feminist discourse, the United States has rarely been identified as a prominent exponent of a radical politics. What, then, explains the exceptionalism of American Catholic feminism? Why have American feminists in the church insisted so on a language of "radical equality" that combines a critique of societal inequalities, racism, patriarchy, imperialism, and militarism with a sharply etched critical analysis of institutional hierarchy and clericalism?[9]

In this chapter, I consider several alternative accounts of American Catholic feminism's adherence to a vision of "radical equality." Casual onlookers are likely to offer an explanation that approximates some version of "people of the church are driven by principle, by a prophetic tradition, rather than by pragmatics"—hence the affinity to radicalism. Although this proposition has its merits, I do not dwell on it; while morality impels many women and men of faith to disregard the kinds of self-preserving considerations that may weaken the resolve of the less religious, this account cannot address why feminists in different religious traditions and in different national contexts act so differently.

I focus, instead, on what feminists in the church as well as their critics are apt to say themselves. Both cite, approvingly or disapprovingly, the influence of Vatican II. Women religious also tend to point to the influence of the commitment to training and education of the earlier (1950s) Sister Formation Movement. I have no quarrel with this account as far as it goes. The prophetic tradition of the church in general, the educational momentum initiated by the Sister Formation Movement, and the unleashing of self-questioning precipitated by Vatican II provided both opportunities for activism and identity-forming norms that shaped the development of a feminist voice in the church.

What these explanations do not account for, however, is the exceptionally outspoken and organized activism of feminists in the *American* Catholic Church.[10] This comparative question directs our analytical lens toward the ways that the identities of American sisters, specifically, were influenced by the social movements of the times—the civil rights, antiwar, and women's movements—and in particular by liberation theology brought back from South and Central America by North American sisters who went to serve in missionary schools and religious communities. American sisters were different from their European counterparts in being exposed to the identity-constructing influences of the 1960s movements. Unlike their counterparts in other American institutions such as the military, it should be added, they were offered no solace or solution by the law. Unlike military activists, moreover, feminists in the Catholic Church enjoyed some structural autonomy, protected places where women were somewhat shielded from the counterpressures of the institution. In making any such comparisons, however, one must understand both opportunities for activism and the sources of identity-formation that shape what feminist activists imagine for themselves.

"EXIT, VOICE, AND LOYALTY"
AMONG FEMINISTS IN THE CHURCH

Just as it takes exceptional courage within the military for women activists to speak out against institutional discrimination, it takes a fiercely intrepid spirit to voice criticism of the institutional church. To choose voice over either loyalty or exit requires enormous personal fortitude, given the monitoring of those deemed to be questioning the views of clerical authority and the sanctions imposed on religious (clerics and sisters) who are viewed as disobedient. The church's efforts in recent times to stifle those who advance a critique of church doctrine are astonishing to someone used to the freedom of a secular American academic institution.

Strategies of Control

In order to contain the expression of allegedly heterodox ideas (feminist, among others), the church has used three strategies of control: (1) punitive—invoking the church's power of excommunication, dismissal, silencing, denial of promotions and appointments, transfers, and reprimands, among other means of chastisement; (2) institutional—setting up counterorganizations or weakening institutions where resistance can be housed; and (3) discursive—providing official interpretive responses to feminist challenges.

Right from the early 1980s, it became clear that the Vatican was prepared to utilize punitive mechanisms to regulate the conduct of American sisters. Punishment was particularly swift where the Vatican could identify sisters who had taken public positions that appeared supportive of reproductive choice.[11] Three Sisters of Mercy—Agnes Mary Mansour, Elizabeth Morancy, and Arlene Violet—were made into examples of the Vatican's readiness to act harshly and with dispatch. All three had undertaken political offices or appointments with the prior permission of their communities and their respective bishops.[12] When word of their public involvement with issues of abortion reached the Vatican, however, officials lost little time in forcing them to choose between their religious vocations and their commitment to public service. The case of Agnes Mary Mansour received the most publicity. President of Mercy College for twelve years, Sister Agnes Mary had run for public office. Although unsuccessful in her electoral bid, in 1983 she was appointed to head Michigan's Department of Social Services, which dispensed funds for Medicaid abortion. Shortly after her appointment, Rome's Congregation for Religious and Secular Institutes (CRIS), with the apparent approval of the pope, informed Mansour that she would need to resign or else be subject to dismissal from the Sisters of Mercy. Mansour was not herself pro-choice but believed that ". . . in a morally pluralistic society, one must respect the fact that other people may conscientiously come to other decisions regarding abortion."[13] Summoned by an emissary of the Vatican, Mansour was given no chance to explain her own position. What was expected of her was absolute obedience.[14] Mansour chose to resign from the religious community to which she had belonged for thirty years.[15]

In the same year, two other Sisters of Mercy were given the same choice—to resign from politics or to separate from their order.[16] Elizabeth Morancy was a state representative in Rhode Island with a prochoice voting record. Arlene Violet was, after dispensation from her vows, to become attorney general in Rhode Island. Such pressures were not limited to those holding electoral or appointed office but were also employed against other publicly visible individuals. Mary Ann Sorrentino, formerly the executive director of Planned Parenthood in Rhode Island, was informed of her excommunication at the close of a session in which her daughter, a few days before her confirmation, was summoned to the parish rectory to be cross-examined about her own views on abortion.[17]

These events were followed closely by the "Vatican 24" controversy. In 1984, twenty-six nuns joined close to a hundred well-known Catholic scholars and social activists, and a few priests, as signatories to an advertisement that appeared in the *New York Times* recognizing the "Diversity of Opinions regarding Abortion [That] Exists among Committed Catholics."[18] The full-page advertisement supported "candid and respectful discussion on this diversity of opinion within the Church."[19] The ad was followed later by a second declaration of solidarity that criticized the "reprisals" that have had a "chilling effect" on the "right to responsible dissent within the church."[20]

For some of the sisters who signed the ad, the reason for making such a statement public, in the *New York Times*, was the very political role the church hierarchy had played in 1984, an election year. The request for signatures circulated at a time when Archbishop (later Cardinal) John O'Connor had begun a "single-issue" attack on then vice presidential candidate Geraldine Ferraro for her stand on abortion. As one of the signees, Patricia Hussey, recalls:

> At that point in 1984 it seemed very clear the public and vocal hierarchy members were staffed with Republicans basically. Some of these men were definitely on Reagan's team, buying his death-dealing policies, hook, line and sinker, and yet judging Geraldine Ferraro for her single issue of pro-choice abortion.
>
> In view of that political climate, and because we work day-in-and-day-out with people who are poor and affected by Reagan's policies, absolutely we would sign the ad.[21]

Shortly after the advertisement's appearance, the church hierarchy moved quickly to discipline those who had signed. Invitations to speak or participate in church-sponsored events were withdrawn,[22] and within two months the Vatican wrote the heads of the religious congregations of the signees stipulating that they seek a retraction from their community members whose names appeared on the ad or else subject the sister(s) to dismissal.[23] What ensued was a nearly two-year-long spate of discussion, memo writing, visits by Vatican representatives, and intense exchanges. In some ways, the debates were not about abortion itself, which most of the nun-signers saw as a regrettable, even morally sickening choice that circumstances (poverty, ill-health, rape, incest) sometimes forced women to make.[24] The questions that were discussed at length and that caused deep emotional tribulation were more about the obligation of nuns to their community, and that of the religious community to nuns who exercise individual freedom of conscience. Should individual nuns be free to speak publicly in ways that might jeopardize the standing of their communities?[25] What is the obligation of a religious community to support nuns who speak out of their own moral conscience? If a congregation supports the right of its own members to speak out, should abortion be the issue on which communities decide to take such a stand, given the widespread belief among women religious that abortion is morally wrong?[26]

By March 1986, nearly a year and a half after the appearance of the *New York Times* statement, fifteen of the twenty-four cases of the sister signers were still unresolved. Of those whose cases were no longer pending, some had signed statements that clarified their position on abortion to the satisfaction of Rome. Others never saw the statements purportedly representing their views made by their community leadership and sent to Rome. To hasten the resolution of the still outstanding cases, representatives of the Vatican arranged to meet with the relevant leadership of the religious communities as well as with some of the signers.[27] The statement signed by the six Loretto sisters in the presence of the Vatican representatives was pronounced by the Vatican in a press release as a "public declaration of adherence to Catholic doctrine on abortion."[28] This was followed several days later by a press release signed by eleven nuns (including the Loretto sisters) who "categorically denied that they had ever made 'public declarations of adherence to Catholic doctrine on abortion.'"[29] Two sisters, Barbara Ferraro and Patricia Hussey, were adamant in their refusal to play what they felt were word games with Rome or to compromise what they believed to be their right and obligation to speak as their individual consciences directed them. Although their community, the Sisters of Notre Dame, had resisted acquiescing to Rome's bidding (dismissal in the face of noncompliance), Ferraro and Hussey felt that they did not have their communities' support. Feeling isolated, they chose to resign. It is not surprising that the emotional and psychological impact of these events is still palpable within the religious communities of the nun-signers. There have been extensive discussions of the "lessons" conveyed by the signing and the subsequent struggles with Rome.[30] But what was indisputable, as the Mansour, Morancy, Violet, and Vatican 24 cases made clear, was the punitiveness with which the Vatican could pursue nuns who were publicly associated with a pro-choice position on reproductive rights.

In its willingness to control dissent through repressive measures, the Vatican has been in most ways an equal opportunity employer: Male clerics and theologians in the United States have also for decades paid a high price for opposing official doctrinal positions of the church.[31] The expression of clerical support for a married priesthood, women's ordination, and greater choice in reproductive and sexual matters has precipitated Vatican sanctions for male as for female religious. Charles Curran was barred from teaching theology at Catholic (and non-Catholic) universities under Vatican pressure initially for his public reflections on the papal birth control ban set out in *Humanae Vitae*.[32] The expression of liberal views on issues of gender and sexuality explains in no small part why Archbishop Weakland has been denied honorary degrees,[33] Father Richard McBrien's writings have come under official fire,[34] Father Joseph Breen has been silenced by his bishop and Matthew Fox by the Dominicans,[35] and Father William R. Callahan was dismissed by the New England Jesuit Province and forbidden to preach or hear confessions in the Washington archdiocese where the Quixote Center, which he codirects, is located; why Archbishop Raymond Hunthausen's episcopal powers were partially transferred elsewhere; why the Jesuit priest John McNeill was ordered by the Vatican not to speak on the subject of homosexuality.[36] But as Ann Ware points out, the penalties for male religious are different at least in one respect: "Punishment for members of religious communities is threat of expulsion, not from the Church but from their communities. If this threat does not bring them to heel, they are to be demoted to the laity. No such punishment exists for unruly bishops, who remain in the episcopate, or for priests, who remain in the priesthood."[37]

The constraints that feminists in the church face in their day-to-day existence is a function partly of direct Vatican monitoring but also of the attention paid and restrictions imposed by local priests or bishops (increasing numbers of whom are appointees of John Paul II). There are a plethora of stories. Their message is that clerical discipline is particularly immediate and harsh for those who contravene Vatican teaching on abortion, but other issues (clerical attire, inclusive language, support for ordination) may also invite the ire of church authorities. A sampling:

In 1993, The Detroit Archdiocesan Office of Parish Life canceled plans to invite Edwina Gately as a speaker after a picture of her appeared in the *National Catholic Reporter* showing her "vested."[38] Gately is certainly not alone is being reported to church authorities for having worn an article of clothing that resembles too closely that to which either priests or ordained deacons are singularly entitled.[39] Wearing a collar, chasuble, or stole (clerical "trappings" that some women pastors of their own accord reject)[40] can invite trouble.

A Boston priest, using inclusive language in a baptism ceremony, was directed to inform the families whose babies he had baptized that the ceremony was invalid. Paulist Father William Larkin substituted ". . . in the name of God our Creator, through Jesus Christ in the power of the Holy Spirit" for "I baptize you in the name of the Father and of the Son and of the Holy Spirit." A visiting priest reported on Larkin's apparent malfeasance to the Boston archdiocese.[41]

In April 1995 Sister Carmel McEnroy was fired from St. Meinrad Seminary (although she was a tenured associate professor) for the apparent reason that she had signed an advertisement supporting women's ordination that appeared in the *New York Times*. The statement, drafted by WOC, read, "The denial of gender equality in our church is a serious, ongoing scandal for faithful, believing Catholics . . . ."[42] This action prompted an astonished response from some who knew McEnroy. "She's a feminist," one priest remarked who was a St. Meinrad alumnus, "but she's not a radical. She wants people to think, to grow in a way that is faithful to the tradition of the Church."[43]

Less surprisingly, women-led Eucharists have provoked sanctions, although few take place in a church setting and most that occur in a living room or other nonchurch meeting place simply do not come to the attention of church authorities. In 1990 in Minneapolis, when Roy Bourgeoise, MM, invited three women to come to the altar and say the eucharistic prayer with him, he was ordered out of the archdiocese.[44] By contrast, what was striking about the St. Meinrad case was that McEnroy had "merely" signed a letter; this is indicative of the seriousness with which the church hierarchy responds to feminist "discursive" power.[45]

The Vatican's efforts to contain the reach of feminism have relied largely on disciplinary tactics, but Rome has also deployed other institutional as well as discursive measures.[46] The institutional approach was transparently at work when Rome took the step in June 1993 of setting up a parallel organization to the Leadership Conference of Women Religious (LCWR).[47] The establishment of a new canonical organization, the Council of Major Superiors of Women Religious in the United States of America, was at least in part an attempt to dilute the authority of the LCWR that has sometimes vigorously, sometimes watchfully, endeavored to express the feminist perspectives of many American sisters.

The new council brought together superiors of eighty-four religious congregations that represented slightly over 10,000 of the close to 100,000 women religious represented by the LCWR. Vatican officials denied any intent to undermine the LCWR, indicating that their purpose was merely to ensure that a diversity of views among American nuns have an authoritative outlet for expression. But the Vatican's approval of a new organization of nuns was certainly read as a hostile act both by the LCWR and by the Conference of Major Superiors of Men (CMSM). The LCWR and CMSM together issued a statement indicating that they were "saddened and profoundly disappointed" by the Vatican's "decision to establish another canonically recognized organization for women religious leaders . . . [which can only] open old wounds within congregations and between congregations."[48] The existence of the new council enables the overrepresentation of conservative voices of women religious: At the October 1994 Synod on the Consecrated Life in Rome, for instance, only three women religious spoke. One was the head of the Sisters of Mercy of the Americas; the other two were brought from the new council.[49] Whether "constructive" or "punitive," the message is the same: feminism is considered a hostile force in the eyes of the present-day Vatican.

Institution-shaping measures were also at work when in November 1993 the pope handed down an encyclical stipulating that the church leaders were empowered to recognize an organization as "Catholic" or to refuse such recognition. Shortly thereafter a committee of the National Conference of Catholic Bishops declared that Catholics for a Free Choice was not "an authentic Catholic Organization." The CFFC "attracts public attention by its denunciations of basic principles of Catholic morality and teaching—denunciations given enhanced visibility by media outlets that portray CFFC as a reputable voice of Catholic dissent."[50] What might allow an organization to be in dissent "reputably" was not spelled out, although the implication was that disagreement could rightfully concern only those issues which were not basic principles of church teaching. The columnist Anna Quindlen termed the bishops' action "organizational excommunication." Clearly incensed, Quindlen snapped, "According to the bishops, Catholics for a Free Choice 'can in no way speak' for all members of the church in the United States. The real crisis is that neither can the bishops."[51]

Appointment of cardinals and bishops is also, of course, one of the most important institutional methods by which control is exerted over the openness of the church hierarchy to feminism.[52] The process of appointment is heavily influenced by the pro-nuncio (once called the apostolic delegate to the United States), who investigates the background, character, and views of the candidates. This is done secretly, with the referees being told that "any violation of this secret not only constitutes a grave fault, but is also a crime punishable with a corresponding ecclesiastical penalty."[53]

The Vatican has also used discursive methods to counter the claims of American Catholic feminism. Part of this approach is to characterize feminism as extreme by associating the term (feminism) with its most (in Catholic terms) extreme goddess- or nature-worshiping form. Thus, in an address to the American bishops, the pope said about feminism,

> It is not simply that some people claim a right for women to be admitted to the ordained priesthood. In its extreme form, it is the Christian faith itself which is in danger of being undermined. Sometimes forms of nature worship and the celebration of myths and symbols take the place of the worship of the God revealed in Jesus Christ. Unfortunately, this kind of feminism is being encouraged by some people in the church, including some women religious, whose beliefs, attitudes and behavior no longer correspond to what the Gospel and the church teach.[54]

Deeming it insufficient to criticize the feminists' support of women's ordination, greater choice in reproductive and sexual matters, and language and rituals in the church that are less exclusive of women, the Vatican has sought to denounce feminism by tarring it with the brush of extremism. As Rosemary Radford Ruether observes, "Since the 1970s and 1980s, women's spirituality has become a very feminist, creative base-community movement operating outside the edge of traditional Christianity, communicating with Christian symbols but also in dialogue with post-Christian symbols. This also means that the new way of attacking Christian feminists is to say that they're pagan. And if you're pagan, it is assumed that you're also a witch and a devil-worshiper."[55]

Explicitly avoiding any affirmation of "feminism" as a term or concept, the Vatican has utilized an alternative phraseology, choosing to appeal to women's faith and support by affirming a "feminine genius." In an open letter published just before the Beijing Fourth World Conference on Women in August 1995, the pope set out the ground on which Catholic women who have felt the sting of injustice and discrimination might find support within the present-day doctrine of the church. The pope praised women's contribution to the "long history of humanity" (particularly in culture and art); he regretted the value placed on women for "their physical appearance [rather] than for their skill, their professionalism, their intellectual abilities, their deep sensitivity." He condemned sexual violence while praising women who, conceiving a child by rape, nevertheless eschew abortion. The pope went on to say, "In these cases [of rape] the choice to have an abortion always remains a grave sin," but in a gesture to the decades of reproductive rights advocacy, he continued, "But before being something to blame on a woman, it is a crime for which guilt needs to be attributed to men and to the complicity of the general social environment. . . ." The letter also set out in fairly explicit terms the measures that must be taken—"equal pay for equal work, protection for working mothers, fairness in career advancements, equality of spouses with regard to family rights"—in the secular environment in order for equality to be achieved outside the church.[56]

The possibility that an ordination-based gender exclusiveness and hierarchy *within* the church might subvert the meaningfulness of secular equality *outside* the church was not addressed. As columnist Nell McCafferty put it in an article that appeared in Dublin's *Sunday Tribune*, "Ach, look, brother John, I'll tell you the full truth: most of my women friends just giggled about you calling for equality while saying no to women priests."[57] This sentiment was echoed by Ferraro and Hussey in a different context: "Apparently equal rights, access for women, freedom of conscience, and freedom of speech were values for *outside* of the Catholic Church only."[58]

The determination not to cede to feminism the semantic terrain on which the debate around gender equality has been framed is evident in the emphasis the Vatican has placed on the language of the 1994 Cairo and the 1995 Beijing conferences. Predictably, the Vatican questioned resolutions including such phrases as "reproductive rights," "fertility regulation, "reproductive health," and "safe motherhood," which Rome saw as endorsing pro-choice positions. But even more indicative of the emphasis the Vatican places on the power of discourse was the war waged around the usage of such terms as "gender." Throughout various drafts of the Beijing Plan of Action, the Vatican and its allies in Beijing requested the bracketing of the word *gender*, perhaps because it was thought to be coded language for homosexuality, but also because it was seen as opposing the belief in a natural feminine essence as distinct from a more constructed view of societal gender roles.[59]

This mission to formulate words and phraseologies that will displace the language of feminism is carried on at different sites within the church by both women and men.[60] Part of the contested terrain is, of course, the liturgy itself. Over the last several decades, perhaps particularly in the United States, the movement toward use of a more "inclusive language" has gathered momentum. In 1990, prompted no doubt by the extensive debates over the Pastoral on women, the U.S. bishops set out criteria for the evaluation of inclusive language. "Words such as 'men,' 'sons,' 'brothers' . . . which were once understood as inclusive generic terms," the report acknowledged, "today are often understood as referring only to males." Recommending the cautious replacement of gendered or solely masculinist terms, the report was couched in a tone clearly evident in the document's section on "Naming God:"

> Great care should be taken in translations of the names of God and in the use of pronouns referring to God. While it would be inappropriate to attribute gender to God as such, the revealed word of God consistently uses a masculine reference for God. It may sometimes be useful, however, to repeat the name of God as used earlier in the text rather than to use the masculine pronoun in every case. But care must be taken that the repetition not become tiresome.[61]

In 1994, however, the Vatican clamped down, withdrawing approval of biblical translations already sanctioned by the U.S. and Canadian episcopal conferences. The use of inclusive language together with the growing inconsistencies of the church's liturgical and catechetical practices reputedly prompted the Vatican's decision. Catholic church historian Gerald Fogarty (also a Jesuit priest) exclaimed that the Vatican move brought back the days before the Council of Trent.[62]

The war of words was transported into the public eye by an advertisement printed in the *New York Times* taken out by the Catholic League for Religious and Civil Rights (housed in the archdiocese of New York) at the time of the pope's 1995 New York visit. The advertisement featured, unusually, a "poem"—a long set of couplets, entitled "Welcome Holy Father; But Can They Hear You?" It read, in part:

> They talk about rights
> You talk about duty
>
> They talk about education
> You talk about wisdom
>
> . . . .
> They talk about equality
> You talk about equity
>
> . . . .
> They talk about gender
>
> You talk about sex
>
> They talk about utility
> You talk about dignity. . . .[63]

These varied attempts by the institutional church to shape the practice of Catholicism—levying penalties, constructing counterinstitutions, reframing discourse—elicit different reactions among feminists. Some "simply" exit—a phrase that belies the grief that can attend the breaking of ties that bind people to their religious birth identities. Exiting may not mean a full break from the church. Many who leave their religious order or their parish or who join an alternative liturgy group still maintain their continued identification with Catholicism. Others, more radically and in far fewer numbers, have chosen to convert or cease altogether to believe. Unfortunately, no estimates exist of numbers in most of these categories, nor is there any fully satisfactory way to assess motivations.

What does exist is ample documentation of the large-scale exit of nuns from religious orders. Marie Augusta Neal's exhaustive study of the transition in religious communities reports that between the mid-1960s and the late 1980s the numbers of nuns had dropped by over 40 percent.[64] In some cases, the exit must have felt massive: As reported by Barbara Ferraro and Patricia Hussey, two of the Vatican 24 nuns, only nine Sisters of Notre Dame remained of the sixty-two who entered when they did in 1962, and, in Hussey's group, at the time of her final vows, only one other nun remained of those who entered with her.[65] At present the numbers of women recruited into religious orders has also dropped precipitously. Between 1958 and 1962, over thirty-two thousand women entered religious orders; now the number of recruits (prenovitiate, canonical novices, second-year novices, and those who are temporarily vowed) is barely more than one thousand.[66] For some sisters—Ferraro and Hussey are dramatic examples—resigning from their religious communities was exactly about being unable to practice their faith within the strictures of their religious order as framed, often, by Vatican pressures.

It would be a mistake, however, to attribute the massive exiting of women religious to the present-day conservatism of Vatican politics. The numbers given dispensation from vows rose precipitously in the 1960s, during Vatican II, well before the papacy of John Paul II.[67] Nor could it be said that the conservative Vatican policies have been a significant cause of lay members' exiting the church. As Andrew Greeley notes, the numbers of Catholic lay "defectors" (those who leave the church and identify with an alternative denomination) have remained essentially unchanged since 1960, although Catholics of Hispanic origin seem to be converting to Protestantism in some small but significant number.[68]

Among those who are discontent with present-day Vatican views, the predominant choice seems to be not so much "exiting" as "defecting in place."[69] One response has been to live Catholicism, as author Tim Unsworth terms it, "on the edge," ignoring, adapting to, and/or resisting confining strictures. This is clearly the approach taken by the nearly three-quarters of all American Catholics who believe you can be a "good

Catholic" without obeying the birth control teaching of the church; by the more than one-half of all American Catholics who believe that the same is true with respect to abortion teachings; and by the two-thirds of Catholics who believe that the laity should be able to participate in the decision about women's ordination.[70] Accounts of religious ritual and practices also indicate that canonical authority is breached not so uncommonly by priests' allowing communion to or officiating at a marriage ceremony of couples whose earlier marriages had not been annulled; by priests' occasionally inviting women parishioners or colleagues to give the homily (sometimes termed "reflection," as Tim Unsworth notes, to forestall inquiries from the chancery office).[71] It is common among priests, Jim Bowman's research suggests, to see their pastoral role as calling for some sort of "bending the rules."[72] Although still uncommon practices, for some nuns and other laywomen who are serving in the pastoral ministry, "defecting in place" may even mean out of exasperation defying canonical law by performing the sacraments for the sick and dying, hearing confessions, or officiating at baptisms.[73] And for those who are disillusioned with the hierarchical, institutional church, "defecting in place" may mean joining liturgical groups and performing nonclerical Eucharists, ceasing to go to Mass, and having little to do with parish life.

To say that rules are in fact bent is not to minimize the pressures against doing so. Although the constraints are both institutional and discursive, those which are directly punitive should not be underestimated. It is impossible as a feminist in the present institutional church not to come into conflict with strictures and invite punitive backlash. To question the Vatican's position on homosexuality (a "person engaging in homosexual behavior . . . acts immorally") is to invite scrutiny at best and censure at worst.[74] To publicly support pro-choice policies can lead to (for a layperson) the cancellation of speaking engagements, the denial of employment, the withholding of pastoral ministry (including communion), and (for a nun) the threat of or actual dismissal from a religious order. Punitive measures are also imposed against those who may endorse inclusive language or women's ordination. Even to invite, as is increasingly common, the participation of altar girls can elicit a bishop's ire, as it did in the Arlington, Virginia, diocese, where the late bishop imposed a ban on girls as altar servers. For speaking out, feminists have been separated from their religious communities, excommunicated, silenced, transferred, refused lecture engagements and job opportunities. At best, they have been berated and patronized. Why, then, do feminists, both religious and lay, continue (as depicted in the previous chapter) to openly, vocally, challenge the church?

WITHOUT RECOURSE TO THE LAW

In the case of the military, the law is both what supports activism and contains it. In the case of the church, the law is simply absent, not there either to support feminism nor to moderate it. It is not that the church is immune to court action. Individuals have sued the church, most notoriously in sex abuse cases. Indeed, the church has been forced to pay large sums in punitive damages in at least three different instances as a result of jury trials in sex abuse cases. One estimate suggests that out-of-court settlements and lawyer fees have cost the Catholic Church over half a billion dollars.[75] In certain cases the church is protected from being sued by virtue of its status as a private organization. The 1984 *New York Times* ad–signers who were later pressured to leave their order, or who were denied speaking engagements, university jobs, or diocesan positions, were simply not constitutionally empowered to claim free speech rights against a private organization.

A number of employment discrimination suits against the church have reached the courts, and in almost none of them have the courts ruled on behalf of the plaintiff. One among the first set of cases involved two suits against St. Ambrose, a Catholic college in Iowa, by Sister Annette Walters and by Sister Ritamary Bradley. Sister Annette Walters died in February 1978, six weeks after the close of hearings on her case. (It was during the decade of the 1970s, as an earlier chapter recounts, that uniformed women were having substantial success in their suits against the military.) Sister Annette Walters's community decided to continue the case in the name of her estate. The case made its way from the Iowa Civil Rights Commission through to the Iowa Court of Appeals, where it was decided against Walters. The case had involved, in part, Sister Annette Walters's application for a sabbatical, which she had hoped to take at Yale to pursue her research in the psychology of conscience and moral development, a subject about which she had already written. (Walters had a Ph.D.) The sabbatical (of which only one, purportedly, could be given that year) was awarded instead to an instructor who had a B.A. and whose acquisition of a terminal degree was deemed by St. Ambrose to be of greater potential benefit to the college. To this day, this instructor has no further degree.

Sister Ritamary Bradley sued the bishop as chair of the board of directors at St. Ambrose, the president of the college, and the academic dean. Her complaint was that she was denied hiring responsibilities that male department and divisional chairs had been granted. In a complicated resolution, parts of the contention Bradley made were accepted in the federal district court's decision and parts were denied. St. Ambrose settled (albeit without any monetary damages) out of court.[76]

Before her death, Sister Annette Walters commented in a communication to Sister Ritamary about two other cases (those of Trudy Champe and of Sister Catherine Fay, BVM) that were then being considered:

> As I write this I am angry, and frightfully grieved at the injustice done to [Trudy and Catherine].
>
> The sin of both was that they were competent. The unforgivable crime they committed was that of being totally unselfish. The deviation for which they must atone is that of excellence.
>
> There was a further limitation, one which neither could overcome. They were women. Strong, vibrant, caring, independent, life-loving women. But they could not and would not flatter men. They loved men, they cared for men. They taught men and taught them superbly. But they did so in the context of their own total personalities. . . .
>
> I weep for Catherine Fay. I weep for Trudy Champe. I weep for all the women who throughout the centuries and still today are the crucified members of the Body of Christ, crucified as was he by the very men he came to save.
>
> I weep for myself. I am a woman.[77]

In 1987, Sister Rosa Marta Zarate, well known in feminist circles for her Spanish songs protesting injustices in church and society, sued the San Bernardino (California) diocese and Bishop Philip Straling for breach of contract and sex and race discrimination. The County Superior Court in San Bernardino ruled against her.[78]

In April 1993, a Denver federal appeals court effectively ruled against a woman who had applied to be a Catholic chaplain at a Veterans Administration (VA) hospital. Although the court declared the VA policy prohibiting women from serving as chaplains to be illegal (since women serve as Catholic hospital chaplains elsewhere), the court upheld the VA policy requiring chaplains to have endorsement from their denomination. The Catholic Church to date has endorsed only priests for positions in the VA system.[79] Throughout the diocesan system itself, employees of the church work in numerous capacities (teaching, administration, health, and social work). A recent *National Catholic Reporter* article recounted the experiences of church employees whose jobs have been eliminated—often, it seems, in the wake of confrontations with church authorities over disagreements that ranged from matters of style to issues of political substance. None to date have led to successful court suits, although one, involving a suit against the Fort Wayne–South Bend diocese is presently in the courts. At a "Call to Action" meeting, Notre Dame's Father Richard McBrien urged the need for more such suits:

> ... until there are dramatically successful lawsuits against priests, bishops, parishes, dioceses, schools, and hospitals, and some costly out-of-court settlements, as there have been to date in the tragic cases of sexual abuse by priests, church employees—the great majority of whom are women—will continue to be abused, intimidated, calumniated, and fired without cause or recourse.[80]

Without the courts' or any legislative bodies' holding the church accountable to existing constitutional or legal standards of justice and equality, the church hierarchy is free to be intransigent to a degree that the military leadership is not. On issues of birth control, homosexuality, reproductive choice, and ordination, the church has remained unyielding. It makes little sense, then, for women in the church to act as an interest group endeavoring to win the support of sympathetic decision-makers. The choice that confronts feminists in the church is to remain reticent or to become radical. Why so many make the latter choice is a question both about political opportunities and about the norms that shape how feminists came to see these choices.

OPPORTUNITY AND NORMS

Vatican II

In contrast to the experience of feminists in the military, the political opportunity for Catholic feminists to raise matters of gender inequality came from within the institution rather than from the courts. This opportunity materialized with the reforms of Vatican II. As helpful as the framework of opportunity structure is, however, it is not entirely adequate to an account of the radicalization and the turn to discursive politics of American Catholic feminism. The opportunity of Vatican II with its call for renewal was, of course, global. And yet American sisters took the opening Vatican II provided in a direction distinct from that taken by religious communities elsewhere—a difference that is understandable in light of the Americans' normative environment, the eruption of U.S. social movement politics, and these women's proximity to liberation theology.

Without question, Vatican II transformed the lives of American nuns.[81] By asking what role the church should assume in the modern world and by inviting the active participation of the laity in the construction of a lived faith, Pope John XXIII and subsequently Pope Paul VI catalyzed vast changes. The Second Vatican Council was convened in 1962. Sixteen documents were issued by the council, of which the 1965

Decree on the Renewal of Religious Life was one of the most immediate goads to change for the lives of women religious. Together with the 1966 *Ecclesiae Sanctae*, the council documents called on all religious orders to reexamine their constitution, directories, ceremonies, and prayers—in short, their entire mission and self-understanding. Equally important, the final document of the Commission on the Church in the Modern World, *Gaudium et Spes*, acknowledged descriptively that women are now claiming "for themselves an equity with men before the law and in fact," and went on to note that sex discrimination was among the prejudices that must be "overcome and eradicated as contrary to God's intent."[82] It is impossible to do justice in a short space to the life-transforming experiences of those who participated in the renewal process and to convey the drama and passions that emanate from first-hand accounts,[83] but the basic outline is as follows: When in response to Vatican II, nuns rewrote their orders' constitutions and recomposed their rituals, they exchanged the old standardization of behavior based on rigid rules of obedience and conformity for new rules that provided at once for greater community and greater individual autonomy. Gone were the requirements to ask the mother superior for permission to take a bath, to use a needle and thread, to read the newspaper, to go outside, to consult a book other than the Bible. No longer were letters between the eighteen-year-old postulant and her mother or father or erstwhile boyfriend opened, read, and maybe not delivered. Gone was the ban on "particular friendships" and community built on the equality of isolated individuals. Gone were the arbitrary assignments to jobs and locations arrived at through closed deliberations to which the nun-assignee was not privy. Writing of her earlier experience, Joan Chittister recalled the chemistry teacher taken out of her high school laboratory and transferred to teach fourth grade, the concert pianist sent to teach beginning piano students, the typing teacher made a high school principal overnight. Chittister writes:

> The important thing to remember is that the examples aren't bizarre. They were the norm. In a society where everyone dressed the same, looked the same, lived the same, functioned the same and believed the same, there was no reason to imagine that individual gifts and needs lurked anywhere beneath the surface, or should, at least, be given any attention. Work undertaken in the "spirit of obedience" would be blessed and that was enough.[84]

As nuns deliberated over the call to renewal of Vatican II, some chose to remain cloistered, preferring the contemplative over the activist life. Many more responded to the call of Vatican II by moving out "into the world." From the mid-1960s on, sisters were running soup kitchens, marching against racism, demonstrating against the Vietnam War, working in peace and justice centers, working with migrants, joining in actions against nuclear testing, running the sanctuary movement. Some remained in parochial schools, in parish jobs, in church-run hospitals, schools, and universities. Others took jobs in the secular world—as accountants, technicians, administrators, editors, social workers, school and college counselors. Most abandoned the habit, dressing in skirts and pants, and moved into apartments to live with roommates, in small groups, or alone. The move out of the convent was a metamorphosis.

Vatican II had opened the way. If the Vatican's declaration of the church as the people of God was a "call," the "response" mouthed by increasingly exasperated feminist sisters and laywomen was: "and it is us—Women-Church." But Vatican II cannot explain the American feminist reaction in full. The council's injunction to activism was sent out from Rome to all corners of the globe, and the reaction of lay and religious to Vatican II was certainly not everywhere the same. Why the American feminist response took the form it did—profuse in its printed expression, readier to challenge the clerical hierarchy, and, as elsewhere, committed to egalitarianism in the church and in society—cannot be explained without further analysis.

Movement Politics

A second vital part of the story of American Catholic feminism's emergence is located in its account of the normative context in which American sisters were reacting to Vatican II's call for renewal. Women religious in the United States deliberated on the meaning of Vatican II in the midst of the already flourishing civil rights movement and the other newly burgeoning social movements of the 1960s. There is less documentation of how the civil rights movement may have influenced the emergence of a feminist consciousness in the Catholic Church than there is of the role played by the women's movement and by liberation theology. But scattered accounts suggest that the exhortations of Martin Luther King, Jr., to build a world founded on justice through nonviolence had resonance for many sisters. Margaret Traxler, School Sister of Notre Dame, describes the 1965 march on Selma where sisters were among those facing the lines of state troopers. She describes the projects bringing northern teachers into southern Black schools and colleges, observing that the National Catholic Conference of Interacial Justice, then in Chicago, placed over two hundred Catholic sisters, most with Ph.Ds., in 112 predominantly Black colleges around that period.[85]

Feminism outside and inside the Catholic Church intersected at many different nodal points. It cannot be argued that the women's movement somehow delivered a particular feminist ideology, neatly packaged, to the door of the Catholic Church. Catholic feminism did not fasten onto a particular set of writings (liberal feminist, socialist feminist, or radical feminist); nor did Catholic feminists associate themselves with one particular organizational section of the women's movement to the exclusion of another. What did happen was that women's movement organizations provided a forum within which women were provoked to ask questions about the role religious institutions played in their lives. The National Organization for Women (NOW), for instance, had established a "women and religion task force" that was already in place by 1968. Participating in the spirit of demonstrative protest of the 1960s, the task force issued a recommendation for an Easter Bonnet Protest: "Whereas the wearing of a head covering by women at religious services is a custom in many churches and synagogues, whereas it is a symbol of subjection, the task force on Women and Religion of N.O.W. recommends . . . a national unveiling." On 10 April 1969, six women in a Milwaukee Catholic church took off their Easter hats and placed them on the communion rail, an act that was termed "immature exhibitionism" by a Milwaukee paper two days later.[86]

The task force continued to speak in words that could only have startled the Catholic hierarchy to which they were addressed. Drawing largely on women from Detroit and Chicago[87] and other Midwestern cities, the task force addressed itself in a press conference held on 28 April 1971 to the National Conference of Catholic Bishops meeting in Detroit. Elizabeth Farians read from a prepared press release:

> The Catholic Church is a sexist institution. As a result it is also racist and warmongering. It is unchristian in the worst sense of the word. . . . It would be difficult to distinguish between the Church and the Pentagon. Both are examples of an over-masculinized culture in which the so called male characteristics have dominated. Assertiveness, arrogance and authoritarianism, pomp, power, and privilege are its characteristics.[88]

Some religious orders specifically urged their membership to become involved in women's movement organization. In 1970, the Lorettos urged their membership to learn about the movement firsthand, to join organizations such as NOW and the League of Women Voters, as well as organizations of sisters that were taking up issues about sex discrimination, such as NCAN and NARW, and to work for laws that would protect women in society. Virginia Williams, a Loretto sister herself, speculates that it was the order's work as Christian educators (as secondary and college teachers) that pushed many Loretto sisters to educate themselves about feminism. Looking back over early documents, Williams observed that Loretto sisters saw the women's movement as lacking "a Christian presence." Rather than see this absence as a reason to eschew movement activities, however, Loretto sisters apparently believed that a Christian presence was something they could bring to the movement.[89]

Activist sisters and laywomen looking for ways to involve themselves in the movement founded and worked in battered women's shelters, federal credit unions for women, counseling, training, and empowerment workshops for women prisoners or homeless women. Maureen Fiedler, then a Sister of Mercy and later a Sister of Loretto, was one of the eight women who fasted in silent witness in 1982 in a futile but courageous attempt to urge the Illinois state legislature to pass the ERA.[90]

Religious communities also brought ideas from the movement into the deliberations, resolution making, and practices of the order. Community assemblies discussed at length the meanings of feminism, passed proposals for action (about the ERA, for example), adopted commitments to the use of inclusive language in official communication within the order.[91]

The educational attainments of many sisters brought them into contact with feminist ideas outside the church. Since the Sister Formation Movement in the 1950s, women religious have been acquiring advanced degrees in abundance. By 1980, over 40 percent of American sisters had at least a master's degree and 94 percent had bachelor's degrees (numbers far higher than those for priests).[92] This education brought sisters into the lay world at a time—in the 1960s, 1970s, and 1980s—when writings on feminism and other social movements were burgeoning.

But the most profound influence of the women's movement is probably the least traceable. The questioning of hierarchy and inequality that was provoked by the movement and that found expression in multiple channels of communication (secular and religious books, magazines, television, organizational meetings, demonstrations, private conversations) was "out there" to be picked up and applied to religious life wherever women and men experienced it. One small example speaks as pointed testimony to the diffusion of feminist consciousness. A woman parishioner tells the story:

> Ten years ago I was of the mentality, "Oh, com'on . . . what's all the fuss? Who cares whether it's Chairman or Chairperson? Besides, Chairperson sounds ridiculous!"
>
> I can probably pinpoint the day when I crossed the border from "it really-isn't-that-important" to "Hey, wait-a-minute!" I was at Mass hearing the parable of the loaves and fishes read for the umpteenth time in my life. But now, after several years of reading the Bible on my own, I was not just being read *to*, I was reading along *with*. I thought I knew the story backwards and forwards. Father got to the line (Matt. 14:15–21), "Then the disciples took up

twelve baskets full of what was left over. The number of men who ate was about 5,000, not counting women and children." At that precise moment I remember turning to my husband (who always seems to bear the brunt of my outbursts) and saying, "Why?"

"Why what? he answered.

"Why weren't they counted?"

"Who?" He was perplexed.

Somebody turned around frowning.[93]

The messages of feminism by the 1970s were broadly diffused throughout society. Whether by joining women's organizations, by reading, by attending workshops, by going to classes, by compiling lesson plans and book lists for their students, women religious and lay Catholic women encountered the ideas of the women's movement. As Sister Kaye Ashe, a Dominican, put it: "Feminist thought took root in American religious communities during the period of renewal. It was impossible not to see how the feminist critique applied to church institutions."[94]

The exposure of women religious and laywomen in the Catholic Church to the feminist movement broadly conceived helps to explain the readiness of Catholic activists to question the inequalities in their immediate environment. But that part of Catholic feminism which is concerned with issues of poverty and economic marginality is not traceable to roots in the women's movement, specifically. When feminist activists in the church cite women's movement literature or refer to speakers they have heard, they mention liberal feminists such as Betty Friedan, Gloria Steinem, Eleanor Smeal, and difference-feminist Carol Gilligan,[95] but they do not mention some of the socialist feminist writing that was part of the earlier women's studies corpus.[96] When groups such as the Loretto order talked of the "Women's Liberation Movement" they spoke largely of liberal feminist organizing (as pressure groups, to change laws and public policies).[97]

The radical strains of Catholic feminism that are based on a view of the structural underpinnings of economic inequality are less directly derived from the women's movement than from a combination of the founding service-to-the-poor charism of many religious orders and the powerful influence beginning in the 1960s of Latin American liberation theology. At least some of this influence was transmitted through the presence of U.S. sisters who were sent to work throughout Latin America. Already by 1961, the church hierarchy had appealed to religious communities in the United States to send 10 percent of their community members to missions in Latin America.[98]

The Loretto experience, as related by Elaine Prevallet, vividly depicts one process by which ideas of liberation theology migrated north. As Loretto sisters became exposed to the Latin American interpretation of

Vatican II that was embodied in liberation theology, their view of their own role shifted from a more traditional understanding of "mission" work to a belief in a broad, populist coming to faith in a common struggle for justice.[99] Even before 1961, the Lorettos had been planning on establishing a site in La Paz, Bolivia. After some deliberation, a school for girls was opened in 1961. Colegio Loreto drew from the privileged strata of society—the military, politicians, and professional families. But very soon, the sisters who were running the school began to reassess its purposes. A 1963 meeting of Latin American bishops in Cuernevaca exhorted religious orders to link education to social justice work. The 1968 Medellín conference was further to reaffirm the "preferential option for the poor" that defined the Latin American reaction to Vatican II.[100] By the latter part of the 1960s, the La Paz sisters were also in touch with Loretto projects in Chile and Peru. Several of the sisters had studied in Cuernavaca under Ivan Illich, and the debates about renewal in North America had reached an intense pitch. At the Colegio, Loretto sisters were divided over the degree to which the school should be made over in a more democratic mode with tuitions scaled and curriculum planned to include experiential learning that would expose students to the realities of inequality in Bolivian life. These debates between radicalism and reformism were brought back into the North American Loretto community, where the Executive Committee and the General Assembly of the religious order became involved in considering the future of the school.

By the 1980s, many sisters were traveling to Central and South America. Many worked as teachers and health workers in El Salvador, Nicaragua, and elsewhere throughout Latin America.[101] The 1980 rape and murder by members of the National Guard of two Maryknoll sisters, one Ursuline sister, and a laywoman who had been working with local communities in El Salvador sent shock waves through the religious communities of North America and undoubtedly intensified further the attention that religious groups were directing to events in Latin America.[102] In the 1980s, Sister Marjorie Tuite, much revered by activist sisters, established the Women's Coalition against United States Intervention in Latin America and the Caribbean. She made frequent trips to Central America and Cuba, taking groups of women religious with her to be "present in the struggle."[103] The National Assembly of Religious Women (NARW), which Tuite founded, shared offices with an organization working with Guatemalan women and continued to act in alliance with women like Renny Golden who were active in the sanctuary movement. Network, the Catholic lobbying group in Washington run by sisters, made U.S. policy in Central America one of their primary issues. Deeply committed to a common struggle for social justice, the entire Loretto order's Assembly voted to spend significant amounts of money on Latin American projects: $30,000 in humanitarian aid to Nicaragua in 1979; $20,000 for two projects in El Salvador in 1980; $23,5000 for aid to refugees from "repressive Central American countries" in 1981.[104] But even for those women who had no direct experience in Latin America, the writings of Paulo Freire and the practices of *conscientiazation*[105] reverberated in the methodologies of discussion and reflection used in meetings of women religious. "Speak outs," breaking up into small groups—methods of discussion incorporated into the Assemblies of many religious orders during the 1970s—were all at least partly a result of teachings that had come to the United States through liberation theology.

THE NORMATIVE REINFORCEMENT OF SEPARATE STRUCTURES

In order to make sense of the American brand of Catholic feminism (outspoken and prolific in its criticism of the church, of society, and of itself), it is helpful to think about one final contributing element: women's autonomous structures within the church. Incorporated within the separate environment of women's communities, radicalism gained legitimacy. It is hard to imagine Catholic feminism's being what it presently is without a considerable degree of both autonomy and collective support for those who exercise their conscience in the face of institutional repression.

The autonomy that is required is both individual and structural. Militancy (however defined) demands a willingness to sacrifice. Those who are single, without responsibilities for children, or those with spouse and children who are willing to make family relationships secondary have always been considered the core of militant movements and radical, organizational work.[106] This is no doubt what accounts in some part for the prevalence of nuns and priests at different historical moments among those who have been committed activists.

But when church authority tries to curb this activism, some degree of structural autonomy from the mechanisms of institutional repression is also critical. Women's religious orders or at least subcommunities within them provide something of a buffer. Religious communities are economically self-sufficient (some might say self-sufficient to be poor) in the sense that the salaries earned by their members are what supports the sisters of that community.[107] (Many sisters do not have bank accounts themselves; salary checks from employers are either made out directly or written over to the community; sisters make out a budget, mostly at poverty levels, on which they then subsist.) The decision about how an order's funds are to be spent is made within the community itself by a process that varies from one community to another. At the same time, financial oversight by Rome exists. Indeed, for canonical orders, Rome must approve all large community expenditures and sale of property just as it must also approve the constitutions of all religious orders.

This has certainly resulted in feelings of dependency for religious communities. But it is still the case that church clerical authority does not directly control the salary checks of many individual sisters. In the military, those who speak out risk finding themselves transferred or their job prospects stymied. In the church the "job" is often not the issue, except where a sister or layperson works directly *for* the church as a teacher in a Catholic school or college, as a pastoral assistant, and so on. Overall, however, the community provides some economic autonomy.

But the canonical status of religious community is a decisive hindrance to independent thinking within religious communities.[108] Rome, as the earlier discussion suggested, can exert control not simply through the budget process but through granting permissions and imposing penalties. The exercise of this power was dramatic with the 1968 Immaculate Heart of Mary (IHM) sisters of Los Angeles, where church intervention helped widen a split in the community. The split resulted in four hundred sisters' "asking" for collective dispensation from their vows (in place of facing, as they were likely to, loss of canonical status).[109] The IHM events in 1968, the Agnes Mary Mansour case, the prohibition against tubal ligations in hospitals run by the Sisters of Mercy of the Union,[110] and the Vatican 24 cases of the mid-1980s are all reminders that the heavy hand of church authority curbs the autonomy of women religious. As Sister Maureen Fiedler commented about the Vatican 24, "I do not believe that [Patricia Hussey and Barbara Ferraro's Sisters of Notre Dame] community leaders would ever consider dismissing members for speaking their consciences if Rome weren't watching every move and if the community did not worry about its status with Rome."[111] At the same time, in the most recent case of the Vatican 24, there was at least considerable effort and discussion (whether successful or not is a matter of debate) among religious communities who wished to avoid acting as handmaidens of Rome; this indicates some greater awareness and readiness on the part of communities to exercise what autonomy they have than was true some decades earlier.

The autonomy, however incomplete, of religious orders has been essential to the sustenance of feminist independent thinking; so too is the existence of community. Although religious orders have been, sometimes deeply, divided by differences (over wearing the habit, decision-making structures in the community, relations with Rome, the support of individuals who conscientiously dissent from church teachings), they have also provided extraordinary sustenance to their members.

By community, I mean, at its simplest, associational linkages. Mary Segers points out that in the United States there were 232 Catholic women's colleges and universities and that most of these were run by sisters. No such network of highly educated Catholic women trained in leadership has existed in other countries.[112]

But community is also more than networks. A number of activist sisters write about the vital importance of mutual commitment and friendships. In pre–Vatican II days, Joan Chittister writes, "We lived with people we never spoke to and wanted to talk to people who were missioned elsewhere and told to stay there for the year. We all lived alone together."[113] Although many sisters now live outside the community, residing in small groups and even singly, the provincial communities (the suborders), particular associations such as the Loretto women's network, liturgy groups, and the religious order itself are sometimes the "family" to which sisters are deeply attached. Sister Maureen Fiedler writes eloquently of the connection between her political commitments and these communities:

> I have begun to learn just a bit of what this solidarity means. It is more than just reading, writing, giving workshops. Sometimes, it involves suffering, fasting, jail, and ultimately a willingness to give life itself. Even more difficult, it can involve loss of reputation and misunderstanding from friends and family. Somehow that all rings true with what Jesus did. And as I learn more about risk, I am grateful for the community support of Loretto and Quixote that makes it all imaginable.[114]

When feminist sisters and laywomen speak about community (pastoral ministers excepted), they rarely talk about their parish. Instead, they speak far more often about communities of women and in some cases small liturgy or organizational groups of feminist women and men. If the church were parishes alone, it is hard to imagine that the American form of Catholic feminism would have thrived as it has.

CONCLUSION

If Vatican II had occurred in the 1950s, it would have been an "opportunity" for activism that American sisters might have responded to simply by intensifying their commitments to the many social betterment projects in which sisters were already engaged. In fact the Sister Formation Conference of the 1950s was in some respects a preview of Vatican II. The conference did encourage women to go outside their orders and acquire educations; it raised some feminist questions, urged American sisters to meet with their Latin American counterparts, and galvanized women religious to think freshly about old questions.[115] But the Sister Formation Conference on its own did not transform religious orders.

Nor would Vatican II have done so, on its own. But in conjunction with the civil rights organizing, the antiwar movement, the women's movement, and the influence of liberation theology, Vatican II afforded not only an opportunity for activism; it also, in interaction with the social movements of the period, shaped the normative and political environment of Catholic women religious and lay in ways that were profoundly transformative.

Vatican II galvanized changes throughout the Catholic world. But for laywomen and sisters, Vatican II had different results in different national settings. The United States was distinctive in the proliferation of Catholic feminist groups, in the explosion of conferences, workshops, liturgies, meetings, books, newsletters, and tapes, and in the directness with which feminists interrogated the patriarchal practices, language, and hierarchy of the church.

To make sense of the discursive radicalism that developed within American Catholic feminism, we must understand how politics creates opportunities, as well as why activists reflect and act on these opportunities as they do. Activist women in the church could not turn to the law, as have women in the military, in any endeavor to hold institutional leadership accountable to norms of nondiscrimination. With "legal" opportunities for political activism foreclosed, Catholic feminists had a choice: leave the church, remain quiescent, or speak up.

Those who spoke up spoke loudly in forthright, no-holds-barred language calling for justice both in the church and in society. They did not have to; they could have spoken in quiet, dulcet tones, cautiously and with diplomatic indirection. Why feminists in the church chose instead to engage in what can be called discursive radicalism is related to the opportunity Vatican II created and also to the normative communities to which women activists looked in the course of rethinking who they were as women in the church. The interaction of the call of Vatican II and the turbulent 1960s movements in the United States, of liberation theology abroad together with the sustenance of women's separate vibrant religious communities of highly educated women religious within the American church, were the norm-setting communities that help to explain why the words of the four women religious cited at the outset of this chapter sound the way they do.

PART FOUR

EPILOGUE

Chapter Seven

A NEW ORDER?

Their sex connects them to the conventional roles of women, while their work connects them unconventionally to the professional roles of men. And in their duality, they are not fully part of either camp. Rather they are mistrusted, often despised by both.

ALTHOUGH these sentences might well have been excerpted from the preceding chapters, this is an account neither of feminists in the military nor of feminists in the church. It is, rather, Mona Harrington's depiction of the now-practicing women graduates of the Harvard Law School Class of 1960. These "women in the law," Harrington maintains, "by their very beings herald a new order even if they arrive with no personal revolutionary intent."[1]

How best might we describe this "new order" that the sometimes unwitting feminism of women's presence or the fully purposive feminism of activists inside institutions may arguably portend? It is clear that protest inside institutions is consistent with what David Meyer and Sidney Tarrow surmise to be the advent of a "social movement society." Protest behavior, they argue, has become integral to modern life. It is "employed with greater frequency, by more diverse constituencies, and is used to represent a wider range of claims than ever before." It has become, they contend, a routinized form of conventional politics.[2]

What is less clear is the significance of this rising tide of claims making for a broader set of political debates: Is it the manifestation of what Robert Putnam has described as the weakened social moorings of American democracy, or is it evidence of the necessary means by which a democratic order more embracing of difference can be reconstituted? America, by Putnam's description, is increasingly a society where people associate less, where trust is on the decline, and where Americans "bowl alone." Arguing that the "vibrancy of American civil society" has "notably declined over the past several decades," Putnam describes the falling memberships of school-related groups (the PTA), institutionally connected church associations, sports clubs (the declining number of bowling leagues), labor unions, and fraternal societies, to name some of the organizations Putnam cites.[3] The rapid waning of popular trust in government, Putnam contends, is partly linked to this fall in civic engagement and declining social capital.

This book argues that the diminution of public trust may be the inevitable and necessary outcome of a process in which the claims of diverse groups gain political legitimacy. Protest inside institutions exposes a new reality of power. When Nathan Glazer writes, "We are all multiculturalists now. . . . we all now accept a greater degree of attention to minorities and women," he is acknowledging this new actuality of power in American society, one that has been fought for rather than conferred.[4] Feminist institutional protest is part of this history, evidence of what Charles Tilly has called the "repertoires of collective action" with which those previously denied resources or recognition make collective claims on authority.[5] In the second half of the twentieth century, protest inside institutions has been one of the most potent "repertoires" with which new groups have made claims on those who have wielded power in the past. Such activism is no longer confined to the once separate spheres of American life or to the realm of party and union politics (which were the designated spaces to which individual groups in the past took their political claims); there is hardly an institution—whether a college, school, hospital, prison, sports team, television broadcasting company, the military, or the church—that is now unacquainted with claims making by a profusion of newly empowered groups. Growing protest by diverse social groups inside institutions is not the familiar "civic" associationalism of much earlier decades, but its different forms and its presence on new terrain record the expansion rather than contraction of a politically active citizenry.

From this book's perspective, the social capital of which Putnam speaks was the foundation of an earlier political order. The parent-teacher associations, many of the church networks, the fraternal societies were socially homogeneous organizations whose purpose was to serve their membership within the boundaries of clearly demarcated segments of society. In many ways they succeeded; in some ways they were not up to the task. But their declining memberships may reveal more about their anachronism in today's claims-making society than it does about a decline in the participatory conditions of democratic society.

The insufficiencies of these earlier forms of civic engagement should not be overlooked. Sometimes, as in the 1930s, even the strongest forms of social capital failed when economic circumstances turned dire. Parishes and civic associations were unable to provide needed support and sustenance[6] in ways that are akin to the present-day difficulty that churches and their associated drug rehabilitation, counseling services, and food kitchens face in today's decaying urban neighborhoods. Civic associationalism was and is no substitute, as Putnam clearly notes, for public action.[7]

But associationalism in the many forms that Putnam names as supporting vibrant communities did so in the context of a different era. The very success of ethnically based networks, of women's groups like the League of Women Voters, of organizations like the PTA, encouraged greater participation by diverse groups in social and political institutions throughout much of the twentieth century. And yet, as elite provinces of society became more diverse, it should not surprise us that the organizations which helped to foster this process could no longer function in the same way. No longer could an organization like the League of Women Voters survive simply as the patron of good citizenship through voter education and election-day turnout drives. Women's issues in the public arena have changed, and the organization had to remake itself (as to some degree it has) or it would find itself swiftly superseded, as have many of the civic associations of an earlier era.

Since the 1950s, as new groups in American society have aspired to a different place within the social order, new forms of collective activity have begun to supplant the old. It would take further research to establish whether other forms of middle-class associationalism—women's bookstores, coffeehouses, gay bars, Hispanic and Black middle-class church congregations, salsa dance studios, as well as the social movement organizations and professional associations that directly target the decision making of policy elites—compensate numerically for the loss of membership in the declining organizations that Putnam names. But it is not surprising that as claims making grows on the part of new groups pursuing new forms of identity in American society, trust in the political institutions that once served an older (more Protestant, male, and white) societal and political order would for a period suffer a decline. The possibility that the aspirations, interests, and identities of these new claimants cannot be absorbed within existing institutional structures and normative frameworks can only be unsettling. Challenges to existing power arrangements invariably are. As political theorist Bonnie Honig has written in a different context, ". . . ungovernability is precisely what difference threatens us with."[8]

A SUMMARY

What makes claims making inside institutions unruly, I have argued, is not its form but its substance. Exactly because this claims making has entered institutions, its "style" resembles neither the associationalism of the early part of the century nor that which we associate with protest in the more recent 1960s era of social movement politics. And yet, if we are to recognize the disruptive potential of feminist politics inside institutions, the character of the claims themselves must be acknowledged no less than their form and place. Whether it takes the form of the most "professional" lobbying or the simplest discursive uttering, feminist activism consitutes protest not because it elicits the reaction common to the 1960s demonstrations "You can't do that here" but because the implied response is still often the same: "Women do not belong here."

In the context of both these two institutions, demanding "to belong" on equal terms is thus to engage in protest politics. In both insititutions, advocates of gender equality insist that no reason other than lack of individual merit should bar women from achieving that which they were traditionally denied on the basis of sex. Exponents of gender equality vehemently adhere to the missions of their institutions. Repudiating any presumption that feminism diminishes an individual's devotion to God, theologian Anne Carr describes a Christian feminist spirituality as primarily a call to "wider visions of human mutuality, reciprocity, and interdependence."[9] Insisting that it is the conservatives, not advocates of gender equality in the military, who lack an understanding of the national interest and national defense, the now-retired aviation squadron commander Rosemary Mariner minces few words in observing that "the conservative right-wing fixation on women in the military is not about national defense, readiness, or military personnel policy, but simply a 'front' in the so-called 'culture war.'"[10] Given the previously rigid gender-caste system in both military and church, and given the continued risks to career, status, and respect that those who challenge gender ascription incur, such women must be fearless to be faithful to their institutions on feminist terms.

Given the similarities in the institutions, it is not surprising that advocates of gender equality would share these personal qualities. But given the institutional parallels, the puzzle is why the politics of feminism in the military and church then evolved so differently. As with the military, the organization of the church is hierarchical. Like the military, the leadership of the Catholic Church makes no pretense of democratic governance.[11] Before the emergence of feminism's second wave, women in both the military and the church sought to empower themselves through an expansion of their roles, which were clearly demarcated as separate from and complementary to men's. With the 1970s, women in both institutions challenged these divisions, but they did so in different ways, as feminism in the church developed in a far more radical and discursive direction than did feminism in the military.

Why this is so has much to do with the proximity of the institution to the state and with the paradoxes of liberal law. In the case of the military, the courts initially provided feminists indispensable support for their political claims. Without the opportunity to take their cases to the courts, it is hard to see how feminism could have acquired the potency it has within the institution of the armed forces. Quiescence, not activism, might well have resulted. The receptivity of the courts and later Congress meant that uniformed women who thought they should be entitled to serve on ships, claim dependency allowances for their spouses, attend military academies, and serve as combat aviators had to be regarded not as outlaws but (if begrudgingly) as legitimate claimants within the institution.

Paradoxically, however, this "access," meant that many women activists inside the U.S. armed forces came to believe in reformist, interest-group politics and saw little need for developing broader alliances with those whose claims to equality were still unrecognized. Feminists did not "need" the support of those fighting discrimination on other fronts. If anything, the narrower their claims, the more acceptable they were.

For women in the church, however, their lack of access to this kind of judicial and legislative oversight was part of how Catholic feminists came to be radicalized. Up against an intransigent church leadership, with no opportunity to appeal to the authority of the state, women in the church had little reason to believe in interest-group politics and evolutionary change. The embryonic lobbying efforts in the 1980s when feminists tracked the views of sympathetic clerics ended almost as soon as they began.[12] Radicalism in the church was shaped by the lack of legal redress.

Those familiar with the Catholic Church might contend, unpersuasively I think, that one might give a more parsimonious account of feminist radicalism by pointing to Vatican II and to the prophetic tradition within the church, a tradition that can hardly be said to exist within the armed forces. But Vatican II and the church's prophetic tradition have shaped Catholicism worldwide and yet feminism among women religious has been particularly vigorous within the United States.

I have attempted to locate, then, as I believe any analysis of institutional change in America's litigation-suffused society must do, the place of the law in the shaping of opportunities for activism. But the law's role goes beyond the provision or withholding of opportunities for claims making, what social science language might designate as opportunity structure. The law's role is also a normative one, shaping the way activists come to define themselves, see the world around them, and prioritize their agendas. For how can we explain otherwise the fact that activists seize some opportunities but not others?

It is not opportunities by themselves but their interactive relationship with norms, beliefs, and values that drives feminist protest within institutions. Liberal legal norms made it easier, for instance, for DACOWITS to define as a problem the "public" world of job discrimination than the "private" world of prostitution, although both strongly impinge on the lives of military women. The irrelevance of the law's regulatory influence in the church meant that the "agenda" of equal opportunity, such as ordination, had no more of a priority for feminism than did the goals urged by the normative influences of liberation theology and the populist exhortations of Vatican II. These normative influences were important but in concert with the absence of the law's regulatory role. Law is thus an important determinant of these norms. But it is not the only one. So are broader currents that are changing society, and this affects how we think of our sense of self, our relationship to others, and our role in creating a more just and equitable world.

The law's recognition of gender and race but the exclusion of class claims within the framework of equal protection litigation is also part of what deters feminism within institutions from assuming a more radical character.[13] Institutional protest has not compensated for the decline of 1960s activism by and on behalf of those in poverty. Feminist protest inside institutions does address cross-class concerns when issues of sexual harassment are invoked, or when claims are made for day care that ensure provisions for low-income families. But institutional protest other than union activism itself rarely addresses the wage concerns of low-income workers, nor is feminist protest inside institutions likely to promote engagement with the concerns of welfare mothers, the homeless, or those beyond the institution's perimeters. If the comparison of the military and the church tells us anything about the general conditions under which feminists inside institutions will engage in radical actions with and on behalf of the poor, it is that the confluence of conditions that radicalized feminist activism in the church (the distance from the law's regulations; the exposure to a range of radical ideologies) is very rare indeed. Nonunion institutional protest does not attend to the same purposes that labor organizing and demonstrative street protests served in the past in making political parties and legislative bodies more responsive to the concerns of the poor.

It would be a serious mistake, however, to underestimate the force of feminist protest inside institutions. Institutional protest has kept feminism alive. Institutional activists have appropriated ideas generated by the autonomous organizations of the 1960s–1980s and have molded them to fit their own experiences and interests. This process of institutionalization has broadened feminism's reach inestimably. Given the difficult times that Washington-based organizations face with the conservative tide that has swept through Congress and the courts, the fact that much of the obvious antidiscrimination legislation is now in place, and the media's declining attention, feminist protest inside institutions has compensated for a slowing down of the mobilizational politics earlier undertaken by autonomous feminist groups.

Although at any given point in time, the barriers to equality can appear impassable, the view over a longer period is quite different. Over the last fifty years, the struggle against gender ascription is best described as one of shifting baselines and disruptive acts. Even in the short span of time since the 1970s, interest-group politics in the military and discursive politics in the church have transmuted long-standing exclusionary practices and beliefs and shifted the struggle for status recognition and economic advancement onto new plateaus.

Past, Present, and Future: The Church

Seen through the prism of five decades, from the 1950s to the present, there has been a metamorphosis in the lives of women religious. Some years back, Betty Friedan remarked that nuns were the "feminine mystique at its most extreme."[14] "Dependence, conformity, and institutionalized living were the marks of religious life."[15] Dressed in habit, many women religious spent their training and early life in community, working, studying, and eating in silence. In the 1950s, the women religious who sought to enhance the lives of vowed women toiled to win the right to and opportunities for further education so that sisters might be better at the work of teaching, nursing, and social work to which their orders had assigned them.[16] In the 1950s, the insistence that women religious should be broadly and professionally educated was radical in and of itself. Over time many women religious acquired college educations and advanced degrees. Little thought was given, at least initially, to whether women religious might wish to explore other occupations or whether there might be some who felt called to priestly ministry. One threshold was reached but new battles were ahead. As the 1960s and 1970s progressed, many of these same religious sisters, now in secular attire, donned armbands, marched, demonstrated, held meetings, lectured, wrote, composed plays, songs, and poetry, turned to non-priest-led liturgies, and dedicated themselves to protesting the many forms of injustice pervasive throughout society and the church. The baseline had moved.

How effective has this discursive politics been?[17] Certainly, the impact of feminist activism in changing the Vatican's stance on gender concerns has been negligible. The most significant Vatican concession in recent years was the 1994 Vatican declaration that no church laws prohibited girls from becoming altar servers.[18] On issues of ordination, reproductive rights, or homosexuality, the Vatican has been unbending.[19] In the United States, the effects of feminism are felt in limited ways at the level of gender representation. Women have slowly begun to play a larger role in parish affairs, with 20 percent of chancellor positions, 4 percent of judgeships, and 8 percent of financial officer positions held by women as of 1993.[20] Two percent of the U.S. parishes in 1991 were headed by nonpriests, three-quarters of whom were women.[21] Feminism's strongest impact has been in shaping the discussions and stimulating deliberation in the public fora of church exchange. The discursive work of feminists in the church has generated intense debates both among women (lay and religious) and within the church hierarchy. Feminists in the church have created a strong counterdiscourse in response to the words, rituals, and symbols that emanate from the Vatican. The voluminous writing by feminist theologians, by feminist leaders of religious orders, and by feminist nuns committed to social justice work has meant that there is hardly a biblical passage, a moment in the Mass, an utterance in the bishops' pastoral letter on women, a clause in a Vatican pronouncement that has not been reflected on, debated, and queried.

Feminist discursive politics has impeded the "mobilization of bias" that would have allowed the hierarchy to keep women's issues off the agenda for public debate. Feminist speech and writing have engaged the Vatican, the American clerical hierarchy, and numerous parishes in public confrontation over women's roles in the church, over exclusionary liturgical language, and over various ecclesiastical and secular forms that the "sin of sexism" (in the concessionary phrase of the bishops' pastoral letter) has assumed. The extraordinary story of the American bishops' pastoral letter is testimonial to the discursive standoff between the more conservative and the feminist forces in the American church. The 1988 letter, originally called "Partners in the Mystery of Redemption: A Pastoral Response to Women's Concerns for Church and Society," went through four full drafts before it was tabled in 1992.[22] Conservatives saw the pastoral as "priest bashing" because of the references to attitudinal changes that clerics might reflect upon. Feminists (from moderate to radical) directed their criticism variously at the bishops' refusal to recommend women's inclusion in the priesthood, to concede any of the feminist arguments over reproductive rights, or to acknowledge the voluminous theological scholarship by feminists, and also to the letter's heavy focus on woman as nurturer, mother, and wife.[23] Unprecedented in the history of pastoral letters in the United States, it failed to win support from the necessary two-thirds of the U.S. Bishops Council. Despite the admonition by the Congregation for the Doctrine of the Faith that any further discussion of women's ordination must end, the bishops have continued both publicly and behind closed doors to discuss, as one reporter called it, "the undiscussable."[24] The public debate over gender issues that feminist discursive work helped to motivate has clearly led to a swing in Catholic lay opinion toward feminist positions. In a 1992 Gallup Poll commissioned by activist groups, nearly 90 percent of the respondents reported the belief that the church should permit couples to make their own decisions about birth control; 70 percent said that Catholics can in good conscience vote for candidates who support legal abortion; 64 percent of all Catholic respondents and 74 percent of those under thirty-five supported women's ordination.[25]

In the future, women religious will likely play a less formative role in discursive protest within the church as their numbers continue to decline. Fewer than 90,000 in 1995 (down from 180,000 in the 1960s), nuns cannot continue to shape feminism in the same way in the years to come. But already lay feminist theologians and lay parishioners have become strong voices for change in organizations such as Call to Action and in local churches. The controversies over the place of women, gays, and lesbians in the church and over the autonomy of local churches in the face of diocesan censorship has come to preoccupy prominent parishes such as Holy Trinity Church in Washington, D.C., and St. Francis Xavier in New York, and to attract broad media attention.[26] The discursive struggle to frame the issues, to provide the words, narrative accounts, and symbols that shape the language of debate, has helped feminists to reach their own diverse self-definitions. For some, this means continuing to go to Mass; for others, it means celebrating Eucharist-like liturgies in small groups outside the parish. For many, it means looking into a future wherein

> Symbols would play a part. Poetry, music and dance would play a part. Language that embraces the feminine as well as the masculine nature of human beings and of God would play a part. And two qualities that especially distinguish feminist theology—relevance to lived experience and inclusivity—would be central and indispensable.[27]

Perhaps Annie Lally Milhaven captured it best in saying, "From an institutional, legal point of view, they [feminists] would seem to be quite powerless. But institutional power does not lie only in possession of control over property and juridical authority. It lies, in the church particularly, in a cultural hegemony to define the meaning of the community and its mission."[28] In resisting any unitary thinking on the meaning of faith and of justice in church and in society, feminist discursive politics has made possible considered reflection and meaningful self-definition.

The Military

Interest-group politics has led to policy shifts in the military that have not occurred in the church, but in contrast to feminism in the church, the low reliance on discursive politics in the military has detracted from the power of uniformed activists to challenge the authority of the institution.

In 1950, military women were 1.5 percent of the armed forces.[29] The army had only just that year desegregated its racially divided companies.[30] Pregnant women and women with children were barred from the service; women were generally assigned to traditionally female specialties and were prohibited by law from serving on ships or in any position designated as combat-related. In the 1950s and well into the 1960s, those who worked to improve the lives of military women did not challenge the presumption of gender difference but sought instead to enhance women's skills, their living conditions, their self-respect within the parameters of a gender-differentiated military.

In the course of the next decades, Black women were to enter the military in unprecedented numbers, becoming close to a third of all women in the military and half of all women in the army;[31] women sued in the courts to open the academies, to be assigned to ships, to serve in the military despite pregnancy and parenthood. Some military women sought out women's groups, their Congressional representatives, and the media to protest discrimination and harassment when they felt ignored by the military chain of command; they lobbied Congress to open up combat positions to women, and DACOWITS transformed itself from its original manifestation as a public relations arm for the military into an often-resented goad, prodding the services to make equal opportunity less of a rhetorical and more of a lived reality. Whether or not the services will move with "all deliberate speed" to integrate women into combat positions remains to be seen.[32] But in 1992, 69 percent of the American public believed a "women should be assigned as a crew member of an aircraft carrier, submarine or destroyer, fighting the enemy from the sea, as a pilot or other crew member on a bomber or fighter aircraft." Thirty-eight percent believed women should be assigned "as infantry soldiers fighting the enemy in close and possibly hand-to-hand combat on the ground."[33]

Feminist interest-group politics in the military has worked inversely from feminist politics in the church. In contrast to the the case of the church, feminist protest in the military has had a clear impact on decision making, driving authorities to open up increasing numbers of positions to women and to change policies on academy admissions, dependency provisions, and a host of other issues. As with feminism in the church, feminist activism in the military has kept a range of issues, such as sexual harassment, on the military's agenda. But unlike discursive feminism in the church, feminist protest in the military has not had great influence over the meaning making that ensues when issues come onto the military's agenda.

Of the media-dramatized exposés (Tailhook, the Kelly Flynn case, Aberdeen), however, not one came to public attention at the behest of those who have organized in support of gender equality. Women activists have, after the fact, been approached by the media for comments, they have been appointed to investigatory commissions, and they have endeavored to use these events as "opportunities" to convey messages that they believe are important. But there is intense pressure in these situations to be one of the "team," never seeking publicity that is not authorized, eschewing any excessively critical verbiage, and staying within the bounds of acceptable inquiry.[34] On the heels of Tailhook, military women used their media appearances to clarify for the public the connection between the demeaning treatment of women in Las Vegas and the exclusion (at that time) of women from the ranks of combat aviation, but their criticism of navy leadership or the judicial process was noticeably restrained.

The role of doing interpretive framing falls largely, in the case of the military, to the civilians who monitor gender and military issues in the women's lobby network (earlier at WEAL and now at WREI, WANDAS, or NOW). The limitations of these networks were evident in situations such as the case of Kelly Flynn, a highly trained aviator whose relationship as an unmarried woman with a married-but-separated civilian led to a threat of court-martial and her resignation from the air force. After realizing that the public seemed to believe that the "punishment did not fit the crime," the air force moved quickly to try to "clarify" the case, insisting that the serious concern was her having disobeyed an order to cease seeing the man in question. Most military women with whom I spoke observed wryly that men are rarely so ordered.[35] Up against the formidable public relations capacities of the air force, however, the limited resources of the women's network were unable to reverse the interpretation that was now being reproduced throughout the mainstream press. Unlike what is seen in the church, the "discursive" capacities and reach of feminists in the military are at present quite limited. Whereas in the case of the church, the *National Catholic Reporter* or other high-circulation newspapers and journals can be counted on to devote extensive space to feminist interpretations of ongoing issues, for feminists in the military there is no comparable public outlet, although the service *Times* papers run scrupulously balanced news and op-ed pieces. Similarly, the military women's organizations do not begin to match the many locations and opportunities for personal and collective narration and political interpretation that are provided to feminists in the church by meetings, workshops, newsletters, and books.

Discursive politics is likely to grow in importance for women in the military. Since 1994, for the first time following the inception of the all-volunteer force in 1973, both houses of Congress were controlled by a Republican majority. This has coincided with what political scientist Ole Holsti has observed is a growing conservatism and an increasingly partisan shift within the military itself.[36] As Tom Ricks of the *Wall Street Journal* noted, "Indeed, there is some evidence of extreme views seeping into military discussions of world affairs," citing illustratively a 1994 statement in the *Marine Corps Gazette*. The article writers deplore what they see as American society in moral decay, concluding that the "next real war we fight is likely to be on American soil."[37] These recent changes have meant that the effectiveness of military women's interest group politics has receded[38] and the need for discursive activism (from conversational exchanges among informal networks to waging opinion battles in the mainstream media) has increased.

In 1997, the behind-the-scenes contest between antifeminists and advocates of gender equality hit the mainstream media with new force. The *Washington Times* broke the "story" that assistant army secretary Sara E. Lister at a Harvard University John T. Olin Institute for Strategic Studies seminar had used the word "extremist" in an off-the-cuff remark describing the marines. The context was a discussion of Tom Ricks's book that depicts the distinctive culture of marine basic training and, in Ricks's words, the " 'culture-war' trend of thinking"[39] that he documents in his book as having grown stronger within sections of the armed forces. Indeed, in another context, many marines might themselves have proudly pointed to this development and to the service's distinctive culture. A fellow panelist, however, Kate O'Beirne, Washington editor of the *National Review*, sent a tape of Lister's remarks to Elaine Donnelly, a longtime supporter of Phyllis Schlafly's Eagle Forum and head of the conservative Center for Military Readiness. Donnelly faxed a copy to the *Washington Times*, where its publication precipitated enraged protestations from some marine as well as congressional quarters, leading to a vote in the House of Representatives, where conservative congressmen had been looking for opportunities to block army initiatives to integrate women into increasing numbers of army jobs.[40] The House voted to ask for Lister's resignation, to which she acceded.[41]

Advocates of equal opportunity in the military have carried out their own media efforts although largely of a reactive sort. When military women came to know that the army's largest professional organization, the Association of the United States Army (AUSA), contributed $20,000 to Elaine Donnelly's center at the same time that they had contributed a mere $4,000 to the Arlington Cemetery Women's Memorial, they made sure that the mainstream media was informed. As one Pentagon military officer reported it, after Dana Priest of the *Washington Post* broke the story,[42] the AUSA allocated another $50,000 to the Women's Memorial, a "nice first-payment," she quipped.[43]

The future of gender equality in the armed forces depends heavily on how the military and the public come to understand the issues. Will the skeptics who oppose gender equality win the day by focusing on physical standards and framing the debate around the question of whether men and women should meet the same physical standards,[44] or will proponents of gender equality succeed in insisting that this does not pass the "common sense test," that already men and women must meet identical physical requirements for specific jobs, and that there are many high-tech jobs, as well as more routine and manual ones, for which massive upper-body strength is simply not required.[45] Will the debate over gender integration be framed as the sociologist Charles Moskos suggests when he argues that gender equality is less likely to be attainable than race integration in the military? A scholar with considerable influence in military policy circles who has brought to public attention what he and John Sibley Butler argue is the exemplary success of the army's race integration efforts,[46] Moskos strongly cautions against similar optimism with respect to gender: Blacks (men) and whites (men), he argues, "are essentially interchangeable soldiers," whereas "physical differences and privacy concerns" prevent any such realization of sameness between the genders.[47] Will this formulation prevail, or will advocates of gender equality be successful in suggesting as does Commander Rosemary Mariner that "the commonality between race and gender is prejudice,"[48] or as a senior military officer in the Pentagon queries, "Is Moskos asking the wrong question?" In the words of this senior official, "What policymakers and the public should be considering is how differences *can* often contribute to an organization. The military has an extraordinarily diverse set of careers. The question is in which can women effectively serve. Are women being considered in all the capacities in which military effectiveness warrants their serving? What is natural is that people are uncomfortable with other people who are different and we can change that working at it over time. We did that with race. And we should expect ourselves as a nation to be pluralistic."[49] Given the escalating war of meanings and interpretations that is building within the military environment, it would not be surprising to see advocates of gender equality stepping up their efforts to influence media coverage, whether through existing organizations or through the establishment of new nonprofit organizations staffed by some of the growing numbers of well-placed soon-to-retire uniformed women.

The foregoing comparison of feminist protest in the military and the church suggests several propositions that might be considered in further studies of institutional change and feminist politics:

- The more closely nested an institution is within the equal rights framework of American law, the more likely it is that its activism will take a more interest-group, moderate political form and the less likely that it will turn to a discursive and more radical politics. The degree to which protest within institutions is embedded within the equal rights formulations of the law (the nested character that I refer to here) is a function both of the "opportunities" for activism that the law provides and also of the normative environment that the law shapes, and out of which values and preferences are developed.
- The more accountable activists are (financially, organizationally, and discursively) to authority within the institution, the more their ability to act politically depends on activists outside the institution.
- Interest-group protest aimed at shaping law and policy and discursive protest aimed at reshaping existing understandings empower groups in different ways. The law offers the opportunity to advance a group's objectives. Less directly and often less visibly to activists, it also shapes the very nature of the group. Discursive politics offers fewer concrete opportunities for advancement. It does, however, help activists to move directly in developing a sense of collective confidence in their autonomous ability to judge their own interests and aspirations. Forms of feminism in the church and in the armed forces are instructive because they exaggerate one or the other. And yet they remind us of the importance of both processes in the politics of all movements for change.

These three propositions emerge from the different experiences of feminism in the military and in the church. But their commonalities bear even greater emphasis. Whether through interest-group or discursive means, feminist protest has raised fundamental questions about the space institutions provide for difference. In the construction of standards by which ideas and conduct are judged in the realms of institutional life, feminist protest inside institutions has contested (to borrow the words of Sandra Bem) the exclusionary reliance on male "biographies" and male "biology."[50] Most fundamentally, protest inside the military and the Catholic Church has challenged the process by which gender difference is naturalized. Whatever the range of institutional responses, there is no possibility that institutions can be, either now or in the future, immune to the claim that assignments based merely on gender ascription lack functional justification and moral worth.

What, then, stands between the still deeply institutionalized inequalities of gender and a future in which gender difference does not require women's subordination? In a sweeping analysis of American history, Rogers Smith argues against the Tocquevillean premise that equality will be realizable when the deployment of liberal ideas can be brought in line with liberal principles.[51] American history is not, for Smith, the vacillation between periods in which the polity abides more closely by the creedal promises of liberalism and periods in which the abrogations of these promises prevail. For Smith, there is not one but multiple traditions—both liberal and exclusionary—braided throughout American history. The inexorable persistence of gender inequality, racism, and economic oppression reflects the periodic failure of liberalism to overcome the competing forces of exclusionary ideologies and practices whose place in American history is no less preeminent than that of liberalism itself.

This book's discussion takes partial issue with Smith's unproblematized portrayal of liberalism—a portrayal that unites his own views with those of the Tocquevillean scholars (Myrdal and Hartz) whose positions he criticizes. As numerous feminist and critical race scholars have argued from an abundance of different perspectives, and as I have also endeavored to contend in this book, liberal tenets of equal rights and the distinction liberalism draws between public and private have *both* egalitarian and inegalitarian implications.[52] Liberal law does incite claims making and sets in sharp relief the hypocrisy of ascriptive practices. In institutional settings where the legal stipulations of liberalism can be invoked (the military, not the church), certain claims of equality are more likely to be realized. It is for this reason that there were women on ships before there were women altar-servers, women generals before women archbishops, and that there are likely to be openly gay admirals before there is a Vatican counterpart. But just as rights doctrine in liberalism licenses claims making, it obscures what is amiss in other realms of inequality. The poor may not be denied equal opportunity; but they may not be able to afford it. Women and men may be entitled to equal opportunities, but gender differences may make that "equality" perverse: Paula Coughlin may not have been denied an equal opportunity to enjoy the fun in the squadron suites of the Las Vegas Hilton. But she was at far greater risk than her male colleagues to become, a bit later, the object of that very same "merriment." A navy officer who fails to promote a more competent woman sailor is discriminating. What he does "on liberty" in the military-regulated campgrounds of prostitution has no name within liberalism that might implicate the promise of gender equality.

This book's claims, however, also affirm the importance of Smith's multiple-traditions thesis in another sense. Institutional locations embody very different mixes of ideological beliefs and liberal or exclusionary practices. In historical perspective, the family, the church, and the military are total, hierarchical institutions that once regulated public life. As Susan Okin has observed in her work on the family, and as I also observe in this study of the military and the Catholic Church, these are major illiberal institutions in a liberal state.[53] Emerging out of different historical heritages, illiberalism is deeply rooted in the institutions of America. Nested in different national and transnational environments and institutional settings, the kinds of claims making that are both desirable and possible are certain to be different.

The importance of this difference is twofold and cannot be overestimated: It is a caution to feminists to heed what political theorist Uday Mehta, in his writing on Edmund Burke, emphasizes as "circumstance."[54] Universals pale against context. What gender means—the defining and self-defining, the imagining of both desire and possibility, the dialogue between derogation and affirmation—unfolds largely within institutional locations. Whether the institutional constraints and possibilities are portrayed as "choice sets" (the language of rational choice), as the visible offshoot of deeply rooted economic systems (the framework of Marxism), or as discursively created (the Foucauldian perspective), the meanings of gender and of feminism must be recognized as institutionally contingent. Gender interacts invariably with race, ethnicity, class, and a myriad of other identities. An institutional approach no less than the "difference" perspective stressing race and gender specificities is a critique of a unitary understanding of gender and of a homogeneous version of feminism. Unlike the emphasis on the genealogies of race and gender, however, the focusing on institutions trains our analytical lens on how such categories are constructed through politics, thus limiting the risks of an essentialist interpretation. Situating the discussion of the "culture wars" in the institutional location, where power is contested on a daily basis, an institutional analysis of protest also grounds the discussion of moral disagreements in a political context.[55]

Protest has taken root within institutions. This is where much of the contemporary conflict over status and resources in American society is being contested. Given the differences in institutions—their distinctive relationship to history, to the state, and to transnational environments, there will continue to be significant divergences between the norms of the institution and the norms of the law in their multiple expressions. This creates a space for politics inside and outside of institutions, a space that feminism now occupies.

NOTES

PREFACE

1. Interview by author with Captain Mary Humphries, 23 November 1988.
I subsequently came across a number of other instances of former nuns who had
joined the military. One sister, a longtime veteran of peace and justice causes,
remarked on having attended the promotion ceremony of a former nun who had
joined the air force and who had been selected for colonel. With an affectionate
laugh, the sister commented, "We don't often go *in* the Pentagon. We picket
outside. It's a measure of how much we care for her that we actually made our
way inside" (interview by author with Sister Maureen Fiedler, SL, 7 January
1998, about promotion ceremony for Colonel Rosanne Greco, USAF). The
person to whom I refer as the first nun I interviewed was Sister Judy Vaughan,
CSJ.

2. All "women religious" take vows of poverty, chastity, and obedience
within a religious community following the charism (or vision) of the community's founder as interpreted and reinterpreted over the years. The linguistic distinction often made is between nuns as cloistered, living a life of prayer within
a monastery, and sisters, engaged in active ministry, serving in a range of capacities within the institutional church and outside: as parish administrators, health
workers, campus chaplains, spiritual directors, as well as accountants, school-
teachers, and university professors in a variety of settings, to list only a few of the
kinds of occupations pursued. It is also common to see the terms *women religious, nuns,* and *sisters* used interchangeably, as I use them in this book. I should
note that some sisters/nuns prefer not to be denoted as "women religious" lest
there be an intimation that vowed women in the church are in some way an elite
class that is more faithful or "religious" than nonvowed members of the church.
Nuns/sisters are nonordained and are therefore, strictly speaking, laywomen.

CHAPTER ONE
PROTEST MOVES INSIDE INSTITUTIONS

1. The importance of dramatic, on-the-streets, political protest is largely associated with the writings of Richard A. Cloward and Frances Fox Piven (Piven
and Cloward 1971 and 1977). In a more recent essay, Piven and Cloward observe that the "continuities between conventional social life and collective protest" that the literature on resource mobilization has described have been useful.
The essay, however, warns against "blurring the distinction between normative
and nonnormative forms of collective action" (Piven and Cloward 1992, 301).
The large literature on protest politics is usefully synthesized in Tarrow 1994.

2. See, for instance, the discussion of Black women's efforts to acquire voting
rights within the First African Baptist Church, in Brown 1997, 343–76.

3. See the discussion of farmer's movements and the demand for a more accessible education in McConnell 1953 and Summers 1996. (Mary Summers is a doctoral candidate in political science, Yale University.)

4. During one of the major discussions of educational reform in the 1930s, for instance, an appeal was issued by three presidents of Black colleges urging the federal government to consider the "moral obligation which binds a central government to exercise special solicitude for disadvantaged minorities . . . " (Fass 1989, 118–19). But no claims were voiced to make *white*-dominated colleges and universities more responsive to the concerns and interests of Black students or faculty. For a discussion of the construction of alternative/separate institutions, see McGreevy 1996 and Cohen 1990. Richard Polenberg writes about the decades before World War II, "It was by no means unusual for a person's entire life to be encompassed by the ethnic community, for his social world to be defined by it" (Polenberg 1980, 1). I am grateful to Lizabeth Cohen, R. Laurence Moore, and M. Elizabeth Sanders for their guidance here and for endeavoring to caution me about relying on generalities that, I recognize, oversimplify a hugely complex and varied history.

5. For a brief discussion of Du Bois's Harvard career, see Rudenstine 1996. Rudenstine draws on Aptheker 1973. Du Bois taught economics and sociology briefly at Atlanta University and then went on to become the editor of the *Crisis*, the journal of the NAACP. On Black historians, see Novick 1988, 231–32. By contrast, Novick describes some of the confrontations *inside* the academy leveled by Black historians beginning in the late 1960s (475–76).

6. See, for instance, Lamb 1993, 491–521. Lamb describes how Harvard, Yale, and Princeton sought to "stabilize" their Jewish and Catholic enrollment, increasing the number of legacies. Between 1900 and 1922, Jewish student enrollment at Harvard had risen from 7 to 21 percent. The fear was that a tipping point might cause these colleges to be labeled "Jewish institutions" (493). See also Karabel 1984, 1–40.

7. See, by contrast, the 1997 dispute at Yale described in Glaberson 1997, 45.

8. Shklar 1989, 5.

9. Cohen 1990, 218–49.

10. See Byrnes 1991, 34; O'Brien 1972; and Greeley and Rossi 1966.

11. In private four-year colleges, enrollments between 1976 and 1996 rose for Whites from 1,878,800 to 2,213,900; for Blacks from 182,000 to 279,700; for Hispanics from 44,300 to 138,700; and for Asians from 31,200 to 153,200. The comparable figures for four-year public institutions are as follows: for Whites 4,120,200 to 4,303,300; for Blacks 421,800 to 572,500; for Hispanics 129,300 to 346,800; for Asians 87,500 to 329,300 ("The Nation" 1997, 18).

12. Between 1960 and 1990, Andrew Hacker reports Black representation among telephone operators to have risen from 2.6 percent to 19.7 percent; for aircraft mechanics, from 4.6 percent to 9.8 percent; for accountants, from 1.6 percent to 7.4 percent; for electricians, from 2.2 percent to 6.2 percent; for lawyers, from 1.3 percent to 3.2 percent. The numbers of Black physicians rose in the same period, but their percentage of the profession declined from 4.4 percent to 3.0 percent (Hacker 1992, 113).

13. Rix 1990, n.p., table 19.

14. The explosion of civil rights cases in the federal courts, doubling from 10,000 in the mid-1970s to 20,000 in the mid-1980s, speaks to this search for new institutional structures. See Ginsberg and Shefter 1990, 8. In an analysis that counters the conservative view of "identity" politics as the creation of "political liberals," Michael Piore traces the rise of "identity" politics to the reign of conservatives themselves. The decay of the manufacturing sector aggravated by the Reagan administration's policies, which drove down blue-collar wage rates and weakened union activism, meant that full-time workers unable to be self-supporting and those dependent on a male worker's wage were forced to take their political claims elsewhere. Piore links the disappearance of the "family" wage (by which men could alone support their wives, aged parents, and children) to the "decline of the family as an integrating social institution." "A key aspect of this decline," Piore writes, "has been a process in which categorically defined financially and/or emotionally burdensome members have been encouraged to leave the household unit and move into living arrangements where they associated with other people categorized like themselves." This process helped drive different groups (the aged, women, single mothers, the blind or hearing-impaired) out of the household in search of alternative sites where their political needs could be met. A changed economy and family structure (the decline of manufacturing, union strength, and the family support system), it could be argued, has contributed to a new set of dependencies and a search by new social groups for political voice (Piore 1995).

15. I place the term in quotation marks because I do not believe that what are often referred to as identity movements are in any sense exclusively about identity. Nancy Whittier defines identity politics as that "in which one's membership in social categories prompts and defines one's politics." I agree with her entirely when she says that debates about "political correctness" and identity politics ". . . obscure the fact that identity is central to all social movements whether they claim to be about identity or not and dissent over the borders of identity categories exists within movements as well as outside them" (Whittier 1995, 250–51). This activism has come to be dubbed "identity" politics whether the claims that are advanced are about jobs, pay, or resources or about something more amorphous in the form of societal position, dignity, or self-definition. The reason for this is, no doubt, that this activism occurs outside the realm of union and labor politics so that the often distinctly concrete, material nature of the claims is less readily apprehended. Many people understand identity politics to refer to movements whose participants are concerned primarily with status, self-definition, and self-naming. The presumption often is that such politics (not being presumably interest-based and therefore instrumental) does not lend itself to negotiation or compromise. I am convinced that many so-called identity-politics movements have a large interest-based component, and that many interest-based movements of the past were as doctrinaire or uncompromising as "identity" movements are believed to be.

16. Tilly 1978, 151–59.

17. Piven and Cloward 1971, 1977, 1979, 24–27.

18. Piven and Cloward, as a careful reading of their work will show, do not do this. But their focus on movements that have relied heavily on strikes, demonstrations, riots, and so on, make it easy to interpret them as saying that protest is synonymous with a particular set of movement tactics, e.g., marches, rent strikes, boycotts, and riots.

19. So-called political process studies of social movements have used protest events as the "staple" signifier of movement stages. I am grateful to David Meyer for helping me to see this point.

20. In an earlier *Signs* article, in which I used the term "unobtrusive mobilization," I grouped together rather than attempting as I do here to make a distinction between groups inside institutions (owing accountability primarily to their parent institution) involved in very visible and disruptive protest and those groups that are much less noticed and, I would argue, much less likely therefore to be disruptive. Katzenstein 1990a, 27–52.

21. Hartmann 1998.

22. Tocqueville 1969.

23. Sarah Slavin has compiled an enormously helpful and painstaking list of all directories of women's associations. Her recent book provides a fascinating profile of over 150 women's interest groups (Slavin 1995). See viii for a listing of other directories, including the 1993 *Encyclopedia of Women's Associations Worldwide* by Gale Research International, which enumerates 3,400 women's groups. *National Women's Organizations* (1993) includes 477 groups. Although it would be possible to trace the individual birth and demise of particular organizations through these reference materials, it is not feasible to use them as a means through which the overall growth or decline of women's associations can be measured, because each works from a very different population base.

24. Shapiro 1991, 44.

25. See their newsletter, *WISP'R* (later renamed). The organizational goals are described in vol. 2, no. 2 (n.d.). The early history of the organization is recounted by Orr 1990a, 2–3, and 1990b, 2–6. I am grateful to Joan Catapano for making the WISP newsletter available to me. For information on other organizations in the media world, see the description of the Women's Caucus (of the *New York Times*), in Robertson 1992. The Women's Caucus, born over a luncheon in 1972, initiated, first, a series of meetings with the paper's management and, subsequently, a lawsuit. The *Washington Post* had a mother's group that met intermittently and acted as a support network, initiating planning meetings with newsroom management to facilitate part-time options and greater sensitivity toward family issues. Some of the other women's media organizations include the Women's Institute for Freedom of the Press, which describes itself as "promoting the radical restructuring of the communications system"(3306 Ross Place, NW Washington, DC 20008), the American News Women's Club (1607 22d Street, Washington, DC 20008—an organization that rather assiduously avoids polemics in its newsletter, *Shop Talk*) the American Women in Radio and Television (for women in the broadcast media), Women in Communications, Inc. (an older organization dating back to presuffrage days, with 11,000 members and 186 professional and student chapters), and JAWS (the Journalism and Women Symposium, a much smaller network of journalists that met annually in

Colorado: P.O. Box 3100 Estes Park, CO 80517). Many of the groups have a specialized membership, such as the Association for Women in Sports Media. On Women in Film, see Anne Thompson 1993, 25.

26. Hall 1990, 53–60.

27. Jepson 1993, A10.

28. Messing 1988, 3.

29. Johnston 1993, A11.

30. Glaberson 1992, A20.

31. See the brief discussion of the WBA in Rosenberg, Perlstadt, and Phillips 1990, 19–45.

32. Mentioned in Boles 1986, 1–30. Boles remarks that the Women's Caucus of the APHA was organized in 1971 to combat sex discrimination in health service delivery. She also refers to the Planning and Women Division of the American Planning Association, founded in 1980 to monitor women's issues (12). Many such organizations were founded in the 1970s and 1980s, produced by and, in turn, reenergizing the wave of organizational and discursive activity begun in the mid-1960s.

33. Putnam 1995.

34. In the course of my interviewing, I heard of no lawyer who was actually court-martialed for failure to participate in a prosecution of a gay or lesbian servicemember, but I was told of a male JAG (judge advocate general) member who resigned. In a later chapter I cite examples that I learned of in my interviews of the daily rumor persecution to which feminists and many nonfeminist women as well are subject. Other writings document this extensively. See, for instance, Francke 1997; Miller 1997, 32–51.

35. The officer ranks in the navy, at least some data suggest, are composed of disproportionately high numbers of Catholics. Based on tracking sheets, for instance, that Naval Academy midshipmen fill out on induction day when they are sworn in, 40 percent of the brigade reports itself as Roman Catholic, twice as high as the 20 percent of Catholics in the U.S. population overall (communication with Respondent 3, 1996). When I would mention to interviewees in the navy that I was also writing about the Catholic Church, frequently a respondent would, smiling, remark on being Catholic herself or on the other "cradle Catholics" in the service.

36. Interview by author with Rosanne Greco, 29 July 1996.

37. I owe this phrase to a discussion with Martha Minow. For a definition of discursive politics and the role, particularly, of feminist publishing and authotheoretical texts, see Young 1997. See also Fraser 1990, 56–79.

38. This phrase is widely utilized by feminists in the church. See, for example, the conference materials from the Women's Ordination Conference 1995, in Crystal City, Virginia.

39. Defense Advisory Committee 1994, 1.

40. Interview by author with Major Michelle Johnson, April 1992.

41. Interview by author with Colonel M. C. Pruitt, 29 October 1995.

42. Interview by author with Captain Pat Gormley, 8 August 1997.

43. Interview by author with Respondent 3, 1989.

44. "Military and the Women" 1997, A14.

45. Bond 1993, E7. See the discussion in McMichael 1997, 54–55.

46. Francke 1993, 218.

47. In addition to those in the military itself who might object to being called feminist when they themselves do not use that nomenclature, there are some who believe that being feminist and in the military is oxymoronic—that to be trained in the use of violence (particularly violence wielded by a national world power with a history of interventions on the soil of other nations) undermines any effort to pursue feminist principles of equality, justice, and peace-through-nonviolence.

48. The words of one Sister of Mercy who was asked by the *New York Daily News* to comment on the work of Mother Teresa help to illuminate the ways that an understanding of structural inequality is central to this vision:

> Before I opened my mouth I knew I was about to get myself in trouble. I had no idea how much.
> Carefully, I began:
> "I think Mother Teresa is a holy and compassionate woman. There is no minimizing the good that she does for Calcutta's abandoned poor and dying. But I think she does many sisters a disservice by allowing the media and ecclesiastical authorities to promote her as the role model for all religious throughout the world, especially in the United States."

The reporter pressed her to explain herself. She continued,

> We confront different needs, a variety of injustices. . . . Sisters here—as in other places—must discover corporately and by themselves what needs exist and how to address them. And even in Calcutta, someone ought to be figuring out who or what it is that causes so many people to perish in the streets. There have got to be direct ministers in the streets, but there must also be people who invade high places to learn why people die in the streets. There must also be sisters who find ways to change the killing systems wherever they are. There have got to be yet others who expose the evil. (D'Arienzo 1985, 33)

49. See the discussion in chapter 6, just before the superscript for n. 50.

CHAPTER TWO
LEGALIZING PROTEST

1. Selznick 1957, 6–7, as quoted in Scott 1995, 18.

2. Sara M. Evans and Harry C. Boyte's important book *Free Spaces: The Sources of Democratic Change in America* (1986) provided my original understanding of the importance of protected environments within institutions. It is important to note, however, that these spaces do not always feel safe and protected; that there often is, as anyone connected with feminist activism can attest, enormous disagreement, contention, and vulnerability *within* such spaces. I use the term *habitat* in part to invoke Pierre Bourdieu's use of *habitus* and its implication of bounded intellectual frames (Bourdieu 1972, 1977). But see Calhoun 1996, 302–5, and Coombe 1989 on the concept of *habitus* (60–123).

3. Cott 1990, 162. Cott observes, "Too great a focus on the achievement of the Nineteenth Amendment, however, obscures the similarities in women's political behavior before and after it and the relation of that behavior to broader political and social context" (154). See also Cott 1987.

4. Muncy 1991, xii.

5. Anderson argues that women's entry into electoral politics "not only extended the life of progressivism" (Anderson 1996, 153) but also shifted the agenda of politics in the direction of greater "good citizenship," introducing a more interest-group form of political participation (170). In a related but potentially very different line of argument, Liette Gidlow argues specifically for women in the 1920s and Lizabeth Cohen for the 1930s more generally that citizenship became increasingly associated with consumerism. See Gidlow 1997, Cohen 1990.

6. Ware 1981. As quoted in Scott 1991, 173.

7. The Medical Women's National Association supported the Sheppard-Towner Act; this put them at odds with their male-dominated parent organization, the AMA (Hummer 1979, 119).

8. Lemons 1972, 67–68.

9. Equal Rights Amendment discussions did mobilize groups to fight protective legislation, successfully so in California and several other states. There are numerous accounts of the division within feminism between supporters of protective legislation and the National Women's Party/equal rights supporters. See, for instance, Cott 1987, 117–42. Lemons 1973, 181–208.

10. Lemons 1973. In California and Indiana, the National Federation of Businesswomen and Professional Women's Clubs worked actively to oppose protective legislation (200–204).

11. Stetson 1991, 184.

12. Hummer 1979, 93.

13. Ibid., 118.

14. Cott 1987, 231.

15. Many more women law graduates were in noncertified schools. Hummer 1979, 144; Cott 1987, 231.

16. *Bradwell v. Illinois* (1873). Judge Bradley wrote, "It certainly cannot be affirmed, as a historical fact, that this has ever been established as one of the fundamental privileges and immunities of the sex. On the contrary, the civil law, as well as nature herself, has always recognized a wide difference in the respective spheres and destinies of man and woman. Man is, or should be, woman's protector and defender. The natural and proper timidity and delicacy which belongs to the female sex evidently unfits it for many of the occupations of civil life."

17. *Muller v. Oregon* (1908).

18. The court returned to *Muller* in the *Radice v. New York* (1924) decision made the same year. For a useful discussion of the characteristics distinguishing the social reform activists' understanding of gender difference, that of the lawyers' who represented them, and the legal discourse promulgated by the court as well, see Lipschultz 1991, 209–28. See also Erickson 1982, 155–87.

19. Parkinson 1923, 131–36 (131), as Baer 1991, 24.

20. Barrett 1987, 107.

21. Brenner 1996, 27.

22. Costello and Krimgold 1996, 339, 327.

23. Herz and Wootton 1996, 64–65.

24. Fuchs 1988, 14.

25. Rupp and Taylor 1987. See also Lynn 1992.

26. *Reed v. Reed* (1971).

27. Deborah Rhode writes that in "some jurisdictions, wages fell an estimated one-third to one-half after the decision and maximum hour laws restricted workers' ability to make up the difference" (Rhode 1989, 43).

28. These questions fill corpulent law school texts on sex discrimination. See, for instance, Frug 1992 and Babcock 1975. Good texts covering the range of constitutional and statutory law regarding sex discrimination used in undergraduate classrooms include Goldstein 1979, 1988; Baer 1991.

29. Bem 1993. See also Eisenstein 1988. See also the related discussion of the "reasonable man" standard in Unikel 1992, 326–75.

30. *General Electric Company v. Martha Gilbert* (1976).

31. *EEOC v. Sears, Roebuck & Co.* (1986; 1988). See Schultz 1992, 298.

32. See Kimberlé Crenshaw's discussion of the General Motors Case in Crenshaw 1988, 1331–87. Crenshaw's discussion of intersectionality and the historical construction of racial tropes that work differently for white women and women of color also helps to counter essentialist thinking (Crenshaw 1992; 1989; 1991, 1241–99). See Eisenstein 1994.

33. See *San Antonio Independent School District v. Rodriguez* (1973); *Lindsey v. Normet* (1972); and *Dandridge v. Williams* (1970).

34. This is, of course, a central concern of critical legal studies.

35. Tarrow 1994, 18. Providing a synthesis of a large body of literature, Sidney Tarrow defines the structure of political opportunity as "consistent—but not necessarily formal or permanent—dimensions of the political environment that provide incentives for people to undertake collective action by affecting their expectations for success or failure" (Tarrow 1994). Tarrow draws on Eisinger 1973, 11–28. See also Tarrow 1989; Kitschelt 1986, 57–85; Tilly, Tilly, and Tilly 1975, 254; Meyer 1995b; Costain 1992; Kriesi, Koopmans, Dyvendak, and Giugni 1995; and McAdam, McCarthy, and Zald 1996. Political process theory also stressed external opportunities stipulating that social movement organization is related to the receptivity of external institutions or processes. See McAdam 1982. The focus on political opportunity along with the focus on resource mobilization shifted the study of social movements away from grievances (widely held and often existing in the absence of activism), arguing that opportunities can better explain why only some groups are able to transpose an aggrieved group of people into an organized movement able to secure the attention of political elites. But see the interesting discussion on the "comeback" of grievances in the analysis of social movements and the comparison of the nuclear energy issue in different European states in Kriesi, Koopmans, Dyvendak, and Guigni 1995, 145–64.

36. As William Gamson and David Meyer argue, movements create opportunities as well as exploit them. See Gamson and Meyer 1996. See also Tarrow 1994, 81–99, his chapter on "seizing and making opportunities." The civil

rights movement, Gamson and Meyer note, by working for voting rights enlarged the political opportunities for future generations. They propose a schema that distinguishes between relatively volatile and relatively enduring aspects of the political system, and between cultural and institutional characteristics, in order to specify what makes movements more or less able to shape the opportunities before them, sharpening the analysis of social movements as agents of change.

37. See Meyer 1995a, 173–92. See the unpublished paper by Sawyers and Meyer 1993. For example, it is not for lack of opportunity in this day of catalog shopping and mail-order gun purchases that women's movements rarely utilize violence. An explanation of the fact that women sometimes employ terrorist methods when they participate in male-led revolutionary or nationalist movements but not in feminist movements requires going beyond "opportunities" to an understanding of the normative environment within which activists operate.

38. Banaszak 1996, 41. In her interesting study, she describes the Swiss and American suffrage movements as confronted with similar opportunities but as operating in different ways because of the different values, beliefs, and preferences activists held.

39. See also Jane Jenson's discussion of the interactive effect of constitutions and ethnic/nationalist identity formation (Jenson 1995), Eisenstein 1988. Eyerman and Jamison 1991.

40. Costain 1992, 98–99, 137–38.

41. Robert O. Keohane defines institutions as "persistent and connected sets of rules (formal and informal) that prescribe behavioral roles, constrain activity, and shape expectations" (Keohane 1989, 3). See also Peter Hall's definition of institutions as "the formal rules, compliance procedures and standard operating practices that structure the relationship between individuals in various units of the polity and economy" (cited in Thelen and Steinmo 1992, 2).

42. Powell and DiMaggio 1992, 1.

43. March and Olsen 1989.

44. The renewed interest in institutions has generated such an outpouring of studies that there is now a growing "literature about the literature." W. Richard Scott's *Institutions and Organizations* provides a particularly clear and comprehensive analysis. Scott suggests (although I am necessarily oversimplifying his summary here) that scholarship about institutions rests on three "pillars." The economists tend to stress the regulative function of institutions; the early sociologists and some recent political scientists emphasize the normative character of institutional life; and much recent sociology stresses the cognitive work that goes on within institutions. Regulative approaches discuss how institutions constrain and regularize behavior (Scott 1995, 35). Institutions thought to be based on normative systems define goals and appropriate means governing behavior. According to normative frameworks, institutions constrain but they also enable, Scott notes (37–38). Scott writes that "Cognitive theorists emphasize the extent to which choice is informed and constrained by the ways in which knowledge is constructed" (51). Scott also discusses three types of institutional carriers (cultures, regimes, and organizations) and six kinds of levels of analysis at which the study of institutions is carried out. He locates various schools of

institutional theory in these classifications (e.g., economists, economic historians, historical institutionalists, traditional sociologists, newer cognitive sociologists, neo-institutional economists). The tables in chapter 3 provide a brilliant synthesis of a huge amount of literature (Scott 1995). See also the useful review by Hall and Taylor, 1996. Describing historical institutionalism in terms that are similar to the political opportunity emphasis of social movement theory, Hall and Taylor note that historical institutionalism (one of the three schools of institutionalism they review) finds explanations for distinct national outcomes in "the way the institutional organization of the polity and economy structures conflict so as to privilege some interests while demobilizing others" (6).

45. See Aggarwal 1985, Tsebelis 1990.

46. Meyer 1995c.

47. Discussion with historian, Professor Mary Beth Norton, 3 November 1996. See also Zinsser 1993.

48. For an enumeration of the questions that institutional analysis takes up, see Scott 1995, xiii–ix.

49. There is now a large body of literature on gendered management styles. See, for instance, Rosabeth Moss Kanter's classic, *Women and Men of the Corporation* (Kanter 1977). There is another body of literature about the incompatibility of bureaucracy and egalitarian norms and practices. See, for instance, Ferguson 1984. Many studies explore the attempts of feminists to create alternative organizational models. See Martin 1990, 182–206; and Ferree and Martin 1995. Some additional useful studies include Franzway, Court, and Connell 1989; Savage and Witz 1992; and Mills and Tancred 1990. In an overview of gender and organizational studies, Karen M. Hult states that "for all the[ir] richness, diversity, and insight," many studies make arguments that are inapplicable to large organizations and many do not differentiate nongovernmental from governmental organizations (Hult 1995, 128–42). In the genre of organizational studies, there are some extremely interesting analyses of those who are at odds with the organizational culture or who challenge organizational policies, but they often focus on individual experience, perception, and purposes rather than on collective efforts at organizational change. See, for instance, Meyerson and Scully 1995, 585–600.

50. Historical studies that ask how past policies provide or foreclose opportunities for particular class, occupational, or group actors to influence subsequent policy processes offer one way of thinking about institutional activism. Victoria Hattam, for instance, describes how differences in the British and American courts produced different labor union strategies both by affording workers distinct political opportunities and also by shaping how workers understood their interests (Hattam 1992, 188–217). Sociologists tend to be more interested in issues of identity construction. Yasemin Soysal, for instance, looks at how the diffusion of international norms of citizenship growing out of the ascendant attention to human rights reshapes national identities such that nations that might otherwise repudiate migrant rights undertake the incorporation of migrants into national polities. Although she does not focus on agency (the role that activists play in the policy process), her analysis suggests that the remaking of citizenship identities in the face of international understandings about migrant

rights provided opportunities for the exertion of political influence on behalf of domestic exponents of migrant rights (Soysal 1994). Opportunities and identities come together in critical ways in this mode of institutional analysis.

51. No note can do justice to what are now whole libraries of material on the analysis of the origins of gender inequality. A sample: For a discussion of the biological bases (or lack thereof) of gender difference, including debates over essentialism, see Rich 1976; Fuss 1989; Smith 1994; Nicholson 1990; Harding 1986, 1991. For a discussion of the materialist and psychological or object-relations underpinnings of standpoint theory as discussed both in terms of gender difference and race difference, see Hartsock 1985; Hirschmann 1992; Collins 1991; Spelman 1988. On discursive accounts, see Riley 1988; Butler 1990; Fuss 1989.

52. Drawing on the work of Thomas Metzger, David Laitin observes that in any given culture there are "diverse strands of opinion and conflicting values." To understand a culture, Laitin proposes, it is necessary to understand not so much what is agreed upon as what are common points of concern. Metzger 1977; Laitin 1988, 589.

53. Jeffords's portrayal of the post-1960s rediscovery of Vietnam and Faludi's account of a broad societal backlash focus on the ideological encounter between feminist ideas and the view of feminism as the preeminent threat to "traditional American values." Jeffords argues that nationalism is interlaced with the reassertion of masculinity (Jeffords 1989; Faludi 1991).

54. Social movement theory has long talked about informal networks as crucial to recruitment of movement activists and supporters. See McAdam 1982. See also Whittier 1995.

55. Lipsky 1968, 1144-58.

56. Within the literature on feminism, there are now a number of excellent discussions of movement activists engaging with state institutions or operating within these institutions. See in particular Eisenstein 1996; Reinelt 1995, 84-104; and Spalter-Roth and Schreiber 1995, 105-28. See also Scott 1981 and Merton 1972, 9-47. For an important critique of the kind of argument presented here, see Piven and Cloward 1992.

57. Goffman 1961; Coser 1974; and Segal 1986, 1995.

58. Referring to the definition of outsider status as designating those who mobilize on behalf of new, previously unmobilized constituencies, they cite Gamson 1990, 16. Referring to the definition of outsiders as those without formal representation, Burstein, Einwohner, and Hollander 1995 cite Tilly 1984, 306.

59. Burstein, Einwohner, and Hollander 1995, 278. McAdam 1982.

60. Although activist groups could also be described as having different degrees of "autonomy," it is probably more accurate to speak of multi-institutional accountability, since activists are financially, organizationally, and discursively dependent on *some* group or network that is part of *some* institutional environment, if not the one to which it is most closely tied. This is the Foucauldian point about there being no "outside" a system of organizations and ideas.

61. Mansbridge 1995, 27-35.

62. Eisenstein 1995, 74-75.

63. Collins 1991.
64. Reinelt 1995, 84–104; Morgen 1990, 169–73.
65. Reinelt 1995, 101. See also Spalter-Roth and Schreiber 1995, 105–28.
66. Gilkes 1988, 53–76.
67. Díaz-Cotto 1996.
68. In fact, mainstream occupations may or may not be consonant with continued political activism. Tom Hayden, a former leader of the Students for a Democratic Society, became active in grassroots California politics and then in the Democratic Party. Bernadine Dohrn was the head of the Central Committee of the Weather Underground. A lawyer, she now runs an institute on juvenile justice at Northwestern University. Tom Jones, one of the African-American student leaders (photographed emerging from the student union carrying guns) in the Willard Straight Takeover at Cornell University in 1969 is now a highly positioned manager of the investment umbrella group TIAA-CREF.
69. Sidney Tarrow notes, for instance, the role played by the student movement in Italy; he writes that the student movement was ". . . part of a cultural transformation that would 'light new fires', in Touraine's image, and act as the University detachment of a 'revolutionary workers' party that does not exist' in Schnapp and Vidal-Naquet's equally picturesque language . . ." (Tarrow 1989a, 166).
70. Morris 1992, 370–71.
71. Taylor 1989, 761–75.
72. Martin 1988, 9–10.

CHAPTER THREE
INTEREST-GROUP ACTIVISM

1. Morden 1990, 214; Holm 1992, 192.
2. The Defense Advisory Committee on Women in the Services (DACOWITS) is reachable through the Pentagon switchboard. The Women's Research and Education Institute (WREI), 1700 18th Street, NW, Suite 400, Washington, DC 20009, (202) 328–7070, publishes regular reports on women in the military. The Servicemembers Legal Defense Network, codirected by Michelle M. Benecke, Esq., and C. Dixon Osburn, Esq., monitors the infringement of rights of uniformed men and women charged with or suspected of being gay or lesbian: P.O. Box 53013, Washington, DC 20009 (sldn1@aol.com). Dr. Linda Grant De Pauw edits *Minerva*: 20 Granada Road, Pasadena, MD 21122 (minervacen@aol.com). WANDAS Fund and WANDAS Watch contacts are Susan Barnes and Wendy Davis (susanatty@aol.com and denver-wend@aol.com); WANDAS is located in Denver at 1410 Grant St. Ste A-101, Denver, CO 80203. Nancy Duff Campbell, copresident at the National Women's Law Center, 11 Dupont Circle, NW, Washington, DC 20036. The staff attorneys at the ACLU Women's Rights Project have also served in a critical role in important discrimination cases. A civilian network of military counselors that dates back to the Vietnam War–era GI coffeehouses is known as the GI Rights Network; they also counsel military women (1-800-FYI 95GI).

3. Interview by author with Mark Forman, 24 April 1992. The following account is based on interviews with Forman, Lisa Moreno of Representative Pat Schroeder's Office, Carolyn Becraft, Nancy Buermeyer, Michelle Benecke, Lieutenant Colonel M. C. Pruitt, DACOWITS director, and several servicemembers who wished to remain unidentified, as well as the cited newspaper accounts.

4. U.S. Congress, Title 10, U.S.C. 6015 (applying to the navy and marine corps) and 8549 (applying to the air force) dating from 1948 stated that women may not be assigned to aircraft engaged in combat missions.

5. DACOWITS had first recommended repeal of the combat exclusion rules in 1969. "News Briefs" 1995, 9.

6. Thirty-two thousand is the figure cited by Gomez 1991, 6–7. See also Presidential Commission 1992; Jeanne Holm reports that Desert Storm Department of Defense figures at last tabulation were 40,782, 7 percent of those deployed (Holm 1992).

7. Spelts 1991, 1–5; also "News Briefs" 1995, 6; Ralston 1991, 52–62.

8. As Jeanne Holm's account reminds us, Major Marie T. Rossi had been interviewed on CNN, 24 February 1991, before her Chinook helicopter crashed in bad weather. "Sometimes you have to disassociate how you feel personally about the prospect of going into war and . . . possibly see the death that is going to be out there. But . . . this is the moment that everybody trains for . . . —that I've trained for—so I feel ready to meet the challenge" (Holm 1992, 460). See also Enloe 1990.

9. Ibid., 477.

10. Ibid., 445–49.

11. For a comparison of the gay/lesbian ban with the combat exclusion and the role of "mortal sacrifice," see Katzenstein 1996.

12. Army soldier Melissa Rathbun-Nealy was captured on 31 January when her flatbed truck came under fire close to the Saudi Arabia–Kuwait border. Interview by author with Carolyn Becraft, February 1991.

13. Senator John McCain, Republican from Arizona, had commented to colleagues that women should be able to pilot combat planes and serve on combatant ships (Holm 1992, 474). McCain was subsequently to oppose the repeal bill. Air force personnel chief Lieutenant General Thomas J. Hickey also indicated that it was only the law that was preventing women from acceding to jobs they were perfectly capable of performing (475).

14. H.R. 2100.

15. U.S. Senate 1991, 45.

16. Senators John Glenn and Sam Nunn led the opposition. Reportedly Schlafly's promise of support for the next electoral campaign of Senator John McCain led him to reverse his earlier endorsement of the legislation. Senator Glenn had also earlier indicated that he might support such legislation, commenting that female pilots "have proven themselves to be just as capable as men," and that "a good case could be made that women should not be barred from flying any aircraft for which they can qualify" (Gellman 1991a and 1991b). But Senator Glenn later led the opposition recommendation for a National Commission that he hoped would forestall a vote on the Roth bill.

17. McConagha 1991, A10; as quoted in Holm 1992, 480.

18. Becraft's group and the Women Military Aviators not only organized the logistics; equally important was the fact that such groups can brace individuals who face potential recrimination and need to know that there is strength in numbers—hence the importance of *organized* activism.

19. Heather Wilson graduated from the third Air Force Academy class to accept women as a vice wing commander, the second-ranking position for a cadet. She went to Oxford as a Rhodes Scholar, where she won a seat as a rower on Oxford's international caliber Blue Boat. She served as director for European defense policy and arms control on the National Security Council.

20. Prepared by Carolyn Becraft (Becraft 1991).

21. There was a core group of about eight to ten pilots. Somewhere between fifteen and thirty military women did the rounds of congressional offices.

22. General Merrill McPeak, chief of staff of the air force, had conceded that women and men have a "similar or identical ability to pull Gs." He went on to say that it was the law (not women's differential abilities) that was preventing women from serving in air combat positions—law that, given his "personal prejudice," he found comforting. See response to Senator Cohen, 18 June 1991 (U.S. Senate 1991).

23. As related by Forman, 24 April 1992. The exclusion policy, it appears, has led some of the service's best women pilots to leave the military (Gellman 1991b, 1).

24. According to a *New York Times* report, "Pentagon spokesman, Pete Williams, said last week, 'The Department welcomes this legislation because it gives the Department of Defense the authority to decide where the line should be drawn rather than having Congress set the limits on the role of women in combat'" (Schmitt 1991, 32).

25. See Presidential Commission on the Assignment of Women in the Armed Forces 1992. The commission did delay Pentagon action, taken finally in spring 1993.

26. Interview by author with Colonel M. C. Pruitt (USAF), 29 October 1995.

27. According to some navy women who were on the Hill, air force women were told not to appear, then not to appear in uniform. Mostly there were navy and army aviators. Only one air force woman was there—a woman in the reserves.

28. According to Carolyn Becraft, military aviators were poised to bring the issue of combat exclusion to the courts. This was a case, Becraft said, of "being all dressed up with nowhere to go." Military women needed to do something if their careers as aviators were not to be permanently attenuated by the foreclosure that combat exclusion imposed (Berkshire Conference on Women's History, 1993: "Roundtable on Citizenship, Gender and Militarization: Comparing South Africa and American Perspectives," panel discussion, 11–13 June).

29. As mentioned earlier, numerous studies over the years of women in the military had been conducted, and there was nothing in the mandate of this legislation that suggested this would cover new territory. Feminists also feared, rightly, that the commission would be filled with conservative Bush appointees. Elaine Donnelly of the Coalition for Military Readiness, a Phyllis Schlafly

associate, was one of a five-person bloc on the commission. Another was retired marine corps general Ronald Ray, who later described sitting on the commission seeking "direction from the Bible. I am keenly aware that these two world views, feminism and Christianity, are in opposition" (Zimmerman 1995, 139).

30. The line components are sometimes, mistakenly, referred to as the women's "auxiliaries." During World War II, as part of the mobilization effort, women in the navy held reserve status whereas army women telephone operators, for instance, were civilian. The 1948 Women's Armed Services Integration Act authorized the continuation of the segregated Women's Army Corps (WAC), to which all army women except nurses and medical specialists were assigned. The Women Accepted for Volunteer Emergency Service (WAVES), which included navy and marine women, and the Women Airforce Service Pilots (WASPs) were also covered by different promotional procedures although they were not officially, like the WACs, in a segregated corps. For a brief and very clear history, see Segal 1989, 102–24.

31. Morden 1990, 3.

32. Women have, as Binkin and Bach note, served in civilian status in earlier times as "nurses, cooks, laundresses, seamstresses and other acceptable feminine pursuits" (Binkin and Bach 1977, 5). Enloe notes that women have also served as mothers, wives, sweethearts, prostitutes (1983). In World War I, the navy and marine corps utilized women as telephone operators and clerical workers, according them military rank and status, but they were demobilized immediately after the war.

33. Morden 1990, 19.

34. Ibid., 33

35. Morden writes that Colonel Hobby, for instance, urged the rapid demobilization of women, concerned that women return quickly to find civilian jobs since their military status was not assured and since they had no reemployment rights (ibid., 26).

36. Holm 1982, 1992, 195–96.

37. Holm 1992, 183–84.

38. During World War II, in the early planning stages of the women's services, the navy in particular sought to demonstrate the well-heeled character of its recruiting efforts. The leadership was chosen from women's colleges. Virginia Gildersleeve, dean of Barnard College, headed an advisory council on the recruitment and training of women. The Midship School for officer training was established at Smith College and later at Mount Holyoke. Training for enlisted women was set up at Hunter College. Mildred McAfee, president of Wellesley, was selected to head the WAVES.

39. See Morden's description of General Elizabeth P. Hoisington, WAC director (Morden 1990, 233, 240).

40. Ibid., 403

41. Ibid., 233, 393.

42. She did, however, support the end of the WAVES as a separate women's service, commenting that even the term implied a notion of a ladies auxiliary. Holm 1992, 280–81.

43. Helen Rogan's assessment is based on her interviews with former WACs in Rogan 1981, 156.

44. Interview by author with Evelyn P. Foote, May 1989.

45. Molyneux 1985, 227–55.

46. Holm 1993, 193.

47. Katzenstein 1990b, 174.

48. Hoffman papers. As it turned out, the committee had little effect in mobilizing the desired numbers or "quality" of women for military duty during the Korean War. The intention had been to recruit 72,000 additional women. Only 6,000 came forward (Holm 1982, 151; Mitchell 1989, 19).

49. Eastman 1972. In 1975, an *Air Force Times* article reporting on DACOWITS's requesting a tour of military academies which were claiming that they did not have the facilities to handle women students noted that DACOWITS ". . . is becoming more militant" ("DACOWITS Fired Up" 1975, 4). In 1980, the *Air Force Times* ran a piece headed, significantly, "DACOWITS Gaining New Clout" (1980, 15).

50. Mitchell 1989, 127.

51. Air force major general Jeanne Holm was the one director who supported integration.

52. "DACOWITS Fired Up" 1975, 4.

53. Retired major general Jeanne Holm of the air force, one of the widely recognized advocates of women's interests, was appointed in 1977. Judith Hicks Stiehm, an academic who worked on gender and military issues, was also appointed in this period. In the 1950s, the women appointees tended to be wives of illustrious men; by the 1970s, women appointees were high-powered women drawn from corporate circles, Washingtonian or state government networks, and occasionally from academia (Cutler 1982, 21).

54. Interview by author with M. Kathleen Carpenter, May 1989.

55. The committee urged that women be appointed to the Court of Military Appeals, that they be assigned to Minuteman and Titan missile crews, and that women's uniforms and equipment be redesigned. They criticized the lack of privacy in barracks and campaigned to legalize abortions in military hospitals. The committee reported during much of the 1980s and into the middle of the 1990s to the office of the secretary of defense (through the assistant secretary of defense for force management and personnel).

56. Defense Advisory Committee n.d.

57. Mitchell 1989, 94.

58. Interview by author with M. Kathleen Carpenter, May 1989.

59. Another of Carpenter's dramatic ventures was her inquiry into complaints that military boots issued to women were causing serious foot injuries. Many dismissed these complaints as women's whining. Carpenter visited the Philadelphia factory that produced the last on which women's boots were fitted, demanding to see the last and confirming that men's lasts were being used to make women's boots.

60. Respondent 1.

61. Ibid.

62. Stiehm 1989, 55–56.

63. Judith Stiehm writes, "Some might attribute the absence of backlash in the Navy's accessions to its successful resistance to earlier forces for change, but even the Navy had increased women enlisted personnel from about 6,000 in 1972 to almost 30,000 in 1980" (ibid., 57).

64. Ibid., 129–30.

65. Holm 1982, 409–10.

66. Interview by author with Colonel Diane Ordes (USAF), 15 May 1989. See also Holm 1993, 405.

67. The press, according to Judith Stiehm, labeled the army's retrenchment "womanpause" (Stiehm 1989, 65–66).

68. Ibid., 125.

69. During the mid- to late 1980s, for example, Captain Kathy Bruyere of the OP-O1W office (where she was special assistant for women's policy), Captain Patricia Gormley (a lawyer with the Inspector General's Office), and Captain Jill Usher in the Equal Opportunity Office constituted an energetic trio that "worked" the institution from the inside.

70. The association began as an informal network in 1978 that met periodically to host luncheons at which speakers were asked to address issues of concern to navy/marine women. In January 1984, WOPA incorporated and a formal board of directors was installed. WOPA's charter identifies several organizational purposes. It is intended to (and does successfully) facilitate the fostering of contacts and advisory networks that are helpful in guiding younger officers to appropriate career choices. At the informal gatherings, WOPA members also find support, fellowship, and a chance to air questions about work issues that are not easily discussed in the office context or brought up with the chain of command—issues such as women's uniforms, sexual harassment, and pregnancy policy. In addition, the more formally scheduled speeches serve an informational function and have at times galvanized political consciousness around gender issues. In addition to the "Lehman event" described a bit later in the text, there was a smaller-scale controversy around the remarks by assistant secretary of the navy for manpower and reserve affairs Chase Untermeyer, who stressed the suitability of women for staff duty in the Pentagon in the face of the ban, then in existence, against women's serving on combat and many combat support ships (Purcell 1984, 28).

71. During the 1980s, the other services also had organizations designed to bring active-duty and retired military women together, but there were none quite comparable in levels of activism to WOPA. The Women's Army Corps holds a biennial reunion for active-duty and retired army women at Fort McClellan, attended by about seven hundred women; but they do not generally address themselves to current issues about gender and military policy (Rogan 1981, 162–64); the Women's Marines Association (WMA), founded in 1960, meets biannually. There are now a number of organizations of women Vietnam veterans groups; see Gigowski 1985, 17–20. Organizations such as the Women's Military Pilot Association were few in number and relatively low-profile. WOPA's early organization seemed due not to women's grievances

being more severe than those of their counterparts in the other services or to the absence of consciousness of gender inequities in the other services. Rather, as Carolyn Becraft, formerly the director of the Women in the Military Project at the Women's Equity Action League (WEAL) argues: Women officers in the navy are stationed on either coast, close to each other, and there is a relatively large cluster of women assigned to Washington for somewhat extensive periods. Navy women, therefore, get to know each other in more familiar ways, and the possibilities of a network's forming are thus substantially enhanced.

72. Another organization that was very active in the 1980s was the Ex-Spouses of Servicemen/women for Equality (EXPOSE), which fought to secure equity in military pensions. Because wives generally followed their military husbands to new assignments, moving frequently, few had a chance to establish long-term jobs or careers. The economic devastation of divorce for women married to servicemen was particularly acute. Congresswomen Patricia Schroeder worked hard to support legislation intended to allow military spouses (which, in the 1980s, meant primarily wives) to share in pensions in the event of divorce. There was also extensive litigation over this issue. Other women's movement organizations have addressed issues of domestic violence on military bases.

73. See, for example, the *Air Force Times* article from 1973, "Ladies May Get More Back Pay," that appears next to a large photo of Patricia Barrett, *Penthouse*'s "Pet of the Year" in a "fetching pose" ("Ladies" 1973, 3). See also the photo in *Soldiers* of the "Playmate" Surrey Marsha (courtesy *Playboy*) on the inside back cover of the March 1975 issue. By 1980, *Soldiers* was running a full-length story on "The Army's Assault on Sexism" (Bant 1980, 6–10). At the same time in the early 1970s as the service papers were running pinups, carrying sexist cartoons, and reporting on the military's efforts to recruit more "ladies" or "gals," they were also covering the *Frontiero v. Richardson* (1973) case and reporting on the Equal Rights Amendment controversy and on the availability of abortions, among other feminist issues. See Cavanaugh 1973, 5–7; on "gals," see "Holm Outlines Women's Role" 1973, 6; "Abortions to Increase" 1973, x; Foster 1973, 18. By the 1980s, pinups had disappeared, as had references to "gals"; and articles on women's numbers, promotions, and gender equality issues were standard fare. I am grateful to Jill Lepore for reading hours of microfilm of the *Air Force Times* and reporting to me on the changes in tone, language, and subject matter that she observed.

74. Correspondents, during the 1980s, regularly covering women and military issues included Richard Halloran and Eric Schmitt of the *New York Times*, and Molly Moore of the *Washington Post*. Rosemary Purcell reported on women's issues for the *Navy Times* for much of the first half of the 1980s.

75. Removed from the hub of lobbying activity, the journal is the creation of a full-time academic and historian, Linda Grant Depauw, who teaches at George Washington University. First published in March 1983, the journal is produced from Depauw's home. For many years a one-person operation, it has, nevertheless, a sizable circulation of between five and six hundred (one-third to libraries) and is an important source in keeping readers current on issues, events, and debates coming from a broad cross-section of political viewpoints. The journal's

ideology is summed up on every cover in its description of the publication's logo:

Helmeted, golden-haired Minerva was the Roman goddess of war and wisdom. Her presence on a battlefield meant that the contest would be decided by sound strategy, cool courage, and military skill rather than by sheer animal strength and blood lust, the qualities represented by Mars, the god of battle. Unlike Mars, Minerva took no pleasure in combat and did not exult in victory. . . . Minerva's broad intellectual interests embraced all the arts and sciences; she brought special inspiration to poets and orators, and she took a keen interest in spinning, weaving, and sewing—activities symbolic of networking.

Minerva does not take policy positions, and Depauw is not involved in the policy-making network. Its self-described mission is to bridge the concerns of uniformed women, military spouses, civilian academics, and defense analysts and even conscientious objectors and peace activists. Any given issue may include historical articles on women's role in earlier military encounters, a present-day study, for instance, of sexual harassment on the job, an update on the last DACOWITS meeting, a book review of an antimilitarist text; its politics are eclectic. As Linda Grant Depauw describes her intentions:

Minerva is an intellectual enterprise. I see things in broad contexts. I tend to see many sides—not just one, two, but many. I simply believe that providing information and encouraging thinking benefits everyone. Feminist academics are skeptical of anything involving the military which to them smacks of militarism. I have been a member of WEAL; I haven't ever really been active. I give money to various causes. But from what I can see as an outsider, the politics [of feminism] have been fierce. (Interview by author with Linda Grant Depauw, 25 April 1992)

Describing the links between her decision to undertake *Minerva* and feminism in the early 1980s, DePauw commented, " I was a historian. When I started learning about women's history I was fascinated. In those days, as these things were opening up, you just *were* a feminist. The intellectual challenge was so great and the military seemed like the last frontier."

76. When I interviewed WOPA members in the late 1980s, they observed that the navy's recognition of the politicizing potential of the group was evident from the rapid reaction at top levels that fences needed mending after the Lehman presentation. This recognition is also evident in the attempts sometimes made at lower levels of the bureaucracy to discourage servicewomen from joining WOPA. A number of WOPA members report that their immediate supervisors or those of their nonmember colleagues were less than supportive when they expressed an interest in attending WOPA luncheon meetings. According to some WOPA members, marine women in particular were in that period (late 1980s) discouraged from joining.

77. DACOWITS Conference Query/Reply 1984.

78. Maze 1984, 9.

79. The *Navy Times* reported the dismayed reactions of navy women. See Purcell 1982, 2. According to a *Navy Times* report, Gregory L. Vistica's book *Fall from Glory: The Men who Sank the U.S. Navy* (1995) claims that Lehman, "a reserve bombardier-navigator" who continued to fly as a weekend warrior even while he was Navy secretary," was complicit in the kind of sexual misconduct that was exposed in Tailhook '91. Vistica mentions two eyewitnesses who "described Lehman entering one of the squadron suites where a stripper was performing and participating in her performance." "That's what I call leadership," the *Navy Times* quotes from Vistica's eyewitnesses. "It's just the wrong kind" (Pexton 1996, 8).

80. Brownmiller 1975, 15.

81. Davis 1987, 3.

82. Davis and Carolyn Becraft from WEAL testified before the Military and Personnel Subcommittee of the Committee on Armed Services in the House of Representatives.

83. Chief of Naval Operations 1988; Chief of Naval Operations 1991.

84. Respondent 3.

85. On the early days of WEAL, see Parr 1983, 238–50.

86. Interview by author with Colonel Diane Ordes (USAF), 15 May 1989.

87. "Bring Me Men," is taken from a poem by Sam Walter Foss entitled "The Coming American." The ramp is where cadets march going to and from the parade ground, where first-year students initially enter, and where cadets are picked up or discharged by car. The phrase is taken from a subsection of the poem that reads, "Bring me men to match my mountains; / Bring me men to match my plains, / Men with Empires in their purpose, / and new eras in their brains." The poem itself begins, "On the Fourth of July we all love to dilate, /With the thought that we are all inexpressibly great; / That we're all legatees of fate's fairest bequest, / And that destiny's egg has been laid in our nest;/That we've climbed up the sides, up the roof, and sublime, / We stand on the top of the ridge-pole of time." Members of the Air Force Academy have at times suggested that the poem's quality or the claim that tradition would be shattered offer weak grounds for preserving the maxim.

88. Burke 1992, 18–20. Although Burke's article was denounced by the academy administration at a faculty meeting, the publicity her material received has meant that the proscription on the use of these kinds of marching chants or ditties (whether "playful" or official) is, at least for now, being enforced (according to one faculty member who asked not to be cited by name).

89. Burke 1996, 209.

90. Roush 1997, 42–44. Followers of Webb at the Naval Academy refer to themselves as Webb-ites. Webb's article in the November 1975 issue of the *Washingtonian*, "Women Can't Fight," has become by some accounts something of an icon among many male midshipmen at the academy (Webb 1975, 142–82). The exchange of letters following the Roush article in the subsequent issues of the 1997 *Proceedings* gives a sense of how fractious and intense the debate over the gender-integrated military still is.

91. Levi and Edwards 1990, 141–73. Available from the Institute of European Studies, Uris Hall, Cornell, Ithaca, NY 14853.

92. See Schneider and Schneider interviews with Carolyn Becraft, Washington, DC, 25 April 1985, stored in Schlesinger Library, Radcliffe College.

93. Becraft 1978.

94. Ibid., 6.

95. Interview by author with Captain Georgia Sadler (USN—ret.), 5 May 1992.

96. Ibid. Under pressure from Admiral Zumwalt, Sadler was accepted as the first woman professor at the Naval Academy. At the time (the early 1970s) officers at the academy ate in Bancroft Hall, where women were permitted only at holidays. The matter of admitting women to the officers' dining facility then had to be taken up with the superintendent.

97. Ibid.

98. Interview by author with Captain Carolyn Prevatte (USN—ret.), 13 November 1995.

99. On the early days of WEAL, before Becraft's tenure, see Parr 1983, 238–50.

100. When efforts to block Webb's appointment failed and he subsequently took office, Becraft arranged for a meeting in order to impress upon him the seriousness of military women's concerns. In their conversation she insisted that his term as secretary was set to fail unless he did better by navy women than had his predecessors or than his own reputation might predict. As Becraft told it, "it was an offer he couldn't refuse." Two months before Webb resigned, he had "nearly tripled to fifteen thousand the number of seagoing combat support jobs open to women . . . and ordered a Navy-wide crackdown on sexual harassment" (interview by author with Carolyn Becraft, May 1989). See also Timberg 1995.

101. Doreen Celli had been prevented from testing submarine repairs at sea and thus from advancement in her job by the navy's policy barring civilian women from submarines (WEAL Washington Report 1987). WEAL also regularly filed amicus briefs—including one in an important case involving an ex-military spouse who sought a share of her former husband's pension after their twenty-three-year marriage ended (Edwards 1988, 8). Becraft testified at numerous hearings of the House Committee on Armed Services on the issues of military wives, combat exclusion, harassment, prostitution, and numerous others. See, for instance, the Hearings before the Military Personnel and Compensation Subcommittee of the Committee on Armed Services, House of Representatives, 1 October, 19 November 19 1987 and 4 February 1988 (U.S. House 1988).

102. Quoted in Jowers 1992, 60.

103. Interview by author with Carolyn Becraft, May 1989. Becraft also mentions that she decided not to touch the issue of women's needing a high school diploma for entry to the services, whereas men do not, on the same logic—that it was not a winning issue.

104. Discussion by author with Colonel M. C. Pruitt (USAF) and Captain Carolyn Prevatte (USN—ret.), 13 November 1995.

105. Katzenstein 1990b, 175.

106. One appointee, described by a fellow committee member as "from the Eagle Forum camp," was clearly ready to support the curtailment of women's

integration. But the committee as a whole vociferously resisted retrenchment. Instead, the committee criticized the army review group for failing to keep DACOWITS informed of its deliberations; it berated the services for the sinking morale of military women during this period of what the press had labeled "womanpause"; and after reviewing the published WITA report, DACOWITS charged the army with a lack of objectivity and an attempt to reach its own pre-ordained conclusions. See the letter to Defense Secretary Weinberger from the chair of DACOWITS, Dr. Mary Evelyn Bragg Huey, as quoted in Stiehm 1989, 65–66.

107. Davis was then executive vice president at the Institute for Foreign Policy Analysis in Cambridge, Massachusetts. See the résumé of her background in *Minerva* (Spring 1986): 82–83. See also Ferrey 1987, 36.

108. After every meeting, for instance, the committee issues requests for information that obligate the services to investigate a situation and provide the relevant data. At the spring 1989 conference, for instance, twenty-three requests for information were issued, including one asking for a briefing on how the Department of Defense recommendations related to combat exclusion issues were being implemented, a request that the coast guard provide a written report regarding the possible limitation of women's assignment to ships, a request for a written report from the marine corps on the possible limitation on women's assignments to foreign missions because of presumed inadequacy of housing, etc. These very specific requests for information keep the services "on their toes" and regularly unearth problem areas that are then hard for the services to ignore. The committee also issues specific recommendations and expressions of "continuing concern."

109. The full committee meets twice yearly; the executive committee quarterly; the subcommittees, of which there are three (then including force utilization, career development, quality of life), meet several times a year. In addition, members make a number of visits to installations as part of the committee obligation. Members serve for a three-year term. One-third of the approximately thirty-five-member committee rotates off each year. Members are nominated by DACOWITS members, members of Congress, the White House, and Department of Defense officials. The final selection is made by the secretary of defense.

110. Memorandum to General Anthony Lukeman, USMC, from Jacquelyn K. Davis, 26 August 1987 (Davis 1987, 1).

111. Respondent 3.

112. Manning and Griffith 1998, 11–12, tables 3 and 4.

113. The committee has, more recently, attempted to assess whether the drawdown of military personnel was having a disparate impact on white women and on women of color.

114. Whether DACOWITS or other advocacy groups are representative of the concerns of military women across the ranks is a complicated issue. Laura Miller, a sociologist at the University of California at Los Angeles, observes that feminist efforts to open up combat roles to women do not represent army women in general, who, her survey work shows, often express "resentment toward officers and civilian activists who are attempting to open combat roles to women" (1995, 14). She attributes this difference between "rights-based feminist activists" and army women more generally to "social location," part of

which may be career- and job-related. Three-quarters of all women, according to Miller's data "support allowing women who are interested to *volunteer* [emphasis in original] for the combat arms" (15). This suggests, I would argue, that a clear majority of enlistees *do* accept the "rights-based" aspect of the feminist position. What makes rights-based feminism nonrepresentative, then, is that most women do not want to be assigned involuntarily to combat-related military occupational specialties, nor do most women wish to fight. (Rights-based feminists with whom I spoke point out that this is often the case for men as well.) What, then, *should* be the position that an organization like DACOWITS might take? Miller proposes several alternatives, arguing herself for an intermediate strategy in which rights-based feminists advocate allowing women (alone) to volunteer for the combat arms if they so qualify. (See also Mansbridge 1986, 1997, for an important analysis of gender differences across both race and class.)

115. This can be a superficial rhetorical gesture, as in the inevitable references to "race-class-and-gender." But these linguistic exigencies at least keep some attention to diversity on the table.

116. Interview by author with Ellen Press Murdoch, 10 June 1993. This shift seems to have registered with those who report on DACOWITS. See Compart 1997, 11. Compart reports that DACOWITS "has stepped up efforts to look at issues affecting black women."

117. It is important to acknowledge that raising issues about racism has not been easy. In 1988, for instance, Jacquelyn Davis, then DACOWITS chair, did address racism in her report on the committee's European trip. Her phraseology was relatively innocuous: "I have a growing impression that the race issue has not been solved by the Services. In my discussions with women of sexual harassment and discrimination, the issue of race kept coming up. Across the Services, both from a Black-White/Hispanic-White and a Black/Hispanic perspective, subtle (and not so subtle) harassment is felt. While the women to whom I spoke could not, many times, be specific, they seem to feel that 'race' plays a role in harassment situations, although it is not as noticeable a factor as is gender" (Davis 1989, 43). Parts were nonetheless expurgated by the Department of Defense before the report was officially released. Once again, the women's network saw to it that the report in its entirety was placed in the hands of the press. The *Washington Post* ran the original and censored versions of the report side by side. For a comparison of the original and expurgated reports, see the Kennedy School of Government Case Program account written by Mary Schumacher (Schumacher 1988, Exhibit 5).

118. In anticipation of the lobbying on the Hill, a number of representatives from different women's groups, including DACOWITS, met at WREI to hash out a political strategy. The NOW woman present pushed to have the issues on the table simultaneously. The other women insisted that this effort had to be single-focused, on combat. One of these women averred, "It doesn't mean that we are homophobic. It's not that we're saying we don't believe in your cause. But if we take on other issues here we will be distracted from getting what we want to get done. It's a question of having this priority . . . of facing the combat exclusion at work and not being able to do what we want to be able to do. We have to deal with this issue first" (interview by author with Colonel M. C. Pruitt, 29 October 1995). On 18 February 1993, Barbara Pope, then assistant secretary

of the navy, addressed the women naval officers at a meeting of WOPA. According to Jean Zimmerman's account, Pope indicated that she regretted that the women's issue and the gay issue were getting rolled up together. When Pope said, "We're both in uniform—but being female is not the same as being gay," Zimmerman reports that the reaction of the WOPA audience was "not just a ripple but a wave of nervous laughter" possibly because "the mere public mention of homosexuality was enough to set off the WOPA members, or else that there were enough female gay officers (present that day or in the ranks) to make Pope's denial unintentionally ironic. Perhaps the audience members couldn't help but recognize that the situation of military women and that of gay servicemembers were in almost every sense identical, from their innate marginality to the types of discrimination suffered" (Zimmerman 1995, 198–99).

119. Yard testified before the Subcommittee on Military Personnel and Compensation of the House Committee on the Armed Services, House of Representatives, 20 March 1990 when she was asked to talk about H.R. 3863 (Army Test Program of Women in Combat).

120. Michelle Benecke of the Servicemembers Legal Defense Network has remarked, however, that it is sometimes astonishing how determined lesbians in the military are, often at great risk, to insist on their identity, whether that means the display of rainbows in car windows or the use of other symbols of gay/lesbian identity.

121. There is now an enormous literature on gay and lesbian issues in the military, including autobiographies by Margarethe Cammermeyer, Joseph Steffan, and others. For an accessible way to get at the most recent studies, see the bibliography in Rimmerman 1996.

122. Phone conversation by author with Michelle Benecke, Esq., 30 October 1995.

123. There is some alliance building. Brigadier General Evelyn (Pat) Foote (USA—ret.), for instance, one of the most active and respected members of the network of women challenging sex discrimination in the military, also serves on the advisory board of the SLDN and has expressed public criticism of the homosexual exclusion. For an interview (from earlier days) with Foote, see Foote 1993, 122–29. Other military women from the network of activists on women's issues have worked behind the scenes, sometimes in coded ways. One woman, for instance, in her Christmas message to those under her command at a military base, rather than extending traditional holiday greetings to their "families" offered holiday greetings to servicemembers on the base and to "their loved ones" (while being pictured holding her cat).

124. Schlafly 1989.

125. Ibid., 8.

CHAPTER FOUR
LIVING BY THE LAW

1. Zimmerman 1995, 121.
2. Zamichow 1990, A3.
3. Hirschman 1970.

4. Olson 1965.

5. Schneider and Schneider 1988 (reprint, 1992). The transcribed interviews on which the Schneiders' study is based were generously deposited by them in the Schlesinger Library, Radlcliffe College, Cambridge, Massachusetts. Barkalow with Rabb 1990; Zimmerman 1995; Cammermeyer 1994; Humphrey 1988. See also appendix A, "I Am a Veteran," of Stiehm 1989. And see the earlier news columns over the last decades of Eric Schmitt and Barton Gellman in the *New York Times*, Molly Moore and Dana Priest in the *Washington Post*, and Tom Ricks in the *Wall Street Journal*.

6. Women in the military provide voluminous stories. They range from the daily annoyances (the male air force cadet who asks a female classmate standing by a store window, "Do you suppose a 'real' woman would like this blouse?") to the possible slander that followed the death of aviator Kara Hultgreen, whose F-14A plunged into the sea just short of its carrier landing. In official navy simulated replays of the accident, eight of nine navy F-14 pilots also crashed, although according to Charles Moskos, in his introduction to William H. McMichael's book on Tailhook, (unnamed) critics charge that these simulations were designed to make it impossible for the navy pilots to perform more successfully than Hultgreen had (McMichael 1997, xii). Hultgreen's mother released training records that showed her daughter as having graduated from flight training in the upper half of her class. Whatever the truth in this debate, another double standard clearly does exist: those who are skeptical about women's capacities to perform well as aviators refuse to engage the possibility that the many deaths of male F-14 pilots—ten in the three-year period between 1992 and 1995 (Zimmerman 1995, 294) and one pilot from the Hultgreen carrier and numerous other combat jets (Francke 1997, 257)—might be attributable specifically to masculinist traits: to excessive risk-taking behavior of young, aggressive male pilots. The possibility that male pilots, self-described as "hot sticks" or "hot dogs," socialized according to typical gender norms, might lack the maturity of judgment necessary to refrain from such risk taking has been considered in at least one media story. See "Lt. Hultgreen and the 'Hot Dogs'" 1995. The training records of the flier, Lieutenant Cary Lohrenz, who was Hultgreen's cotrainee were taken and released to the press and eventually included in a report ("Double Standards in Naval Aviation") by Elaine Donnelly's Center for Military Readiness, later released to the press in an attempt to show that women fliers were rushed through training and were unqualified. Donnelly's center and the navy are being sued over the illegal release of these records. A naval inspector general investigation was carried out after the Pacific Fleet IG investigation was considered deficient. In a section of the report titled "Male Perceptions in the TACAIR Community" (6), the IG remarks on the strong opposition in the TACAIR (elite fighter) community to the admission of women into the community, and the perception among male aviators that they were "abandoned," following Tailhook, by senior leaders. They cite the withdrawal of Admiral Arthur's name for consideration as commander-in-chief, Pacific, on account of his decision to remove a female helicopter pilot from flight training as evidence that the senior leadership has supported a "lowering of standards." The report is particularly interesting for its description of the way a "gender neutral" train-

ing approach was misapplied (my reading) in the Pacific but used fairly and with better effect in the TACAIR deployment on the East Coast, USS *Eisenhower*. See Department of Defense, Naval Inspector General 1997.

On rape: The massive survey done on sexual harassment in the services in the late 1980s also asked questions about sexual assault and rape. The results of the harassment question were reported in full. It would be important to know more about the results of the data on rape. In the course of my interviews, military women told me on several occasions about unreported rape. One air force graduate indicated that only the academy nurse would know the extent of this problem in the academy. To the best of my knowledge, the academy nurses are not asked this question. Clearly, this is an issue in society generally. Madeline Morris, professor of law at Duke University, has completed a carefully researched manuscript indicating that rape within the military occurs at lower rates than in civilian society but at higher rates than other forms of criminal behavior in the military (Morris 1996, 651–781). The recent episode at Aberdeen Proving Ground, Maryland, suggests that unreported rapes are a significant problem. See Ricks 1996, A20.

7. U.S. House 1992, 20–21. Dorn was referring to the events at the "Flag Panel," an open forum in which several admirals spoke and audience members posed questions to the panel. One navy woman asked about the likelihood that women would be flying combat aircraft. Her question was greeted, according to the inspector general report, with "strong reactions from the attendees" (according to one report I heard, audience members began chanting, "No woman in TACAIR") and a "Hoo-boy" from Vice Admiral Dunleavy, who (the Tailhook Association's own report acknowledged) "first displayed some unease in addressing the issue" and then responded that the navy would do as Congress directed (Department of Defense Inspector General 1993, B-4). A 1997 naval inspector general report was considerably more blunt: "A number of TACAIR aviators had strongly and often publicly opposed the admission of women into their community. Few senior TACAIR leaders attempted to counter these feelings. For example, at the 1991 Tailhook Symposium, some male aviators publicly displayed buttons proclaiming 'not in my cockpit.' A female aviator who attempted to ask a panel of flag officer aviators about the navy's plans to integrate women into combat positions was shouted down, and the response of the navy's senior aviator made it clear to all present that he did not support the concept." Department of Defense Naval Inspector General 1997, 6. This indifference and, on occasion, outright opposition was persistently reported to me by military women with whom I spoke. An anecdote recounted by a former West Point army captain illustrates this kind of rebuff. The captain expressed concern to her commander that her exclusion as a woman from combat specializations severely compromised her opportunities for promotion. He replied, "Well, you have a problem." What he meant, she said, was "That's your problem." "It was not the military's problem, not his problem, but my problem" (interview by author with Major Dana Isaacoff, 1995).

8. See Webb 1992, A23. See also the satirical article that appeared in *Proceedings*, a journal of the U.S. Naval Institute, about the fictional carrier *Boorda*, the reference being to the late Admiral Boorda who as chief of naval operations

called for a servicewide stand-down after a number of incidents involving race and gender offenses had rocked the navy. The story features a seaman "of IndoUgric heritage" who sues his supervisor for "insensitivity to diversity"—a matter difficult for "old timers" to adjust to "after spending so many years learning that individuality had nothing to do with military readiness" (cited in Blazar 1995), 9. The late Admiral Mike Boorda, chief of naval operations, was the target of criticism by James Webb at a mid-1990s West Point commencement address, shortly before his tragic suicide following the reports that he wore military badges which he had not in fact been awarded.

9. General Accounting Office 1994, 21.

10. United States Naval Academy Board of Visitors 1990, 13.

11. Respondents 4 and 5.

12. Respondent 6.

13. The material on WUBA jokes was collected by Carol Burke, formerly a civilian instructor at the Naval Academy and a folklorist. WUBA stands for "Working Uniform Blue Alpha," which, Burke explains, "first appeared in 1976 to describe the freshly issued uniforms of the first female midshipmen" but was soon deployed as a derisory term for unattractive women at the academy and is sometimes understood to mean "women used by all" (Burke 1996). Respondent 7.

14. Bennett 1992. Four different study reports, following the incident, including one commissioned by the academy itself, suggested that the Dreyer incident betrayed patterns of hostility in the academy that required addressing.

15. Schmitt 1992b, 28.

16. Barkalow with Raab 1990, 168.

17. Every single woman academy graduate I talked with could relate at least one anecdote about these kinds of comments.

18. Barkalow with Raab 1990, 85.

19. Interview by author with Brynnen Hahn, May 1991.

20. General Accounting Office 1994, 37. The figures I report are averages of the three service academy responses. The table breaks down the responses by academy location.

21. As any military woman will recount, officer or enlistee, the choice of sexual roles is overshadowed constantly by the lesbian-whore binary. Turn down a date: you're a dyke. Alternatively, accept a date (with more than one man): you're a whore. Respondent 8.

22. Osburn and Benecke 1996, i.

23. SLDN reports that the 850 people the Department of Defense discharged under "Don't Ask, Don't Tell, Don't Pursue" in 1996 was the highest rate of discharge since 1987. Women accounted for 29 percent of gay discharges despite making up 13 percent of the active duty force. In the army, women accounted for 41 percent of gay discharges, three times their presence in the service. Osburn, Benecke, and Childress 1997, i.

24. Osburn and Benecke 1996, 6–7.

25. Clifford Alexander, former secretary of the army, speaks concisely of the capacity of military authority to curb racism/sexism when leadership is committed to doing so: "I do feel, however, that because of the command orientation

of the army as well as its task nature, race played a less significant role than in the private sector" (Alexander 1986).

26. Twice within eight years, for instance, the commanders of the salvage ship U.S.S. *Safeguard* were found to have been themselves perpetrators of harassing behavior. On *Safeguard I*, see Schumacher 1988; on *Safeguard II*, see "Navy Commander Is Relieved" 1992, 19.

27. Fear of bad publicity was probably one of the reasons why prompter action was not taken after Paula Coughlin first reported her experience to her commanding officers. The obstruction of investigation and prosecution due to the refusal of those at Tailhook to provide information on what they or others had done or seen was clearly part of the problem as well. For an analysis of sexual harassment in the military more generally, see Skaine 1996. See also Department of Defense Inspector General 1993. Interviewees with whom I spoke cited incidents, for instance, of a commanding officer who failed to act on the knowledge that someone under his command was behaving recklessly owing to alcohol addiction, because he was worried that evidence of personnel problems would reflect badly on the unit. The individual was then, later, in an accident and is partially paralyzed. Another interviewee noted that all of the close to a dozen women in her squadron had eating disorders. Because those with eating disorders can be suspended temporarily or dismissed from the military, there is pressure on both the individual and the individual's commander not to report a problem (respondent 9). In a 1988 Committee Hearing, Congresswoman Patricia Schroeder commented, ". . . I know for example with sexual harassment, I remember chaplains and base commanders telling me that the problem was that if they reported the incidents on their base, then it went on their record that they were not running their bases well" (U.S. House 1988, 165). This is also an issue mentioned in the Dellums Report on race discrimination in the armed forces: U.S. House 1995.

28. Dunivin 1988, 43.

29. Ibid., 61–62.

30. Schneider and Schneider 1988, 176–89.

31. Ibid., 180.

32. Ibid., 43.

33. Dunivin 1988, 44–47.

34. Ibid., 46.

35. Levin 1990, 1010–61.

36. *United States v. Stanley* (1987).

37. Ibid. Stanley claimed to have been severely debilitated by the LSD—experiencing hallucinations, memory loss, disorientation, and eventually the breakup of his marriage and discharge from the service.

38. Levin 1990, 1014.

39. *Parker v. Levy* (1974).

40. The case was decided by a five-justice majority opinion written by Justice Rehnquist. The dissent expressed dismay at the utilization of a separate standard of review for the military, different from that which might have been applied in a civilian context. But as Marilyn A. Gordon and Mary Jo Ludvigson point out, the court did not hesitate to inquire into the constitutionality of military actions

(Gordon and Ludvigson 1990, 51–85). Gordon and Ludvigson thus argue that *Parker* would have been among the cases that women might have cited had the constitutionality of combat exclusion been challenged in the courts.

41. *Brown v. Glines* (1980); and *Secretary of the Navy v. Huff* (1980). These cases involved the service requirement that prior approval by a commanding officer be given before petitions could be circulated. Justice Brennan points out in his dissent that this requirement pertained to bases that were not operating "under combat or near-combat conditions" and that the application of such stringent standards to these "rear-echelon" situations should be considered particularly questionable (as discussed in Levin 1990, 1017–18).

42. *Goldman v. Weinberger* (1986).

43. The *Stanley* case was brought both under constitutional law and as a tort. The Federal Tort Claims Act (FTCA) is the instrument through which the government can be sued for negligence or wrongful acts. See Levin 1990, 1011 n. 6. See the discussion, as well, in Stiehm 1989.

44. See the excellent discussions of equal protection litigation by Goodman 1979, 243–83; and by Stichm 1989, 108 34.

45. *Frontiero v. Richardson* (1973).

46. *Schlesinger v. Ballard* (1975).

47. *Waldie v. Schlesinger* (1974). The appeals court ordered the case to trial, but it was dropped when Congress took action the following year. See also Morden 1990, 320.

48. *Crawford v. Cushman* (1976); *Struck v. Sec'y of Defense* (1971a; 1971b; 1972); *Robinson v. Rand* (1972); *Gutierrez v. Laird* (1972); *Flores v. Sec'y of Defense* (1973). The *Cushman* case did not decide military policy, however. Well into the 1980s, the services continued to debate the issue of whether pregnancy should result in a military woman's discharge. The services have no common policy on the issue of aviators and undetected or undiagnosed pregnancy. This is likely to continue to be debated over the next years.

49. *Owens v. Brown* (1978).

50. Ibid., 301.

51. Ibid., 302.

52. Morden 1990, 321–22.

53. Holm 1992 (1993 ed.), 305–12; Mitchell 1989, 305 12. Secretary of defense Melvin Laird supported the opening of the academies to women. ROTC programs had been opened to women in the early 1970s.

54. Stiehm 1989, 117.

55. Holm 1992 (1993 ed.), 294. Up until the 1970s, it was not just pregnancy but *parenthood* that required a military woman to leave the service. A military woman who married a man with children under eighteen was required to be discharged unless (as in the latter years) she could secure a waiver. See Holm's discussion (299–302).

56. Ibid., 332–35.

57. This was despite the fact that Quigley, in charge of women's affairs, opposed these policy changes (ibid., 280–82).

58. Captain Kathy Bruyere, USN, then Kathy Byerly, notified her commanding officer that she had been asked to join the *Owens* class action suit. Rather

than attempting to dissuade her from joining the suit, he endorsed her decision with the query: How else were the services going to be made to change?

59. See, for example, WEAL and ACLU's testimony before the 1979 Military Personnel Subcommittee of the House Armed Services Committee.

60. National Organization for Women 1981, 2.

61. Ibid. at 20.

62. Congressional hearings, however, continued to be important in keeping the military aware of their accountability to the public.

63. *Rostker v. Goldberg* (1981).

64. Brundage n.d.

65. *Rostker v. Goldberg* (1981).

66. "Navy Sued" 1987, 4; Inuzuka 1987, 6; Inuzuka 1989, 8.

67. *Chappell et al. v. Wallace et al.* (1982).

68. *Willas v. Rapal* (1987) as reported in the Women's Equity Action League 1987, 4.

69. Nalty 1986, 345.

70. Stiehm 1989, 129–32.

71. *Ben-Shalom v. Marsh* (1989); citing *Gilligan v. Morgan* (1973).

72. Interview by author with Captain Pat Gormley (USN—ret.), 8 August 1997.

73. The predominance of white women on DACOWITS and of black male personnel in the EO offices means that any distinctive concerns of uniformed women of color are unlikely to be clearly identified or prioritized by either the EO offices or DACOWITS. As Major Gwen Hall has noted, data collection measuring the specific impact of the military's drawdown, of appointments and promotions within the academies and in particular job slots, often does not register the specifics of the situation for women of color. It is an interesting mental exercise to think about the issues that might be prioritized by a DACOWITS that was 30 percent African-American (the percentage of African Americans among military women) or by an office that consisted predominantly of women of color.

74. Interview by author with Captain Lory Manning (USN—ret.), 18 September 1997.

75. Abrams 1993, 217–43. There is beginning to be recognition of the intersection of issues. Equal opportunity training programs that had formerly focused on race issues are now addressing issues of race discrimination together with sexual harassment. One of the complaints voiced in the Dellums Report, however, was that equal opportunity training overlooked issues about racial discrimination emphasizing sexual harassment (U.S. House 1995, 3). DACOWITS is beginning to make race issues part of its regular agenda. The committee for the first time called for a service briefing about race differentials in the progress of military women ("News Briefs" 1995, 9–10). It is unfortunate that the intended congressional follow-up study on gender that was to constitute part 2 of the Dellums report on race discrimination in the military was aborted at the hands of the 1994 Congress.

76. The 1990s may be the first time, given the Republican-controlled Congress and a Democrat-controlled executive, that the military is ready to take on

certain issues and is being pressured to hold back by the Congress. Congressman Steve Buyer (R-Ind.), for instance, as chair of the Subcommittee on Military Personnel of the House Committee on National Security Affairs (what was the old House Armed Services Committee) used the army report on sexual harassment following the Aberdeen incidents to query military personnel and the army secretary about different physical fitness standards. Military personnel attempted to explain that different standards are a useful way of measuring similar aerobic capacities, defending the procedures used to advance women in the military (interview by author with Captain Lory Manning [USN—ret.], 19 October 1997). The hearings were held on 1 October 1997. On the army report on sexual harassment, see Secretary of the Army 1997.

77. Gaventa 1980; Lukes 1974.

78. Department of Defense Inspector General 1993, I-1.

79. McMichael 1997, 49. Ludwig's letter goes on to admonish participants in a few sentences for the $23,000 damage bill and a handful of reports (five) about abuse of women during "the Gauntlet."

80. Vistica 1995, 308.

81. Castaneda and Stone 1993, A1.

82. The *MacNeil/Lehrer Newshour* reported (summary by Jim Lehrer) that 28 officers of 140 charged received some kind of administrative punishment, as did 33 admirals. *MacNeil/Lehrer Newshour* 1994, 6. Not one of the 140 was court-martialed. The *New York Times* reports that "most of the complaints have resulted in small fines or reprimands" ("Plaintiff in Tailhook Case" 1994, 1). According to another *New York Times* report, by Neil A. Lewis, 3 admirals received censure, less serious action was taken against 30 other senior officers, and about 40 lower-ranking officers have been fined or disciplined (Lewis 1993, 1). Tailhook I (the investigation by the Department of Defense) has fairly scathing criticisms of the investigations conducted by the navy: two investigations ran in parallel—one conducted by the Naval Investigative Service and the other by the Naval Inspector General Office. The poor example of naval leadership was something that the navy's own investigative service could hardly address. The fact that this behavior had a history was also something that needed official recognition. See Vistica 1995.

83. Kelso was present at the Las Vegas hotel but claimed to be unaware of any untoward behavior.

84. His retirement at four-star rank was supported by many military women in DACOWITS and the Women's Officers Professional Association (WOPA) because they saw Kelso as having advocated for women's issues—supporting sensitivity training, toughened penalties for sexual harassment, and expanded job opportunities for women. But see, on women in the Senate, Schmitt 1994c, 1. Both Barbara Pope, former assistant secretary of the navy, and Commander Rosemary Mariner made a point of praising Admiral Kelso's record on women's issues on *MacNeil/Lehrer*, 15 February 1994.

85. Paula Coughlin reached an out-of-court settlement with the Tailhook Association for $400,000. A jury awarded her $5.2 million in her lawsuit against the Hilton hotel. "Six more Tailhook Victims" 1995, 5.

86. Schmitt 1994a, A15. This dismissal was expected for three reasons. First, under the Feres doctrine (a 1950 Supreme Court ruling that bars servicemembers from suing the government for harm due to negligence or malpractice), few plaintiffs succeed in suing the military for damages. Second, the government could (and did) disclaim liability by insisting that Tailhook was a private association. How private an association it was, in fact, might be questioned, given the fact that Tailhook's headquarters in California were located, rent free, on a military base. Tailhook participants were flown to Las Vegas, in some cases, in military transport. Some Tailhook attendees, furthermore, attended the planning sessions and conference while on military payroll. Third, unit cohesion (the same unit cohesion that military spokesmen have said would be disrupted by uniformed homosexuals) made it impossible to obtain the kind of evidence necessary for a proper trial or convictions.

87. Schmitt 1993, 1; but see Cates 1993, 16.

88. Garrison 1996, 4. See also North 1996, 70. The Senate panel left the decision about Strumpf in the hands of Dalton, who struck down the promotion, a decision that is the target of David North's editorial criticism.

89. Many military women I spoke with alluded to the harassment that Paula Coughlin suffered in her post-Tailhook postings and to how the insufferable experiences she later had must have led to her resignation. See Paula Coughlin's own account in Noble 1994, A18.

90. *MacNeil/Lehrer Newshour* 1994, 4–5, 6. Order from Strictly Business, P.O. Box 12803, Overland Park, KS 66212. Schroeder noted that the military court had itself in fact believed Admiral Kelso to have been dissembling when he said that he had been unaware of what was happening in the Hilton hospitality suites, a view presumably based on the testimony of many of those present at Tailhook to the effect that Kelso was allegedly on the patio just a few yards from signs advertising leg shaving. See Schmitt 1992a, 1. Schroeder derided the military for dismissing the findings of its own court:

> I want to ask you, is there anywhere else in society where someone could be so damned by a decision—and this [the military court] was a very damning decision about Admiral Kelso's role in this and the role in the cover-up—can you think of any place else where you could just say, well, we don't go along with that decision, that decision wasn't right? Of course, we're not going to appeal it and prove we were right because, you see, it would just take more time and money. [The navy decided not to appeal what was essentially a ruling against navy leadership (Weiner 1994, 1).] Everything is fine. I'll just retire a couple of months early. Have a nice day. Meanwhile the women who supposedly are now operating under much better conditions and so forth, we see the leading spokesman, Paula Coughlin, saying I've had it [and resigning]. (*MacNeil/Lehrer Newshour* 1994, 5)

The lesson, she said, is that ". . . justice in the Navy is for the admirals, by the admirals, and of the admirals." "I thought," Schroeder continued, "one of the cartoonists in Denver captured it the best. They had a picture of a sinking ship with Tailhook written on it, and all the officers out in a little life boat, all the male officers, saying 'Well it's a Navy tradition. The women always go down with the ship.'" (4). Vice Admiral Robert Dunn(USN—ret.), said in retort, "Well, I'm very saddened that Congresswoman Schroeder has an attitude like that, and she's had that attitude for some time. And nothing we do seems to be able to change that attitude" (4). See also "Command Presents" 1994, A14; Schmitt 1994b, 1; "Tailhook Group Settles Lawsuit" 1995, A22.

91. Webb 1992, A23. An editorial in the *Denver Post* insisted that Tailhook was a tempest in a teapot: "What the young aviators did was not to be con-doned. Jerks will be jerks. But it is not as though KGB files were uncovered revealing an espionage ring. Admirals resign over issues where national security is compromised, not over some guys under their command acting like bawdy fraternity boys" (Rosen 1992, 11b). See also Werner 1992, 10b. See also "I'm a Scapegoat" 1993, 9. Apparently President Bush did not share the view that this was a tempest in a teapot, inviting Paula Coughlin to the White House and indicating through Marvin Fitzwater that he was very upset at the navy's investi-gation (Lewis 1992, 12). See also two highly critical *New York Times* editorials, "The Tailhook Fiasco" 1994, A22; and an editorial criticizing the Senate Armed Services Committee for protecting Admiral Kelso: "Command Presents" 1993, A14.

92. See comment, for instance by Rosemary Mariner: *MacNeil/Lehrer Newshour* 1994, 5. Even if Mariner was right about the "anomaly" of the Tail-hook gauntlet/assaults, it is surprising that she declined the occasion of *Mac-Neil/Lehrer* to make the linkage that she and others had repeatedly made on other occasions, the connections between Tailhook and the *systemic, structural* problem of women's combat exclusion. Perhaps there were "strategic" reasons why military women offered only tempered public commentaries on Tailhook. Military women knew that they would have to face the wrath of male col-leagues—the same shunning and derision that ultimately drove Paula Coughlin out of the navy. See Noble 1994, A18. They may have also realized that the media and others were, for once, doing their job for them. And they may have been reluctant to go to lengths in public to support Coughlin, who was per-ceived by some as having taken few risks as a feminist before Tailhook.

93. *U.S. v. Virginia et al.* (1996).

94. Ibid. at 2275. The court cites *Reed v. Reed* (1971) as setting the pivotal decision in which the court holds unconstitutional a law that would deny equal opportunity to women because they are women, ignoring individual talent and capacity.

95. As quoted in Mandelbaum and Wyckoff 1995, 14. Sara Mandelbaum and Mary Wyckoff are staff attorneys at the ACLU Women's Rights Project.

96. Justice Ginsburg states, "The notion that admission of women would downgrade VMI's stature, destroy the adversative system and, with it, even the school, is a judgment hardly proved, a prediction hardly different from other 'self-fulfilling prophec[ies].' . . ." 116 S. Ct. 2264 (1996) at 2280.

97. One fourth circuit court judge who reviewed the Citadel's case suggested that the exclusion of women was not really about the character of military educa-tion at all, a claim given particular weight by the fact that only 18 percent of Citadel graduates, reportedly, go on to a military career (Rosen 1996, 25). Sug-gesting (in a view that had little influence over the judgment of the court) that

the schools' all-male environment was really about the preservation of existing hierarchies of power, Judge Kenneth Hall commented,

> In fact, though VMI, the Citadel, and their advocates have ceaselessly insisted that education is at the heart of this debate, I suspect that these cases have very little to do with education. They instead have very much to do with wealth, power, and the ability of those who have it now to determine who will have it later. The daughters of Virginia and South Carolina have every right to insist that their tax dollars no longer be spent to support what amount to fraternal organizations whose initiates emerge as full-fledged members of an all-male aristocracy. (*Faulkner v. Jones* [1995], 440)

98. When the arguments were presented before the Supreme Court, Judge Stephen G. Breyer commented that he took it as a given that the integration of women into the VMI program would force the "adversative" mode of education to change. Whether the adversative model has been significantly altered at the academies is a matter of much dispute.

99. Rosen 1996, 25.

100. How much are the Citadel and VMI likely to change under such a ruling? The Citadel president, Claudius E. Watts III, replied to Wilson's article, which he called defamatory. But it is significant that while he sought to correct Wilson's portrayal of the institution by listing the famous graduates of the Citadel, he chose not to reply in any way to the observations about hazing or student conduct (Watts 1995, 31). It is telling that Vice Admiral James Stockdale, who spent years as a prisoner of war in the so-called tiger cages of North Vietnam, served less than two years as Citadel president. See Wilson 1995, 29. Stockdale found the hazing present in the academy a form of "personalized malevolence and dictatorial vengeance." He quit as president, frustrated at being unable to alter established practices in the school.

101. "Army Doctor Jailed" 1992, 25.

102. Schmitt 1993, A20.

103. Interview by author with Lieutenant Colonel M. C. Pruitt, 21 November 1991.

104. See Eisenstein 1988.

CHAPTER FIVE
DISCURSIVE ACTIVISM

1. Unless otherwise indicated, the comments that are quoted in the report on the WOC conference are based on my own interviews during the three-day event.

2. Fiorenza 1993.

3. Women's Ordination Conference 1995a (WOC, P.O. Box 2693, Fairfax VA 22031, [703] 352-1006).

4. Steinfels 1995a.

5. This quotation is from notes I took during the workshop, 11 November. Interview by author with Sister Maureen Fiedler, 13 November 1995.

6. Some Saturday afternoon focus groups did take up the question of strategy—"How to Build a Feminist Christian Coalition Challenging the War on Women and the Poor: Grass Roots Organizing"; "Ordination into Patriarchal Ministry: Pros and Cons"; "Fundraising with Feminist Values." But most of the focus groups were more exercises in analysis and truth seeking than explorations of strategy.

7. Comment at WOC meeting by Sister Joan Sobala, 14 November 1996.

8. Schaeffer 1995, 9.

9. Steinfels 1995a, A17.

10. This was sung at the "Re-imagining" Conference in Minneapolis, 4–7 November 1993, which a number of people present at the WOC conference had also attended (Hunt 1994, 1).

11. Words and music © by Fulmer, 1995.

12. Words and music © by marsie silvestro, 8/9/95. Reprinted by permission from MoonSong Productions, 127 Eastern Ave., Suite 8008 212, Gloucester, MA 01930.

13. Another marsie silvestro song.

14. Schaeffer 1995, 10.

15. Ibid., 9.

16. See, for instance, the draft pledge in Women's Ordination Conference 1995b.

17. Weaver 1986, 113.

18. Quoted in Papa 1978. Papa reports the reactions of several women attending the conference who were distressed at the fact that the meeting had taken on broad social justice aims (which could be pursued "elsewhere") rather than limiting itself to the issue of ordination (see also Weaver 1986, 112–16). The changed tone of the conference began to elicit criticism in the usually liberal Catholic newspapers (McCarthy 1978; Moan 1978, 433).

19. Kane states. "Maybe two weeks before the visit, I got a phone call from the priest at the national shrine. All he said to me was, 'The pope will be giving a prayer service to the sisters, and as the president of LCWR, we would like you to give the greeting.' So I said, 'Can you tell me how long it will be?' He said, 'Well very brief, Sister. They're really coming to hear the Holy Father.' And I thought, 'Well, I know that.' So he said two or three minutes. Now that was all the conversation I had with him. He said, 'What's your name? We want to put your name on the program.'" See Rogers 1996, 225.

20. Ibid.

21. Milhaven 1987, 6.

22. Kane 1987, 613.

23. Hays 1984, 1.

24. A workshop in Washington drew from mostly moderate, liberal quarters (Giveu 1986; Hansen 1987). The speakers addressed topics that focused largely on issues within the institutional church. The talks were forthright and posed clear challenges, covering topics such as "Relationships between U.S. Women Religious and Hierarchical Authority" and "To Face or Not to Face Sexism: Consequences for the Institutional Church." To the extent that one can read

through the invective, a useful and detailed report of the first (1986) Time Consultant conferences (held in the Shoreham hotel, Washington, D.C.) is provided in Steichen 1991, 123–54.

25. In this account, I am relying on three reports of the conference: Martinez 1993a, 3–4; Martinez 1993b, 5; Walsh 1993, 6–7. In November 1993, the "Reimagining" conference was also held in Minneapolis, Minnesota. The majority of participants were Protestant, but over 240 Roman Catholics also participated (Hunt 1994, 1).

26. Martinez 1993a, 3–4.

27. Gramick wrote this in the newsletter of the National Coalition of American Nuns, as reported by Demetria Martinez (ibid., 3).

28. As quoted in Martinez 1993b, 5.

29. Walsh 1993.

30. See the essays in Ware 1995. The book can be acquired through the Book Department, Loretto Motherhouse, Nerinx, KY 40049-9999. See Williams 1995, particularly 245–46, on the origins of the Loretto Women's Network. The Adrian Dominicans have a commission for women. Similarly, the Sisters of Charity of the Blessed Virgin Mary have a Network for Women's Issues—loosely held together through small group discussions, personal contact, and a newsletter.

31. An excellent description of these organizations can be found in Weaver 1995. Donna Steichen's sarcastic account of feminism in the Catholic Church (Steichen 1991) also contains useful information. The credibility of much of her analysis is severely diminished, however, by the dismissive commentary that she intersperses throughout her discussion. Much of her description is so specific as to names of speakers, their affiliations, the networks to which they appear to belong, that it is hard not to believe that her intent is as much a watchdog one, facilitating the capacities of church authorities to track the statements of feminists, as it is any attempt at actual scholarly analysis. Steichen is intent on protecting her sources "whose help has been invaluable but whose lives might become more difficult than they already are if their names are mentioned" (403), but she seems to have no qualms about liberally naming and quoting anyone with whom she disagrees without regard for the consequences that might ensue.

32. See the final issue of *Probe* (1995) for a history of NARW.

33. For a history of NCAN, see Traxler and Ware 1989 (NCAN, 7315 S. Yale, Chicago, IL 60621).

34. Weaver 1986, 84–85.

35. Eighth Day Center was founded in 1974 by twenty religious communities as an organization directed to work for social justice ("systemic change through research, educational outreach, direct action, legislative action, coalition building, and networking"). Call to Action describes itself as "A Catholic movement of 10,000 laity, religious, and clergy advocating peace, justice and love in our world, our church, and ourselves in the spirit of Vatican II and the U.S. Catholic Bishops' 1976 Call to Action Conference." CTA produces three quarterly publications. On Ash Wednesday 1990, CTA took out a full page in the *New York Times*, "A Call for Reform" in the Catholic Church. These de-

scriptions are from *Renewing Our Church* (Call to Action 1996). Directory available from CTA, 4419 N. Kedzie, Chicago IL 60625. The Quixote Center, founded in 1976, is a Catholic-based justice center located in Hyattsville, Maryland. Maureen Fiedler, Sister of Loretto, and Dolly Pomerleau have been two of the women most prominently associated with the center. Network and Center for Concern are two additional multi-issue organizations. Network was founded in 1971 as a lobbying organization that tries to influence Washington decision making on social justice issues. Sister Carol Coston, OP, and more recently Sister Nancy Sylvester, IHM, have been the two national directors. Center for Concern was founded by three Jesuit priests in 1971 as a social justice think tank and has housed a women's project. This by no means exhausts the list of feminist organizations. For an excellent brief history, for instance, of the Grail, an older organization that became feminist in the 1970s, see Weaver 1986, 123–27. In 1984, Women-Church Convergence was formally renamed, growing out of the Women Church Coalition.

36. Interview by author with Maureen Gallagher, 11 November 1995.

37. Some examples: NARW's bimonthly was *Probe*; WOC's *New Women, New Church* is a quarterly with four thousand readers. WATER publishes *WATERwheel*; the Loretto Women's Network puts out *couRAGE*; Las Hermanas produces *Informes*. The National Coalition of American Nuns has a newsletter; Chicago Catholic Women regularly produces information, calendars, and announcement sheets; CFFC produces numerous working papers, brochures, and the newsletter/journal *Conscience*. For some further information, see Vidulich 1993, 2.

38. The writings of feminist historians, sociologists, and political scientists throughout the 1980s were also very important in the creation of an epistemic community. Some prominent examples from the roster of names of present/ former women religious include Sister Marie Augusta Neal, SND de Namur, Department of Sociology, Emmanuel College, Helen Rose Ebaugh, Department of Sociology, University of Houston; Ruth Wallace, Sociology, George Washington University, but the literature produced by the vast numbers of M.A. and Ph.D. women religious documenting, reanalyzing, and reconstructing (in the 1970s and 1980s) the history of women in the church is far too great and too important to represent within a note. Part of what is extraordinary about some of that literature, which is highly scholarly, is that it was done by women who had neither the salary nor the free time provided by academic institutions. Lay academics have also been significant contributors to this community of scholars, including historians Mary Jo Weaver, professor of religion at Indiana, and Margaret Thompson, Syracuse, as well as political scientists Mary Segers, Rutgers, and Jo Renee Formicola, Seton Hall University.

39. Daly's book *The Church and the Second Sex* presented a view of the church as deeply misogynist (Daly 1975). Curran was known, already by 1967, for a critical view of church teachings on birth control.

40. Rosemary Radford Ruether is at the Garrett-Evangelical Theological Seminary in Chicago; Elisabeth Schüssler Fiorenza at Harvard Divinity School; Anne Carr at the University of Chicago Divinity School. Some Catholic institutions have appointed feminists to their faculty: Diana Hayes in theology at

Georgetown; Sandra M. Schneiders, IHM, at the Jesuit School of Theology, Berkeley; and Joan Wolski Conn at Neumann College are some of a growing number of such appointees.

41. From this early stage in which feminist theologians came to be recognized and widely read (1970s and 1980s), I include only a sampling of theological writings. Regular reviews of theological writings appear in the September and February issues of *National Catholic Reporter*. More complete writings are easily traced through such bibliographical sources as the *Catholic Religion and Periodical Index*. See, for instance, Daly 1973, 1975, 1984; Ruether 1974, 1975, 1983, 1985; Ruether with McLaughlin 1979; Fiorenza 1983; 1984; Carr 1988; Swidler and Swidler 1977. For an analysis of some of these writings from this period, see Weaver 1986. This has been republished, with a new introduction, by Indiana University Press (1995); see also Weaver's own more recent and very interesting theological explorations, Weaver 1993. See also Graff 1993. Note the importance to this process of institutionalization of such presses as Harper and Row, Simon and Schuster, and, of course, Beacon Press, which has long specialized in the writings of feminist theologians and feminists writing about spirituality.

42. Baumgaertner 1988, 90–92; as quoted in Wallace 1992, 5.

43. Ruth Wallace's study (Wallace 1992) looks at the effect of women pastors on the development of nonsexist attitudes in the parish community. She does not report on whether the twenty women pastors she interviewed consider themselves to be feminist, but her observations about their words and behavior certainly suggest that they do.

44. Ibid., 13. There may, Wallace suggests, be an underreporting of such parishes.

45. Fox 1995, 234.

46. The figures on women's employment in U.S. Catholic dioceses are discouraging, however, particularly when compared to progress in professions and secular administrative and political positions. See Hudson 1995. Only two parishes in the United States apparently explicitly prohibit girls from being altar servers, although many more "by custom" have only boys.

47. Comment at WOC Conference by St. Harold group member, 11 November 1995.

48. CFFC also makes an effort to keep in touch with key Washington policy players and has, along with other groups, submitted *amicus* briefs in recent court cases.

49. See discussion in Steichen 1991, 169–72, on lobbying the church. CFFC has had a "Bishop Watch," but this kind of activism is significant more for its exceptionalism than for its frequency.

50. In an extraordinary decision, the Vatican Congregation for Institutes of Consecrated Life and Societies of Apostolic Life recognized a new Council of Major Superiors of Women Religious meant to function as a parallel organization to the LCWR. This action gave canonical recognition to U.S. women religious who embrace more conservative views of church and society and who did not feel themselves to be represented through the LCWR. The LCWR reaction

expressed apprehension that the Vatican's creation of this alternative council will "open old wounds within congregations and between congregations." The president of the Conference of Major Superiors of Men also sent a letter to the heads of men's orders in the United States, commenting that the new council "declared themselves more authentically religious [than the women in LCWR] and more loyal to the Holy See. . . . We feel that the special recognition given to a small group who declare themselves more authentic is offensive and is not unifying" ("New Council of Major Superiors" 1992, 157).

51. Marjorie Tuite, OP, was an extraordinary activist who played key roles in the founding of NAWR, WOC, and Church Women United, and in efforts to support those persecuted in Central America; her death was hastened, some said, after she joined with others in signing the 1984 *New York Times* advertisement that supported a diversity of views over abortion, because of her distress at the way the issue of "retraction" had been handled. Tuite, by all accounts, was an inspiration to many activist women in the church.

52. Interview with Ruth McDonough Fitzpatrick in Milhaven 1987, 41.

53. Ferraro and Hussey with O'Reilly 1990, 153–55.

54. Ibid. See also Quinn 1992 in Lieblich 1992, 86–155.

55. "Battling Sexism" 1986, 10–11; "Ash Wednesday Protest" 1996, 11. Notification about Chicago protests drawn from a single sheet of material circulated by Chicago Catholic Women, 5249 N. Kenmore, Chicago, IL 60640. Protests staged outside major cathedrals during ordination ceremonies for male seminary graduates and outdoor liturgies were more a feature of the 1980s than of the 1990s.

56. As quoted in interview with Margaret Traxler, SSND (of NCAN), by Unsworth 1995, 105.

57. Conversation with a nun from Chicago, Crystal City, Virginia, 12 November 1995. Evidence of this alienation was provided by the discussion in anticipation of the Women-Church Convergence meetings in Albuquerque, New Mexico, in 1993 about whether to invite a priest to perform Mass as one of perhaps twenty or so services to be offered on the last day of the conference. The proposal was ultimately rejected by the planning board, with the assertion that those who might want a traditional male-led Eucharist could go to any of the churches in town, but that at the conference site itself it would be important for the model to be women-led Eucharists (Martinez 1993a, 4). I do not address myself in this study to the issue of women's relationship, more generally, to the Roman Catholic Church. But see Winter, Lummis, and Stokes 1994.

58. As quoted in Houppert 1995, 37.

59. Moran and Schwarz 1987.

60. Ruether 1985, 62–63.

61. Ibid., 7.

62. Quiñonez and Turner 1992.

63. Ibid., 21.

64. Ibid., 27.

65. Ibid., 28.

66. Ibid., 133.

67. Ibid., 46.

68. Ibid., 110.

69. Ibid., 88.

70. Ibid., 111.

71. Ibid., 129.

72. Isasi-Díaz 1992b, 46; Moody 1997.

73. Isasi-Díaz 1992a, 106.

74. Ziegenhals 1989, x.

75. I do not attempt in these chapters to treat theological writings, but for an introduction to the work of women of color, Walker 1983; Fabella and Oduyoye 1988; King 1994. See also Cannon 1995; Moody 1996; and Hayes 1996.

76. At NARW conferences, speakers were introduced without the usual weighty litany about a speaker's advanced education, degrees, and publications (the kind of discourse that can discourage the participation of those present who may lack these "credentials"); the facilitator role was rotated; and women were encouraged to speak from their own experiences. In ways reminiscent of the earlier feminist "small-group" activism in the women's movement, democratic processes were often strictly heeded. Individuals were discouraged from dominating discussion; panel participants introduced each other rather than privilege a single chair or moderator; care was taken to encourage broad participation and sharing of tasks; and self-evaluations by the group at the end of the meetings were routine. Much of this participatory ethic is now standard in many organizational meetings by feminist groups in the church.

77. See, for instance, Ann Patrick Ware's critical discussion of the history of the Loretto Sisters, Ware 1995a.

78. Women-Church Convergence 1991.

79. Martinez 1993b, 5.

80. Fitzgerald 1993, 5.

81. Interview by author with Sister Cornelia Bührle, rscj, June 1996.

82. The transparency of radicalism on the Left as distinct from radicalism on the Right (as exemplified by the secret meetings and conduct of *Opus Dei* organizing) is one characteristic of church politics.

83. Weaver 1992, 201.

84. Huels 1993, 21.

CHAPTER SIX
IN THE LAW'S ABSENCE

1. For the full text of *Ordinatio Sacerdotalis*, the pope's apostolic letter, see John Paul II 1994, 7. In November 1995, the Vatican Congregation for the Doctrine of the Faith invoked the word "infallible" in once again restating that only men can be ordained. See Steinfels 1995b, 1.

2. The other two incidents Chittister discusses are the elimination of the feminine in the new catechism and the Pennsylvania Supreme Court's ruling that a woman must show evidence of having physically resisted for an assault to

be judged as rape. About the first, she says, "If we do not talk about women, we do not think about them, and if we do not think about them, we will never notice that they are missing. Missing from the parliaments of the world, missing from the synods of the world, missing from the altars of the world, missing from the boardrooms of the world, missing from the documents of the world, missing from the consciousness of the men of the world." About the second, she says, "Call it the St. Maria Goretti Law. She died of wounds incurred resisting rape" (Chittister 1994, 12).

3. For Chittister reference, see previous note. For Kane, Foley, and Carroll references, see Vidulich 1994, 3. The quotations were compiled by Sister of St. Joseph of Peace Dorothy Vidulich, a correspondent in NCR's Washington bureau.

4. Thirteen women's groups in Lima, Peru, for instance, wrote a public letter to the pope in 1985 on the occasion of his visit to Peru, critiquing the "oppressive" teachings of the church on issues of sexuality (Carroll 1995. 11–14). See also Fabella and Oduyoye 1988. Gene Burns usefully discusses Latin American liberation theology and American feminism in the church, which he describes as the "challenge of American sisters," as presenting two kinds of radicalism. American sisters focus on patriarchal hierarchy, liberation theology in Latin America on sociopolitical change (Burns 1992, particularly 157)

5. Troch 1988/89, 113–28.

6. After the Vatican approved the presence of altar girls, Ursuline Sister Bernadette Mbuy Beya, an African theologian, stated wryly that this change was designed to "tranquilize" women. The *National Catholic Reporter* writes that "After practically running two parishes back home, she said to now be told that she can be an altar girl is hardly 'thrilling'" (Edwards 1994, 7).

7. Soon after the formation of the Women's Ordination Conference, for instance, the Vatican issued a "Declaration on the Question of the Admission of Women to the Ministerial Priesthood" (Vatican City: Sacred Congregation for the Doctrine of the Faith, 1976) prohibiting episcopal discussion of the ordination question. Vatican delegations have been sent to the United States to monitor and resolve to Vatican satisfaction the cases of Sister Agnes Mary Mansour, the Loretto signees to the 1984 *New York Times* advertisement, and then-Sisters Barbara Ferraro and Patricia Hussey. See McAvoy 1995; Ferraro and Hussey 1987, 65–83; and Ferraro and Hussey, with O'Reilly 1990.

8. For a discussion of this term at the WOC conference, see the previous chapter. Also, see Fiorenza 1993, 368.

9. Gene Burns suggests in *Frontiers of Catholicism* (Burns 1992) that American sisters, in their critique, focus more on the internal structure of the church but, in comparison to liberation theology in Latin America, have a less fully developed sociopolitical criticism of society and economy.

10. For a discussion of feminism in the European Catholic Church, see Brotherton 1992.

11. Any public association with a pro-choice position regularly triggers punitive measures. Mary Ann Sorrentino, executive director of Planned Parenthood of Rhode Island, was excommunicated in 1985 (Milhaven 1987, 243–62); in

1989, Luch Killea, a California assemblywoman, was refused communion by Bishop Leo Maher of San Diego ("Assemblywoman Refused Communion" 1989, 457). Bishop Rene Gracida of Corpus Christi, Texas, excommunicated a clinic director and clinic physician who worked in abortion facilities (Wilkes 1991, 53). It is ironic, as feminist theologians point out, that wife murder, terrorism, rape, the fatal beating of an infant, and the savagery of dropping bombs do not precipitate such punitive steps (see Milhaven 1987, 199).

12. Carroll 1995, 13.

13. Milhaven 1987, 66.

14. Ibid., 71.

15. Congressman Robert Drinan of Massachusetts (a Jesuit priest) did resign after being told that because of his support for Medicaid funding of abortion he could not occupy public office while still a priest. Drinan resigned and was succeeded in office by Barney Frank, whose outspoken support for a variety of liberal issues (gay rights, abortion) could not have pleased the critics of Father Drinan.

16. Morancy 1985.

17. Milhaven 1987, 243–62; Kolbenschlag 1986: largely a collection of documents and analysis of the Mansour decision.

18. Although the group became known as the Vatican 24, there were at least two more nuns who signed the advertisement. One was not identified by the Vatican, and one belonged to a noncanonical community. This account is based on the narratives provided in Ware 1993, obtainable from NCAN, 7315 S. Yale, Chicago IL 60621, (312) 651-8372; Fiedler 1987; Ferraro and Hussey, with O'Reilly 1990; Hunt and Kissling 1993; McAvoy 1995; and Cunningham 1995.

19. For the full text of the statement, see Milhaven 1987, app. A, p. 265 (reprinted from the *New York Times*, 7 October 1984).

20. Ibid., app. B, p. 266.

21. Ibid., 221. See also Ferraro and Hussey, with O'Reilly 1990, 216–20.

22. See statements by Via 1987, 12.

23. The letter asked the head of the religious community to direct the member of the community to "make a public retraction." "In the event that the religious refuse and in fact do not make a public retraction, you are to procede (sic) in accordance with Canon 696, I and as directed by Canon 697 to warn the religious with an explicit threat of dismissal from the Institute" (Ware 1993, 5).

24. For discussion of the views of feminist nuns on abortion, see Ferraro and Hussey, with O'Reilly 1990, Milhaven 1987, Traxler and Ware 1989, 41 and 57–59. See also Ware 1993.

25. As Maureen Fiedler reviewed, numerous "scenarios" were rehearsed about what could happen to the religious communities whose cases were not settled. "What if the signers don't settle, and the leaders refuse to dismiss them? Would CRIS depose the leaders? Would the community then lose canonical status? What would happen to the retired sisters, the community property and the assets built for so long with women's labor? Rome's power operated from within us very effectively" (Fiedler 1987, 8).

26. Many women religious, including those who consider themselves to be feminist, were reluctant to make abortion "the issue" around which they were to be asked to come together to stand firmly against Vatican imposition. In reaction to this sentiment, Patricia Hussey commented: " 'You say again, now is not the time for religious communities to stand firm and strong.' . . . We kept voicing these sentiments. And we said if now is not the time, and abortion is not the issue, when are we going to stand firm? Is homosexuality going to be the issue that will get us to stand firm? Is ordination of women the issue that will make all of us stand firm?" (Milhaven 1987, 224). In my interviews, sisters raised many other questions relating to the Vatican 24: Should the advertisement have been more direct in espousing pro-choice rights? Were some of the signers being "used" by pro-choice organizations that were less concerned with the value of community?

27. For an account of these exchanges, see Ware 1993 and Ferraro and Hussey, with O'Reilly 1990.

28. The statement read: "We had no intention of making a pro-abortion statement. We regret that the statement was misconstrued by some who read it in that way. We hold, as we have in the past, that human life is sacred and inviolable. We acknowledge this as teaching of the church." Sister Ann Patrick Ware explains in her account that the wording of this statement intentionally does not talk about fetal life but about the sacredness and inviolability of human life which was meant to recognize the moral autonomy and the claims of women, denied by the church's official stand on abortion. See Ware 1993, 34–35.

29. Ibid., 37.

30. See Ann Ware's extremely thoughtful discussion, ibid., 38–48.

31. For an absolutely chilling account of the experience of being silenced by the Vatican, see the discussion of Brazilian Leonardo Boff (Cox 1988).

32. He was ousted, in a much publicized case, from Catholic University in Washington, D.C. More recently, allegedly under church pressure, the president of Alabama's Auburn University overruled a faculty committee that had recommended Curran for a chair (Windsor 1990, 4).

33. Weakland was to have been awarded an honorary degree at the University of Fribourg, but the Vatican apparently interceded. See Wilkes 1991, 38–59.

34. McBrien, a professor of theology and former chairman of the theology department at the University of Notre Dame, has, according to the Committee on Doctrine of the National Conference of Catholic Bishops, "overemphasized the plurality of viewpoints in the church." See Schaeffer 1996b, 3.

35. Gibeau 1993, 5. On Fox, see Carroll 1995, 11–14.

36. On Callahan, see "On File" 1991, 730; Hunthausen's "pastoral openness" was evident in his allowing members of Dignity (a Catholic gay and lesbian group) to celebrate the Eucharist in the Seattle Cathedral. See Hunt and Kissling 1993, 20. McNeil defied the ban and was expelled by the Jesuits after a controversy within the order.

37. Ware 1993, 41.

38. "CTA 'We are the Church'" 1994, 3. Gately had copresided at the Call to Action Eucharistic celebration, October 1993 (and had received the highest score of fifty speakers rated by CTA attendees). She composed this poem, included in the article just cited following the Eucharistic celebration:

They said I could not celebrate
For woman I was born.
They said I must not proclaim nor preach
For woman I was born.
They said I could not lead worship
For woman I was born.
Then they closed the door and said no more
For woman I was born.

So, woman born, I crept away
Into a silent place
And stretched my woman body
On the naked moist-wet earth
There, cradled by the darkness
Beneath a purple sky
I opened wide my woman legs
And heaved an anguished cry.
Then from my woman body slipped
The tiny perfect form
Of the one they call the Living God
Of woman body born.

39. Such stories are not uncommon. A woman chaplain at Smith College was reputedly reported to her local bishop for wearing the alblike apparel worn by priests (Respondent 10).

40. Wallace 1992, 130.

41. "Inclusive Language" 1993.

42. Bole 1995, 3. See Sister Carmel Elizabeth McEnroy's own account in McEnroy 1996, 273–79.

43. Bole 1995, 3.

44. Farrell 1990, 7.

45. This certainly appeared to raise the ante over earlier measures. In 1985, Archbishop Pio Laghi had sent letters to women religious whose orders funded the 1985 WOC conference in St. Louis, asking them what their sponsorship had meant and who gave them the authorization to extend it. The firing of a signee from her job escalated the level of response significantly and may have had a chilling effect on the attendance at the WOC 1995 conference (Jones 1994, 4; Bole 1995).

46. For a discussion of the pressures Rome exerted over the contemplative orders (convents), see the useful discussion in Weaver 1995, 102–8. For a discussion of the ways Rome attempted, before John Paul II, to contain the power of the Sister Formation Movement, see Carroll 1985, 59.

47. An earlier organization, Consortium Perfectai Caritatis, had endeavored

to represent the view of those sisters who opposed the kinds of renewal precipitated by Vatican II. The consortium dissolved, but its views were represented in part by the Institute of Religious Life (Carroll 1985, 65–66).

48. "New Council" 1992, 159.

49. Unsworth 1995, 106.

50. Quindlen 1993, A27.

51. Ibid.

52. Of the 123 cardinals who are eligible to elect a successor to the present pope, 106 are appointees of Pope John Paul II.

53. Reese 1992, 6.

54. John Paul II 1993, 124–25.

55. "Can Women Stay" 1994, 11.

56. See "To the Women" 1995, E7.

57. McCafferty 1995, 15 ff. This piece first appeared in the *Sunday Tribune* (Dublin) on 16 July 95. McCafferty begins, "Dear brother Pope, Thank you for the letter and for the apology for the harm done to women by the Catholic Church. I accept the apology and I think your compliment to feminism was handsome. 'I cannot fail to express my admiration for those women of good will . . . demonstrating courageous initiative at a time when this was considered extremely inappropriate, the sign of a lack of femininity, a manifestation of exhibitionism and even a sin!' That wee exclamation mark at the end showed a nice touch of self deprecating humour, which I like in a man. It also subtly suggests an acknowledgment of papal fallibility. . . ." (15). See also Redmont 1995, 11.

58. Ferraro and Hussey, with O'Reilly 1990, 265.

59. Kissling 1995/96, 16–22; Lefevere 1994, 5. "Front Woman?" 1995, 25. Several countries joined with the Vatican effort to bracket the term *gender* in Beijing. They included Benin, Guatemala, Honduras, and Malta (Cook 1995, 33).

60. Prof. Mary Ann Glendon, who teaches at the Harvard Law School, and Dr. Janne Haaland Matlary, a senior researcher at Oslo University, have served in official capacities as part of the Holy See's delegation to Beijing. They speak of themselves as working to describe a true Catholicism with regard to women. Matlary speaks of working to "overcome selfishness and self-centeredness," working to foster a supportive family structure that includes a husband who shares in the work of the household, and social policies that make it possible for women to be mothers and to compete on the same terms as men in the paid workforce. See Matlary 1995. Dr. Matlary's address is Senior Researcher, ARENA, Oslo University, Box 1143 Blindern, 0317 Oslo, Norway; Fax 4722857832.

61. "Inclusive Language in Liturgy" 1990, 407.

62. For a discussion of the papal decision, see the special report in the *National Catholic Reporter*: Fox 1994, 1 ff.; and Fogarty 1994, 14–15.

63. "Welcome, Holy Father" 1995, 13. See also "'Radical Feminism'" 1989, 6. In this article, Cardinal Bernard Law is quoted as saying that radical feminists have "difficulty in accepting complementarity because of an assumption that equality and difference are fundamentally incompatible with each other."

64. Neal 1990, 32.

65. For Ferraro's comment, see Milhaven 1987, 218. Hussey's remark is taken from Ferraro and Hussey, with O'Reilly 1990, 164.

66. Ebaugh 1993a, 69 n. 1. See also Ebaugh 1977. Ebaugh writes in the latter work that the highest rate of dispensation of vows was from relatively liberal, change-oriented religious orders where women felt that "they could achieve the same goals in a secular life [e.g., dedication to social justice concerns] and not be restricted by such institutionalized demands as celibacy" (82).

67. Helen Rose Ebaugh suggests that the growth and decline of Catholic religious orders is related to educational and career opportunities in secular society. Her case is an interesting and convincing one, but it needs to account for the decline in numbers of male religious as well (Ebaugh 1993).

68. Greeley 1991. Greeley notes that in the early 1970s, 77 percent of Hispanics report being Catholic. By the mid-1980s, the number declines to 71 percent. He suggests two explanations related to the responsiveness of the church to "problems of ordinary people" and their "native" (and married) clergy and to the role of Protestantism in signifying a path to upward mobility (53–54).

69. Winter, Lummis, and Stokes 1994.

70. Wallace 1993, 28.

71. Unsworth 1995, 146. The pastors interviewed by Ruth Wallace indicate that another way around the proscription preventing laywomen/men from giving the homily is to have the priest say a few words after the gospel section of the service, followed by a woman's or nonordained man's preaching. Wallace 1992, 127.

72. Bowman 1994.

73. See Wallace 1992, 135–36.

74. For a statement of the Vatican's position on homosexuality, see the Congregation for the Doctrine of the Faith 1986. This is reprinted in Gramick and Furey 1988, 1–10. Father Robert Nugent and Sister Jeannine Gramick have been repeatedly queried by the Vatican about their writing and teaching on homosexuality. See Schaeffer 1996a, 10. Others, such as Father John McNeill, whose ministry to gays and lesbians included the explicitly forbidden act of making church premises available to gay and lesbian groups, have been treated more punitively still. McNeill, the founder of the gay/lesbian Catholic group Dignity, and an early challenger of the magisterial position on homosexuality, was silenced for ten years and then expelled from the Jesuits.

75. Wirpsa 1996, 4.

76. Sister Ritamary Bradley says that she and Sister Annette pursued these cases lest women of the future will ask: "Why did not women—with education and in a position to take risks . . . why did they not 'do something.' Actions like these are intended to show that we did indeed try to do something. We certainly did not 'win' the cases. But let us hope the record of what we tried to do will make a difference in some broader way" (letter to author from Sister Ritamary Bradley, 2 July 1996).

77. Sister Annette Walters, CSJ, written in August 1977 and shared with author by Sister Ritamary Bradley in personal communication, 2 July, 1966.

78. Interview by author with Rosa Marta Zarate, 11 November 1955 WOC meeting. Zarate joined the diocese as coordinator of the Department of Evangelization and Catechesis for Hispanics (DECH). She worked with Father Patricio Guillen, who was also dismissed from his job in the Community Program. Guillen had been director of DECH in the diocese. Followers of liberation theology, the two worked with the poor, traveling to parishes in rural communities setting up Spanish-language social and religious programs and organizations.

79. "Women Still Cannot Serve" 1995, 8.

80. McCarthy 1994, 17.

81. See Neal 1990. This book has an extensive bibliography of studies and firsthand accounts documenting the process of transition. See also Ebaugh 1977; Chittister et al. 1977.

82. See the discussion of *Gaudium et Spes* in Ruether 1990, 261.

83. See Ware 1985; Curb and Manahan 1985.

84. Chittister 1985, 9.

85. Traxler 1995, 133. For more on the NCCIJ, see Kopp 1985, 211.

86. Document located in the collection of the National Organization for Women 1969.

87. Perhaps this is related to these cities' later becoming the site for much activity around ordination and women-church (Weaver 1986, 112).

88. Opening statement by Elizabeth Farians, Ph.D. (Farians 1972). With her were two other members of the Chicago and Detroit organizations of NOW. See collection of NOW. papers stored in the Schlesinger Library, Radcliffe College, Carton Farians 72-8-82 M211. Also in the NOW cartons are materials such as the card suggesting that "women tithe for women." A card designed for deposit in the collection basket reads, "I cannot give financial support to any organization that discriminates against women. ——— discriminates against women in the following ways (list sexist practices) I am therefore withholding my contribution of (dollar amount) and am instead donating the amount to (name of nonsexist, nonracist organization). Signature not necessary" (designed by Denyse Barbet). See National Organization for Women n.d.

89. Williams 1995, 233–34.

90. Ibid.

91. Ibid.

92. Wittberg 1989, 531. Wittberg offers an interesting analysis of the importance of nuns' moving into the work world and having to compete with men, and coming to a realization of discrimination through these experiences.

93. Zullo 1988, 8.

94. Ashe 1985, 224.

95. Interestingly, Marian McAvoy, a sister of Loretto, writes about citing Carol Gilligan's *In a Different Voice* in trying to explain to the Loretto community why some sisters would choose to sign the 1984 abortion advertisement (McAvoy 1995, 212).

96. Writers such as Nancy Hartsock, Heidi Hartmann, Zillah Eisenstein, or Juliet Mitchell, whose earlier works could be classified in this fashion. I base this

observation on the more than twenty-five interviews I did with activists and the writings by members of the National Coalition of Nuns, the National Assembly of Religious Women, the Women's Ordination Council, Mary's Pence, and Chicago Catholic Women. This generalization probably applies less well to feminist theologians who rely in their work on a broader spectrum of women's studies writings.

97. See Williams 1995.

98. Prevallet 1995, 91.

99. This account is based entirely on Prevallet's research. Ibid., 91–113.

100. See "The Post-Vatican II Church" 1991, 233–45.

101. See the very moving story of friendship and love between two Loretto sisters. Ann Manganaro taught barefoot doctor techniques in El Salvador in the late 1980s until her death in 1993 (Crawley 1995, 115–37).

102. See Neal 1990, 39; Ferraro and Hussey, with O'Reilly 1990, 197.

103. Ibid., 196. See the National Assembly of Religious Women's newsletter, *Probe*, of which Tuite was the first editor, for a sense of the deep involvement of some women religious in Latin American social justice issues, in combating U.S. imperialism, and in assisting with the sanctuary movement.

104. Ware 1995b, 75.

105. A Brazilian educator, Freire wrote *Pedagogy of the Oppressed* (Freire 1970), which laid out methods of consciousness-raising that could be incorporated within literacy classes.

106. See Hellman 1987, 132–53.

107. The financial crisis facing religious communities that now have few members under forty and many sisters in retirement and facing health care needs is real. There are numerous studies, which I do not list here. One, the study by the William M. Mercer consulting firm, suggests that retirement benefits of male and female religious are underfunded by $6.3 billion (Karr 1994, A2).

108. A number of noncanonical communities exist, including the Immaculate Heart of Mary (IHM) in Los Angeles and the Sisters for Christian Community. Some think that noncanonical experimental communities are likely to be the way religious orders are kept alive in the future. Margaret Thompson, a historian at Syracuse, points out that religious orders had earlier sought canonical status in order to attain a greater autonomy than had been typical in earlier periods, when religious communities were accountable to the local bishops and under diocesan supervision (Thompson 1994).

109. Carroll 1985, 64–65; Weaver 1986 and 1995, 93–94.

110. In the early 1980s, the Sisters of Mercy undertook a study for themselves to try to come to some resolution about whether tubal ligations should be performed in their hospitals. Some sisters (not identified) sent the study document to Rome. Rome then undertook an investigation. Catholics for a Free Choice have addressed themselves in recent years to the issue of Catholic hospitals and health care. In most Catholic hospitals, neither abortions nor in vitro fertilization services are performed. There is variation, however, on the availability of contraceptive counseling, AIDS support, "medically necessary" tubal ligations and vasectomies, and the dispensation of a morning-after pill to rape victims. CFCC has numerous publications on the subject. See, for instance, Catholics for a Free Choice 1995.

111. Fiedler 1987, 8.

112. I am grateful to Professor Mary Segers for pointing this out in conversation.

113. Chittister 1985, 8. See also Sylvester 1997.

114. Fiedler 1985, 51.

115. Burns 1992, 133. Burns cites the work of Mary Schneider (Schneider 1986). See also Beane 1993.

CHAPTER SEVEN
A NEW ORDER?

1. Harrington 1993, 7.

2. Meyer and Tarrow 1998; the theme of social movement diffusion is also explored in the final chapter, "A Movement Society?" in Tarrow 1994.

3. Putnam 1995, 65. In another article Putnam writes briefly about the "repositories of social capital within America's minority communities" (primarily the churches and associated organizations) (Putnam 1994). See Putnam 1993.

4. Glazer 1997.

5. Tilly 1978.

6. Cohen 1990.

7. Putnam is clear in saying that voluntary associationalism cannot replace governmental activity. "Social capital is not a substitute for effective public policy but rather a prerequisite of it and, in part, a consequence of it" (Putnam 1994, 18).

8. Honig 1996, 258.

9. Quoted in Brennan 1997, 108.

10. Comment to the Minerva list on the World Wide Web (H-Minerva@ h-net.msu.edu), 7 January 1998, followed by personal communication from Rosemary Mariner, 9 January 1998.

11. Even the Second Vatican Council did not confront the internal hierarchy of the ruling structure of the church. Vatican II divided its consideration of reforms into two separate sections, "one dealing with the church ad extra and the other with the church ad intra." The relations of the church to the external world were redrawn, but not the internal organization. See Baum and Vaillancourt 1991, 31-32.

12. Comment at WOC Conference by St. Harold group member, 11 November 1995.

13. See the discussion of the supersession of class politics by identity politics in Gitlin 1995.

14. Quoted in Ebaugh 1993b, 134. Ebaugh notes, however, that "despite stereotypes and the outward demeanor of nuns, in three ways Catholic nuns were unwitting feminists: as role models for Catholic girls in immigrant communities, as professional women in various career settings, and as single women in a society where the wife-mother role was normative" (134).

15. Beane 1993, 1.

16. I am referring here, of course, to the Sister Formation Movement. The very act of seeking more education for sisters was highly controversial. Its leaders

sought to "prepare women religious [to] be competent, creative, and able to serve . . ." (ibid., 4).

17. I have discussed this question elsewhere in terms of Gaventa's three-dimensional view of power (the power to make decisions, the power to set the agenda of policy and public debate, and the power—through the control of "social myths, language, and symbols"—to shape the way people define their concerns and options). In Gaventa's account of Appalachia, all three dimensions of power converge to render the population quiescent. These three forms of power, however, need not operate in synchrony. The discursive politics of feminists in the church illustrates the capacity of protest politics to mount a counter-offensive within the second and third arenas of power, even as the first realm of decision making appears impervious to protesters' claims. See Katzenstein 1995.

18. The Vatican does not require diocesan bishops to permit girls to serve as altar servers. In the United States the dioceses of Lincoln, Nebraska, and Arlington, Virginia have refused to do so. Conservatives argue that allowing girls to serve will discourage boys from doing so, diminishing the already thin stream of young men considering the priesthood as vocation. Some also argue that this will unfairly raise girls' expectations and hopes about becoming priests. See Ribadeneira 1997, A1.

19. There was apparently a debate at the highest levels about whether the "definitive" 1995 declaration by Pope John Paul II reinforcing the ban on women's ordination belongs to the "deposit of faith" and is therefore taught "infallibly." The use of the word "definitive" (teaching that was to be "definitively held by all the church's faithful") fell short of the language of "irreformable" that was apparently being considered. Nevertheless, the Vatican Congregation for the Doctrine of the Faith released a response signed by Cardinal Joseph Ratzinger, prefect of the doctrinal congregation, and Archbishop Tarcisio Bertone, congregation secretary, to a question about the pope's 1995 declaration *Ordinatio Sacerdotalis* asserting that it had been an "infallible" teaching. There is some suggestion that an earlier representation of American bishops urged against any statement of infallibility. See Wessinger 1996. See also Steinfels 1995b, 1.

20. Edwards 1994, 7.

21. Wallace 1994, 15.

22. Steinfels 1992, E3.

23. The pastoral did attempt to portray Mary as a champion of the oppressed, and it spoke of the "sin of sexism"—a linguistic frame that on the whole met with feminist approval.

24. At the November 1994 National Conference of Catholic Bishops, the bishops did not refute the papal ban on women's ordination but issued a statement calling for "alternative ways in which women can exercise leadership in the church" (Wessinger 1996, 27; Roberts 1996, 5). In 1995, the Jesuits meeting in Rome spoke of a need to "align themselves in solidarity with women" through "genuine involvement of women in consultation and decisionmaking" and affirmed the need for inclusive language (Wessinger 1996), 28. In June 1997 Catholic theologians voted in favor of a resolution to support continued debate over the issue of women's ordination (Schaeffer 1997, 3).

25. Goldman 1992, A16. See also "U.S. Catholicism: Trends" 1993, 21–32. For a more recent poll, which shows a trend toward even greater liberalization, see "Survey Finds Catholics Want More Say" 1996, 4.

26. Naughton 1997 provides a gripping narrative of "the standing" at Holy Trinity in which some parishioners remained on their feet throughout Mass to protest women's exclusion from the priesthood, although the controversy that has beset the parish involves a broad range of issues in addition; McKinley 1998; Fiedler 1998.

27. Murphy 1997, 14.

28. Milhaven 1987, xi.

29. Goldman 1973, 132.

30. Moore 1996, 121.

31. Ibid., 129. See also Moskos and Butler 1996.

32. But see Priest 1997b and 1997c on the slow pace of integration into combat jobs.

33. Roper 1992, 55.

34. This pressure exists even for civilians when they are serving in an official capacity. In the recent inquiry into sex discrimination in the army following the Aberdeen Proving Ground events, for instance, Secretary Togo West appointed a panel that included civilian advisers to make recommendations. The limita tions on even a civilian role in such a situation were evident when two women resigned from the panel: Dr. Leora N. Rosen, a social anthropologist at the Walter Reed Army Institute of Research, had urged the panel to include ques tions on the sexual harassment survey that would have explored the linkages between harassment and soldiers' frequenting of strip joints and pornography viewing. The second panelist, Dr. Madeline Morris, who had come to Secretary West's attention through her academic research on military culture and rape, also resigned under pressure. Morris also urged Secretary West to retain the sur vey questions. After she spoke with the press about her work and after her law review article was misrepresented in a *Washington Times* piece (3 and 7 April 1997)—the latter took out of context her scholarly analysis of the higher rates of rape than of other criminal activity within the military—she came to be viewed as a liability. See Schmitt 1997, 15. See Morris 1996, 651.

35. There are expressions in the navy, for instance, like "What goes on on shore, stays on shore" (tales of adultery are not to be taken home) or "Rings off" (before hitting port).

36. As reported in Ricks 1997a, A20. See also Ricks 1997b, 278–82.

37. Ricks 1997a, A20.

38. One major setback was the Nancy Kassebaum Baker report that recom mended the resegregation by gender of significant portions of service training (Myers 1997, A1).

39. Ricks 1997b, 295.

40. There was also apparently some apprehension in conservative congres sional circles that Lister was in line for the army secretary appointment left va cant by Togo West's departure.

41. McAllister and Priest 1997c, A1.

42. Priest 1997a, A13.

43. Interview by author with Respondent 11.

44. Donnelly 1995.

45. See the remarks by army brigadier general Evelyn P. Foote in Kitfield 1997, 2128. See the comprehensive discussion in Ginburg 1997, 14–15.

46. Moskos and Butler 1996.

47. Moskos's exact words are "The main argument for the integration of women in the armed forces must be the same as it was for blacks: Does it make for a more efficient military? The bottom line is that blacks and whites are essentially interchangeable soldiers. But when physical differences and privacy concerns matter—and they do—men and women are not" (Moskos 1998, C1). Moskos is one of the most influential academic scholars in military circles. His writings shaped the formulation "Don't Ask, Don't Tell, Don't Pursue."

48. Interview by author with Commander Rosemary Mariner, 16 January 1998.

49. Interview by author with Respondent 12.

50. Bem 1993. See also Bem 1995.

51. Smith 1993; Smith 1989, 229–93. See also the response to Smith in Stevens 1995.

52. One of the most careful critiques, which treats both the strengths of rights doctrine and its deficiencies, is Crenshaw 1988. And see Minow 1991; MacKinnon 1987, 1989, 1993; Eisenstein 1988. This list scarcely begins to enumerate the sources that have contributed to a critique (both positive and negative) of the liberal premises of American law.

53. Okin 1989.

54. The phrase is Burke's. See Mehta forthcoming (1999).

55. Hunter 1991.

REFERENCES

The individuals listed here by name, as well as some whose names I have not recorded, are the core source material in this book. In the text, I list the uniformed service personnel with whom I spoke by their rank at the time at which we met. I have designated simply as "respondent" some individuals who preferred not to have their names used. In their cases, I withhold the dates of the interviews to avoid any association with the interviews that are listed by dates.

INTERVIEWEES

Military

Gerald Alfred
Vicki Almquist
Trish Beckman
Carolyn Becraft
Michelle Benecke
Barbara Brehm
William Brundage
Kathy Bruyere
Nancy Buermeyer
Carol Burke
Lillian Burke
Rani Bush
Bobbie Carleton
M. Kathleen Carpenter
Antonia Chayes
D. O. Cooke
Diane Davis
Linda Grant Depauw
Tanya Domi
Karen Dunivin
Ann Eidson
Andreas Elesky
Andy Feinstein
Evelyn P. Foote
Mark Forman
Barney Frank
Pat Gormley
Rosanne Greco
Brynnen Hahn
Gwendolyn Hall
Richard Halloran

Kelly Hamilton
Claiborne Haughton
Karen Heath
Jacaranda Henkel
Jeanne Holm
Rosemary Howard
Mary Humphries
Dana Isaacoff
Ron Joe
Kathy Johnson
Michelle Johnson
Deborah Kamin
Joanne Kauffeld
Mike Kehoe
Lawrence Korb
Carolyn Kresek
Jeanne Lang
Pam Le Baron
Barbara Lee
Robyn Lippner
Lory Manning
Rosemary Mariner
Melanie Martindale
Ann McGee
Gail McGinn
Colleen McKenzie
Linda McTague
Brenda Moore
Derek Moore
Betty Morden
Lisa Moreno
Linda Netsch

Diane Ordes
Ellen Press-Murdoch
Carolyn Prevatte
M. C. Pruitt
Aline Quester
Paul Roush
Georgia Sadler
Sue Guenter-Schlesinger
Jill Singleton
P. J. Sottile
David Super
Patricia Thomas
Elizabeth Toupin
Bill Walton
Mitzi Wertheim

Church

Anita Baird
Ritamary Bradley
Cornelia Buhrle
Tim Byrnes
J. Cocuzzi
Carol Cook
Patty Crowley
Kathleen DeSautels
Connie Driscoll

Marita Estor
Barbara Ferraro
Maureen Fiedler
Maureen Gallagher
Renny Golden
Chris Gould
Pat Hussey
Mary Therese Johnson
Gregory Lebel
Kathryn Messina
Suzanne Mettler
Laurie Michalowski
Marie Augusta Neal
Laverne Nickson
Mary Oates
Kathy Osberger
Mary Jude Postel
Mary Karen Powers
Donna Quinn
Lora Ann Quiñonez
Maureen Reiff
Mary Segers
Margaret Traxler
Mary Daniel Turner
Judy Vaughan
Virginia Williams

BOOKS AND PERIODICALS

"Abortions to Increase." 1973. *Air Force Times*, 7 February: x

Abrams, Kathryn. 1993. "Gender in the Military: Androcentrism and Institutional Reform." *Law and Contemporary Problems* 56, no. 4 (Autumn): 217–43.

Aggarwal, Vinod K. 1985. *Liberal Protectionism: The International Politics of Organized Textile Trade*. Berkeley and Los Angeles: University of California Press.

Alexander, Clifford L., Jr. 1986. "Blacks and the Military." In *Black Voices in American Politics*, ed. Jeffrey M. Elliot. New York: Harcourt, Brace, Jovanovich.

Anderson, Kristi. 1996. *After Suffrage: Women in Partisan and Electoral Politics before the New Deal*. Chicago: University of Chicago Press.

Aptheker, Herbert, ed. 1973. *The Education of Black People*. Amherst: University of Massachusetts Press.

"Army Doctor Jailed for Conscience Sees Need for Peace Education." 1992. *Boston Globe*, 12 April: 25.

Ashe, Kaye. 1985. "Looking Back, Looking Ahead." In *Midwives of the Future: American Sisters Tell their Story*, ed. Ann Patrick Ware, 218–26. Kansas City, MO: Leavan Press.

"Ash Wednesday Protest." 1996. *National Catholic Reporter*, 1 March: 11.

"Assemblywoman Refused Communion." 1989. *Origins* 19, no. 28 (14 December): 457.

Babcock, Barbara Allen. 1975. *Sex Discrimination and the Law*. Boston: Little, Brown.

Baer, Judith A. 1991. *Women in American Law: The Struggle towards Equality from the New Deal to the Present*. New York: Holmes and Meier.

Banaszak, Lee Ann. 1996. *Why Movements Succeed or Fail: Opportunity, Culture and the Struggle for Woman Suffrage*. Princeton: Princeton University Press.

Bant, Bruce N. 1980. "Working Together: The Army's Assault on Sexism." *Soldiers* (October): 6–10.

Barkalow, Carol, with Andrea Rabb. 1990. *In the Men's House: An Inside Account of Life in the Army by One of West Point's First Female Graduates*. New York: Poseidon.

Barrett, Nancy. 1987. "Women and the Economy." In *The American Woman 1987–88: A Report in Depth*, ed. Sara E. Rix. New York: W. W. Norton.

"Battling Sexism in Pittsburgh."1986. *Soujourners* 15, no. 6 (June): 10–11.

Baum, Gregory, and Jean-Guy Vaillancourt. 1991. "The Church and Modernization." In *Religion and the Social Order*, vol. 2, *Vatican II and U.S. Catholicism*, ed. Helen Rose Ebaugh, 31–32. Greenwich, CT: JAI Press.

Baumgaertner, William L., ed. 1988. *Fact Book on Theological Education: 1987–88*. Vandalia: Association of Theological Schools in the United States and Canada.

Beane, Marjorie Noterman, Ph.D. 1993. *From Framework to Freedom: A History of the Sister Formation Conference*. Lanham, MD: University Press of America.

Becrafi, Carolyn. 1978. "The Woman's Movement: Its Effects on the Wives of Military Officers." M.A. thesis. Course: EDHP-590B, 13 June. University of Southern California.

———. 1991. "Women in the U.S. Armed Services: The War in the Persian Gulf." Washington, DC: Women's Research and Education Institute.

Bem, Sandra Lipsitz. 1993. *The Lenses of Gender: Transforming the Debate on Sexual Inequality*. New Haven: Yale University Press.

———. 1995. "Dismantling Gender Polarization and Compulsory Heterosexuality: Should We Turn the Volume Down or Up." *Journal of Sex Research* 32, no. 4: 329–34.

———. 1996. "Transforming the Debate on Sexual Inequality: From Biological Difference to Institutionalized Androcentrism." In *Lectures on the Psychology of Women*, ed. J. C. Chrisler, C. Golden, and P. D. Rosee, 9–21. New York: McGraw Hill.

Bennett, James Gordon. 1992. "Shock Waves at the U.S. Naval Academy." *Glamour* 90, no. 6 (June): 42 ff.

Bernstein, Mary. 1997. "Celebration and Suppression: The Strategic Uses of Identity by the Lesbian and Gay Movement." *American Journal of Sociology* 103, no. 3 (November): 531–65.

Binkin, Martin, and Shirley Bach. 1977. *Women in the Military*. Washington, DC: The Brookings Institution.

Blazar, Ernest. 1995. "Senior Navy Leaders Feel Essay's Sting." *Navy Times*, 9 September: 9.

Bohlen, Celestine. 1998. "John Paul Appoints 22 More Cardinals; 2 Are from the U.S." *New York Times*, 19 January: A1.

Bole, William. 1995. "Bishops Want Feminist Professor Fired." *National Catholic Reporter* 31, no. 22 (31 March): 3.

Boles, Janet K. 1986 "The Women's Movement and the Redesign of Urban Services." Remarks prepared for the annual meeting of the American Political Science Association, Washington, D.C.: 1–30.

Bond, Ruth M. 1993. "The Civilian Old Salt Who Took on the Navy's Cover-up of Tailhook." *New York Times*, 16 May: E7.

Bordo, Susan. 1990. "Feminism, Postmodernism, and Gender Scepticism." In *Feminism/Postmodernism*, ed. Linda J. Nicholson, 133–57. New York: Routledge.

Bourdieu, Pierre. 1972, 1977. *Outline of a Theory of Practice*. Trans. Richard Nice. New York: Cambridge University Press.

Bowman, Jim. 1994. *Bending the Rules: What American Priests Tell American Catholics*. New York: Crossroad.

Brennan, Margaret, IHM. 1997. "No Two Exactly Alike." In Sisters, Servants of the Immaculate Heart of Mary, *Building Sisterhood: A Feminist History of the Sisters, Servants of the Immaculate Heart of Mary*, 95–113. Syracuse: Syracuse University Press.

Brenner, Johanna. 1996. "The Best of Times, the Worst of Times: Feminism in the United States." In *Mapping the Women's Movement*, ed. Monica Threlfall, 17–73. London: Verso.

Brooke, James. 1995. "For Most G.I.s Only Few Hints of Hate Groups." *New York Times*, 21 December: A14.

Brotherton, Anne, ed. 1992. *The Voice of the Turtledove: New Catholic Women in Europe*. Mahwah: Paulist Press.

Brown, Elsa Barkley. 1997. "Negotiating and Transforming the Public Sphere: African American Political Life in the Transition from Slavery to Freedom." In *Women Transforming Politics: An Alternative Reader*, ed. Cathy J. Cohen, Kathleen B. Jones, and Joan C. Tronto, 343–77. New York: New York University Press.

Brownmiller, Susan. 1975. *Against Our Will: Men, Women, and Rape*. New York: Simon and Schuster.

Brundage, William. n.d. (forthcoming). Ph.D. diss., Department of Government, Harvard University.

Burke, Carol. 1992. "Dames at Sea." *New Republic*, 17 and 24 August: 18–20.

———. 1993. "Sex, G.I.s and Videotape." Paper at Women and the Military Workshop, Peace Studies Program, Cornell University, Ithaca, New York.

———. 1996. "Pernicious Cohesion." In *It's Our Military Too! Women and the U.S. Military*, ed. Judith Hicks Stiehm, 205–19. Philadelphia: Temple University Press.

Burns, Gene. 1992. *The Frontiers of Catholicism: The Politics of Ideology in a Liberal World*. Berkeley and Los Angeles: University of California Press.

Burstein, Paul, Rachel L. Einwohner, and Jocelyn A. Hollander. 1995. "The Success of Political Movements: A Bargaining Perspective." In *The Politics of Social Protest: Comparative Perspectives on States and Social Movements*, ed.

J. Craig Jenkins and Bert Klandermans, 275–96. Minneapolis: University of Minnesota Press.

Butler, Judith. 1990. *Gender Troubles: Feminism and the Subversion of Identity.* New York: Routledge.

Butler, Judith, and Joan W. Scott, eds. 1992. *Feminists Theorize the Political.* New York: Routledge.

Byrnes, Timothy A. 1991. *Catholic Bishops in American Politics.* Princeton: Princeton University Press.

Calhoun, Craig. 1996. "A Different Poststructuralism." *Contemporary Sociology: A Journal of Reviews* 25, no. 3 (May): 302–5.

———, ed. 1994. *Social Theory and the Politics of Identity.* Oxford: Blackwell.

Call to Action. 1996. *Renewing Our Church: A National Directory.* Chicago.

Cammermeyer, Margarethe. 1994. *Serving in Silence.* New York: Viking Penguin.

Cannon, Katie Geneva. 1995. *Womanism and the Soul of the Black Community.* New York: Continuum Publishing Company.

"Can Women Stay in the Church?" 1994. *Witness* (July): 8–11.

Carr, Anne E. 1988. *Transforming Grace: Christian Tradition and Women's Experience.* San Francisco: Harper and Row.

Carroll, Elizabeth. 1985. "Reaping the Fruits of Redemption." In *Midwives of the Future: American Nuns Tell Their Story,* ed. Ann Patrick Ware, 53–68. Kansas City, MO: Leavan Press.

———. 1995. "Anger with the Church." *New Women, New Church* 18, no. 2 (Fall): 11–14.

"Case Being Built against Aviators." 1993. *New York Times,* 7 February: 20.

Castaneda, Carol, and Andrea Stone. 1993 "Tailhook May Claim Admirals." *USA Today,* 8 February: A1

Cates, G. L. 1993. Letter to the Editor. *Chicago Tribune,* 17 May: 16.

Catholics for a Free Choice. 1995. *Risky Business: The Community Impact of Catholic Health Care Expansion.* Washington, DC: Catholics for a Free Choice (CFCC).

Cavanaugh, Mildred. 1973. "Coffee, Teas, but without Me." *Air Force Times,* 1 August: 5–7.

"Cheney Would Expand Women's Roles." 1991. *Washington Times,* 26 April.

Chief of Naval Operations. 1988. "Study Group Report on Equal Opportunity in the Navy." Washington, DC (July).

———. 1991. "1990 Navy Women's Study Group: An Update Report on the Progress of Women in the Navy" (March).

Chittister, Joan D. 1985. "No Time for Tying Cats." In *Midwives of the Future: American Sisters Tell their Story,* ed. Ann Patrick Ware, 4–22. Kansas City, MO: Leavan Press.

———. 1994. "One, Two, Three Strikes, You're Out in the Ol' Boys' Game." *National Catholic Reporter* 30, no. 32 (17 June): 12.

Chittister, Joan, et al. 1977. *Climb along the Cutting Edge: An Analysis of Change in Religious Life.* New York: Paulist Press.

Cohen, Lizabeth. 1990. *Making a New Deal: Industrial Workers in Chicago, 1919–1939.* Cambridge: Cambridge University Press.

Collins, Patricia Hill. 1991. *Black Feminist Thought: Knowledge, Consciousness, and the Politics of Empowerment.* New York: Routledge.

"Command Presents." 1994. Editorial. *New York Times*, 18 April: A14.

Compart, Andrew. 1997. "DACOWITS New Goal: Shatter Glass Ceiling." *Navy Times*, 28 April: 11.

Congregation for the Doctrine of the Faith. 1986. "Letter to the Bishops of the Church on the Pastoral Care of Homosexual Persons." Reprinted in *The Vatican and Homosexuality*, ed. Jeannine Gramick and Pat Furey, 1–10. New York: Crossroad (1988).

Cook, Rebecca J. 1995. "The Elimination of Sexual Apartheid." *Conscience*, 14 no. 3 (Autumn): 31–33.

Coombe, Rosemary J. 1989. "Room for Manoeuver: Toward a Theory of Practice in Critical Legal Studies." *Law and Social Inquiry* 14, no. 1 (Winter): 60–123.

Coser, Lewis. 1974. *Greedy Institutions: Patterns of Undivided Commitment.* New York: Free Press.

Costain, Anne N. 1992. *Inviting Women's Rebellion: A Political Process Interpretation of Women's Movement.* Baltimore, MD: Johns Hopkins University Press.

Costello, Cynthia, and Barbara Kivimae Krimgold, eds., for the Women's Research and Education Institute (Betty Dooley, president). 1996. *The American Woman, 1996–1997.* New York: Norton.

Cott, Nancy F. 1987. *The Grounding of Modern Feminism.* New Haven: Yale University Press.

———. 1990. "Across the Great Divide: Women in Politics before and after 1920." In *Women, Politics, and Change*, ed. Louise Tilly and Patricia Gurin, 162. New York: Russell Sage Foundation.

Cox, Harvey. 1988. *The Silencing of Leonardo Boff: The Vatican and the Future of World Christianity.* Oak Park, IL: Meyer Stone Books.

Crawley, Martha. 1995. "Salvador: Land of Love, Land of War." In *Naming Our Truth: Stories of Loretto Women*, ed. Ann Patrick Ware, 115–37. Inverness, CA: Chardon Press.

Crenshaw, Kimberlé Williams. 1988. "Race, Reform, and Retrenchment: Transformation and Legitimation in Antidiscrimination Law." *Harvard Law Review* 101, no. 7 (May): 1331–87.

———. 1989. "Demarginalizing the Intersection of Race and Sex: A Black Feminist Critique of Anti-Discrimination Doctrine, Feminist Theory and Antiracist Politics." *University of Chicago Legal Forum*, 139–67.

———. 1991. "Mapping the Margins: Intersectionality, Identity Politics, and Violence against Women of Color." *Stanford Law Review* 43, no. 6 (July): 1241–99.

———. 1992. "Whose Story Is It Anyway? Feminist and Antiracist Appropriations of Anita Hill." In *Race-Ing Justice, En-Gendering Power: Essays on Anita Hill, Clarence Thomas, and the Construction of Social Reality*, ed. Toni Morrison. New York: Pantheon Books.

"CTA 'We Are the Church' Conference Draws 2,300." 1994. *Call to Action News* 15, no. 3 (January): 3.

Cunningham, Mary Ann. 1995. "From Silence to Speech: Finding My Voice." In *Naming Our Truth: Stories of Loretto Women*, ed. Ann Patrick Ware, 139–61. Inverness, CA: Chardon Press.

Curb, Rosemary, and Nancy Manahan. 1985. *Lesbian Nuns: Breaking Silence*. Tallahassee, FL: Naiad Press.

Cutler, Katie. 1982."All about DACOWITS." *Airman* (April): 21.

DACOWITS Conference Query/Reply. 1984

"DACOWITS Fired Up over Academy Issue." 1975. *Air Force Times*, 7 May: 4.

"DACOWITS Gaining New Clout." 1980. *Air Force Times*, 26 March: 15.

Daly, Mary. 1973. *Beyond God the Father: Toward a Philosophy of Women's Liberation*. Boston: Beacon Press.

———. 1975. *The Church and the Second Sex: With a New Feminist Post-Christian Introduction*. New York: Harper and Row.

———. 1984. *Pure Lust: Elemental Feminist Philosophy*. Boston: Beacon Press.

D'Arienzo, Camille. 1985. "My Pact with Camillus." In *Midwives of the Future: American Sisters Tell Their Story*, ed. Ann Patrick Ware, 22–36. Kansas City, MO: Leavan Press.

Davis, Flora. 1991. *Moving the Mountain: The Women's Movement in America since 1960*. New York: Simon and Schuster.

Davis, Jacquelyn. 1986. Profile in *Minerva* 4, no. 1 (Spring): 82 83.

———. 1987. "Memorandum to General Anthony Lukeman, USMC: 1987 WESTPAC visit of the Defense Advisory Committee on Women in the Services." (Letter in possession of author). (26 August): 1.

———. 1989. "DACOWITS European Trip, Summer 1988." *Minerva: Quarterly Report on Women and the Military* (Summer): 43.

Defense Advisory Committee on Women in the Services. 1994. *Defense Advisory Committee on Women in the Services Issuebook from the 1994 Fall Conference*. Virginia Beach, Virginia.

———. N.d. *Thirty-fifth Anniversary Highlights of the Defense Advisory Committee on Women in the Services: Thirty-five Years of Service to the Department of Defense* (no publication information); material printed and distributed by the DACOWITS office.

Department of Defense. 1988. Report of the Task Force on Women in the Military" (January).

Department of Defense Inspector General. 1993. *Tailhook 91, Part 2: Events at the Thirty-fifth Annual Tailhook Symposium*. (February). Washington, DC: GPO. III-1, B-4.

Department of Defense Naval Inspector General. 1997. "Integration of Women into Carrier Air Wing Eleven." Report of Investigation, Case No. 951297. 10 February. Obtained through Freedom of Information request to navy inspector general.

Díaz-Cotto, Juanita. 1996. *Gender, Ethnicity, and the State: Latina and Latino Prison Politics*. Albany: State University of New York Press.

Donnelly, Elaine. 1995. "Social Experimentation in the Military." Heritage Lectures. Wasington, DC: Heritage Foundation.

Dunivin, Karen O. 1988. "There's Men, There's Women, and There's Me: The Role and Status of Military Women." *Minerva* 6, no. 2 (Summer): 43 ff.

Eastman, Margaret E. 1972. "DACOWITS: A Nice Little Group That Doesn't Do Very Much." *Army Times Family Supplement* 32 (15 March).

Ebaugh, Helen Rose Fuchs. 1977. *Out of the Cloister: A Study of Organizational Dilemmas.* Austin: University of Texas Press.

————. 1993a. "The Growth and Decline of Catholic Religious Orders of Women Worldwide: The Impact of Women's Opportunity Structures." *Journal for the Scientific Study of Religion* 30 (March): 68–75.

————. 1993b. *Women in the Vanishing Cloister: Organizational Decline in Catholic Religious Orders in the United States.* New Brunswick, NJ: Rutgers University Press.

Edwards, Donna. 1988. "WEAL Supreme Court Brief Helps Ex-Military Spouse Seek Pension Share." *WEAL Washington Report* 17, nos. 4–6 (Winter): 8.

Edwards, Robin T. 1994. "African Bishops Offer Wish Lists to Synod." *National Catholic Reporter* 30, no. 26 (29 April): 7.

Eisenstein, Hester. 1995. "The Australian Femocratic Experiment." In *Feminist Organizations; Harvest of the New Women's Movement,* ed. Myra Marx Ferree and Patricia Yancey Martin, 69–84. Philadelphia: Temple University Press.

————. 1996. *Inside Agitators: Australian Femocrats and the State.* Philadelphia: Temple University Press.

Eisenstein, Hester, and Alice Jardine. 1991. *Gender Shock: Practicing Feminism on Two Continents.* Boston: Beacon Press.

Eisenstein, Zillah R. 1988. *The Female Body and the Law.* Berkeley and Los Angeles: University of California Press.

————. 1994. *The Color of Gender: Reimaging Democracy.* Berkeley and Los Angeles: University of California Press.

Eisinger, Peter K. 1973. "Conditions of Protest Behavior in American Cities." *American Political Science Review* 67, no. 1 (March): 11–28.

Enloe, Cynthia. 1983. *Does Khaki Become You: The Militarization of Women's Lives.* Boston: Southend Press; republished by Pandora Press, 1988.

————. 1990a. *Bananas, Beaches, and Bases: Making Feminist Sense of International Politics.* Berkeley and Los Angeles: University of California Press.

————. 1990b. "Womenandchildren." *Village Voice,* 25 September.

————. 1996. "Spoils of War." *Ms.* (March/April): 15.

————. 1999. *Maneuvers: The International Politics of Militarizing Women's Lives.* Berkeley and Los Angeles: University of California Press.

Erickson, Nancy S. 1982. "Historical Background of 'Protective' Labor Legislation: *Muller v. Oregon.*" In *Women and the Law: The Social Historical Perspective,* ed. D. Kelly Weisberg, 2:155–87. Cambridge: Schenkman Publishing Co.

Evans, Sara M., and Harry C. Boyte. 1986. *Free Spaces: The Sources of Democratic Change in America.* New York: Harper and Row.

Eyerman, Ron, and Andrew Jamison. 1991. *Social Movements: A Cognitive Approach.* University Park: Pennsylvania State University Press.

Fabella, V., and Oduyoye, eds. 1988. *With Passion and Compassion: Third World Women Doing Theology.* Maryknoll, NY: Orbis Books.

Faludi, Susan. 1991. *Backlash: The Undeclared War against American Women.* New York: Crown.

Farians, Elizabeth, 1972. Opening statement at NOW Ecumenical Task Force on Women and Religion, press conference at National Conference of Catholic Bishops, Sheraton-Cadillac Hotel, Detroit, Michigan, 28 April. NOW. Collection, Carton 1, Farians, 72-8-82 M211, Schlesinger Library, Radcliffe College, Cambridge, Massachusetts.

Farrell, Caroline. 1990. "Who Shall Find a Liberated Woman." *Probe* 18, no. 5 (October/November): 7.

Fass, Paula. 1989. *Outside In: The Transformation of American Education.* Oxford: Oxford University Press.

Ferguson, Kathy E. 1984. *The Feminist Case against Bureaucracy.* Philadelphia: Temple University Press.

Ferraro, Barbara, and Patricia Hussey. 1987. Profile in *Inside Stories: Thirteen Valiant Women Challenging the Church*, ed. Annie Lally Milhaven, 65–83. Mystic, CT: Twenty-Third Publications.

Ferraro, Barbara, and Patricia Hussey, with Jane O'Reilly. 1990. *No Turning Back: Two Nuns Battle with the Vatican over Women's Right to Choose.* New York: Poseidon.

Ferree, Myra Marx. 1992. "The Political Context of Rationality: Rational Choice Theory and Resource Mobilization." In *Frontiers in Social Movement Theory*, ed. Aldon D. Morris and Carol McClurg Mueller, 29–53. New Haven: Yale University Press.

Ferree, Myra Marx, and Patricia Yancey Martin. 1995. *Feminist Organizations: Harvest of the New Women's Movements.* Philadelphia: Temple University Press.

Ferrey, Marie E. 1987. "Task Force on Military Women Called 'Positive' Step." *Air Force Times*, 2 November: 36.

Fiedler, Maureen. 1985. "Riding the City Bus from Pittsburgh." In *Midwives of the Future: American Nuns Tell Their Story*, ed. Ann Patrick Ware, 37–53. Kansas City, MO: Leaven Press.

———. 1987. "Claiming Our Power as Women in the Midst of Political Struggle." Amplified version of a talk delivered at "Women-Church: Claiming Our Power" conference, Cincinnati, Ohio (October). On file at Catholics for a Free Choice, Washington, D.C.

———. 1998. "The Inquisition at Holy Trinity." Aired on WAMU-FM, Washington, DC, 9 December 1997. For more information, contact Maureen Fiedler, Catholics Speak Out, P.O. Box 5206, Hyattsville, MD 20782.

Filteau, Jerry. 1995. "Papal No to Women Priests Is Infallible, Document Says." *National Catholic Reporter*, 1 December: 5.

Fiorenza, Elisabeth Schüssler. 1983. *In Memory of Her: A Feminist Theological Reconstruction of Christian Origins.* New York: Crossroad.

———. 1984. *Bread Not Stone: The Challenge of Feminist Biblical Interpretation.* Boston: Beacon Press.

———. 1993. *Discipleship of Equals: A Critical Feminist Ekkl{{emacron}}sialogy of Liberation*: New York: Crossroad.

Fitzgerald, Constance. 1993. "American Indian Traditionalist's Reflection on the Women-Church Conference." *Probe* 21, no. 2 (May–June): 5.

Fitzpatrick, Ruth McDonough. 1987. Interview in *The Inside Stories: Thirteen Valiant Women Challenging the Church*, ed. Annie Lally Milhaven, 41. Mystic, CT: Twenty-Third Publications.

Fogarty, Gerald P. 1994. "Venerable but Rocky History of U.S. Collegiality." *National Catholic Reporter* 31, no. 4 (11 November): 14–15.

Foote, Evelyn P. 1993. "Evelyn P. Foote: Advocate of Equality in the Military." In *Women in Foreign Policy*, ed. Nancy E. McGlen and Meredith Reid Sarkees, 122–29. New York: Routledge.

Foster, George. 1973. "High Court Hears WAF Equality Case."*Air Force Times*, 31 January: 18.

Fox, Thomas C. 1994. "Vatican Veto: Rejection of Inclusive Language Raises the Question of Who Has Authority to Teach." *National Catholic Reporter* 31, no. 4 (11 November): 1 ff.

———. 1995. *Sexuality and Catholicism*. New York: George Braziller.

Francke, Linda Bird. 1993. "Paula Coughlin: The Woman Who Changed the U.S. Navy." *Glamour* (June): 158 ff.

———. 1997. *Ground Zero*. New York: Simon and Schuster.

Franzway, Suzanne, Dianne Court, and R. W. Connell. 1989. *Staking a Claim: Feminism, Bureaucracy and the State*. Boston: Allen and Unwin; Oxford: Polity Press.

Fraser, Nancy. 1990. "Rethinking the Public Sphere: Contribution to the Critique of Actually Existing Democracy." *Social Text* 8, no. 3; 9, no. 1: 56–79.

Freire, Paulo. 1970. *Pedagogy of the Oppressed*. New York: Continuum.

"Front Woman?" 1995. *Conscience* 16, no. 3 (Autumn): 25.

Frug, Mary Jo. 1992. *Postmodern Legal Feminism*. New York: Routledge.

Fuchs, Victor R. 1988. *Women's Quest for Economic Equality*. Cambridge: Harvard University Press.

Fuss, Diana. 1989. *Essentially Speaking*. New York: Routledge.

Gamson, William. 1990. *The Strategy of Social Protest* 2d. ed. Belmont, CA: Wadsworth.

Gamson, William A., and David S. Meyer. 1996. "Framing Political Opportunity." In *Comparative Perspectives on Social Movements: Political Opportunities, Mobilizing Structures, and Cultural Framings*, ed. Doug McAdam, John D. McCarthy, and Mayer N. Zald, 81–99. Cambridge: Cambridge University Press.

Garrison, Becky. 1996. "Tailhooker Pulled from Promotion List." *Navy Times*, 8 January: 4.

Gaventa, John. 1980. *Power and Powerlessness: Quiescence and Rebellion in an Appalachian Valley*. Urbana: University of Illinois Press.

Gellman, Barton. 1991a. "Combat Role for Women Stalled by Senate Panel." *Washington Post*, 10 July: A4.

———. 1991b. "Women Fliers in Race with Changing Times." *Washington Post*, 29 July: 1.

General Accounting Office. 1994. *DoD Service Academies: More Actions Needed to Eliminate Sexual Harassment*. GAO/NSIAD-94-6 (January).

Gibeau, Dawn. 1993. "Priest Critic of Celibacy Policy Is Silenced by Nashville Bishop." *National Catholic Reporter*, 10 December: 5.

Gidlow, Liette. 1997. "Getting Out the Vote: Gender and Citizenship in an Age of Consumer Culture." Ph.D. diss., Cornell University.

Gigowski, Margaret. 1985. "Women Vietnam Veterans Form Networks." *Minerva* 3, no. 2 (Summer): 17–20.

Gilkes, Cheryl Townsend. 1988. "Building in Many Places: Multiple Commitments and Ideologies in Black Women's Community Work." In *Women and the Politics of Empowerment*, ed. Ann Bookman and Sandra Morgen, 53–76. Philadelphia: Temple University Press.

Gilligan, Carol. 1982. *In a Different Voice: Psychological Theory and Women's Development.* Cambridge: Harvard University Press.

Ginberg, Yana. 1997. "All Things Being Equal: Should Men and Women Meet the Same Physical Standards?" *Navy Times*, 22 September: 14–15.

Ginsberg, Benjamin, and Martin Shefter. 1990. *Politics by Other Means: The Declining Importance of Elections in America.* New York: Basic Books.

Gitlin, Todd. 1995. *The Twilight of Common Dreams.* New York: Metropolitan Books.

Giveu, Dawn. 1986. "Mainline Church Women 'Empowered' by Gathering.' *National Catholic Reporter* 23, no. 1 (24 October): 1.

Glaberson, William. 1992. "Gay Journalists Leading a Revolution." *New York Times* 10 September: A20.

———. 1997. "Five Orthodox Jews Spur Moral Debate over Yale's Housing Rules." *New York Times*, 7 September: 45.

Glazer, Nathan. 1997. *We Are All Multiculturalists Now.* Cambridge: Harvard University Press.

Goffman, Erving. 1961. *Asylums: Essays on the Social Situation of Mental Patients and Other Inmates.* Garden City, NY: Anchor Books.

Goldman, Ari L. 1992. "Catholics Are at Odds with Bishops." *New York Times*, 19 June: A16.

Goldman, Nancy. 1973. "The Changing Role of Women in the Armed Forces." In *Changing Women in a Changing Society*, ed. Joan Huber, 130–50. Chicago: University of Chicago Press.

Goldstein, Leslie Friedman. 1979, 1988. *The Constitutional Rights of Women.* Madison, WI: University of Wisconsin Press.

Gomez, Rita Victoria. 1991. "What Women Did in Operation Desert Storm." *Minerva's Bulletin Board* (Summer): 6–7.

Goodman, Jill Laurie. 1979. "Women, War, and Equality: An Examination of Sex Discrimination in the Military." *Women's Rights Law Reporter* 5, no. 4 (Summer): 243–83.

Gordon, Marilyn A., and Mary Jo Ludvigson. 1990. "The Combat Exclusion for Women Aviators: A Constitutional Analysis." *United States Air Force Journal of Legal Studies* 1: 51–85.

Graff, Ann O'Hara. 1993. "Catholic Feminist Theologians on Catholic Women in the Church." *New Theology Review* 6, no. 2 (May): 6–19.

Gramick, Jeannine and Pat Furey. 1988. *The Vatican and Homosexuality.* New York: Crossroad.

Greeley, Andrew M. 1991. "The Demography of American Catholics: 1965–1990." In *Religion and the Social Order: Vatican II and U.S. Catholicism*, ed. Helen Rose Fuchs Ebaugh, 37–56. Greenwich, CT: JAI Press.

Greeley, Andrew M., and Peter H. Rossi. 1966. *The Education of Catholic Americans*. Chicago: Aldine.

Greenhouse, Linda. 1996a. "High Court Rejects Challenge to the Military's Gay Policy." *New York Times*, 22 October: 1.

———. 1996b. "Justices Appear Skeptical of V.M.I.'s Proposal for Women." *New York Times*, 18 January: A18.

Hacker, Andrew. 1992. *Two Nations: Black and White, Separate, Hostile, Unequal*. New York: Charles Scribner's Sons.

Hall, Betty Jean. 1990. "Women Miners Can Dig It, Too!" In *Communities in Economic Crisis: Appalachia and the South*, ed. John Gaventa, Barbara Ellen Smith, and Alex Willingham, 53–60. Philadephia: Temple University Press.

Hall, Peter A., and Rosemary C. R. Taylor. 1996. "New Institutionalisms." Max-Planck-Institut für Gesellschaftsforschung, Cologne, Germany. MPIFG Discussion Paper 96/6 (June).

Hansen, Susan. 1987. "Catholic Women, Citing 'Sexist' Church Call for 'Much Patience.'" *National Catholic Reporter* 24, no. 4 (November): 1.

Harding, Sandra G. 1986. *The Science Question in Feminism*. Ithaca, NY: Cornell University Press.

———. 1991. *Whose Science? Whose Knowledge? Thinking from Women's Lives*. Ithaca, NY: Cornell University Press.

Harrington, Mona. 1993. *Women Lawyers: Rewriting the Rules*. New York: Penguin.

Hartmann, Susan. 1998. *Feminist Footholds Everywhere: Capturing the Liberal Establishment in the 1960s and 1970s*. New Haven: Yale University Press.

Hartsock, Nancy C. M. 1985. *Money, Sex, and Power; Towards a Feminist Historical Materialism*. Boston: Northeastern University Press.

Hattam, Victoria C. 1992. "Institutions and Political Change: Working-Class Formation in England and the United States, 1820–1896." In *Structuring Politics; Historical Institutionalism in Comparative Analysis*, ed. Sven Steinmo, Kathleen Thelen, and Frank Longstreth, 188–217. Cambridge: Cambridge University Press.

Hayes, Diana L. 1996. *And Still We Rise: An Introduction to Black Liberation Theology*. New York: Paulist Press.

Hays, Charlotte. 1984. "Feminists Rip Sexism, Patriarchal Structures at Chitown Conference." *National Catholic Register* 59 (27 November): 1.

Hellman, Stephen. 1987. "Feminism and the Model of Militancy in an Italian Communist Federation: Challenges to the Old Style of Politics." In *The Women's Movements of the United States and Western Europe: Consciousness, Political Opportunity, and Public Policy*, ed. Mary Fainsod Katzenstein and Carol McClurg Mueller, 132–53. Philadelphia: Temple University Press.

Herz, Diane E., and Barbara H. Wootton. 1996. "Women in the Workforce: An Overview." In *The American Woman 1966–97: Where We Stand*, ed. Cynthia Costello and Barbara Kivimae Krimgold, 44–79. New York: W. W. Norton.

Hirschman, Albert O. 1970. *Exit, Voice, and Loyalty: Responses to the Decline in Firms, Organizations, and States.* Cambridge: Harvard University Press.

Hirschmann, Nancy J. 1992. *Rethinking Obligation.* Ithaca, NY: Cornell University Press.

"History of NARW." 1995. *Probe* 23, no. 2 (Summer).

Hoffmann, Anna Rosenberg. Papers stored in the Schlesinger Library, 83-M162–84-M65, Carton 4, Radcliffe College, Cambridge, Massachusetts.

Holm, Jeanne. 1982. *Women in the Military: An Unfinished Revolution.* Novato, CA: Presidio Press.

———. 1992. *Women in the Military: An Unfinished Revolution.* Rev. ed., 1993. Novato, CA: Presidio Press; Quality Paperback, printed 1993.

———. 1993. In Report on WREI 1993 Conference. 193, 405.

"Holm Outlines Women's Role." 1973. *Air Force Times,* 28 February: 6.

Honig, Bonnie. 1996. "Difference, Dilemmas, and the Politics of Home." In *Democracy and Difference: Contesting the Boundaries of the Political,* ed. Seyla Benhabib, 257–78. Princeton: Princeton University Press.

Houppert, Karen. 1995. "Mother Superior: Bronx Nun Takes on Sins of Sexism." *Village Voice,* 10 October: 37–38.

Hudson, Sarita. 1995. "All Talk and Little Action." *Conscience.* (Spring/Summer): 37–44.

Huels, John M., OSM. 1993. "Women's Role in Church Law: Past and Present." *New Theology Review* 6, no. 2 (May): 19–31.

Hult, Karen M. 1995. "Feminist Organization Theories and Government Organizations: The Promise of Diverse Structural Forms." *Public Productivity and Management Review* 19, no. 2 (December): 128–42.

Hummer, Patricia M. 1979. *The Decade of Elusive Promise: Professional Women in the United States 1920–1930* (1976 diss.). N.p.: UMI Research Press.

Humphrey, Mary Ann. 1988. *My Country, My Right to Serve: Experiences of Gay Men and Women in the Military: World War Two to the Present.* New York: HarperCollins.

Hunt, Mary E. 1994. "Re-Imagining: I Wish You Had Been There." *WATER-wheel: A Quarterly Newsletter of the Women's Alliance for Theology, Ethics, and Ritual* 6, no. 4 (Winter): 1.

Hunt, Mary E., and Frances Kissling. 1993. "The New York Times Ad." *Conscience* 14, nos. 1 and 2 (Spring/Summer): 16–23.

Hunter, James Davidson. 1991. *Culture Wars: The Struggle to Define America.* New York: Basic Books.

"I'm a Scapegoat, Admiral Says of Censure in Tailhook Case." 1993. *New York Times,* 30 October: 9.

"Inclusive Language in Liturgy: Scriptural Texts." 1990. *Origins* 20, no. 25 (29 November): 404–8.

"Inclusive Language Invalidates Baptisms, Church Tells Priest."1993. *National Catholic Reporter* 30, no. 1 (22 October):

Inuzuka, June K. 1987. "Maine Court to Decide Civilian Women's Rights in Navy Jobs." *WEAL Washington Report* 16, no. 5 (October/November): 6.

———. 1989. "Civilian Women Win Court Rulings for Defense Job." *WEAL Washington Report* (Winter): 8.

Isasi-Díaz, Ada-María. 1992a. "Roundtable Discussion: *Mujeristas*—Who We Are and What We Are About." *Journal of Feminist Studies in Religion* 8 (Spring): 105–25.

———. 1992b. "*Mujerista* Theology's Method: A Liberative Praxis, A Way of Life." *Listening* 27 (Winter): 41–54.

Jeffords, Susan. 1989. *The Remasculinization of America: Gender and the Vietnam War.* Bloomington: Indiana University Press.

Jenson, Jane. 1995. "What's in a Name: Nationalist Movements and Public Discourse." In *Social Movements and Culture*, ed. Hank Johnston and Bert Klandermans, 107–27. Minneapolis: University of Minnesota Press.

Jepson, Barbara. 1993. "Sexism in the Brass Section." *Wall Street Journal*, 7 July: A10.

John Paul II. 1993. "'*Ad Limina*' Address: On Parishes, Lay Ministry, and Women." *Origins* 23, no. 8 (15 July): 124–25.

———. 1994. *Ordinatio Sacerdotalis. National Catholic Reporter* 30, no. 32 (17 June): 7.

Jones, Arthur. 1994. "Women React in Anger and Pain." *National Catholic Reporter* 30, no. 32 (17 June): 4.

Jowers, Karen. 1992. "Sexual Politics." *Army Times*, 21 September: 60.

Kane, Sister Theresa. 1987. Quoted in *Commonweal*, 6 November: 613.

Kanter, Rosabeth Moss. 1977. *Women and Men of the Corporation.* New York: Basic Books.

Karabel, Jerome. 1984. "Status-Group Struggle, Organizational Interests, and the Limits of Institutional Autonomy." *Theory and Society* 13, no. 1 (January): 1–40.

Karr, Albert R. 1994. "Pensions Benefits of Nuns, Priests in U.S. Appear Underfunded by $6.3 billion." *Wall Street Journal*, 3 November: A2.

Katzenstein, Mary Fainsod. 1990a. "Feminism within American Institutions: Unobtrusive Mobilization in the 1980's." *Signs* 16, no. 11 (Autumn): 27–52.

———. 1990b. "Organizing the Terrain of Mainstream Institutions: Feminism in the United States Military." In *Going Public: National Histories of Women's Enfranchisement and Women's Participation within State Institutions*, ed. Mary Fainsod Katzenstein and Hege Skjeie, 173–205. Oslo: Institute for Social Research. Available from the Institute of European Studies, Uris Hall, Cornell University, Ithaca NY 14853.

———. 1995. "Discursive Politics and Feminist Activism in the Catholic Church." In *Feminist Organizations: Harvest of the New Women's Movement*, ed. Myra Marx Ferree and Patricia Yancey Martin, 35–53. Philadelphia: Temple University Press.

———. 1996. "The Spectacle of Life and Death: Feminist and Gay/Lesbian Politics in the Military." In *Gay Rights, Military Wrongs: Political Perspectives on Lesbians and Gays in the Military*, ed. Craig A. Rimmerman, 229–49. New York and London: Garland Press.

Keohane, Robert O. 1989. *International Institutions and State Power: Essays in International Relations Theory.* Boulder, CO: Westview.

King, Ursula, ed. 1994. *Feminist Theology from the Third World: A Reader.* Maryknoll, NY: Orbis Books.

Kissling, Frances. 1995/96. "From Cairo to Beijing and Beyond." *Conscience* 16, no. 4 (Winter): 16–22.

Kitfield, James. 1997. "Front and Center: Like It or Not, Women Are Transforming the Military." *National Journal* 43 (25 October): 2124–29.

Kitschelt, Herbert. 1986. "Political Opportunity Structures and Political Protest: Anti-nuclear Movements in Four Democracies." *British Journal of Political Science* 16, no. 1: 57–85.

Kolbenschlag, Madonna, ed. 1986. *Authority, Community, and Conflict.* Kansas City, MO: Sheed and Ward.

Kopp, Lillanna Audrey. 1985. "Don't Fence Me In." In *Midwives of the Future: American Sisters Tell their Story*, ed. Ann Patrick Ware, 206–17. Kansas City, MO: Leavan Press.

Kriesi, Hanspeter, Ruud Koopmans, Jan Willem Dyvendak, and Marco G. Giugni. 1995. *New Social Movements in Western Europe: A Comparative Analysis.* Minneapolis: University of Minnesota Press.

"Ladies May Get More Back Pay." 1973. *Air Force Times*, 3.

Laitin, David. 1988. "Political Culture and Political Preferences." *American Political Science Review* (June): 589–97.

Lamb, John D. 1993. "The Real Affirmative Action Babies: Legacy Preferences at Harvard and Yale." *Columbia Journal of Law and Social Problems* 26, no. 3 (Spring): 491–521.

Lefevere, Patricia. 1994. "Vatican Is Ridiculed at Population Meet." *National Catholic Reporter* 30, no. 29 (20 May): 5.

Lemons, J. Stanley. 1973. *The Woman Citizen: Social Feminism in the 1920s.* Charlottesville: University Press of Virginia.

Levi, Margaret, and Meredith Edwards. 1990. "The Dilemmas of Femocratic Reform." In *Going Public: National Histories of Women's Enfranchisement and Women's Participation within State Institutions*, ed. Mary Fainsod Katzenstein and Hege Skjeie, 141–73. Oslo: Institute for Social Research. Available from the Institute of European Studies, Uris Hall, Cornell, Ithaca, NY 14853.

Levin, Stephanie A. 1990. "The Deference That Is Due: Rethinking the Jurisprudence of Judicial Deference to the Military." *Villanova Law Review* 35, no. 6: 1010–61.

Lewis, Neil A. 1992. "President Meets with Female Officer in Navy Incident." *New York Times*, 28 June: 12.

———. 1993. "Tailhook Affair Brings Censure of Three Admirals." *New York Times*, 16 October: 1.

Lieblich, Julia. 1992. *Sisters: Lives of Devotion and Defiance.* New York: Ballantine Books.

Lipschultz, Sybil. 1991. "Social Feminism and Legal Discourse, 1908–1923." In *At the Boundaries of Law: Feminism and Legal Theory*, ed. Martha Albertson Fineman and Nancy Sweet Thomadson, 209–28. New York: Routledge.

Lipsky, Michael. 1968. "Protest as a Political Resource." *American Political Science Review* 62: 1144–58.

"Lt. Hultgreen and the 'Hot Dogs': A Bad Year for Navy Flyers." 1995. *Minerva's Bulletin Board* (Summer).

Lukes, Steven. 1974. *Power: A Radical View*. London: MacMillan.

Lynn, Susan. 1992. *Progressive Women in Conservative Times: Racial Justice, Peace, and Feminism 1945 to the 1960s*. New Brunswick, NJ: Rutgers University Press.

MacKinnon, Catharine A. 1987. *Feminism Unmodified: Discourses on Life and Law*. Cambridge: Harvard University Press.

———. 1989. *Toward a Feminist Theory of the State*. Cambridge: Harvard University Press.

———. 1993. *Only Words*. Cambridge: Harvard University Press.

MacNeil/Lehrer Newshour. 1994. Transcript of Show 4864 (15 February).

Maisels, Amanda, and Patricia M. Gormley. 1994. *Women in the Military: Where They Stand*. Women's Research and Education Institute, Washington, DC.

Mandelbaum, Sara, and Mary Wyckoff. 1995. "Note." In *Minerva's Bulletin Board* (Fall): 14.

Manning, Lory, and Jennifer E. Griffith. 1998. *Women in the Military: Where They Stand*. 2d ed. A Women in the Military report of the Women's Research and Education Institute.

Mansbridge, Jane. 1986. *Why We Lost the Era*. Chicago: University of Chicago Press.

———. 1995. "What Is the Feminist Movement?" In *Feminist Organizations: Harvest of the Women's Movement*, ed. Myra Marx Ferree and Patricia Yancey Martin, 27–35. Philadelphia: Temple University Press.

———. 1997. "You're Too Independent!: Gender, Race and Class in the Production of Plural Feminisms." Kennedy School of Government, Harvard University.

March, James G., and Johan P. Olsen. 1989. *Rediscovering Institutions: The Organizational Basis of Politics*. New York: Free Press.

Martin, Biddy. 1988. "Feminism, Criticism, and Foucault." In *Feminism and Foucault: Reflections on Resistance*, ed. Irene Diamond and Lee Quinby, 9–10. Boston: Northeastern University Press.

Martin, Patricia Yancey. 1990. "Rethinking Feminist Organizations." *Gender and Society* 4, no. 2 (June): 182–206.

Martinez, Demetria. 1993a. "Women-Church: 'Adrift' from Catholicism?" *National Catholic Reporter* 29, no. 24 (16 April): 3–4.

———. 1993b. "Celebrating Diversity of Catholic Women." *National Catholic Reporter* 29, no. 26 (30 April): 5.

Matlary, Janne Haaland. 1995. "To Be a Woman on Women's Own Terms: A Catholic Perspective on Challenges Facing Western Women." Lecture at the Club de Debate of the Universidad Complutense, Madrid, 7–8 November.

Maze, Rich. 1984. "Services Support Women's Aid Groups." *Air Force Times*, 14 May: 9.

McAdam, Doug. 1982. *The Political Process and the Development of Black Insurgency, 1930–1970*. Chicago: University of Chicago Press.

———. 1988. *Freedom Summer*. Oxford: Oxford University Press.

McAdam, Doug, John D. McCarthy, and Mayer N. Zald, eds. 1996. *On Social Movements: Political Opportunities, Mobilizing Structures, and Cultural Framings*. Cambridge: Cambridge University Press.

McAllister, Bill, and Dana Priest. 1997. "Under Fire, Army Assistant Secretary Resigns." *Washington Post*, 15 November: A1.

McAvoy, Marian. 1995. "The Only Way Available." In *Naming Our Truth: Stories of Loretto Women*, ed. Ann Patrick Ware, 207–29. Inverness, CA: Chardon Press.

McCafferty, Nell. 1995. "It's a Nice Try Your Holiness, but You Need to Do More for the Sisters." *NewWomen, NewChurch* 18, no. 2 (Fall): 15 ff.

McCarthy, Abigail. 1978. "Sanity and Sister Says." *Commonweal* 105, no. 24 (8 December): 773–75.

McCarthy, Tim. 1994. "Church Accused of Workplace Injustices." *National Catholic Reporter* 30, no. 12 (21 January): 17–19.

McConagha, Alan. 1991. "Family Is at Stake, Critics Claim." *Washington Times*, 18 June: A10.

McConnell, Grant. 1953. *The Decline of Agrarian Democracy*. Berkeley and Los Angeles: University of California Press.

McEnroy, Sister Carmel Elizabeth. 1996. *Guests in Their Own House: The Women of Vatican II*. New York: Crossroad.

McGreevy, John T. 1996. *Parish Boundaries: The Catholic Encounter with Race in the Twentieth Century Urban North*. Chicago: University of Chicago Press.

McKinley, Jesse. 1998. "Traditions Collide at a Chelsea Catholic Church." *New York Times*, 2 January: A17.

McMichael, William H. 1997. *The Mother of All Hooks: The Story of the U.S. Navy's Tailhook Scandal*. New Brunswick, NJ: Transaction Publishers.

Mehta, Uday Singh. Forthcoming (1999). *Liberalism and Empire*. Chicago: University of Chicago Press.

Merton, Robert K. 1972. "Insiders and Outsiders: A Chapter in the Sociology of Knowledge." *American Journal of Sociology* 78 (July): 9–47.

Messing, Suzanne. 1988. "Women Cops Sue for Equality." *New Directions for Women* 17, no. 2 (March/April): 3.

Metzger, Thomas. 1977. *Neo-Confucianism and China's Political Culture*. New York: Columbia University Press.

Meyer, David S. 1995a. "Framing National Security: Elite Public Discourse on Nuclear Weapons during the Cold War." *Political Communication* 12, no. 2 (April–June): 173–92.

———. 1995b. "Institutionalizing Dissent: The United States Structure of Political Opportunity and the End of the Nuclear Freeze Movement." *Sociological Forum* 8, no. 2: 157–76.

———. 1995c. "Political Opportunity and Nested Institutions." Unpublished paper.

Meyer, David S., and Sidney Tarrow. 1998. "A Movement Society: Contentious Politics for a New Century." In *The Social Movement Society: Contentious Politics for a New Century*, ed. David S. Meyer and Sidney Tarrow. Lanham, MD: Rowman and Littlefield.

Meyerson, Debra E., and Maureen Scully. 1995. "Tempered Radicalism and the Politics of Ambivalence and Change." *Organizational Science* 6, no. 5 (September–October): 585–600.

Milhaven, Annie Lally. 1987. *The Inside Stories: Thirteen Valiant Women Challenging the Church*. Mystic, CT: Twenty-Third Publications.

"The Military and the Women." 1997. Editorial. *Wall Street Journal*, 21 February: A14.

Miller, Laura. 1995. "Feminism and the Exclusion of Army Women from Combat." In Project on U.S. Post Cold-War Civil Military Relations, Working Paper No. 2, Harvard University John M. Olin Institute for Strategic Studies, Cambridge, Massachusetts. December.

———. 1997. "Not Just Weapons of the Weak: Gender Harassment as a Form of Protest for Army Men." *Social Psychology Quarterly* 60, no. 1: 32–51.

Mills, Albert J., and Peter Tancred, eds. 1990. *Social Analysis*. Newbury Park, CA: Sage.

Minow, Martha. 1991. *Making All the Difference: Inclusion, Exclusion and American Law*. Ithaca, NY: Cornell University Press.

Mitchell, Brian. 1989. *Weak Link: The Feminization of the American Military*. Washington, DC: Regnery Gateway.

Moan, Frank, SJ. 1978. "Growing Pains." *America* 139, no. 19 (9 December): 433.

Molyneux, Maxine. 1985. "Mobilization without Emancipation? Women's Interests, the States and Revolution in Nicaragua." *Feminist Studies* 2, no. 2 (Summer): 227–55.

Moody, Linda A. 1996. *Women Encounter God: Theology across the Boundaries of Difference*. New York: Orbis.

———. 1997. *Women Encounter God: Theology across the Boundaries of Difference*. New York: Orbis.

Moore, Brenda L. 1991. "African-American Women in the U.S. Military." *Armed Forces and Society* 17, no. 3 (Spring): 364–84.

———. 1995. "Changing Laws and Women of Color in the U.S. Military." *Minerva: Quarterly Report on Women and the Military* 13, nos. 3–4 (Fall–Winter): 15–25.

———. 1996. "From Underrepresentation to Overrepresentation: African American Women." In *It's Our Military Too!: Women and the U.S. Military*, ed. Judith Hicks Stiehm, 115–36. Philadelphia: Temple University Press.

Moraga, Cherrie, and Gloria Anzaldua, eds. 1981. *This Bridge Called My Back: Writings by Radical Women of Color*. Watertown, MA: Persephone Press.

Moran, Barbara, and Karen Schwartz. 1987. "Living on the Edge: Women and Catholics." *Probe* 15, no. 3.

Morancy, Elizabeth, RSM. 1985. "Politics as a Mission of Mercy." In *Between God and Caesar: Priests, Sisters, and Political Office in the United States*, ed. Madonna Kolbenschlag. New York: Paulist Press.

Morden, Bettie J. 1990. *The Women's Army Corps, 1945–1978*. Washington, DC: Center of Military History, United States Army.

Morgen, Sandra. 1990. "Two Faces of the State: Women, Social Control, and Empowerment." In *Uncertain Terms: Negotiating Gender in American Culture*, ed. Faye Ginsburg and Anna Lowenhaupt Tsing, 169–73. Boston: Beacon Press.

Morris, Aldon D. 1992. "Political Consciousness and Collective Action." In *Frontiers of Social Movement Theory*, ed. Aldon D. Morris and Carol McClurg Mueller, 370–71. New Haven: Yale University Press.

Morris, Madeline. 1996. "By Force of Arms: Rape, War, and Military Culture." *Duke Law Journal* 45, no. 4: 651–781.

Moskos, Charles. 1998. "The Folly of Comparing Race and Gender in the Army." *Washington Post*, 4 January: C1.

Moskos, Charles C., and John Sibley Butler. 1996. *All That We Can Be: Black Leadership and Racial Integration the Army Way*. New York: Basic Books.

Muncy, Robyn. 1991. *Creating a Female Dominion in American Reform*. New York: Oxford University Press.

Murphy, Margaret. 1997. "Women's Priesthood? Few Women Agree." *National Catholic Reporter*, 31 January: 14.

Myers, Steven Lee. 1997. "Pentagon Is Urged to Separate Sexes." *New York Times*, 16 December: A1.

Nalty, Bernard C. 1980. *Strength for the Fight: A History of Black Americans in the Military*. New York: Free Press; London: Collier Macmillan.

"The Nation." 1997. *Chronicle of Higher Education*, 29 August.

National Organization for Women. 1969. Recommendation for Easter Bonnet Protest and Milwaukee newspaper editorial, 12 April. NOW Collection, Carton 1, Farians, 72-8-82 M211. Schlesinger Library, Radcliffe College, Cambridge, Massachusetts.

———. 1981. Brief for *Amicus Curiae, Rostker v. Goldberg* 60 L. ED. 2c478 at 487.

———. N.d. Collection Deposit Card. NOW. Collection, Carton 4, #35, 84-M216. Schlesinger Library, Radcliffe College, Cambridge, Massachusetts.

Naughton, Jim. 1997. *Catholics in Crisis: The Rift between American Catholics and Their Church*. New York: Penguin.

"Navy Approves Retention of Lesbian Officer." 1995. *Minerva's Bulletin Board* (Summer): 6.

"Navy Commander Is Relieved in Inquiry on Sex Harassment." 1992. *New York Times*, 22 July: 19.

"Navy Sued for Inaction on EEOC Order."1987. *WEAL Washington Report* 16, no. 2. (April/May): 4.

Neal, Marie Augusta, SND de Namur. 1990. *From Nuns to Sisters: An Expanding Vocation*. Mystic, CT: Twenty-Third Publications.

"New Citadel Challenger Pronounces Herself Physically Ready." 1995. *New York Times*, 10 September: 37.

"New Council of Major Superiors of Women Religious." 1992. *Origins* 22, no. 9 (23 July): 157–59.

"News Briefs: WANDAS Forum."1995. *Minerva's Bulletin Board* (Fall): 6, 9–10.

Nicholson, Linda J., ed. 1990. *Feminism/Postmodernism*. New York: Routledge.

Noble, Kenneth. 1994. "Woman Tells of Retaliation." *New York Times*, 15 October: A18.

North, David M. 1996. "U.S. Navy Should Protect Its Own." *Aviation Week and Space Technology*, 22 January: 70.

Novick, Peter. 1988. *That Noble Dream: The Objectivity Question and the American Historical Profession.* Cambridge: Cambridge University Press.

O'Brien, David J. 1972. *The Renewal of American Catholicism.* New York: Oxford University Press.

Okin, Susan. 1989. *Justice, Gender, and the Family.* New York: Basic Books.

Olson, Mancur. 1965. *The Logic of Collective Action: Public Goods and the Theories of Groups.* Cambridge: Harvard University Press.

"On File." 1991. *Origins* 20, no. 45 (18 April): 730.

Orr, Carol Wallace. 1990a. "Wisp: The Beginnings, Part I." *WISP* 11, no. 2 (December/January): 2–3.

———. 1990b. "WISP: The Beginnings, Part II." *WISP* 11, no. 3: 2–6.

Osburn, C. Dixon, and Michelle M. Benecke, Esqs. 1996. *Conduct Unbecoming: The Second Annual Report on "Don't Ask, Don't Tell, Don't Pursue" Violations March 1, 1995–February 27, 1996.* Washington, DC: Servicemembers Legal Defense Network.

Osburn, C. Dixon, Michelle M. Benecke, and Kirk Childress, Esqs. 1997. *Conduct Unbecoming: The Third Annual Report on "Don't Ask, Don't Tell, Don't Pursue" February 28, 1996–February 26, 1997.* Washington, DC: Servicemembers Legal Defense Network.

Papa, Mary. 1978. "Women Mix Social Changes, Ordinational Aims." *National Catholic Reporter*, 24 November: 1.

Parkinson, Thomas J. 1923. "Minimum Wage and the Constitution." *American Labor Legislation Review* 13 (June): 131–36.

Parr, Carol C. 1983. "Women in the Military." In *Women in Washington: Advocates for Public Policy*, ed. Irene Tinker, 238–50. Beverly Hills, CA: Sage Publications.

Pexton, Patrick. 1996. "Tailhook, the Book, Blames Lehman." *Navy Times*, 26 February: 8.

Piore, Michael. 1995. *Beyond Individualism.* Cambridge: Harvard University Press.

Piven, Frances Fox, and Richard A. Cloward. 1971. *Regulating the Poor: The Functions of Public Welfare.* New York: Pantheon Books.

———. 1977. *Poor People's Movements: Why They Succeed, How They Fail.* New York: Pantheon Books; New York: Vintage, 1979.

———. 1992. "Normalizing Collective Protest." In *Frontiers in Social Movement Theory*, ed. Aldon D. Morris and Carol McClurg Mueller, 301–26. New Haven: Yale University Press.

"Plaintiff in Tailhook Case Wins $1.7 Million Damages." 1994. *New York Times*, 29 October: 1.

Polenberg, Richard. 1980. *One Nation Divisible: Class, Race, and Ethnicity in the United States Since 1938.* Harmondsworth, Middlesex: Penguin.

"The Post-Vatican II Church in Latin America." 1991. In *Religion and the Social Order: Vatican II and U.S. Catholicism*, ed. Helen Rose Fuchs Ebaugh, 233–245. Greenwich, CT: JAI Press.

Powell, Walter W., and Paul J. DiMaggio. 1992. *The New Institutionalism in Organizational Analysis*. Chicago: University of Chicago Press.

The Presidential Commission on the Assignment of Women in the Armed Forces. 1992. *Women in Combat: Report to the President, Presidential Commission on the Assignment of Women in the Armed Forces*. Washington, DC: Brassey.

Prevallet, Elaine. 1995. "Testing the Roots: The Story of *Colegio Loreto* in La Paz." In *Naming Our Truth: Stories of Loretto Women*, ed. Ann Patrick Ware, 91–113. Inverness, CA: Chardon Press.

Priest, Dana. 1997a. "Service Group Gave $20,000 to Foe of Women in Combat." *Washington Post*, 8 November: A13.

———. 1997b. "A Trench between Women, Jobs." *Washington Post*, 28 December: A1 (first of three articles on three consecutive days).

———. 1997c. "Women Filled Few Jobs Tied to Combat: Despite Order to Military to Open Opportunities, Results Are Negligible." *Washington Post*, 21 October: A1.

Purcell, Rosemary. 1982. "SecNav Criticized for Terming DOPMA 'Non-Issue' for Women." *Navy Times*, 25 January: 2.

———. 1984. "WOPA Members Divided by Untermeyer Speech." *Navy Times*, 22 October: 28.

Putnam, Robert D. 1993. *Making Democracy Work: Civic Traditions in Modern Italy*. Princeton: Princeton University Press.

———. 1994. "Social Capital and Public Affairs." *Bulletin of the American Academy of Arts and Sciences* 47, no. 8 (May): 5–20.

———. 1995. "Bowling Alone: America's Declining Social Capital." *Journal of Democracy* 6, no. 1 (January): 65–78.

Quindlen, Anna. 1993. "Authentic Catholics." *New York Times*, 18 November: A27.

Quinn, Sister Donna. 1992. Interview in *Sisters: Lives of Devotion and Defiance*, ed. Julia Lieblich, 86–155. New York: Ballantine Books.

Quiñonez, Lora Ann, and Mary Daniel Turner. 1992. *The Transformation of American Catholic Sisters*. Philadelphia: Temple University Press.

"'Radical Feminism' Criticized."1989. *National Catholic Reporter*, 24 March: 6.

Ralston, Jeannie. 1991. "Women's Work." *Life* 14, no. 5 (May): 52–62.

Redmont, Jane. 1995. "'Letter to Women' Bares John Paul's Isolation." *National Catholic Reporter* 31, no. 35 (28 July): 11.

Reese, Thomas J., SJ. 1992. *A Flock of Shepherds: The National Conference of Catholic Bishops*. Kansas City, MO: Sheed and Ward.

Reeves, Connie L. 1995. "Dual-Service and Single Parents: What about the Kids?" *Minerva: Quarterly Report on Women and the Military* 13, nos. 3–4 (Fall–Winter): 25–68.

Reinelt, Claire. 1995. "Moving onto the Terrain of the State: The Battered Women's Movement and the Politics of Engagement." In *Feminist Organizations: Harvest of the New Women's Movements*, ed. Myra Marx Ferree and Patricia Yancey Martin, 84–104. Philadelphia: Temple University Press.

Rhode, Deborah. 1989. *Justice and Gender*. Cambridge: Harvard University Press.

Ribadeneira, Diego. 1997. "Altar Girls on the Rise: Role Largely Welcomed at Parishes." *Boston Globe*, 29 July: A1.

Rich, Adrienne Cecile. 1976. *Of Woman Born: Motherhood as Experience and Institution*. New York: Norton.

Ricks, Thomas E. 1996. "Soldiers at Army Facility Are Charged with Sexual Attacks against Women." *Wall Street Journal*, 8 November: A20.

———. 1997a. "Duke Study Finds Sharp Rightward Shift in Military." *Wall Street Journal*, 11 November: A20.

———. 1997b. *Making the Corps*. New York: Scribner.

Riley, Denise. 1988. *Am I That Name? Feminism and the Category of "Women" in History*. Minneapolis: University of Minnesota Press.

Rimmerman, Craig, ed. 1996. *Gay Rights, Military Wrongs: Political Perspective on Lesbians and Gays in the Military*. New York and London: Garland Press.

Rix, Sara E. 1990. "American Women Today: A Statistical Portrait." In *The American Woman 1990–91: A Status Report*, ed. Sara E. Rix, table 19, "Women as a Percentage of All Workers in Selected Occupations." New York: W. W. Norton for the Women's Research & Education Institute.

Roberts, Tom. 1996. "Behind Closed Doors, Bishops Discuss Women's Ordination." *National Catholic Reporter* (12 July): 5.

Robertson, Nan. 1992. *The Girls in the Balcony: Women, Men and the New York Times*. New York: Random House.

Rogan, Helen. 1981. *Mixed Company: Women in the Modern Army*. New York: G. P. Putnam's Sons.

Rogers, Carole Garibaldi. 1996. *Poverty, Chastity, and Change: Lives of Contemporary American Nuns*. New York: Twayne Publishers.

The Roper Organization. 1992. "Attitudes regarding the Assignment of Women in the Armed Forces: The Public Perspective." Conducted for the Presidential Commission on the Assignment of Women in the Armed Forces, August.

Rosen, Jeffrey. 1996. "Like Race, Like Gender." *New Republic*, 19 February: 25, 21 ff.

Rosen, Michael. 1992. "Tailhook: A Tempest in a Teapot." *Denver Post*, 7 August: 11b.

Rosenberg, Janet, Harry Perlstadt, William R. F. Phillips. 1990. "Politics, Feminism and Women's Professional Orientations: A Case Study of Women Lawyers." *Women and Politics* 10, no. 4: 19–45.

Roush, Colonel Paul E., U.S. Marine Corps (retired). 1997. "A Tangled Webb." *Proceedings* (August): 42–44.

Rudenstine, Neil L. 1996. "Diversity and Learning." In *The President's Report 1993–1995*. Cambridge: Harvard University.

Ruether, Rosemary Radford. 1974. *Religion and Sexism: Images of Women in the Jewish and Christian Traditions*. New York: Simon and Schuster.

———. 1975. *New Woman, New Earth: Sexist Ideologies and Human Liberation*. New York: The Seabury Press.

———. 1983. *Sexism and God-Talk: Toward a Feminist Theology*. Boston: Beacon Press.

———. 1985. *Women-Church: Theology and Practice of Feminist Communities*. San Francisco: Harper and Row.

———. 1990. "The Place of Women in the Church." In *Modern Catholicism: Vatican II and After*, ed. Adrian Hastings, 260–66. New York: Oxford University Press.

Ruether, Rosemary Radford, and Eleanor McLaughlin, eds. 1979. *Women of Spirit: Female Leadersip in the Jewish and Christian Traditions*. New York: Simon and Schuster.

Rupp, Leila J., and Verta Taylor. 1987. *Survival in the Doldrums: The American Women's Rights Movement, 1945 to the 1960s*. New York: Oxford University Press.

Ryan, Mary P. 1990. *Women in Public: Between Banners and Ballots, 1825–1880*. Baltimore: Johns Hopkins University Press.

Savage, Mike, and Anne Witz, eds. 1992. *Gender and Bureaucracy*. Cambridge: Blackwell.

Sawyers, Traci M., and David S. Meyer. 1993. "Missed Opportunities: Social Movement Abeyance and Public Policy." September (unpublished paper).

Schaeffer, Pamela. 1995. "WOC Gathers to Promote Women's Ordination amid Conflicting Visions, Goal." *National Catholic Reporter*, 1 December: 9, 10.

———. 1996a. "Vatican Has More Questions for Priest, Nun." *National Catholic Reporter*, 16 February: 10.

———. 1996b. "Bishops Take Aim at McBrien's Catholicism." *National Catholic Reporter*, 12 April: 3.

———. 1997. "Theologians Opt for Diplomacy in Dispute." *National Catholic Reporter*, 20 June: 3.

Schlafly, Phyllis. 1989. "The Feminization of the U.S. Military." *Phyllis Schlafly Report* 23, no. 2, sec. 1 (September): 8.

Schmich, Mary. 1993. "'Unit Cohesion' Gave Us Tailhook." *Chicago Tribune*, 28 April: 1.

Schmitt, Eric. 1991. "Head of Army Sees Chance of Female Fliers in Combat." *New York Times*, 2 June: 32.

———. 1992a. "Navy Chief Admits to Being Close By during Lewd Party." *New York Times*, 17 June: 1.

———. 1992b. "Fort Bragg. . . ." *New York Times*, 2 August: 28.

———. 1993. "Military Chaplain Fights a Battle over Loyalties." *New York Times*, 21 December: A20.

———. 1994a. "Judge Dismisses Some Claims in Tailhook Suit." 1994. *New York Times*, 21 April: A15.

———. 1994b. "Judge Dismisses Tailhook Cases, Saying Admiral Tainted Inquiry." *New York Times*, 9 February: 1.

———. 1994c. "Senate Women Would Reduce a Four-Star Rank." *New York Times*, 19 April: 1.

———. 1997. "Army Criticized on Survey on Harassment." *New York Times*, 27 June: 15.

Schneider, Dorothy, and Carl J. Schneider. 1988. *Sound Off! American Military Women Speak Out*. New York: E. P. Dutton. Reprinted 1992 by Paragon House.

Schneider, Mary. 1986. "The Transformation of American Women Religious: The Sister Formation Conference as a Catalyst for Change (1954–1964)." Working Paper Series 17, no. 1. Notre Dame: University of Notre Dame, Cushwa Center for the Study of American Catholicism.

Schultz, Vicki. 1992. "Women 'Before' the Law." In *Feminists Theorize the Political*, ed. Judith Butler and Joan M. Scott, 297–341. New York: Routledge.

Schumacher, Mary. 1988 "Women in the Navy." Kennedy School of Government Case Program Account C16-88-853.0, Exhibit 5. Copyright by President and Fellows of Harvard College, Cambridge, Massachusetts.

Scott, Anne Firor. 1981. "What Happens When Outsiders Become Insiders." Address delivered to the Symposium in Celebration of the Twentieth Anniversary of the Mary Ingraham Bunting Insitute of Radcliffe College, Cambridge, Massachusetts, 11 April.

———. 1991. *Natural Allies: Women's Associations in American History*. Urbana: University of Illinois Press.

Scott, James C. 1985. *Weapons of the Weak: Everyday Forms of Peasant Resistance*. New Haven: Yale University Press.

Scott, Joan Wallach. 1996. *Only Paradoxes to Offer*. Cambridge: Harvard University Press.

Scott, W. Richard. 1995. *Institutions and Organizations*. Thousand Oaks, CA: Sage Publications.

The Secretary of the Army. 1997. *Senior Review Panel Report on Sexual Harassment* 1 (July) and 2 (Data Report—28 July).

Segal, David R. 1989. *Recruiting for Uncle Sam: Citizenship and Military Manpower Policy*. Lawrence: University Press of Kansas.

Segal, Mady. 1986. "The Military and the Family as Greedy Institutions." *Armed Forces and Society* 13: 9–38.

———. 1995. "Women's Military Roles Cross-Nationally: Past, Present, and Future." *Gender and Society* 9, no. 6 (December): 757–75.

Selznick, Philip. 1957. *Leadership in Administration: A Sociological Interpretation*. New York: Harper and Row.

Shapiro, Laura. 1991. "Why Women Are Angry." *Newsweek*, 21 October: 44.

Shklar, Judith 1989. *A Life of Learning*. Charles Homer Haskins Lecture. American Council of Learned Societies (ACLS) Occasional Paper no. 9 (6 April): 5.

"Six More Tailhook Victims Settle Lawsuits."1995. *Minerva* (Summer): 5.

Skaine, Rosemarie. 1996. *Power and Gender: Issues in Sexual Dominance and Harassment*. Jefferson, NC: McFarland and Co.

Slavin, Sarah. 1995. *U.S. Women's Interest Groups: Institutional Profiles*. Westport, CT: Greenwood Press.

Smith, Anna Marie. 1994. "Rastafari as Resistance and the Ambiguities of Essentialism in the 'New Social Movements.'" In *The Making of Political Identities*, ed. Ernesto Laclau, 171–204. London: Verso.

Smith, Barbara, Gloria T. Hull, and Patricia Bell Scott. 1982. *All the Women Are White, All the Blacks Are Men, but Some of Us Are Brave: Black Women's Studies*. Old Westbury, NY: The Feminist Press.

Smith, Dorothy E. 1987. *The Everyday World as Problematic: A Feminist Sociology*. Boston: Northeastern Press.

Smith, Rogers M. 1989. "'One United People': Second-Class Female Citizenship and the American Quest for Community." *Yale Journal of Law and Humanities* 1: 229–93.

———. 1993. "Beyond Tocqueville, Myrdal, and Hartz: The Multiple Traditions in America." *American Political Science Review* 87, no. 3 (September): 549–66.

Soysal, Yasemin Nuhoglu. 1994. *Limits of Citizenship: Migrants and Postnational Membership in Europe*. Chicago: University of Chicago Press.

Spalter-Roth, Roberta, and Ronnee Schreiber. 1995. "Outsider Issues and Insider Tactics: Strategic Tensions in the Women's Policy Network during the 1980s." In *Feminist Organizations: Harvest of the New Women's Movements*, ed. Myra Marx Ferree and Patricia Yancey Martin, 105–28. Philadelphia: Temple University Press.

Spelman, Elizabeth V. 1988. *Inessential Woman: Problems of Exclusion in Feminist Thought*. Boston: Beacon Press.

Spelts, Doreen. 1991. "Women Casualties of the Gulf Operations." *Minerva's Bulletin Board* 4, no. 1 (Spring): 1–5.

Steichen, Donna. 1991. *Ungodly Rage: The Hidden Face of Catholic Feminism*. San Francisco: Ignatius Press.

Steinfels, Peter. 1992. "Bishops' Valued Consensus Lost; Pastoral Fails." *New York Times*, 21 November: E3.

———. 1995a. "Women Wary about Aiming to Be Priests: Feminists Consider New Catholic Model." *New York Times*, 14 November: A17.

———. 1995b. "Vatican Says the Ban on Women as Priests Is 'Infallible' Doctrine." *New York Times*, 19 November: 1.

Stetson, Dorothy McBride. 1991. *Women's Rights in the U.S.A.: Policy Debates and Gender Roles*. Pacific Grove, CA: Brooks/Cole Publishing Company.

Stevens, Jacqueline. 1995. "Beyond Tocqueville, Please!" *American Political Science Review* 89, no. 4 (December): 987–90.

Stiehm, Judith Hicks. 1989. *Arms and the Enlisted Woman*. Philadelphia: Temple University Press.

Stimpson, Catherine R. "The Women's Studies Movement." In *The Humanities in the Schools*. New York: American Council of Learned Societies, Occasional Paper no. 20.

Summers, Mary. 1996. "What the Public Ought to be Taught: Visions, Conflicts, and Forgetting in the Development of Agricultural Science and Education." Social Science History Association Annual Meeting. New Orleans, Louisiana, October.

"Survey Finds Catholics Want More Say." 1996. *National Catholic Reporter* 32, no. 32 (14 June): 4.

Swidler, Leonard, and Arlene Swidler. 1977. *Women Priests: A Catholic Commentary on the Vatican Declaration*. New York: Paulist Press.

Sylvester, Nancy, I.H.M. 1997. "PFs: Persistent Friendships." In Sisters, Servants of the Immaculate Heart of Mary, *Building Sisterhood: A Feminist History of the Sisters, Servants of the Immaculate Heart of Mary*, 173–93. Syracuse: Syracuse University Press.

"The Tailhook Fiasco." 1994. Editorial. *New York Times*, 17 February: A22.

"Tailhook Group Settles Lawsuit by 6 Who Charged Sex Assault."1995. *New York Times*, 23 June: A22.

Tarrow, Sidney. 1989a. *Democracy and Disorder: Protest and Politics in Italy 1965–1975.* Oxford: Oxford University Press.

———. 1989b. "Struggle, Politics, and Reform: Collective Action, Social Movements and Cycles of Protest." Western Societies Paper no. 21, Cornell University, Ithaca, NY.

———. 1994. *Power in Movement: Social Movements, Collective Action and Politics.* Cambridge: Cambridge University Press.

Taylor, Verta. 1989. "Social Movement Continuity: The Women's Movement in Abeyance." *American Sociological Review* 54: 761–75.

Thelen, Kathleen, and Sven Steinmo. 1992. "Historical Institutionalism in Comparative Politics." In *Structuring Politics: Historical Institutionalism in Comparative Analysis*, ed. Kathleen Thelen, Sven Steinmo, and Frank Longstreth. Cambridge: Cambridge University Press.

Thompson, Anne. 1993. "Hollywood Is Taken to Task by Its Women." *New York Times*, 17 January: 25.

Thompson, Margaret. 1994. "The Validation of Sisterhood: Canonical Status and Liberation in the History of American Nuns." In *A Leaf from the Great Tree of God: Essays in Honor of Ritamary Bradley*, ed. Margot H. King. Toronto: Peregrina Publishing.

Tilly, Charles. 1978. *From Mobilization to Revolution*. Reading, MA: Addison-Wesley Publishing Co.

———. 1979. "Repertoires of Contention in America and Britain, 1750–1830." In *The Dynamics of Social Movements: Resource Mobilization, Social Control, and Tactics*, ed. Mayer Zald and John McCarthy, 126–55. Cambridge: Winthrop Publisher.

———. 1984. "Social Movements and National Politics." In *Statemaking and Social Movements*, ed. C. Bright and S. Harding, 297–317. Ann Arbor: University of Michigan Press.

Tilly, Charles, Louise Tilly, and Richard Tilly. 1975. *The Rebellious Century 1830–1930*. Cambridge: Harvard University Press.

Timberg, Robert. 1995. *The Nightingale's Song*. New York: Simon and Schuster.

Tocqueville, Alexis de. 1969. *Democracy in America*. Trans. G. Lawrence. New York: Anchor Books.

"To the Women of the World: An Affirmation of 'Feminine Genius.'"1995. *New York Times*, 16 July: E7.

Touraine, Alain. 1981. *The Voice and the Eye: An Analysis of Social Movements*. Cambridge: Cambridge University Press.

Traxler, Margaret Ellen. 1995a. "Great Tide of Returning." In *Naming Our Truth: Stories of Loretto Women*, ed. Ann Patrick Ware, 129–39. Inverness. CA: Chardon Press.

———. 1995b. Interview in *Catholics on the Edge* by Tim Unsworth, 105. New York: Crossroad.

Traxler, Margaret, and Ann Patrick Ware, eds. 1989. "If Anyone Can, NCAN: Twenty Years of Speaking Out." *NCAN Anniversary Issue*, 19, nos. 3–4 (Summer and Fall).

Troch, Lieve. 1988/89. "The Feminist Movement in and on the Edge of the Churches in the Netherlands: From Consciousness-Raising to Womenchurch." *Journal of Feminist Studies in Religion* 5 (Fall): 113–28.

Tsebelis, George. 1990. *Nested Games: Rational Choice in Comparative Politics.* Berkeley and Los Angeles: University of California Press.

Unikel, Robert. 1992. " 'Reasonable' Doubts: A Critique of the Reasonable Woman Standard in American Jurisprudence." *Northwestern University Law Review* 87, no. 1 (Fall): 326–75.

"U.S. Catholicism: Trends in the 90s." 1993. *National Catholic Reporter*, NCR Gallup Poll Supplement. 8 October: 21–32.

U.S. Congress. Title 10, U.S.C. 6015 (applying to the navy and marine corps) and 8549 (applying to the air force).

U.S. House. 1988. Military Personnel and Compensation Subcommittee of the Committee on Armed Services. *Hearings before the Military Personnel and Compensation Subcommittee of the Committee on Armed Services.* 1 October, 19 November 1987 and 4 February 1988. H.A.S.C. no. 100-52. Washington, DC: GPO.

———. 1992. Military Personnel and Compensation Subcommittee and the Defense Policy Panel of the Committee on Armed Services. *Hearings before the Military Personnel and Compensation Subcommittee and the Defense Policy Panel of the Committee on Armed Services.* 102d Congress, 2d session, 29–30 July.

———. 1995. Committee on Armed Services. *An Assessment of Racial Discrimination in the Military: A Global Perspective* ("Dellums Report"), 30 December 1994. Washington, DC: GPO.

United States Naval Academy Board of Visitors. 1990. "Report of the Committee on Women's Issues." 9 October.

U.S. Senate. 1991. Hearings before the Manpower and Personnel Subcommittee of the Senate Armed Services Committee. *Females in Combat: LEGISLATE Report for the 102d Congress.* 19 June: 45. Copyright, Federal Informations Systems Corporation.

Unsworth, Tim. 1995. *Catholics on the Edge.* New York: Crossroad.

Via, Jane. 1987. "Breaking the Conspiracy of Silence." *Probe* 15, no. 5 (November): 12.

Vidulich, Sister of St. Joseph of Peace Dorothy. 1993. "Underground, Women's Press Multiplies." *National Catholic Reporter* 29, no. 2 (15 January): 2.

———. 1994. "Catholic Women Speak Out." *National Catholic Reporter* 30, no. 32 (17 June): 3.

Vistica, Gregory L. 1995. *Fall from Glory: The Men Who Sank the U.S. Navy.* New York: Simon and Schuster.

Walker, Alice. 1983. *In Search of Our Mothers' Gardens: Womanist Prose.* New York: Harcourt Brace Jovanovich.

Wallace, Ruth A. 1992. *They Call Her Pastor: A New Role for Catholic Women.* Albany: State University of New York Press.

———. 1993. "Catholic Women More Open to Change Than Catholic Men." *National Catholic Reporter* 29, no. 28 (8 October): 28.

———. 1994. "The Social Construction of a New Leadership Role: Catholic Women Pastors." In *Gender and Religion,* ed. William H. Swatos, 15–26. New Brunswick, NJ: Transaction Publishers.

Walsh, Catherine. 1993. "Bang the Drum—Not: Women-Church in the Desert." *Commonweal* 120, no. 11 (4 June): 6–7.

Ware, Ann Patrick. 1993. "A Case Study in Oppression: A Theological and Personal Analysis." Chicago: The National Coalition of American Nuns.

———. 1995a/b. "Loretto's Hispanic Tradition: Lights and Shadows." In *Naming Our Truth: Stories of Loretto Women,* ed. Ann Patrick Ware, 53–91. Inverness, CA: Chardon Press.

Ware, Ann Patrick, ed. 1985. *Midwives of the Future: American Sisters Tell their Story.* Kansas City, MO: Leavan Press.

Ware, Susan. 1981. *Beyond Suffrage: Women in the New Deal.* Cambridge: Harvard University Press.

Watts, Claudius E. III. 1995. "'Good Ol' Boys' Have Long Made the Citadel Proud." *Navy Times,* 18 September: 31.

WEAL Facts. Updated 1986. "Organizations Concerned with Women and the Military."

WEAL Washington Report. 1987. Vol. 16, no. 4 (August/September).

Weaver, Mary Jo. 1986. *New Catholic Women: A Contemporary Challenge to Traditional Religious Authority.* New York: Harper and Row.

———. 1992. "Widening the Sphere of Discourse: Reflections on the Feminist Perspective in Religious Studies." In *Horizons on Catholic Feminist Theology,* ed. Joann Wolski Conn and Walter E. Conn, 191–207. Washington, DC: Georgetown University Press.

———. 1993. *Springs of Water in a Dry Land: Spiritual Survival for Catholic Women Today.* Boston: Beacon Press.

———. 1995. *New Catholic Women: A Contemporary Challenge to Traditional Religious Authority.* Rev. ed. Bloomington: Indiana University Press.

Webb, James. 1975. "Women Can't Fight." *Washingtonian* (November): 142–82.

———. 1992. "Witch Hunt in the Navy." *New York Times,* 6 October: A23.

Weiner, Tim. 1994. "The Navy Decides Not to Appeal Dismissal of Last Tailhook Cases." *New York Times,* 11 February: 1.

"Welcome, Holy Father." 1995. *New York Times,* 1 October: 13.

Wendt, Alexander. 1992. "Anarchy Is What States Make of It: The Social Construction of Power Politics." *International Organization* 46, no. 2 (Spring): 391–425.

Werner, A. Matt, Capt., USAF (reserve). 1992. Letter to Editor. *Denver Post,* 7 August: 10b.

Wessinger, Catherine, 1996. "Women's Religious Leadership in the United States." In *Religious Institutions and Women's Leadership: New Roles Inside the Mainstream,* ed. Catherine Wessinger, 3–39. Columbia: University of South Carolina Press.

Whittier, Nancy. 1995. *Feminist Generations: The Persistence of the Radical Women's Movement.* Philadelphia: Temple University Press.

Wilkes, Paul. 1991. "The Education of an Archbishop— I." *New Yorker*, 15 July: 38–59.

Williams, Virginia. 1995. "Loretto and the Women's Movement: From 'Sister' to Sister." In *Naming Our Truth: Stories of Loretto Women*, ed. Ann Patrick Ware, 229–59. Inverness, CA: Chardon Press.

Wilson, George C. 1995. "Others Have Found the Citadel Wanting." *Navy Times*, 4 September: 29.

Windsor, Pat. 1990. "Curran Is Denied Tenure at Auburn." *National Catholic Reporter*, 21 September: 4.

Winter, Miriam Therese, Adair Lummis. and Allison Stokes, eds. 1994. *Defecting in Place: Women Claiming Responsibility for Their Own Spiritual Lives.* New York: Crossroad.

Wirpsa, Leslie. 1996. "Archdiocese Fined More Than $1 Million." *National Catholic Reporter*, 1 March: 4.

Wittberg, Patricia. 1989. "Feminist Consciousness among American Nuns: Patterns of Ideological Diffusion." *Women's Studies International Forum* 12, no. 5: 527–39.

Women-Church Convergence Planning Committee. 1991. Undated letter.

Women's Ordination Conference. 1995a. *Discipleship of Equals: Breaking Bread, Doing Justice.* Conference Program: 10–12 November, Crystal City. Arlington, Virginia.

———. 1995b. "Hand in Hand, a Declaration of Radical Equality." In *Discipleship of Equals: Breaking Bread, Doing Justice*, 33. 10–12 November, Crystal City. Arlington, Virginia.

"Women Still Cannot Serve as Catholic Hospital Chaplains." 1995. *National Catholic Reporter* 29, no. 25 (23 April): 8.

Young, Stacey. 1997. *Changing the Wor(l)d: Discourse, Politics, and the Feminist Movement.* New York: Routledge.

Zamichow, Nora. 1990. "For Her, Sky's No Limit." *Los Angeles Times*, 25 June: A3.

Ziegenhals, Gretchen E. 1989. "Meeting the Women of Women-Church." *Christian Century*, 10 May: x.

Zimmerman, Jean. 1995. *Tailspin: Women at War in the Wake of Tailhook.* New York. Doubleday Press.

Zinsser, Judith P. 1993. *History and Feminism: A Glass Half Full.* New York: Twayne Publishers.

Zullo, Harriet. 1988. "What about Jazmin?" *Chicago Catholic Women Newsletter* (Summer): 8.

COURT CASES

Ben-Shalom v. Marsh 881 F.2d 454 (7th Cir. 1989).

Bradwell v. Illinois 83 U.S. 442 (1873).

Brown v. Glines 444 U.S. 348 (1980).

Chappell et al. v. Wallace et al. 462 U.S. 296 (1982).

Crawford v. Cushman 531 F.2d 114 (2d Cir. 1976).

Dandridge v. Williams 397 U.S. 471 (1970).

EEOC v. Sears, Roebuck & Co. 628 F. Supp. 1264 (N.D. Ill. (1986), aff'd F.2d 302 (7th Cir. 1988).

Faulkner v. Jones 51 F.3d.440 (4th Cir., 1995 at 451).

Flores v. Sec'y of Defense 355 F. Supp. 93 (N.D. Fla. 1973).

Frontiero v. Richardson 411 U.S. 677 (1973).

General Electric Company v. Martha Gilbert 429 U.S. 125 (1976).

Goldman v. Weinberger 475 U.S. 503 (1986).

Gutierrez v. Laird 346 F. Supp. 289 (D.D.C. 1972).

Lindsey v. Normet 405 U.S. 56 (1972).

Muller v. Oregon 208 U.S. 412 (1908).

Owens v. Brown 455 F.Supp. 291 (1978).

Parker v. Levy 417 U.S. 733 (1974).

Radice v. New York U.S. 292 (1924).

Reed v. Reed 404 U.S. 71 (1971).

Robinson v. Rand 340 F. Supp. 37 (D. Colo. 1972).

Rostker v. Goldberg 60 L. Ed. 2d 478 at 487 (1981).

San Antonio Independent School District v. Rodriguez 411 U.S. 1 (1973).

Schlesinger v. Ballard 419 U.S. 498 (1975).

Secretary of the Navy v. Huff 444 U.S. 453 (1980).

Struck v. Sec'y of Defense 460 F.2d 1372 (9th Cir. 1971a), cert. granted, 409 U.S. 497 (1971b), vacated and remanded, 409 U.S. 1071 (1972).

United States v. Stanley 483 U.S. 669 (1987).

U.S. v. Virginia et al. 116 S. Ct. 2264 (1996).

Waldie v. Schlesinger 509 F.2d 508 (D.C. Cir. 1974).

Willas v. Rapal 1987. As reported in the Women's Equity Action League Washington Reporter (June–July): 4.

INDEX

abortion: American Catholics on, 145; excommunication over issue of, 135–37, 217–218n.11; Vatican on rape and, 141–42; women religious's position on, 137, 219n.26. *See also* Catholics for a Free Choice (CFFC); *New York Times* abortion advertisement (7 October 1984); the Vatican

abortion advertisement (*New York Times*, October 1984), 126–27, 136–38, 146

Abrams, Kathryn, 95

accountability: gatekeeping through chain-of-command military, 85–86; multidimensional nature of, 38

ACLU, 64–65

ACT UP, 122

Adkins v. Children's Hospital, 27

adversative model (VMI), 99

advocates of gender equality, 21

African Americans: institutional changes for, 4, 5, 6, 22, 178n.12; suing over military discrimination, 93–94

African-American women: as outsiders within, 38–39; within U.S. military, 75–76, 170; of the USS *Norton Sound* episode, 94

Air Force Academy, 45, 68, 82

All-Volunteer Force (AVF), 45, 52, 54

Almquist, Vicki, 73

altar servers (female), 167–68, 226n.18

American Agri-Women, 74

American Association of University Women, 91

American Catholic Church: appointment of bishops/cardinals for, 140–41; "bending the rules" by, 145; clerical discipline by, 138–39; comparison of military feminism and that of, 12–16, 170–74; discursive politics of feminism in, 19; discursive radicalism feminism in, 16, 21–22; effectiveness of feminism on, 167–68; exit of nuns from, 144; feminist radicalism in, 165; Hispanics within, 20, 118, 127–30, 222n.68; institutionalization of feminism in, 117–20; lay defectors from, 144–45,

222n.68; move into American mainstream by, 5; papal birth control ban and, 138; "Partners in the Mystery of Redemption" pastoral letter of, 168; strategies of control exercised by, 135–45; VA sexual discrimination policy and, 147; women's autonomous structures within, 155–57. *See also* Catholic Church; feminist activism (American Catholic Church); ordination debate

American Historical Review, 4

American Jewish Congress' Commission for Women's Equality, 11

American Medical Association, 25

American Nurses Association, 50

American Women's Hospitals, 26

Anderson, Kristi, 25

Anglo-Saxon ideal, 5

Arlington Cemetery Women's Memorial (Women in Military Service to America—WIMSA), 173

Armed Services Committee, 98

Army Times, 58

Ashe, Sister Kaye, 153

Ash Wednesday protests, 122

associational activism, 11–12

associationalism. *See* civic associationalism

Association of the United States Army (AUSA), 173

autonomous organizations, 9

Banaszak, Lee Ann, 32–33

Barkalow, Carol, 84

Batjer, Marybel, 97

Becraft, Carolyn, 50, 68, 70–71, 72–73

Beijing Fourth World Conference on Women (1995), 141, 142

Beijing Plan of Action, 142

Bem, Sandra, 31

Benecke, Michelle, 76

"Berks" (Berkshire conference), 34

Berry, Gail, 59

birth control ban, 138, 144–45, 224n.110

Black Women's Health Project, 10

Bledsoe, Glenda, 93

"Equality Management" (DACOWITS), 75–76

Equal Pay Act (1963), 6, 29

equal rights: comparison of gender/racial, 173, 228n.47; gained during 1920s, 24–28; gained during 1970s, 28–32; liberalism and, 175; papal statement on, 142; politics and institutionalization of, 32; progress of military women's, 54–62. *See also* gender equality; racial equality

Equal Rights Amendment of 1973 (ERA), 29, 33, 59, 90, 117, 152, 183n.9

European Catholic feminist activism, 130, 133

excommunication: "organizational," 140; pro-choice position punished by, 217–218n.11; as strategy of control by church, 135–38; used against feminists by church, 13

Executive Order 11246 (1965), 29

Executive Order 11375 (1968), 29

Ex-Spouses of Servicemen/women for Equality (EXPOSE), 194n.72

Faludi, Susan, 35

Farians, Elizabeth, 151

Fay, Sister Catherine, 147

Federally Employed Women, 66

Federation of Women Dentists, 26

feminist activism: comparison of interest group/discursive protest, 174; comparison of military and church, 16, 170–71, 174; habitats and, 35, 63–70, 117–20; institutionalization as de-radicalization of, 70–77; institutional protest and, 8–12, 164, 166–67; opportunities and, 32–33; resistance by, 8. *See also* interest-group politics

feminist activism (American Catholic Church): on antiracism and women of color, 127–30; autonomous church structures and, 155–57; church strategies of control over, 135–45; compared to European feminist activism, 130, 133–34; discursive acts of, 120–24; discursive methods used by Vatican against, 141–45; discursive radicalism of, 130; effectiveness of, 167–68; exceptionally outspoken/organized nature of, 134; habitats available to, 117–

20; language of, 126; the law and, 146–48; of LCWR, 124–27; within liturgy groups and base communities, 120; movement politics and, 150–55; organizations promoting, 117–19; within parishes, 119–20; as outside of parish politics, 122–23; radicalization of, 165; Vatican concerns over, 132–33; Vatican II reforms and, 148–50; of Women-Church, 115, 116–17, 123–24. *See also* Latin American Catholic feminist activism; women religious

feminist activism (U.S. military): attacks against women's, 59–60; backlash (1980s) against, 92–95; denial of feminism label within, 86–87; features of, 45–46, 53–54; gatekeeping/rebuff modes against, 81–86; habitats available to, 63–70; homosexual exclusion and, 64, 73, 75, 76–77; interdependence of inside/outside, 62–69; interest-group, 47, 170–74; media and, 65–69; within military offices/organizations, 63–64; pressures to conform and, 81–86; by Rosemary Mariner, 79–80. *See also* servicewomen

feminist politics: institutionalization of equal rights and, 32; Republican Party marginalization of, 32–33

feminist protest: institutionalization of, 23–24; during the 1920s, 24–28; in U.S. military/Catholic Church, 12–16. *See also* protest

"feminists by any other name," 20–21

Ferraro, Sister Barbara, 122, 137, 142, 144

Ferraro, Geraldine, 16, 136

Fiedler, Sister Maureen, 108, 121, 152, 156

Fiorenza, Elisabeth Schüssler, 108–9

Fitzpatrick, Ruth McDonough, 121

"Flag Panel," 202n.7

Flynn, Kelly, 171

Fogarty, Gerald, 143

Foley, Sister Nadine, 132

Foote, Evelyn P., 56, 57, 77

foot washing (Holy Thursday), 122

Forman, Mark, 48

Fort Bragg, 84

Fort McClellan, 56

Foucault, Michel, 36, 41

Fourteenth Amendment, 30

PRINCETON STUDIES IN AMERICAN POLITICS:
HISTORICAL, INTERNATIONAL, AND COMPARATIVE PERSPECTIVES

The Origins of the Urban Crisis: Race and Inequality in Postwar Detroit
by Thomas J. Sugrue

*The Road to Nowhere: The Genesis of President Clinton's Plan
for Health Security* by Jacob Hacker

*Imperiled Innocents: Anthony Comstock and Family Reproduction
in Victorian America* by Nicola Beisel

Morning Glories: Municipal Reform in the Southwest by Amy Bridges

*The Hidden Welfare State: Tax Expenditures and Social Policy
in the United States* by Christopher Howard

*Bold Relief: Institutional Politics and the Origins of Modern
American Social Policy* by Edwin Amenta

*Parting at the Crossroads: The Emergence of Health Insurance in the
United States and Canada* by Antonia Maioni

*Forged Consensus: Science, Technology, and Economic Policy in the
United States, 1921–1953* by David M. Hart

Faithful and Fearless: Moving Feminism into the Church and Military
by Mary Fainsod Katzenstein

About the Author

MARY FAINSOD KATZENSTEIN is a professor of government and a member of the faculty of the Women's Studies Program at Cornell University. She is the author of *Ethnicity and Equality: The Shiv Sena Party and Preferential Policies in Bombay* and has cowritten and coedited several books, including, with Carol McClurg Mueller, *The Women's Movements of the United States and Europe.*